# The Social Psychology of Prejudice

# The Social Psychology
# of Prejudice

*John Duckitt*

PRAEGER

New York
Westport, Connecticut
London

**Copyright Acknowledgments**

The author and publisher are grateful for permission to use the following material:

Table 8.2 in Chapter 8 and Tables 9.1 and 9.3 and Figure 9.2 in Chapter 9 are reprinted from Duckitt, J. (1991). Prejudice and racism. Chapter 6 in D. Foster & J. Louw-Potgieter (Eds.), *Social psychology in South Africa*. Isando, South Africa: Lexicon. Reprinted by permission of the publisher.

Figure 9.1 in Chapter 9 is reprinted from Duckitt, J. (1988). Normative conformity and racial prejudice in South Africa. *Genetic, Social, and General Psychology Monographs, 114*, 413–438. Reprinted with permission of the Helen Dwight Reid Educational Foundation. Published by Heldref Publications, 4000 Albemarle St., N.W., Washington, D.C. 20016. Copyright © 1988.

**Library of Congress Cataloging-in-Publication Data**

Duckitt, J. H.
    The social psychology of prejudice / John Duckitt.
        p.     cm.
    Includes bibliographical references (p.    ) and indexes.
    ISBN 0–275–94241–4 (alk. paper)
    1. Prejudices.  2. Prejudices—South Africa.  3. Racism.
    4. Racism—South Africa.    I. Title.
    HM291.D77     1992
    303.3′85—dc20         91–33889

British Library Cataloguing in Publication Data is available.

Library of Congress Catalog Card Number: 91–33889
ISBN: 0–275–94241–4

First published in 1992

Praeger Publishers, One Madison Avenue, New York, NY 10010
An imprint of Greenwood Publishing Group, Inc.

Printed in the United States of America

The paper used in this book complies with the
Permanent Paper Standard issued by the National
Information Standards Organization (Z39.48–1984).

10 9 8 7 6 5 4 3 2 1

# Contents

# Preface

Growing up in South Africa and living with the injustices of Apartheid inevitably confronts one with the question of how such wrongs come into being and endure for so long. My personal attempts to confront this question very soon led to the depressing realization that racism and prejudice were not just South African phenomena. The cruelty and absurdity of prejudice, with its often tragically destructive consequences, pervade human history. How can we explain phenomena that are so often harmful and which may seem so completely irrational? It has only been in the past seventy years that the social sciences have begun to make a determined effort to understand the nature and causes of prejudice, yet already important advances have been made. This book is about that effort.

In preparing this book I have undoubtedly drawn more heavily on South African illustrations and research than would have been the case for a non–South African writer. However, this book is not intended to be about South Africa and its unhappy contribution to the history of racism. It is intended to be a general book about the nature and causes of prejudice. First, it sets out to try and provide a concise but reasonably comprehensive overview of the state of our knowledge on the subject. As such, I hope it may be useful for persons with a general or professional interest in the area, as well as for people who are teaching or taking courses on prejudice, racism, and related topics. Second, it proposes a general framework to integrate this knowledge in a coherent and meaningful fashion. The critical argument here is that the currently fashionable cognitively based paradigm for understanding intergroup behavior and attitudes, like the preceding paradigms, only provides a partial understanding. It illuminates certain issues while it obscures others. What is needed is a framework to pull together the different paradigms that have contributed to explaining prejudice—the insights of the present and the past—into a broader and more coherent understanding. I hope the proposals made here may make some contribution to that objective.

I would like to express my gratitude to Graham Tyson for his advice and criticism throughout the preparation of an earlier version of the manuscript. I was also fortunate to receive insightful commentary and a great deal of encouragement from Bob Altemeyer and Don Foster. I am afraid I did not always follow their advice, and they certainly cannot be held responsible for any of the deficiencies of the final version. My wife, Inez, did a great deal of proofreading and made many valuable stylistic suggestions; Ian Samson set up the tables and figures; and Laetitia du Toit spent a good deal of time getting the final manuscript into the right format. I also wish to thank my mother, who provided a very quiet back room where I was able to work completely undisturbed for several very critical months.

# The Social Psychology
of Prejudice

# 1

## Introduction and Overview

A great deal of human history has been a record of antagonism and conflict between groups. Indeed, the most terrible atrocities committed by humans have often not been the acts of criminals or madmen but of ordinary, loyal citizens acting in the presumed interests of their group against another group. As Tajfel (1984) pointed out:

If I confess that last week I killed two individuals for my own private benefit or the benefit of my family, there would be no moral argument in most of the societies that are familiar to us, no disagreement about my guilt. If I confess that last week I killed or caused to be killed two thousand people for the benefit of my "group"—national, tribal, racial, social, political, or religious—the least that can be said is that in some cultural contexts there would be a controversy about the moral propriety of my action; in other cultural contexts the question of culpability would perhaps not even arise. (p. 704)

The immense advances in science and technology during the past few centuries have not diminished the intensity and frequency of intergroup hatreds and violence. In fact, the growth of military and political power has introduced a scale of massacre and despoliation that makes the efforts of previous centuries seem modest by comparison. Isaacs (1975), examining a mere two decades of the mid-twentieth century, found:

It is a somber catalogue: mutual massacring of Hindus and Muslims in India; tribal wars in Nigeria, the Congo, Chad, Sudan; Indians killing Nagas in north-eastern Assam; Malays killing Chinese in Malaysia; Indonesians killing Chinese in Indonesia; Chinese killing Tibetans in Tibet; Tutsis and Hutu killing each other in Burundi; Catholics and Protestants killing each other in Ulster; Turks and Greeks in Cyprus; Kurds and Iraqis in Iraq; Papuans fighting Indonesians in New Guinea; Israelis and Arabs; Telenganas and Andhras and other such groups in India; Filipino Christians and Filipino Muslims; and so on and on and on. One attempt to count the "ethnic/cultural fatalities" in such clashes between 1945 and 1967 listed thirty-four "major" blood-lettings and hundreds of lesser collisions and came up with an estimated total of 7,480,000 deaths. (p. 3)

Yet these are still exceptional events. It is only under particular circumstances that intergroup animosities erupt into open violence and killing. Underlying these periodic eruptions are patterns of intergroup dislike, resentment, discrimination, and denigration that are all too unexceptional. Prejudiced attitudes and beliefs—whether national, tribal, racial, social, religious, or, indeed, based on almost any cue that could conceivably be used to differentiate people into separate groupings—pervade human social life. They are remarkable not in their existence, but in their sheer ubiquity, the ease with which they can be aroused, their variety of expression, and the tenacity with which they are held.

The very pervasiveness of prejudice may be one reason why it has been only in historically recent times that it has come to be seen as a seriously problematic phenomenon that merits scientific investigation. Previously, even social scientists had tended to view prejudice and discrimination as essentially natural and normal. Thus, it was widely believed that "outgroup rejection was inborn or instinctive, derived from 'consciousness of kind' according to Giddings in 1906 . . . , and 'dislike of the unlike' according to Summer in 1906. . . . Humans, like animals were thought to possess a biologically controlled fear of strangers, and, for example, an innate sense of race" (Vaughan, 1988, p. 3).

Two kinds of prejudice have been very influential in stimulating the interest of social scientists and, particularly, psychologists in the study of prejudice. One has been anti-Semitism and its expression in the holocaust in Nazi Germany; the other has been racism, both as a serious social problem in the United States and as a global phenomenon. In twentieth-century society, racism and anti-Semitism have come to epitomize the destructive power of prejudice in human affairs, as well as its tragic irrationality.

The concept of prejudice as a subject of social psychological inquiry emerged around the 1920s (Samelson, 1978; Vaughan, 1988). Research on the topic grew slowly during the 1930s and early 1940s, and it was only after World War II that interest escalated dramatically (Fairchild & Gurin, 1978). Nevertheless, when Gordon Allport's classic, *The Nature of Prejudice*, was published in 1954, a substantial body of research already existed. This was sufficient to indicate the enormous breadth and complexity of the phenomenon. The causes of prejudice had been sought in all of the following: intrapsychic conflicts deep inside the personality, psychological inadequacies and maladjustment, chronic frustrations, ignorance, low intelligence, styles of thinking, social learning and cultural influences, conforming to social norms and traditions, contact experiences with outgroup members, the actual characteristics of outgroup members, conflicts of interest among social groups, the justification of exploitation, the need for scapegoats, economic insecurity, the projection of one's own unacceptable impulses, fear of strangers, dislike of dissimilarity, religiosity, anxiety, aggression, sex, and guilt. This is not even a complete list, merely a sampling of the topics discussed by Allport. Today, almost forty years later, despite a substantial accumulation of research and some important theoretical advances, the study of prejudice, discrimination, and intergroup relations still presents "one of the most difficult and complex knots of problems which we confront in our times" (Tajfel, 1982b, p. 1).

As a social scientific construct, the very idea of prejudice is not an entirely unambiguous one. A large number of definitions have been proposed which raise some extremely complex and difficult issues. The problems involved in defining and conceptualizing prejudice are therefore discussed in Chapter 2, and an attempt is made to clarify them. Chapter 3 considers an equally problematic issue—the relationship between prejudiced attitudes and actual behavior. To what extent is hostile and discriminatory behavior toward outgroups and minorities really related to prejudiced feelings and beliefs about them? Although this problem is frequently noted, it has rarely been considered in detail. Yet it has basic implications for the social and practical relevance of studying prejudice.

The bewildering multiplicity of theories of prejudice has already been mentioned. Many attempts have been made to classify these theories in a systematic manner, but the classifications have been descriptive rather than functional and so have contributed little to the understanding of prejudice. Chapter 4 addresses this problem from a new perspective, by presenting a historical analysis of theorizing about prejudice. This analysis indicates that different kinds of theories were prominent at different historical periods. It also suggests that this represented attempts to answer fundamentally different kinds of questions about the nature and causation of prejudice—questions that important social events and circumstances had made particularly salient for social scientists.

Four such issues emerged from the analysis, suggesting that four qualitatively different but complementary processes are involved in the causation of prejudice and are necessary for its explanation. First, certain universal psychological processes build in an inherently human potentiality for prejudice. Second, social and intergroup dynamics describe the conditions and circumstances of contact and interaction among groups, which then elaborate this potentiality into socially shared or consensual patterns of prejudice within groups. Third, mechanisms of transmission explain how these intergroup dynamics and shared patterns of prejudice are socially transmitted to individual members of the groups. Fourth and finally, individual-difference dimensions determine individual susceptibility to prejudice and so operate to modulate the impact of these social transmission mechanisms on individuals. These four functional processes and the theories pertaining to each are described in Chapters 5 through 8, respectively.

Two of these processes, the social transmission of prejudice and individual differences in susceptibility, are directly relevant for explaining the prejudiced attitudes held by individuals—an issue that has been particularly salient for psychologists. They correspond broadly to the distinction typically made in the psychological literature between social determinants of prejudice on the one hand and psychological, or personality, determinants on the other. The assumption that these two sets of factors interact in determining prejudice has been widespread. Thus, psychological factors would be important when social factors are relatively weak or conducive to tolerance. The opposite would be the case in highly prejudiced societies where social factors would presumably be very powerful; in these groups, it is argued, prejudice becomes a social norm and is enforced by strong conformity pressures. Consequently, the prejudiced attitudes held by individuals are primarily determined by social conformity, and psychological causes of prejudice become correspondingly less important.

Their very high levels of racial prejudice make South African whites a population uniquely suited for investigation of this interactive hypothesis. As a result, this has been an important issue in South African research on prejudice ever since Pettigrew's classic studies (1958, 1959, 1960) first examined the problem. The research relating to this thesis, both in South Africa and elsewhere, is reviewed in Chapter 9. This reveals that, despite the widespread acceptance of the normative conformity hypothesis, most of the research cited in support of it has been very weak methodologically and the findings have been generally ambiguous and inconclusive. New and better South African research has recently examined the issue more directly. The findings clearly refute the idea that social and psychological factors interact in determining prejudice and suggest that they operate in complementary fashion, with the effect of each being independent of the operation of the other. Chapter 9 concludes by considering some other important implications of these findings for our understanding of prejudice.

Finally, Chapter 10 considers the future of prejudice. There are important gaps in our knowledge about prejudice that require systematic research. Despite the inadequacies of our knowledge, there are important practical issues that need to be confronted. The significance of prejudice can be located within the context of the evolution of human society.

Originally, prejudice may have been adaptive for human groups. It may have helped engender loyalty to the ingroup and a distrust of outgroups; it may have facilitated a readiness to defend and if necessary die in the interests of the group. The evolution of mass societies and highly destructive weaponry has changed this from an evolutionary advantage to perhaps the most serious threat to the continued survival of human society and civilization.

Can the social scientific knowledge that has been amassed about prejudice help alleviate this threat? Although it is unlikely that the universal psychological processes that underlie a fundamentally human propensity for prejudice can be changed, the degree to which they come to be expressed in prejudice can be. This would require action at three different levels, corresponding to the three causal processes described in Chapters 6, 7, and 8. Thus, change would be required first at the level of social structure and intergroup relations, second in the social influences to which individuals are exposed, and third in individual susceptibility. The possible strategies that emerge from our state of knowledge at each these three levels are discussed and briefly evaluated. It is concluded that a world in which prejudice has been completely eliminated has little likelihood of being realized in our future, or perhaps ever. Nevertheless, societies in which prejudice is not a significant social problem and in which a considerable degree of tolerance is normative are by no means unfeasible.

# 2

# The Concept of Prejudice

A number of concepts have been used by social scientists to describe and understand intergroup relations and intergroup conflict. These include ethnocentrism, tolerance, stereotype, social distance, racism, discrimination, and prejudice. Although the cognitive perspective in psychology has resulted in an emphasis on the concept of stereotype in recent years (Hamilton, 1981a; Messick & Mackie, 1989; Miller, 1982), in general, social psychologists, and often sociologists as well (e.g., Lever, 1978; Simpson & Yinger, 1985) have accorded primacy to the concept of prejudice. This involves the assumption that, from a psychological perspective at least, the feelings and attitudes involved in intergroup hostility and conflict are particularly crucial for its understanding.

Prejudice, however, is a complex construct, and its definition involves several awkward problems. As a result, a large number of different definitions have been proposed. The issues involved in defining prejudice will be discussed in the next section, but first it seems advisable to briefly define and explain several other closely related concepts.

*Ethnocentrism.* In his classic account, Sumner (1906) described ethnocentrism as a "view of things in which one's own group is the centre of everything, and all others are scaled and rated with reference to it. . . . Each group nourishes its own pride and vanity, boasts itself superior, exalts its own divinities, and looks with contempt on outsiders" (p. 12). In essence, then, ethnocentrism consists of a belief in the unique value and rightness of one's ingroup and a disdain for outgroups to the extent that they differ from the ingroup (Brewer, 1981; Lanternari, 1980; LeVine & Campbell, 1972).

*Tolerance.* In the literature on political science and democratic theory the term tolerance describes adherence to specific democratic principles (Jackman, 1977). In the literature on intergroup relations it is used differently to mean "the lack of group prejudice, a willingness to evaluate individuals as individuals" (Martin, 1964, p. 11). In this sense, tolerance indicates a tendency to be generally free of prejudice, irrespective of the outgroup or situation. Intolerance, on the other hand, refers to a generalized tendency to be negative to outgroups. In contrast to the term ethnocentrism, the term intolerance has no implication about the orientation to the ingroup.

*Stereotype.* Ashmore and DelBoca (1981) defined the concept of stereotype as "a set of beliefs about the personal attributes of a group of people" (p. 16). This illustrates two important shifts in the conceptualization of stereotype (Brewer & Kramer, 1985; Messick & Mackie, 1989; Stephan & Rosenfield, 1982). First, stereotypes are no longer defined as being incorrect, irrational, rigid, or morally wrong in some way. Instead, they are seen as arising out of essentially normal and adaptive cognitive processes. Second, stereotypes are not limited to personality trait descriptions (e.g., "Germans are conscientious and hardworking") but can include any personal attribute—physical, affective, visual, or behavioral—that can be seen as characteristic of that group ("Germans are fair and tall").

*Social distance.* Originally social distance was defined as reflecting the degree of "sympathetic understanding and intimacy" between groups or individuals (Bogardus, 1925; Park, 1924). The social distance questionnaire developed by Bogardus (1925) asks respondents whether they would be willing to admit members of some other group to "classifications" such as "close kinship by marriage," "to my street as neighbors," "to employment in my occupation," and "to citizenship in my country." It has been argued that inferring "sympathetic understanding and intimacy" from responses to these items is not entirely justified and that the definition of social distance should more closely reflect the manner in which it has been operationalized and measured (e.g., Lever, 1978). On this basis, social distance can be defined as reflecting the preferred degree of closeness in interpersonal contact and relationships with members of another group (cf. Harding, Proshansky, Kutner, & Chein, 1969; Lever, 1978; Simpson & Yinger, 1985).

*Racism.* Psychologists have often used the concept of racism as synonymous with racial prejudice (e.g., Bagley, Verma, Mallick & Young, 1979; Milner, 1981). Sociologists, on the other hand, have given it a more specific meaning. For example, Wilson (1973) provides a reasonably representative definition of racism as "an ideology of racial domination or exploitation that (1) incorporates beliefs in a particular race's cultural and/or inherent biological inferiority, and (2) uses such beliefs to justify and prescribe inferior or unequal treatment for that group" (p. 32).

Most traditional definitions of racism have included these two ideas—that is, a belief in inferiority and support for discriminatory treatment (e.g., Bowser, 1985). More recently, however, it has been suggested that a new kind of racism, termed symbolic or modern racism, may have emerged which does not involve these components, at least in this form (Kinder, 1986; Kinder & Sears, 1981; McConahay, Hardee, & Batts, 1981; McConahay & Hough, 1976). This issue will be discussed later in this chapter.

*Discrimination.* Simpson and Yinger (1985) described discrimination as "drawing an unfair or injurious distinction" (p. 23), a distinction that is based solely on membership in a particular group with effects favorable to ingroup members and/or disadvantageous to outgroup members (cf. Feagin & Eckberg, 1980). Psychologists have typically discussed discrimination as an intentional act. Stephan and Rosenfield (1982), for example, described discrimination as "the behavioral expression of racial and ethnic attitudes" (p. 93). Sociologists, however, have also proposed the existence of institutional discrimination or racism (Carmichael & Hamilton, 1967). This refers to social and institutional practices that affect outgroup members negatively but which do not necessarily involve any conscious discriminatory intent in those who benefit from or implement them.

## DEFINING PREJUDICE

A large number of definitions of prejudice have been proposed. In fact, Milner (1981) has suggested that "there are almost as many definitions of the term as writers who employ it" (p. 112). A reasonably representative sample of definitions proposed by psychologists and sociologists is presented in Table 2.1. Even a cursory scrutiny of this list indicates some marked differences between definitions. An important suggestion, which enables some degree of clarification, was made by Ashmore (1970), who identified four basic points of agreement common to most definitions. These are:

1. Prejudice is an intergroup phenomenon.
2. Prejudice is a negative orientation.
3. Prejudice is bad.
4. Prejudice is an attitude.

These four elements, Ashmore argued, could be combined to give a consensually acceptable definition of prejudice. On this basis, prejudice could be defined as a negative intergroup attitude which is bad, unjustified, or irrational in some way or other. It is evident that the first three components of such a definition do not seem to pose any problem. The fourth, however, does.

Ashmore suggested that prejudice was bad and fundamentally irra-

**Table 2.1**
**Some Definitions of Prejudice**

---

Prejudiced attitudes . . . are irrational, unjust, or intolerant dispositions towards other groups. They are often accompanied by stereotyping. This is the attribution of supposed characteristics of the whole group to all its individual members (Milner, 1975, p. 9).

It seems most useful to us to define prejudice as a failure of rationality or a failure of justice or a failure of human-heartedness in an individual's attitude toward members of another ethnic group (Harding et al., 1969, p. 6).

An emotional, rigid attitude (a predisposition to respond to a certain stimulus in a certain way) toward a group of people (Simpson & Yinger, 1985, p. 21).

Thinking ill of others without sufficient warrant (Allport, 1954, p. 7).

An unsubstantiated prejudgment of an individual or group, favorable or unfavorable in character, tending to action in a consonant direction (Klineberg, 1968, p. 439).

A pattern of hostility in interpersonal relations which is directed against an entire group, or against its individual members; it fulfills a specific irrational function for its bearer (Ackerman & Jahoda, 1950, pp. 2--3).

The essential features of prejudice would appear to be its emotional character, in that it serves psychic functions for the individuals who display it, and its rigidity, in that when someone tries to demonstrate that an opinion is false, prejudiced people to not modify their views (Banton, 1967, p. 8).

Hostility or aggression toward individuals on the basis of their group membership (Buss, 1961, p. 245).

Group prejudice is now commonly viewed as having two components: hostility and misinformation (Kelman & Pettigrew, 1959, p. 436).

A set of attitudes which causes, supports, or justifies discrimination (Rose, 1951, p. 5).

An unfavorable attitude toward an object which tends to be highly stereotyped, emotionally charged, and not easily changed by contrary information (Krech, Crutchfield, & Ballachey, 1962).

---

tional because it was an overgeneralized attitude that did not recognize the diversity of abilities, beliefs, and personal attributes among members of the group against whom it was directed. This conclusion is hardly consensual, however. Other writers, as Table 2.1 indicates, have suggested different reasons why prejudice is "bad," creating a major source of disagreement among definitions. More recently, it has also been argued that there may be some very fundamental problems with the idea of prejudice as a pejorative concept. As a result, the idea that prejudice should necessarily be defined as "bad" in some way has been seriously questioned. Two other problems are also relevant to the issue of defining prejudice: One is that there is considerable disagreement over what the concept of attitude means; the other is the problem of whether there are qualitatively different kinds of prejudice. These three problems—the issue of the meaning of attitude, the problem of a pejorative definition of prejudice, and the issue of whether there are different kinds of prejudice—are discussed in more detail in the remainder of this chapter.

## PREJUDICE AS AN ATTITUDE

While there is a great deal of agreement that prejudice is an attitude, there is much less agreement about what the concept of attitude means. Psychologists, for example, employ two quite different models of the concept of attitude: the unidimensional model and the three-component model. In the case of prejudice as an attitude, these two models have quite different implications about the relationship between prejudice and concepts such as stereotype and social distance and about how prejudice influences behavior.

In its early history, the concept of attitude was most commonly viewed as an individual's affective or emotional orientation to an object along the single dimension of favorability–unfavorability. Thurstone and Chave (1929), for example, defined an attitude as "a general evaluation or feeling of favorability or unfavorability" to an object (p. 12). All the major attitude measurement methodologies were based on this unidimensional affective conceptualization of attitude (Guttman, 1944; Likert, 1931; Thurstone & Chave, 1929).

Later, during the 1940s and 1950s, there was a shift away from this early unidimensional concept toward a broader and more complex view of attitude, which was termed the three-component model (Katz & Stotland, 1959; Krech & Crutchfield, 1948; Lambert & Lambert, 1964; Newcomb, Turner, & Converse, 1965; Secord & Backman, 1964). From this perspective, attitudes consisted of three related dimensions: beliefs about the attitude object (the cognitive component); feelings toward it (the affective component); and action tendencies or behavioral dispositions toward it (the conative or behavioral component).

The idea that prejudiced attitudes consisted of these three components was widely adopted (e.g., Allport, 1954; Ehrlich, 1973; Gergen & Gergen, 1981; Harding et al., 1969; Newcomb et al., 1965; Rajecki, 1982; Rosenfield & Stephan, 1981), perhaps because it seemed to integrate several important social psychological concepts within a single broad conceptualization of prejudice. Thus, stereotypes were part of the cognitive component, intergroup dislike and negative evaluation was equivalent to the affective component, and social distance was part of the behavioral component.

The three-component approach, however, involved some important problems. For example, issues such as that of the interrelationship among the three components and how they influenced behavior were never definitively clarified (Ajzen & Fishbein, 1980). If these three components comprise a broader second-order dimension, then it seems logical to expect substantial consistency among them. While consistency has usually been implied by adherents of the three-component model, this has not always been so. Greenwald (1968), for example, suggested that each component might be learned quite differently from the others, making a considerable degree of independence among the components quite feasible.

This model also implies that behavior is jointly determined by all three components, with the behavioral component often seen as the most important. One implication of this, along with the idea that there could be inconsistency among components, was that behavior might not be strongly predictable from attitude measures such as Likert and Thurstone scales which assess only the affective component. Early findings, such as the classic study of LaPiere (1934; cf. also Minard, 1952; Saenger & Gilbert, 1950), which were interpreted as indicating that racial attitudes and behavior could be quite unrelated, were sometimes explained in this way (e.g., Bagley & Verma, 1979; Katz & Stotland, 1959; Krech & Crutchfield, 1948). The three-component model also had little impact on attitude measurement, with attitudes continuing to be measured as unidimensional constructs. In fact, this approach stimulated very little research in general. All these problems may have contributed to a decline in interest in the three-component model during the past two decades and a revival of interest in unidimensional approaches (Ajzen & Fishbein, 1980; Fishbein & Ajzen, 1975; Jaspers, 1978).

These unidimensional approaches see attitude as a purely affective construct that is conceptually and empirically distinct from the cognitive and behavioral components of the tripartite model. For Ajzen and Fishbein (1980), for example, the individual's attitude to an object crystallizes from the evaluative implications of his or her beliefs about the object (e.g., stereotypes). The behavioral component from the tripartite model is split off completely from the attitude concept and is seen as an entirely independent construct, termed behavioral intention. This comprises the individual's consciously formed intentions to behave toward the attitude object, which as Triandis (1967) pointed out, in the intergroup context would include social distance preferences. Ajzen and Fishbein (1980) did not see attitudes as directly influencing behavior; instead, their effect is mediated through the individual's behavioral intentions.

This unidimensional approach also does not expect a strong relationship between an attitude to an object and specific behaviors to that object. To predict a specific act, both the attitude to that act and act-specific social norms need to be considered as well. On the other hand, a generalized attitude toward an object should predict the overall tendency to behave in a generally favorable or unfavorable way toward that object, as aggregating over a variety of different situations and acts should largely average out normative and situational influences. This has important implications for the prediction of discriminatory behavior from prejudiced attitudes—an issue that will be discussed in more detail in the next chapter.

Finally, it is evident that a two-component view of attitude as consisting of cognitive and affective components could also be proposed. Several writers on prejudice, in fact, have suggested this. Levin and Levin (1982), for example, defined prejudice as "a learned disposition consisting of the following components or dimensions: (1) negative beliefs or stereotypes (cognitive component) [and] (2) negative feelings or emotions (affective component)" (p. 66).

To sum up, therefore, three different approaches to the concept of prejudice as an attitude have been presented in the literature. These three models, the unidimensional, the three-component, and the two-component model, and the interrelations specified by each, are illustrated in Figure 2.1. Which of these models is best? Certain general conclusions do seem to emerge from the literature. A two-component model, for example, may have promise, but has thus far attracted little interest, has not yet been given any theoretical basis, and has never been empirically tested. The three-component model has the advantage of integrative breadth. On the other hand, it also has serious disadvantages. It is vague and imprecise concerning the interrelationships among its components and behavior, and it lacks a clear theoretical basis. It has little empirical support. Few studies have tested it, and the few studies that did so in regard to prejudiced attitudes did not support it (Gray & Revelle, 1972; Mann, 1959; Woodmansee & Cook, 1967). Finally, attitudes in general continue to be measured using unidimensional methodologies, and little if any attempt has been made to develop and use tripartite measures in the case of prejudice or any other area.

In contrast, the unidimensional approach specifies the interrelations among concepts, and with behavior, clearly and unambiguously in an empirically testable manner. As a result, there has been a great deal of research on such approaches, including that of Ajzen and Fishbein (1980). Much of this research has been supportive of the general framework of the approach (Ajzen & Fishbein, 1980; Manstead, Proffit, & Smart, 1983; Pagel & Davidson, 1984; Schwartz & Tessler, 1972; Zuckerman & Reis, 1978), though not always in respect of its details (Bentler

**Figure 2.1**
**Three Approaches to the Concept of Prejudiced Attitude**

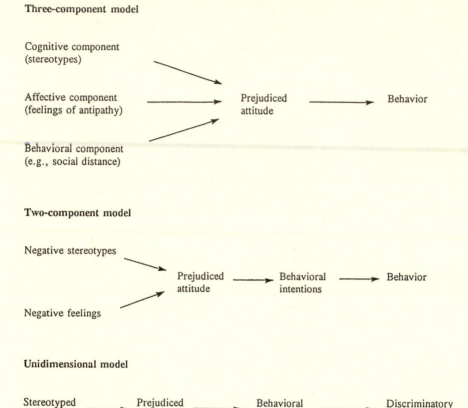

Three-component model

Cognitive component
(stereotypes)

Affective component                          Prejudiced                    Behavior
(feelings of antipathy)                      attitude

Behavioral component
(e.g., social distance)

Two-component model

Negative stereotypes

                          Prejudiced         Behavioral          Behavior
                          attitude           intentions

Negative feelings

Unidimensional model

Stereotyped          Prejudiced          Behavioral          Discriminatory
beliefs              attitude            intentions          behavior

& Speckart, 1981; Fredricks & Dossett, 1983; Gorsuch & Ortberg, 1983). Finally, a good deal of evidence indicates that measures of intergroup affect, stereotypes, and social distance or behavioral intention are not always very closely related, and they are certainly not related to an extent sufficient to justify their integration into a single broad concept of prejudice (Abelson, Kinder, Peters, & Fiske, 1982; Brewer, Campbell, & LeVine, 1971; Brigham, 1971b, 1972; Ewens & Ehrlich, 1972; Gardner, 1973; Jackman, 1977).

Overall, therefore, it would seem that prejudiced attitudes may be best viewed in terms of the affective dimension only, with constructs such as stereotype, social distance, and intergroup behavioral intentions seen as empirically related but conceptually separate—a conclusion recently endorsed by several important reviews (Babad, Birnbaum &

Benne, 1983; Brewer & Kramer, 1985; Stephan, 1983; Stephan & Rosen-field, 1982). Brewer and Kramer (1985), for example, in discussing the relationship of stereotype and prejudice, concluded that "while technically the term 'prejudice' could be applied to the cognitive content of intergroup perceptions as well, typically it is used with reference to the affective or emotional component of intergroup relations" (p. 231).

## PREJUDICE AS "BAD"

It was mentioned earlier that prejudice is usually defined as a "bad" or an "unjustified" attitude. A number of reasons why prejudice is bad have been given, and definitions have differed in emphasizing one or more of these reasons. The following have been most frequently mentioned:

1. Prejudice is based on a faulty or incorrect generalization (Allport, 1954; Jones, 1972; Kelman & Pettigrew, 1959; Peterson, 1958).
2. Prejudice is a rigid or inflexible attitude (Allport, 1954; Krech et al., 1962; Simpson & Yinger, 1985).
3. Prejudice is an overgeneralized attitude (Ashmore & DelBoca, 1976; Marden & Meyer, 1962).
4. Prejudice is an irrational attitude (Ackerman & Jahoda, 1950; Milner, 1983).
5. Prejudice justifies discrimination (Rose, 1951).
6. Prejudice is an attitude that is not based on actual experience or objective evidence (Cooper & McGaugh, 1963; Klineberg, 1968).
7. Prejudice is an unjust attitude (Milner, 1983).

The most elaborate approach to the issue of why prejudice is bad has been that of Harding et al. (1969), which tried to systematize and integrate most points listed above. They argued that prejudice is bad because it violates certain ideal norms, or "standards of conduct that everyone is felt to have some obligation to follow, but are not actually followed by everyone" (p. 5). Three such ideal norms are violated by prejudice: Prejudice violates the norm of rationality by being overgeneralized, rigid, and based on inadequate evidence; it violates the norm of justice because it fails to accord equal treatment to all members of society; and it violates the norm of human-heartedness in denying the basic humanity of others.

The perspective of prejudice as bad arises out of what Rose (1964) and others have termed a social problems approach to intergroup relations. As Harding et al. (1969) pointed out, this means that "the values of the social scientist are inextricably involved in the key concepts of his analysis: 'prejudice' and 'discrimination' are pejorative terms in a way that 'competition' and 'conflict' are not" (p. 2). Although a social problems perspective has been the dominant approach to the study of intergroup relations since the end of World War II, recently there have been indications of change.

The shift away from a social problems perspective is illustrated by a change in the way in which the concept of stereotype is viewed. Traditionally, stereotype was defined as bad in terms very similar to those applied to prejudice. Thus, stereotype was defined as a generalization that was incorrectly learned, rigid, overgeneralized, or factually incorrect (Ashmore & DelBoca, 1981; Brigham, 1971a). During the past decade, this definition has come to be generally rejected in favor of a nonevaluative concept (e.g., Ashmore & DelBoca, 1981; Brewer & Kramer, 1985; Hamilton, 1981c; McCauley, Stitt, & Segal, 1980; Messick & Mackie, 1989).

Ashmore and DelBoca (1981) summarized the three main objections to defining stereotype as bad, and all three appear to be equally relevant to the view of *prejudice* as bad. First, they argued that adding a value judgment to the substantive specification of a stereotype is not parsimonious. Second, defining stereotypes as bad implies that they are "deviant, bizarre, or pathological" and not an outcome of essentially natural cognitive or motivational processes. Third, the badness of stereotypes has simply been assumed and not empirically demonstrated. Thus, there is no evidence indicating that stereotyped beliefs are any more rigid, overgeneralized, or incorrect than any other widely held category-based generalizations.

Although these considerations seem to apply to prejudice as much as to stereotypes, the idea of prejudice as a pejorative concept has been more widespread and more tenacious than was the case for that of stereotype. Whereas it is rare to find stereotype pejoratively defined in contemporary literature, this does still happen in the case of prejudice (e.g., Milner, 1983; Simpson & Yinger, 1985). One reason may be that such a concept of prejudice provides a scientifically awkward, yet ideologically tempting, distinction. This is the distinction between those negative intergroup attitudes that seem reasonable and justifiable to an observer and those that do not. An example would be the antipathy of Jew for German during the period of the Nazi regime as opposed to the antipathy of German for Jew. If prejudice is a social problem, then surely it should refer only to the latter and not to the former phenomenon. In a similar vein, Simpson and Yinger (1985) recently suggested that "for a democrat to be prejudiced against communists and fascists is different from his being prejudiced against Japanese—not entirely different, to be sure, but sufficiently so to require separation in vocabularies (prejudice 1 and prejudice 2). It is the latter type that is the subject of this book" (p. 22).

What makes such a distinction scientifically problematic is that no objective and empirically validated basis has yet been demonstrated for it. As a result, the distinction becomes a purely subjective value judgment almost inevitably influenced by the beliefs, group membership, and biases of the person making it, as well as the social and historical circumstances. To illustrate, Simpson and Yinger's implication that a democrat's dislike of communists may be justified, but not a dislike of the Japanese, may seem reasonable to an American social scientist today. It might not have seemed quite so easy a distinction during World War II when the United States and the Soviet Union were allies against Japan.

Because the idea of prejudice as a bad and unjustified attitude has always been an essentially subjective value judgment, prejudice has never actually been operationalized and measured in that way. Instead, prejudice has simply been measured as a negative intergroup attitude. As a result, the body of scientific knowledge that has emerged on the topic concerns prejudice as a negative intergroup attitude per se, and not prejudice as a particular kind of "bad" negative intergroup attitude.

Such fundamental problems have resulted in a shift away from the social problems perspective of prejudice as a bad or unjustified attitude. One expression of this has been a de-emphasis of the term prejudice in the study of intergroup relations, because of its apparently pejorative connotations. Instead non-evaluative and more neutral terms are favored such as racial or intergroup attitude (e.g., Apostle, Glock, Piazza, & Suelze, 1983), favoritism, or bias (e.g., Messick & Mackie, 1989; Tajfel, 1982b). This has often, at least in the case of the latter two terms, been associated with a more cognitive approach to prejudice and a general de-emphasis of the role of affect in intergroup relations (cf. Hamilton, 1981c).

A second expression of the shift away from a social problems perspective has involved retaining the term prejudice but defining it in an evaluatively neutral rather than a pejorative manner. Some examples are shown in Table 2.2. In essence, they define prejudice as simply a negative intergroup attitude. In contrast to the approach of avoiding the use of the term prejudice altogether, this tends to imply an unambiguous emphasis on the central role of the affective dimension in intergroup relations. This definition has another important advantage: It is consistent with the way in which prejudice has typically been operationalized and measured. As such, it would appear to provide a more appropriate reflection of the phenomenon as it has actually been studied by social scientists.

## ARE THERE DIFFERENT KINDS OF PREJUDICE?

The idea that it might be possible to distinguish between qualitatively different kinds of prejudice has often been raised, particularly in the

Table 2.2
Some Nonpejorative Definitions of Prejudice

---

From a psychological perspective, prejudice can be regarded as a negative attitude toward the members of a minority group (Levin & Levin, 1982, p. 66).

An attitude towards members of a specific group, leading to a negative evaluation of them on the basis of that membership (Vaughan, 1988, p. 2).

A readiness to respond to a person in an unfavorable manner on the basis of his or her class or category membership (Gergen & Gergen, 1981, p. 121).

A negative attitude toward members of socially defined groups (Stephan, 1983, p. 417).

A favourable or unfavourable predisposition toward any member of the category in question (Tajfel, 1982b, p. 3).

Shared feelings of acceptance-rejection, trust-distrust, and liking-disliking that characterize attitudes toward specific groups in the social system (Brewer & Kramer, 1985, p. 230).

---

case of racism (e.g., Allport, 1954; Campbell, 1971; Hamilton, 1972; Kovel, 1970; Rothbart, 1976; Schermerhorn, 1970; Schuman & Harding, 1964; van den Berghe, 1967; Vanneman & Pettigrew, 1972). For example, Schermerhorn (1970) suggested a distinction between maximal and minimal racism: Maximal racism involved a belief in the inherent biological inferiority of blacks, whereas minimal racism saw this inferiority as socially and culturally determined. Kovel (1970), on the other hand, suggested a distinction between the "dominative" racism of the American South and the "aversive" racism of the North. He proposed that these two kinds of racism involved quite different psychodynamics—oedipal and anal, respectively. Thus, the dominative racism of the South permitted intimate interracial contact, with, for example, black women being used as sexual objects while black men were objects to be feared, envied, and castrated. The aversive racism of the North, on the other hand, allowed blacks certain formal rights while it severely circumscribed interracial contact. A third example is van den Berghe's (1967) historically and sociologically based typology. This differentiates between paternalistic racism, which is seen as characteristic of societies in which white domination and superiority is uncontested and consensually accepted, and competitive racism, in which the legitimacy of white domination and superiority is challenged and open intergroup animosity results.

Although many of these typologies seem intuitively plausible, few have any empirical basis. In none of the cases cited above, for example, have the typologies been operationalized and adequate measures of the various types been developed. This makes an assessment of their validity and utility very difficult. A different approach to this problem was taken by Woodmansee and Cook (1967) in the development of their Multifactor Racial Attitude Inventory (MRAI). They used factor and cluster analysis to construct a 100-item racial attitude inventory consisting of 10 empirically distinct subscales. The subscales were assumed to reflect different dimensions of whites' attitudes toward blacks, including dimensions such as derogatory beliefs, ease in interracial contacts, integration-segregation policy, acceptance in status-superior relationships, and so forth. The 10 dimensions were replicated by a later cluster analytic study, which also added two new dimensions (Brigham, Woodmansee, & Cook, 1976).

Whether these subscales measure usefully distinct dimensions, however, can be contested. First, they tend to be highly intercorrelated. The mean intercorrelation of the original ten MRAI scales was .54, and it would presumably have been even higher if one of the subscales ("black superiority"), which had negligible correlations with all the other subscales, had been excluded. As Harding et al. (1969) pointed out, when the MRAI is factor analyzed, like most other measures of racial attitude, it gives a powerful general factor of favorableness versus unfavorableness with correlations between factor scales not much below their reliabilities.

Second, little consistent evidence exists that such dimensions correlate differently with other theoretically pertinent constructs or behavioral variables. In fact, the evidence suggests that although factor-analytically distinct dimensions can be obtained from inventories such as the MRAI, these dimensions have essentially similar patterns of association with other variables (Brigham et al., 1976; Woodmansee and Cook, 1967). This means that these dimensions may not be delineating usefully distinct constructs.

The most important contemporary approach distinguishing different kinds of prejudice has been the theory of symbolic racism. This proposes that old-fashioned or traditional racism in the United States has been largely replaced by a newer kind of racism, termed either symbolic racism (Kinder & Sears, 1981; McConahay & Hough, 1976; Sears & Kinder, 1971) or modern racism (McConahay, 1983; McConahay et al., 1981).

The essential argument here is that racial prejudice in its traditional form was expressed in sentiments of white supremacy, black inferiority, and racial segregation, all of which have become unacceptable in the mainstream of American society. As a result, it has been replaced by symbolic racism, which does not express racist sentiments in an overtly obvious and recognizable manner. Instead, these sentiments emerge as:

a blend of anti-black affect and the kind of traditional values embodied in the Protestant Ethic. Symbolic racism represents a form of resistance to change in the racial status quo based on moral feelings that blacks violate such traditional American values as individualism and self-reliance, the work ethic, obedience, and discipline. (Kinder & Sears, 1981, p. 416)

Symbolic racism was seen as being particularly characteristic of affluent white suburbanites in the American North, whereas traditional, old-fashioned, or red-neck racism would mainly be found among "unedu-cated and lower class Southern whites" (McConahay & Hough, 1976).

A good deal of research indicates the usefulness of this approach. Measures of symbolic racism (with items such as "Negroes are going too far in their push for equal rights") have been shown to be stronger predictors than traditional racism of whites voting along racial lines (Kinder & Sears, 1981), voting for Reagan (Weigel & Howes, 1985), opposition to busing (McConahay, 1982), and opposition to affirmative action (Jacobson, 1985). In addition, affluent white suburbanites readily endorsed symbolic racism items but not traditional racism items (McConahay & Hough, 1976), whereas students tended to find tradi-tional racism items but not symbolic racism items objectionably racist (McConahay et al., 1981; McConahay & Hough, 1976).

The theory of symbolic racism has also produced a good deal of con-troversy, however (e.g., Bobo, 1983; Kinder, 1986; Sears & Kinder, 1985; Sniderman & Tetlock, 1986a, 1986b; Weigel & Howes, 1985). One par-ticularly controversial issue is whether symbolic racism is merely a more contemporary expression of the same basic attitude underlying tradi-tional racism, or whether it is a substantively different construct rep-resenting a new and distinctive kind of racism. Proponents of the theory of symbolic racism have invariably taken the latter position. According to McConahay and Hough (1976): "Symbolic racism is an expression of some of the negative feelings underlying old-fashioned or red-neck rac-ism, but it differs from them in its other psychological roots and in many of its specific forms of expression" (p. 34). The psychological roots re-ferred to here are a blending of conservative, moralistic, and antiblack socialization. It was also suggested that symbolic racism would not be associated with factors associated with traditional racism, such as per-ceived threat from blacks, alienation, dissatisfaction, and powerlessness (Kinder & Sears, 1981; McConahay & Hough, 1976).

An early study by McConahay and Hough (1976) seemed to support the idea that symbolic and traditional racism were relatively independent constructs. Measures of both were administered to a sample of seminary students and found not to be significantly correlated. However, this study has been seriously criticized. Weigel and Howes (1985), for ex-ample, pointed out that the traditional racism scale consisted of eight rather obvious and offensively racist items drawn from only two subscales of the MRAI (negative stereotypes and segregationism). More-over, the sample was atypical and homogeneous: Young seminary students would tend to be particularly liberal and very sensitive to state-ments that openly support segregation and racial inferiority. In fact, nearly 40 percent of the sample refused to answer the traditional racism items, and the variance in response of those who did answer was very limited compared to the other scales used in the study.

The restricted response variance in this study could have been re-sponsible for the failure of the symbolic and traditional racism scales to be significantly correlated. Weigel and Howes (1985) reinvestigated the issue using a more appropriate measure of traditional racism, the short form of the MRAI proposed by its developers, and a community sample randomly selected from a medium-sized American city in the northeast. The correlation between the symbolic and traditional racism scales was very powerful ($r = .67$) and not much below the reliabilities of the two scales. Several other studies have also reported correlations between symbolic and traditional racism: McConahay (1982) found a correlation of .58, McClendon (1985) .65, and Jacobson (1985) .49. These correlations are high and in several cases would be higher after correcting for poor scale reliabilities—for example, in the Jacobson study, traditional racism was measured by an ad hoc scale of only two items. Clearly, these findings do not support the idea that symbolic racism is a distinctively different construct from traditional racism.

On the other hand, however, Kinder (1986) pointed out that factor analyses have generated separate symbolic and traditional racism factors in several studies (e.g., Bobo, 1983; McConahay, 1982, 1986). However, this is not an entirely consistent finding. Jacobson (1985), for example, found that symbolic and traditional racism items loaded on a single factor. Factor analysis is also a purely empirical technique, and the num-ber of factors extracted depends on fundamentally arbitrary decisions. In addition, the degree to which groups of items are semantically similar or different may result in factors emerging that have little theoretical or empirical significance. Whether such factors form usefully distinct con-structs must be ultimately decided by other considerations. Two of these, directly relevant to the present issue, are the degree of correlation be-tween the factors, or scales, and the extent to which the scales predict other theoretically or practically relevant criteria differently.

In the former case, it has already been noted that symbolic and tra-ditional racism scales tend to be very strongly correlated. In the latter case, no evidence has been reported, indicating that symbolic and tra-ditional racism have different patterns of correlation with other impor-tant constructs. In fact, the most important correlates of symbolic racism have been such variables as education, political conservatism, patriot-ism, and social conventionalism (McConahay & Hough, 1976). Without exception, these are also well-established correlates of traditional racism (Ashmore, 1970; Harding et al., 1969; Simpson & Yinger, 1985). Contrary to the idea that symbolic racism would be more common among the better educated, education shows a strong inverse correlation with symbolic racism, just as it does with traditional racism (McClendon, 1985; McConahay & Hough, 1976).

McConahay and Hough (1976) and others (Kinder, 1986; Kinder & Sears, 1981) argued that an important distinction between symbolic and traditional racism was that the former was rooted not just in racist socialization but in a combination of racist and conservative socialization. However, when Weigel and Howes (1985) investigated this, they found that symbolic and traditional measures showed very similar correlations with several measures of conservatism. Sniderman and Tetlock (1986a), in reviewing the issue of whether symbolic and traditional racism can be differentiated in terms of their pattern of correlation with other variables, concluded that "on the information in hand, it appears that every major cause of symbolic racism is, simultaneously, a major cause of old-fashioned racism; and every major cause of old-fashioned racism is a major cause of symbolic [racism]" (p. 137).

In certain instances, however, symbolic and traditional racism have produced correlations with other variables that differ in magnitude, though not in direction. For instance, symbolic racism was a stronger predictor, sometimes to quite a substantial extent, of racially relevant behaviors and policy positions such as voting for white or conservative candidates (Kinder & Sears, 1981; Weigel & Howes, 1985), opposition to busing (McConahay, 1982; Sears, Hensler, & Speer, 1979), and opposition to affirmative action (Jacobson, 1985). These findings, however, do not necessarily mean that symbolic racism is a new and different kind of racism. They are quite consistent with it being simply a more subtle, more socially acceptable, more sophisticated, and more covert expression of racial prejudice. As a result, it should provide a more discriminating measure of prejudice and better prediction of expressions of racism, particularly in social settings where "old-fashioned" racist beliefs are no longer completely socially acceptable.

Overall, therefore, the evidence seems to suggest that symbolic racism is not a qualitatively different kind of racism. It seems probable that it is merely a more contemporary and socially acceptable expression of the same basic antiblack attitude that was expressed in traditional racism. Jacobson (1985) forcefully concluded on the basis of his findings that "what is new is not the new racism, but rather the exclusion of a few generalized items about racial integration (old-fashioned racism) from the usual cluster of racial bigotry items. The new racism may be symbolic, but from the Harris data it appears to be quite old-fashioned" (p. 328).

Several recent reviews of this issue suggested similar conclusions (Sniderman & Tetlock, 1986a; Ward, 1985; Weigel & Howes, 1985). As one of these pointed out, the basic lesson from the debate seems to be that "people justify their discriminatory behavior toward minorities in ways that change over time under the pressure of what society considers respectable" (Weigel & Howes, 1985, p. 124). New social developments bring new ways to express negative intergroup attitudes and a concomitant need for new and updated measures of these attitudes. This has important and obvious implications for attempts to predict behavior from measures of prejudice, which will be taken up in the next chapter.

## CONCLUSIONS

Prejudice has been an important psychological concept for the understanding of intergroup phenomena. However, its definition and conceptualization have involved several awkward problems and a great deal of disagreement. Three issues appear to be of major significance and were discussed in this chapter.

The first issue—whether prejudice should be defined simply as a negative intergroup attitude or as an attitude that is bad in some way—has been the most clearly problematic in the literature. Underlying this problem appears to be the desire to differentiate between intergroup dislike that seems reasonable and justified and that which does not. Thus, there seems to be a difference between the hostility oppressors feel for their victims and that which oppressed peoples feel toward their persecutors. However, although a number of attempts have been made to specify when negative intergroup attitudes are unreasonable, bad, and unjustified, no objectively specifiable or validated criterion has yet emerged. As a result, contemporary approaches have begun to shift to nonevaluative definitions of prejudice as simply a negative intergroup attitude. This approach has the important advantage of being consistent with the way in which prejudice has actually been measured and studied.

A second problem involves the meaning of the concept of attitude. It is generally agreed that prejudice is an attitude, but there is much less agreement over what an attitude is. Psychologists, for example, have used two quite different models of attitude. The three-component model has been most favored, particularly by writers on prejudice. Its primary advantage appears to be its breadth, combining important related concepts such as stereotype, the affective dimension of liking–disliking, and discriminatory behavioral dispositions as expressed in social distance, into a single integrative conceptualization. However, this approach also has a number of serious problems, in particular its vagueness, its lack of empirical support, and the fact that prejudice has rarely, if ever, been measured in this way. Unidimensional approaches that see prejudiced attitudes in terms of the affective dimension only, and which treat concepts such as stereotype and social distance as conceptually distinct, seem to have important advantages. These include greater clarity and precision, more adequate theoretical grounding, and consistency with the way in which prejudiced attitudes have usually been measured.

The third problem is whether different kinds of prejudice can be distinguished. A number of typologies of racism have been proposed, most of which have little if any empirical basis. One approach that has received attention is the theory of symbolic racism. This argues that a new kind of racism has emerged in America which is qualitatively different from traditional racism. However, while factor analytic studies indicate that measures of symbolic and traditional racism often emerge as separate factors, the correlation between them tends to be very powerful and not far below their reliabilities. Symbolic and traditional racism also show very similar patterns of correlation with other variables, though symbolic racism often proves to be a superior predictor of behavioral and other expressions of racism. This suggests that symbolic racism may not be a new and different kind of racism, but, rather, a more subtle, contemporary, and sophisticated expression of racial prejudice. In general, it would seem that the usefulness of typological and multidimensional approaches to racism and prejudice have not yet been clearly demonstrated.

Finally, an important question arises: To what extent is prejudice as a negative intergroup attitude related to intergroup behavior? Social scientists have often assumed that prejudice is closely related to discriminatory behavior, using this to justify the emphasis they have placed on the study of prejudice (e.g., Levin & Levin, 1982). The belief in such an interrelationship has been seriously challenged, however, with some arguing that most of the available evidence indicates prejudice may not be closely related to discriminatory behavior at all. This issue is discussed in the next chapter.

# 3

# Prejudice and Behavior

Traditionally, psychologists assumed that there was a close and direct relationship between prejudiced intergroup attitudes and hostile and discriminatory intergroup behavior. Allport (1954), for example, suggested that although prejudiced people may not always act out their prejudices, there is a strong tendency for this to happen: "It is true that any negative attitude tends somehow, somewhere to express itself in action. Few people keep their antipathies entirely to themselves. The more intense the attitude, the more likely it is to result in vigorously hostile action" (p. 14). He suggested five graduations of increasingly intense behavioral expressions of prejudice: (1) antilocution, or verbally expressing antipathy; (2) avoidance; (3) discrimination by, for example, excluding members of the group in question from certain social rights or privileges; (4) physical attack; and (5) extermination.

In fact, a lower level could well be added to this hierarchy as a variety of extremely subtle and indirect behavioral expressions of intergroup antipathy have since been empirically demonstrated. These include indicators such as voice tone (Weitz, 1972), failing to respect personal space (Brown, 1981), less eye contact, less verbal interaction, less friendliness (Bielby, 1987), and attributional biases such as interpreting negative behavior by outgroup members as dispositionally rather than situationally determined and the reverse for positive behavior (Pettigrew, 1979).

The belief that prejudiced attitudes and negative intergroup behavior are very closely related has often been used to justify the emphasis that social scientists have placed on the study of prejudice. Levin and Levin (1982), for example, stated that: "We are interested in prejudice only to the extent that it is related to actual discrimination" (p. 81). Most social scientists would probably regard this as an overstatement and consider prejudice is an issue that merits attention in its own right.

Nevertheless, the question of the nature and magnitude of its relationship with behavior remains a highly relevant issue.

The belief that prejudice and behavior are closely related has also come to be seriously questioned on empirical grounds. Ehrlich (1973) pointed out that "studies of the relation of prejudice and behavior have almost consistently resulted in a summary statement of the form that prejudice is a poor predictor of discrimination" (p. 8). This conclusion has been widely accepted (e.g., Bowser, 1985; Brigham, 1971b, Feagin & Eckberg, 1980; Green, 1972; Schwarzwald & Yinon, 1978), and it has therefore often been emphasized that the relationship appears to be complex and by no means straightforward (Bowser, 1985; Brigham, 1971b; Ehrlich, 1973; Feagin & Eckberg, 1980; Green, 1972). Merton's (1970) four-category typology interrelating prejudice and discrimination (unprejudiced nondiscriminators, unprejudiced discriminators, prejudiced non-discriminators, and prejudiced discriminators) has been much cited to illustrate this complexity (e.g., Feagin & Eckberg, 1980; Levin & Levin, 1982; Simpson & Yinger, 1985). More recently, however, certain theoretical and empirical developments suggest that this may have been an overly pessimistic conclusion. The remainder of this chapter is therefore devoted to an overview and reappraisal of this issue.

## PREJUDICE AND BEHAVIOR: SOCIOLOGICAL STUDIES

Several early field and ethnographic studies conducted mainly by sociologists raised the possibility that prejudiced attitudes and behavior might often be quite discrepant. Four studies were particularly influential and have been much cited in the literature. These are the studies by LaPiere (1934), Kutner, Wilkens, and Yarrow (1952), Saenger and Gilbert (1950), and Minard (1952).

LaPiere toured the United States with a Chinese couple, stopping at many hotels and restaurants. Although anti-Chinese attitudes were common at the time, they were refused service only once. Six months later he sent questionnaires to the establishments visited, asking whether they would be prepared to accept Chinese as guests. More than 90 percent of those who replied stated that they would not. Kutner et al. (1952) conducted a very similar study. Two white and one black women entered eleven restaurants in a fashionable suburban community in the northeastern United States and were served normally. Later attempts by letter to secure reservations at these restaurants for a racially mixed group were ignored, and telephone calls resulted in either refusals or attempts to dissuade the group from coming.

Saenger and Gilbert (1950) investigated the consequences of introducing black sales personnel in department stores and found that prejudiced customers did not avoid black clerks or the stores employing them. Minard (1952) studied race relations in several American coal mining communities; he found virtually complete racial integration and equality in the work situation and the trade union but strict segregation outside these areas. The majority of white miners accepted this apparent incongruity as perfectly natural, shifting from egalitarianism to white superiority as they moved from one situation to the other.

Overall, these findings seemed to suggest that the way people actually behaved could be quite different from their stated attitudes or intentions. In fact, individuals' behavior appeared to be determined by their roles and situations rather than by their attitudes. On the basis of such findings, Rose (1956), an eminent sociologist, argued that:

It may be desirable to assume that patterns of intergroup relations (including mainly discrimination and segregation) are quite distinct from attitudes of prejudice in that each has a separate and distinct history, cause, and process of change. In other words . . . patterns of intergroup relations on the one hand, and attitudes of prejudice and stereotyping, on the other hand, are fairly unrelated phenomena. (p. 173)

These findings, however, were open to a number of criticisms. In LaPiere and Kutner et al.'s studies, for example, the reaction of proprietors could have been powerfully influenced by the fact that the Chinese and black customers were accompanied by obviously respectable white persons (Linn, 1965). Proprietors may have had no objection to serving respectable, middle-class blacks or Chinese, and they may have refused the reservations because of the activation of cultural stereotypes of blacks and Chinese as rough and uneducated laborers (Lord, Lepper, & Mackie, 1984). In fact, these proprietors may not have been expressing their real attitudes at all in refusing reservations and may only have done so to try and minimize the possibility of incidents that might damage their business. Finally, both LaPiere and Kutner et al.'s studies assessed intention rather than attitude, and they assumed that the latter could simply be inferred from the former.

Overall, the findings from these early field studies were suggestive, but they lacked the precision and control necessary for a definitive assessment of the degree of correspondence between intergroup attitudes and behavior (Green, 1972; Linn, 1965). They did, however, stimulate a series of more systematic, quasi-experimental studies designed to assess the association between antiblack prejudice and actions in a more direct and rigorous manner. These studies, which are summarized in Table 3.1, were conducted mainly in the 1960s and early 1970s. At the time, desegregation and the civil rights movement made the issue of the relationship between prejudiced attitudes and action a particularly salient one in the United States.

**Table 3.1**
**Studies Investigating the Relationship Between Prejudiced Attitudes and Action**

| Study | Sample | Attitude measure | Behavior measure | Attitude-behavior relation |
|---|---|---|---|---|
| DeFleur & Westie, 1958 | 23 high and 23 low prejudice college students | Likert scale of anti-black prejudice | Signing releases to be photographed with blacks for various uses | Significant ($p < .01$), but almost 30% of subjects were inconsistent |
| Linn, 1965 | 34 white female college students | Self-report of readiness to pose for photos with black male and release use of photos | Actual request four weeks later to pose for and permit use of photo | Nonsignificant, and 58% of subjects were inconsistent |
| Fendrich, 1967 | 189 white college students | Likert scale of anti-black prejudice | Signing a pledge to attend NAACP meeting | Significant, Gamma = .71 |
| DeFriese & Ford, 1969 | 262 householders in one U.S. city | Thurstone scale of antiblack prejudice | Signing a public declaration of support or opposition to residential integration | Tau-B = .095 for all responses, and .40 when nonresponses were excluded |
| Warner & DeFleur, 1969 | 121 white college students | Likert scale of antiblack prejudice | Signing pledges to engage in various interracial activities | Significant association ($p < .01$) |
| Warner & Dennis, 1970 | 537 white college students | Self-report of readiness to engage in specific interracial activities | Later solicited by letter to sign a pledge to participate in one of these interracial activities | Overall gamma = .27 but 37% were inconsistent |
| Green, 1972 | 22 high and 22 low prejudice white students | MRAI | Signing agreement to pose for interracial photos to illustrate textbook | Manova indicated highly significant effect |
| Ewens & Ehrlich, 1972 | 83 white college students | Antiblack prejudice (cognitive, affective, and conative) | Signing pledges to participate in 12 civil rights activities | Tau-B ranged from .09 to .52 with 8 of the 12 significant |

All these studies used essentially the same basic research design. Typically, the subjects were white American students. Attitudes were assessed by questionnaires, such as the MRAI, that measured general antiblack sentiments, or in some other cases by quite specific questions about how subjects would behave in hypothetical interracial situations. Behaviors were often assessed some time after the attitude measure, in certain cases weeks or even months later. These criterion behaviors usually involved some kind of social activism regarded as indicative of nonprejudice. Thus, subjects were requested to commit themselves (usually by signing a pledge) to behaviors such as participating in interracial or civil rights activities, or they were asked to sign statements of belief or pose for interracial photographs that could be made public.

The most influential of these studies was conducted by Linn (1965). White female students answered items embedded in a more general survey questionnaire asking if they would pose for photos with a black male for uses involving varying degrees of publicity, ranging from publication in a professional scientific journal to being used in a nationwide campaign for racial integration. One month later, these students were subjected to a carefully contrived behavioral test. During an ostensibly unrelated interview with one white and two black representatives of a "psychological testing corporation" (actually confederates of the experimenter), the subjects were confronted with exactly the same request, now no longer as a hypothetical issue but as a reality. Many of the subjects found the situation an extremely uncomfortable and stressful one, and fully 58 percent behaved differently in the apparently real-life situation from what they had earlier said they would do. In almost every case, the inconsistency arose from subjects who had said they would permit photos to be taken and used, but were then not prepared to do so. Overall, the association between intention and actual behavior was statistically nonsignificant.

Linn's conclusion from this finding was that "statements or predictions of racial behavior based on attitude measurement have little reliability unless first validated empirically" (p. 353). Several of the other studies listed in Table 3.1 also noted marked inconsistencies. Warner and Dennis (1970), using a research design similar to Linn's, found that 37 percent of their subjects were inconsistent, while DeFleur and Westie (1958) reported inconsistency for nearly 30 percent of their subjects. Although these two studies emphasized the inconsistency that was observed, in both cases the overall association between attitude and behavior was highly significant in the direction of consistency. In fact, except for Linn's study, this was the case for all the studies listed in Table 3.1. Overviews of this research, however, tended to stress the inconsistency that was observed (Bowser, 1985; Brigham, 1971b; Ehrlich,

1973; Feagin & Eckberg, 1980; Green, 1972; Warner & Dennis, 1970). There seem to be several reasons for this.

First, although the statistical analyses used in these studies generally did not give direct estimates of effect strength, the associations between attitude and behavior, while clearly significant, typically did not seem very powerful. Second, in most of these studies the behavioral tests might not have appeared to have quite the degree of realism and immediacy, as was the case in Linn's study. Thus, Linn's study might have seemed a more valid assessment than the others.

On the other hand, these studies shared one important problem, which could have resulted in a serious underestimation of the degree of attitude-behavior consistency: in most cases the questionnaire measures of attitude or intention were not anonymous. Because attitudinal and behavioral measures were obtained at different times, subjects were required to write their names on their questionnaires. As a result, their responses would be known, at least to those faculty involved in the study.

At the time, civil rights and desegregation were highly salient issues on American campuses, and many students and faculty espoused strong liberal sentiments. This meant that there could be powerful demand characteristics for undergraduate psychology students to present a liberal image, which might not accurately reflect their underlying attitudes. In fact, in discussing his results, Linn commented that many of his subjects were attempting to play a "university social role as a racial liberal" (p. 363). Clearly, it would be easier to present such an image in responding to a questionnaire than in a realistic behavioral situation that involved a number of costs and implications.

Summing up, therefore, early ethnographic and field studies—of which LaPiere's is the classic example—raised the possibility that intergroup behavior might be primarily determined by roles and situations and thus have little relation to individuals' attitudes. This stimulated a series of more rigorously controlled quasi-experimental studies by sociologists and social psychologists. These indicated a significant, but not necessarily very powerful, degree of consistency between attitudes and behavior. In some studies quite marked discrepancies were also noted. Despite the evidence of at least a moderate degree of consistency, and certain methodological problems that appear to preclude definitive conclusions, reviews of this research emphasized the inconsistency, rather than the consistency, that was found.

## PREJUDICE AND BEHAVIOR: PSYCHOLOGICAL STUDIES

Whereas the more sociological studies listed in Table 3.1 looked at social actions that seemed to indicate prejudice or nonprejudice, psychological studies focused more specifically on discriminatory behavioral responses to outgroup members. In essence, these studies have sought to show that prejudiced individuals respond differently and negatively to those against whom they are prejudiced. A number of such studies have been reported for a variety of potentially discriminatory responses. The results of these studies have not been very consistent; although most have found significant relationships between discriminatory treatment and prejudice, a number have not.

The latter studies have often been cited as showing that prejudice and discrimination do not seem to be related (e.g., Bowser, 1985; Brigham, 1971b; Ehrlich, 1973; Feagin & Eckberg, 1980). However, this conclusion may not be warranted. A good deal of evidence suggests that groups experiencing discrimination are not discriminated against in all situations. This is illustrated by an important review of unobtrusive studies of antiblack discrimination by white Americans in areas such as helping behavior, aggression, and nonverbal communication (Crosby, Bromley, & Saxe, 1980). While discrimination against blacks was found in most studies, it was often not present. In the case of studies investigating helping behavior, for example, whites tended not to discriminate against blacks in situations involving face-to-face contact. On the other hand, discrimination was much more likely in situations in which there was no direct contact with the person to be helped. Overall, discrimination tended to be absent when surveillance was high and discrimination was costly. Conversely, discrimination tended to occur when surveillance was low and discrimination involved no costs for the discriminator.

This has obvious implications for studies investigating the relationship between prejudice and discrimination. If behavior toward outgroup members is generally not discriminatory in a particular situation, one would not expect any relationship between prejudice and that behavior. Studies that found a relationship between prejudice and discriminatory behavior and those that did not are listed in Tables 3.2 and 3.3, respectively. In the latter (Table 3.3), the results indicate that no discrimination overall occurred in seven studies, and insufficient data was reported to ascertain whether discrimination occurred or not in the remaining two. On the other hand, in the former (Table 3.2), discrimination was present for all those studies for which overall data was reported. Thus, it would seem that failures to obtain any association between prejudice and discriminatory behavior can be attributed to discriminatory behavior not occurring in those studies. When discrimination does occur, a relationship with prejudice appears to have emerged fairly consistently.

An interesting point emerges from a comparison of Tables 3.2 and 3.3. The studies in which discrimination tended not to occur and behavior was not related to prejudice usually involved structured tasks with relatively clear-cut goals and procedures: administering punish-

**Table 3.2**

**Studies of the Relationship Between Prejudiced Attitudes and Discriminatory Behavior: Studies in Which Prejudice Is Related to Discrimination**

| Study[a] | Sample | Attitude measure | Behavior measure | Attitude-behavior relation |
|---|---|---|---|---|
| Iverson & Schwab, 1967 (?) | 23 students high and 23 low on ethnocentric dogmatism | California E and Dogmatism scales | Binocular resolution of white/black photos presented by tachistoscope | Subjects low on ethnocentrism obtained binocular fusion more often ($p < .01$). |
| Smith & Dixon, 1968 (?) | 136 high and low prejudice white female students | California E scale | Verbal conditioning to white and black experimenters | Prejudiced subjects conditioned to white but not black experimenters ($p < .01$) |
| Beloff & Coupar, 1969 (D) | 42 Scottish college students | Antiblack prejudice | Estimating the distance of black or white faces shown in a stereoscope | More prejudiced subjects located the black faces further from them ($p < .05$) |
| Melamed, 1970 (?) | 31 white South African college students | Willingness for social contact with blacks | Agreeing to accompany black fellow research subject to refectory | Point biserial correlation of .48 ($p < .01$). |
| Brigham, 1971b (?) | 200 white college students | MRAI | Role-playing a judge evaluating and sentencing whites and blacks | Correlations of .29, .28, and .16 with evaluations and sentences of blacks |
| Richards, & Jaffee, 1972 (D) | 356 college students | MRAI | Response to and rating the performance of black and white supervisors of work groups | Prejudiced subordinates tended to give poorer ratings to black supervisors ($p < .01$) |
| Boyanowsky & Allen, 1973 (?) | 170 white college students | Likert scale of antiblack prejudice | Reducing conformity in Asch group pressure situation with support from black or white confederate | Prejudiced subjects more influenced by whites ($p < .01$) in personal opinions but not in judgments of line length |
| Montgomery & Enzie, 1973 (D) | 40 high and 40 low prejudice white students | California E scale | Amount of agreement on autokinetic judgments with white or black confederates | Highly prejudiced subjects were significantly more influenced by white than black confederates ($p < .01$) |

| Study (year) | Sample | Measure | Task | Results |
|---|---|---|---|---|
| Porter, 1974 (D) | 218 white college students | Likert scale of antiblack prejudice | Persuasive communication from black or white authority to assist anti-delinquency program | More prejudiced subjects were much less likely to comply with black communicator ($r = .61$) |
| Sappington, 1974 (?) | 22 female college students | Liberal-conservative on civil rights self-rating | Simulated participation in interracial video discussion group | $p < .05$ for amount spoken to, negative affect to, and choosing black partner |
| Mabe & Williams, 1975 (D) | 32 white and 20 black second-grade children | Preschool Racial Attitude Measure (PRAM II) | Choosing whites or blacks as partners | Correlation of .52 between color bias and choice of white or black partner |
| Feldman & Donohoe, 1978 (D) | 36 high and low prejudice white students | MRAI | Role-playing a teacher praising a successful black or white student | Prejudiced "teachers" were discriminatory in non-verbal behavior ($p < .05$) |
| Bagley & Verma, 1979 (?) | 38 white high school students | Anti-West Indian attitude scale | Ratings of interaction with black students during school-related activities | $p < .01$ for avoidance of and negative interactions with black students |
| Press, Burt, & Barling, 1979 (D) | 20 black and 20 white South African preschool children | Questionnaire assessment of racial preference | Donating sweets to photographs of black and white children | Correlation of .62 between racial preference and donating sweets |
| McConahay, 1983 (?) | 81 white college students | Modern racism scale | Evaluating the resumés of white and black job applicants | More prejudiced subjects rated blacks less favorably ($r = -.50$) |
| Patchen, 1983 (?) | 1200 black and 1500 white high school students | Likert scale of general attitude to whites/blacks | Self-reported friendly and unfriendly interracial contact, and avoidance | Eta coefficients of .22, .3, and .37, respectively |

[a](?) = Results do not indicate whether or not there was overall discrimination; (D) = Discrimination was observed overall in the study.

**Table 3.3**
**Studies Investigating the Relationship Between Prejudiced Attitudes and Discriminatory Behavior: Behaviors for Which Prejudice Is Not Related to Discrimination**

| Study[a] | Sample | Attitude measure | Behavior measure | Attitude-behavior relation |
|---|---|---|---|---|
| Bray, 1950 (ND) | 150 white college students | Likert scales of antiblack and anti-Semitic prejudice | Amount of agreement on autokinetic judgments with gentile, Jewish, or black confederate | Anti-Semitic or antiblack prejudice did not influence degree of agreement with confederates |
| Malof & Lott, 1962 (ND) | 30 low and 30 high prejudice students | California E scale | Reducing conformity in group pressure situation with support from a black or white confederate | High prejudice subjects were not more influenced by the white than by the black confederate |
| Berg, 1966 (?) | 60 white male college students | F and E scales, and social distance scale | Amount of agreement on autokinetic judgments with white or black confederate | No tendency for prejudice to be related to degree of agreement with the black confederate |
| Boyanowsky & Allen, 1973 (?) | 170 white college students | Likert scale of antiblack prejudice | Reducing conformity in Asch group pressure situation with support from black or white confederate | Prejudiced subjects were not more influenced by the white confederate in judgments of line length |
| Genthner & Taylor, 1973 (?) | 18 high and 18 low prejudice white college students | Holtzman D scale | Administering shock to black or white opponents in a competitive task | Prejudiced whites were generally more punitive but not differentially so to blacks |

34

| | | | | |
|---|---|---|---|---|
| Larsen, Colen, von Flue, & Zimmerman, 1974 (ND) | 40 male white college students | Antiblack scale | Administering shock to blacks and whites for mistakes in a learning task | No tendency for more prejudiced whites to be more punitive to blacks |
| Wexley & Nemeroff, 1974 (ND) | 120 white college students | MRAI | Evaluating the resumés of white and black job applicants | More prejudiced whites did not evaluate black applicants less favorably |
| Rand & Wexley, 1975 (ND) | 160 white college students | Holtzman D scale | Evaluating job applicants on the basis of videotaped employment interviews | More prejudiced whites did not evaluate black applicants less favorably than whites |
| Schwartzwald & Yinon, 1978 (ND) | 96 Israeli high school students of Western origin | Evaluative trait rating scale of Oriental Jews | Administering shock to Oriental or Western Jews in a competitive task | No tendency for more prejudiced Western Jews to be more punitive to Orientals |

[a](?) = Results do not indicate whether or not there was overall discrimination; (ND) = No discrimination was observed overall in the study.

ment in learning and competitive situations, evaluating job applicants, and judging the position of a light or length of a line with a partner. In such situations, criteria other than personal likes and dislikes might be salient. Thus, norms of equity, objectivity, fairness, and suppressing personal biases might be activated, and, perhaps, be particularly strong for American college students in an interracial context. Consequently, such situations could minimize discrimination and the expression of prejudice, especially when surveillance was high or when cues accentuating these norms were present.

On the other hand, the studies in which discrimination tended to occur and was related to prejudice (Table 3.3) generally involved informal social interaction. The criterion behaviors were usually friendliness or choosing partners, or they were behaviors that occur outside conscious awareness, such as verbal conditioning and binocular fusion of stimuli. In such situations, one's personal likes and dislikes might be more salient and seem normatively permissible. Consequently, discrimination and the expression of prejudice could be facilitated.

In the few cases in which discrimination and a relationship with prejudice were found in more structured task situations, cues were clearly present that de-emphasized formal task objectives and made subjects' personal inclinations more salient (i.e., Boyanowsky and Allen, 1973; McConahay, 1983). For example, in McConahay's study, subjects evaluated the resumés of job applicants; however, the instructions to the subjects emphasized that the purpose of the study was not to evaluate the quality of the applicant per se, but to assess the subjective impression that the physical appearance of the resumé (typeface, color of the paper, etc.) made on the reader. The study by Boyanowsky and Allen (1973) used a group pressure situation. Discrimination in accepting support from a black or white confederate was not found when the task involved making judgments of physical stimuli (length of lines, or shape of geometric figures), but it was found when the judgments were about statements of personal opinion and belief.

Summing up, therefore, more formal and structured situations in which task objectives are salient seem to be less likely to generate discriminatory behavior, whereas less formal, less structured, social interactive situations in which personal inclinations are salient seem more likely to result in discrimination. This differentiation partly complements and partly cuts across the one suggested by Crosby et al. (1980) between situations of high surveillance, where discrimination is costly, and situations of low surveillance, where discrimination has little cost. Not surprisingly, when discrimination does not occur, no relationship is found between prejudice and behavior. On the other hand, when discrimination does occur, a relationship between prejudice and discriminatory behavior emerges quite consistently. This raises the question of how strong the relationship is.

The magnitude of the effects reported in the research varies considerably. In some cases the association is weak (e.g., Brigham, 1971b; Patchen, 1983), whereas in others it appears to be quite substantial (e.g., Mabe & Williams, 1975; Press et al., 1979). Often results are reported in a way that does not permit a reliable estimation of effect size. The best overall conclusion would appear to be that the relationship obtained is usually in the weak to moderate range.

This conclusion is similar to the one suggested by the sociologically orientated studies described in the previous section (listed in Table 3.1). Although the relationship between prejudice and action is consistent, it is typically not strong and may be quite weak. Similar conclusions have been drawn for the relationship between attitudes and behavior in general. For example, a number of influential reviews of this issue appeared around 1970 (Deutscher, 1973; McGuire, 1966; Wicker, 1969). The reviews, of which Wicker's was the most influential, all concluded that the attitude-behavior relationship was usually weak and sometimes negligible. This conclusion has been widely accepted for attitudes in general and is typically seen as applying to prejudiced attitudes as well (e.g., Bowser, 1985; Brigham, 1971b; Feagin & Eckberg, 1980; Green, 1972; Schwarzwald & Yinon, 1978).

More recently, however, several theoretical and empirical developments have suggested that these conclusions may not be justified. These developments seem to indicate that the relationship of attitudes in general, and prejudiced attitudes specifically, with behavior may be much more powerful than has been generally assumed and is apparent from the empirical literature. First, Ajzen and Fishbein's (1977) theory proposes that attitudes do predict behavior strongly if the behavioral criterion is assessed at an adequate level of generality. Second, the theory of symbolic racism suggests that the empirically obtained relationship between prejudice and behavior may have been depressed by the use of inappropriately crude, transparent, and "old-fashioned" approaches to measuring prejudice. These two considerations are discussed and evaluated in the remainder of this chapter.

## PREJUDICE AND THE GENERALITY OF BEHAVIORAL CRITERIA

In 1977 Ajzen and Fishbein published an important paper that reexamined Wicker's (1969) conclusions. Their basic point was that attitude measures and behavioral criteria should correspond adequately to each other in order to reveal the degree of relationship between them. In particular, they focused on the issue of correspondence in terms of the degree of generality and specificity.

Most studies of the relation between attitude and behavior had used measures of a generalized attitude to an object to predict single highly specific behavioral acts to that object. Ajzen and Fishbein argued that this was inappropriate. A single act toward an object would be subject to a number of other influences specific to the act and its situational context, besides the overall attitude to that object. Consequently, the general attitude toward the object would not usually predict a single act with much accuracy. In order to predict such an act at a reasonable level of accuracy, they suggested, the specific attitude to acting in that particular way would have to be considered ("attitude to the act"), as well as the normative expectations of others concerning the performance of that act.

On the other hand, a general attitude toward an object should be a powerful predictor of the general pattern of behavior toward that object over a number of different acts and situations. In this case, situation- and act-specific influences should largely average out. This means that, although general attitudes to an object would not predict specific single acts very well, they would be powerful predictors when a number of such acts were aggregated to provide an overall index of the general favorability or unfavorability of behavior to that object. Epstein (1983), in considering the issue of predicting behavior from personality traits, presented an essentially similar argument. Single items of behavior, he argues, have a large component of error of measurement and a small range of generality. This makes it difficult to predict them with much accuracy. Aggregation reduces the error of measurement and broadens the range of generality so that behavior averaged over a sample of situations or occasions can be predicted much more effectively from general attitude or trait measures.

Ajzen and Fishbein (1977) pointed out that many of the studies reviewed by Wicker (1969) had used generalized attitude measures to predict single, highly specific behavioral acts. They reexamined this research to demonstrate that it was precisely these studies in which attitudes had been poor predictors of behavior. On the other hand, when attitudes and behavior corresponded adequately, with highly specific attitude measures predicting specific single acts, or general attitudes predicting broader or more global behavioral criteria, attitudes were very much stronger predictors. A number of empirical studies have supported this. For example, it has been shown that general attitude measures correlate highly with multiple-act behavioral criteria, with correlations typically ranging from .50 to .90 (e.g., Cheek, 1982; Olson & Zanna, 1983; Weigel & Newman, 1976). At the same time, the correlations of these attitude measures with the individual acts comprising the multiple-act criteria tend to be rather weak, averaging out at about the level Wicker (1969) found—that is, below .30.

Research on prejudice and behavior, like the studies reviewed by Wicker (1969), has generally predicted specific behavioral acts from general attitudes toward particular groups. This applies to most of the studies summarized in Tables 3.1, 3.2, and 3.3. According to Ajzen and Fishbein, this would explain why prediction was typically no better than moderate. In no case did any of this research use a true multiple-act criterion aggregated over different behavioral acts and different situations.

Overall, therefore, Ajzen and Fishbein's argument implies that the relationship between prejudice and behavior has not yet been appropriately tested. According to this perspective, an intergroup attitude indicates the overall affective orientation to that group and will influence the overall tendency to behave favorably or unfavorably toward members of that group. Such attitudes cannot be expected to predict single acts very accurately because of influences specific to those acts. They should, however, show a powerful association with behavior aggregated over a variety of acts and situations.

## SYMBOLIC RACISM AND THE MEASUREMENT OF PREJUDICE

Studies of the prejudice-behavior relationship have assessed prejudiced attitudes by means of self-report scales or questionnaires tapping sentiments toward outgroups, usually blacks, in a fairly open and obvious manner. Typically used measures have been the MRAI (Woodmansee & Cook, 1967), the California E, or anti-Negro, scale (Adorno, Frenkel-Brunswick, Levinson, & Sanford, 1950), and the Holtzman D scale (Kelley, Ferson, & Holtzman, 1958). Perhaps because of the very obvious and transparent content of these measures, their validity was unquestioningly assumed in these studies.

During the past decade, however, the validity of such measures has been seriously challenged. Research on the concept of symbolic racism, as discussed in the previous chapter, has suggested that transparent and obvious "old-fashioned" or "traditional" expressions of antiblack racism may have become socially unacceptable in many contexts and settings in the United States. As a result, such measures might no longer be valid or effective indices of antiblack prejudice. More subtle and indirect measures—such as the symbolic racism scale—might have become necessary to assess prejudice adequately.

In support of this argument, several studies have shown that samples of white suburbanites and students were much more ready to endorse symbolic racism items than traditional racism items, which they regarded as socially unacceptable expressions of racist bigotry (McConahay et al., 1981; McConahay & Hough, 1976). Several studies have been even more directly relevant to the issue of the relationship between prejudice and behavior. These studies have shown the symbolic racism scale to be a clearly superior predictor of racially relevant behaviors, such as voting for white or conservative candidates (Kinder & Sears, 1981), opposition to busing (McConahay, 1982; Sears et al., 1979), and opposition to affirmative action (Jacobson, 1985).

These studies suggest that research using "old-fashioned" or "traditional" measures of racial prejudice may have systematically underestimated the strength of the relationship between prejudice and behavior. Presumably, the use of more subtle, indirect measures would have resulted in a much stronger relationship than that found in the studies reviewed in the previous two sections of this chapter. However, there is a possible objection to this argument. Proponents of the theory of symbolic racism have often implied that its emergence in the United States has been relatively recent—perhaps during the 1970s (McConahay et al., 1981). Many studies of the relationship between prejudice and behavior were done before this, particularly during the 1960s, when, according to this assumption, traditional measures of racism would not yet have lost their effectiveness.

This objection may not be entirely valid, however. Most studies of the relationship between prejudice and behavior used American college students as subjects. It seems likely that the liberal atmosphere of most American campuses would have created significant pressures for students to try and avoid creating the impression of being racist from at least the early 1960s when desegregation and the civil rights movement were prominent in the United States. This is illustrated by Linn's (1965) comment, noted previously, that his subjects seemed to have been playing a "university social role as a racial liberal" (p. 363).

Linn's findings also indicate that most of his subjects who scored high on prejudice did behave in a discriminatory fashion (83 percent). The inconsistency in his study was produced by the low scorers, of whom only a minority behaved in a nondiscriminatory fashion (41 percent). Similar findings were obtained by Fendrich (1967): 94 percent of his prejudiced subjects discriminated, whereas only 29 percent of his non-prejudiced subjects were nondiscriminatory. This pattern fits the symbolic racism thesis that in more sophisticated samples low scorers on traditional measures of racism could well have underlying antiblack attitudes. The failure of such subjects to behave in a nondiscriminatory fashion might not therefore indicate inconsistency between attitude and behavior but merely the use of ineffective measures of prejudice.

Overall, it would seem that the use of obvious and transparent measures of traditional racial prejudice with American college students as subjects may have systematically biased the observed relationship between prejudice and behavior downward. Significantly, the one study of this relationship that used a more subtle measure of prejudice, the symbolic racism scale, obtained a relatively powerful correlation of .50 between prejudice and behavior (McConahay, 1983).

## CONCLUSIONS

Traditionally, it was assumed that there was a close and direct relationship between prejudiced intergroup attitudes and hostile and discriminatory intergroup behavior. However, empirical research did not appear to support this. Early field and ethnographic studies, such as that of LaPiere (1934), suggested that interracial behavior might have little, if any, relation to the attitudes or intentions that individuals expressed, and might be primarily determined by situational factors. These findings later stimulated a series of investigations by sociologists, which indicated a generally consistent, though not very strong, relationship between prejudice and racially relevant actions.

Psychologists have focused on the relationship between prejudice and discriminatory behavior toward outgroup members. A number of these studies found no relation between prejudice and discrimination. However, it would seem that no overall discrimination was elicited in these studies. When discrimination did occur, it seems to have been consistently related to prejudice. Once again, however, the relationship was usually not a very powerful one. Finally, studies of the relation between attitudes and behavior in general have suggested a typically weak and sometimes negligible relationship (e.g., Wicker, 1969). Overall, these findings have resulted in a widely held conclusion that prejudice and behavior are not very strongly related (Bowser, 1985; Brigham, 1971b; Ehrlich, 1973; Green, 1972; Schwarzwald & Yinon, 1978).

Two more recent developments suggest that this conclusion may need to be reevaluated. First, research on symbolic racism indicates that subtle and indirect measures of prejudice, such as the symbolic racism scale, are better predictors of racially relevant behaviors in American samples than more transparent traditional measures (Jacobson, 1985; Kinder & Sears, 1981; McConahay, 1982; Sears et al., 1979). Because traditional measures have invariably been used in studies of the relationship between prejudice and behavior, it is possible that this research may have systematically underestimated the strength of the relationship.

Second, Ajzen and Fishbein (1977, 1980) argued that a generalized attitude toward an object will determine the overall tendency to behave favorably or unfavorably to that object. It will not predict specific single acts with much accuracy because of act- and situation-specific influences. However, it should show a very strong relationship with multiple-act criteria—that is, behavior aggregated over a variety of different acts and situations. Research on prejudice and behavior has invariably used single behavioral criteria, suggesting that this relationship may not yet have been appropriately tested and that it may be much more powerful than this research seems to indicate.

This does not imply, of course, that the relationship between prejudice and behavior would be one of unidirectional causality. A good deal of evidence demonstrates that behavior can causally influence beliefs and attitudes (Bem, 1970), as well as the converse (Snyder, 1981). Thus, the relationship between prejudice and discriminatory behavior seems to be most appropriately viewed as one of reciprocal causality and mutual reinforcement, with each influencing and contributing to the other (Levin & Levin, 1982; Simpson & Yinger, 1985). Moreover, although they may be closely interrelated, prejudice and discrimination are conceptually separate.

Basically, it can be argued that both intergroup attitudes of hostility and discriminatory and antagonistic intergroup behavior are important phenomena that require explanation. Traditionally, psychologists have been more interested in prejudice and have proposed a large number of theories to explain it. These are discussed in the next chapter from the perspective of a historical analysis of the development of theorizing about prejudice.

# 4

# Theories of Prejudice: A Historical Analysis and an Integrative Framework

Many theories have been proposed to explain the causation of prejudice. This was illustrated in Chapter 1 by listing some of the topics discussed by Allport in 1954. A great deal of research has been done and there have been several important theoretical developments since that date. New theories have emerged (e.g., Tajfel & Turner, 1979), and older ones have been elaborated (e.g., Altemeyer, 1981). Unfortunately, these developments have not brought much clarification to the overall question of the causation of prejudice. The list of possible causes, and the complexity of the problem, seems to have increased rather than decreased. As a result, one of the best established conclusions in the literature is that "prejudice is a complex phenomenon which is determined by many factors" (Ashmore, 1970; cf. also Condor & Brown, 1988; Harding et al., 1969; Simpson & Yinger, 1985; Tajfel, 1982b).

Most theories focus on only one aspect or manifestation of prejudice. Allport (1954), for example, pointed out that "as a rule most 'theories' are advanced by their authors to call attention to some one important causal factor, without implying that no other factors are operating" (p. 207). Consequently, each theory tends to illuminate only a limited set or subset of causal processes and rarely attempts to provide a complete explanation of prejudice. One response to this by reviewers has been "to simply construct a long list of 'causes' and treat them all somewhat uncritically, assuming that each theory is valid under certain circumstances or to a certain extent" (Ashmore, 1970, p. 256). A much better approach, Ashmore suggested, is to try and classify or "categorize the explanations so we can ascertain how they fit together" (p. 256). Many reviewers have proposed classifications that attempt to simplify and systematize the area in this way.

These classifications have usually been according to level of analysis.

For example, Allport's (1954) classification identified six different levels of explanation: the historical, sociocultural, situational, personality, phenomenological, and stimulus object levels. Although this is one of the most extensive classifications that have been suggested, it has rarely been used by other authors—perhaps precisely because it may have seemed too extensive and rather cumbersome. Most other reviewers have used fewer categories. In fact, many have suggested that only two basic kinds of theory or levels of analysis are needed—societel-level sociological theories on the one hand, and individual-level psychological theories on the other (e.g., Ashmore, 1970; Babad et al., 1983; Ehrlich, 1973).

Simpson and Yinger (1985) provided a tripartite classification in terms of cultural, group, and individual factors, which has been often cited and used (e.g., Nieuwoudt & Nel, 1975). Cultural factors and theories typically involve the idea of prejudice as a cultural tradition or norm and focus on processes such as conformity and socialization. Group influences concern the political and economic functions that prejudice may serve for macrosocial groups, particularly in the context of struggles for power, prestige, and wealth. Finally, individual sources of prejudice include theories and approaches in terms of frustration, projection, status needs, authoritarian personality structures, and so forth.

Classifications in terms of level of analysis assume that theories and approaches at different levels are basically complementary. However, these classifications have been essentially descriptive, merely grouping together those theories that appear to be operating at a similar level. As such, they do not show how theories and approaches at different levels might actually fit together to give a coherent and integrated explanation of prejudice.

Ashmore and DelBoca (1981) took a somewhat different approach. Instead of organizing theories by level of analysis, they emphasized the existence of different theoretical perspectives, each of which subsumes more specific theories and approaches. Although their discussion focused specifically on stereotyping, it is equally relevant to prejudice. They suggested that three distinct perspectives can be identified—the sociocultural, the psychodynamic, and the cognitive. These perspectives are seen as analogous to Kuhn's (1962) concept of "disciplinary matrices," or paradigms. Thus, each perspective provides a distinctive frame of reference that guides the conduct of research, and each involves quite different underlying models and assumptions about the nature of man and the phenomenon of stereotyping (and, by extension, prejudice).

Two of these perspectives, the sociocultural and the psychodynamic, correspond broadly with Simpson and Yinger's cultural and individual categories. The sociocultural perspective, according to Ashmore and DelBoca, rests on a conceptualization of prejudice as a sociocultural norm. It is assumed that people are basically motivated to seek approval, and so to conform to norms and traditions. The psychodynamic perspective, on the other hand, emphasizes unconscious drives that conflict with societal constraints. Prejudice is therefore viewed as an expression of inner conflicts. Finally, the cognitive perspective sees humans as limited-capacity information processors striving to make sense out of a complex environment, through processes such as categorization. When categorization occurs in a social context it leads to stereotyping, intergroup bias, and prejudice. Stereotypes and prejudice thus serve a knowledge function by reducing the complexity of the world and making it more manageable.

Classifications in terms of levels of analysis see theories at each level as basically complementary to those at other levels. Ashmore and DelBoca, on the other hand, stressed the differences between their three perspectives, along with the incompatibility of their underlying models and assumptions. They suggested that these three perspectives are competing rather than complementary paradigms for the explanation of prejudice. Nevertheless, they conceded that none of the three produces a complete explanation of prejudice. Consequently, they accepted that "it is necessary to seek connections between these perspectives . . . and ultimately to integrate the socio-cultural, psychodynamic, and cognitive viewpoints into a more complete picture of stereotypes and intergroup relations" (pp. 31–32).

It is often noted that different perspectives and approaches to prejudice have been dominant in different historical periods (Condor & Brown, 1988; Fairchild & Gurin, 1978; Milner, 1975, 1983). For example, cognitive and cognitively based approaches, such as social identity theory, have been dominant during the past one to two decades. This is well illustrated by the three chapters on intergroup relations that have appeared in the *Annual Review of Psychology* during the 1980s (Brewer & Kramer, 1985; Messick & Mackie, 1989; Tajfel, 1982b), each of which has focused almost exclusively on topics and issues emerging from cognitively based approaches. Earlier noncognitive approaches—such as socialization, conformity, realistic conflict theory, authoritarianism, and other psychodynamic or individual-difference factors—are hardly mentioned. As Messick and Mackie (1989) pointed out in the most recent of these chapters, "the study of intergroup relations, like many other areas of research in social psychology, has acquired a distinctly cognitive tone" (p. 45).

On the other hand, the theory of the authoritarian personality dominated research and thinking during the 1950s (Condor & Brown, 1988; Milner, 1983), but by the mid-1960s, authoritarianism had been displaced from the mainstream of psychological thinking on the causes of prejudice. The primary emphasis then fell on sociocultural processes, such as normative influences, socialization, and conformity (Fairchild & Gurin, 1978).

Why have these shifts occurred? One possible explanation is that they may simply reflect the development of knowledge in the area—the systematic replacement of theories and approaches that have been refuted or shown to be inadequate by better, more useful, and more powerful theories. There may be some truth in this. For example, the theory of the authoritarian personality involved certain conceptual and methodological problems (Altemeyer, 1981), and the failure to resolve such issues as the response set problem may have been partly responsible for the loss of interest in the approach. New approaches generally did show a capacity to explain phenomena that their predecessors could not account for adequately. For example, sociocultural factors could explain group differences in prejudice, whereas authoritarianism and other personality-based approaches could not. The cognitive perspective was able to account for intergroup bias, stereotyping, and competition in minimal group situations where sociocultural or personality-based motivational factors did not appear to be operating.

These shifts in emphasis, however, do not seem to be fully explained in terms of the evolution of knowledge and the emergence of new and better theories. Typically, older perspectives and theories are not refuted or even shown to be seriously inadequate. Although displaced from the mainstream of psychological interest, they are not discarded. In fact, it is widely acknowledged that they remain relevant, and even important, in accounting for prejudice (Ashmore & DelBoca, 1981; Condor & Brown, 1988; Pettigrew, 1981; Simpson & Yinger, 1985). Instead of new perspectives and approaches replacing their predecessors, they appear to illuminate quite different issues and problems. What appears to happen, therefore, are fundamental shifts of interest away from certain issues and problems concerning the causes of prejudice to new or different ones, which require different theories, approaches, and perspectives.

In examining the history of the social psychological analysis of race relations, Fairchild and Gurin (1978) pointed out that "psychologists chose as topics for study those events which were then of local or national importance" (p. 757). Historical events and circumstances, however, might have more profound effects on thinking about prejudice than merely shifting interest to new research topics. These events and circumstances might make salient fundamentally new and different questions about the nature of prejudice, while obscuring others. This could generate a shift in the perception or image of prejudice. It would also elicit new kinds of theories, research orientations, and broad theoretical perspectives.

Thus, the theoretical perspectives at different historical periods could reflect different explanatory goals and objectives. To the extent that these explanatory goals emerged from fundamentally different questions about the nature of prejudice, the resulting perspectives would each make partial, but essential and complementary contributions to understanding prejudice. A historical analysis of theorizing about prejudice could therefore clarify the questions and explanatory objectives that underlie different perspectives of prejudice, and could indicate how the perspectives complement each other. Such an analysis, which is presented in the next section, might have important implications for the development of an overall integrative framework for the explanation of prejudice.

## A HISTORICAL ANALYSIS

From a historical perspective, seven distinct periods in the way in which prejudice has been understood by psychologists can be identified. Each of these periods will be briefly discussed. It will be shown how social circumstances and historical events, interacting with the evolution of knowledge, focused attention on different issues and questions in each period. Each question was associated with a particular image of prejudice, and each generated a distinctive theoretical orientation and research emphasis. The overall analysis is summarized in Table 4.1.

Before considering these stages, two points should be made. First, identifying distinct periods necessarily involves some oversimplification. Each period represents only the main thrust of theoretical and research attention, and is not intended to exhaustively subsume all thinking on the subject. Thus, there are research and theoretical developments that were outside the mainstream of attention at their time and do not fit comfortably into these stages. Finding examples is not difficult. Rokeach's theory of belief congruence (Rokeach, Smith, & Evans, 1960), for example, was formulated at a time when the psychodynamic and personality-based approaches were giving way to a sociocultural emphasis, yet it does not fit into either approach. Altemeyer's (1981, 1988a) work on authoritarianism, which appeared during a period when cognitive perspectives were dominant, is another example.

Second, social psychology in general and the study of prejudice in particular have been largely North American enterprises for most of their history. Thus, the kind of historical circumstances that have had the most influence on mainstream developments in the area have tended to be ones that affect North Americans. Only during the past few decades has a strong European influence become apparent. This means that the historical stages outlined here would not necessarily be relevant in different contexts or societies.

**Table 4.1**

**Historical Evolution of the Psychological Understanding of Prejudice**

| Social and historical problem | Social scientific question | Image of prejudice | Theoretical orientation | Research orientation |
|---|---|---|---|---|
| Up to the 1920s: White domination and colonial rule of "backward peoples" | Identifying the deficiencies of "backward peoples" | A natural response to "inferior peoples" | "Race theories" | Comparative studies of the abilities of different races |
| The 1920s and 1930s: The legitimacy of white domination challenged | Explaining the stigmatization of minorities | Prejudice as irrational and unjustified | Conceptualizing prejudice as a social problem | Measurement and descriptive studies |
| The 1930s and 1940s: The ubiquity of white racism in the U.S. | Identifying universal processes underlying prejudice | Prejudice as an unconscious defense | Psychodynamic theory: defensive processes | Experimental |
| The 1950s: Nazi racial ideology and the holocaust | Identifying the prejudice prone personality | Prejudice as an expression of a pathological need | Individual differences | Correlational |
| The 1960s: The problem of prejudice in the American South | How social norms and influences determine prejudice | Prejudice as a social norm | Sociocultural approach: social transmission of prejudice | Observational and correlational |
| The 1970s: The persistence of American racism and discrimination | How prejudice is rooted in social structure and inter-group relations | Prejudice as an expression of group interests | Sociocultural approach: intergroup dynamics of prejudice | Sociological and historical research |
| The 1980s and 1990s: The inevitably and universality of prejudice and intergroup conflict | What universal psychological processes underlie intergroup conflict and prejudice | Prejudice as an inevitable outcome of social categorization | Social cognitive perspective | Experimental |

## Race Psychology: Up to the 1920s

The idea of prejudice as a social scientific construct meriting serious attention by psychologists only emerged in the 1920s. At that time, the most important and problematic intergroup differences were typically seen as racial differences. As a result, the concept of prejudice rose to scientific prominence largely in the context of understanding racial differences and antipathies (Levin & Levin, 1982; Milner, 1983; Samelson, 1978; Vaughan, 1988).

During the nineteenth century, as Haller (1971) pointed out, "almost the whole of scientific thought in both America and Europe . . . accepted race inferiority" (p. 77). The idea of the superiority of white over black races was well established, and the concept of white prejudice or white racial attitudes was not a scientific issue of any significance. White attitudes of paternalistic superiority or open antipathy to blacks were widely accepted as inevitable and natural responses to the seemingly obvious "inferiority" and "backwardness" of blacks and other colonial peoples.

The connection between these attitudes and white political domination of blacks in the form of European colonialism and American slavery has often been made. Thus, "notions of the superiority of the white race were useful in justifying the subjugation of people of color" (Fairchild & Gurin, 1978, p. 758; cf. also Levin & Levin, 1982; Samelson, 1978). These historical circumstances generated an interest among scientists in delineating and explaining racial differences, and particularly the inferiorities of "backward" races. As a result, "race theories" dominated social scientific thinking about racial differences. Race theories explained black inferiority in terms of such factors as evolutionary backwardness, limited intellectual capacity, and even excess sexual drive (Haller, 1971).

Research, initially in the fields of medicine and anthropology, was largely concerned with demonstrating and describing the pattern of deficiency. When intelligence testing emerged early in the twentieth century, psychologists joined this enterprise. As Samelson (1978) pointed out:

The original purpose of testing had been the study of individual differences. Soon, however, some testers began collecting data on race and found differences—or, if they did not, insisted that further research would. The initial focus of such studies was on black-white comparisons; a number of authors published empirical demonstrations of white superiority, the inferiority of blacks (and Indians), and the increase in native intelligence with increasing admixture of white blood. (p. 266)

In 1925 an influential paper by Thomas Garth in the *Psychological Bulletin* reviewed seventy-three studies on the issue of race and intelligence.

Garth concluded that these studies, "taken all together seem to indicate the mental superiority of the white race" (cited in Samelson, 1978, p. 266).

To sum up, the historical situation of white domination and rule of colonial peoples was associated with an image of prejudice as a natural response to "backward" and "inferior" races. The social scientific paradigm of the period was therefore characterized by race theories. Research concentrated on identifying and explaining racial differences, particularly the supposed inferiorities of "backward" races.

### Race Prejudice: The 1920s and 1930s

During the 1920s the manner in which psychology defined the "race problem" began to change completely. This change in thinking was documented by Samelson (1978), who described it as a profound thematic reversal: "In 1920 most psychologists believed in the existence of mental differences between races; by 1940 they were searching for the sources of 'irrational prejudice.' In a few decades, a dramatic reversal of the dominant paradigm for the study of groups and group relations had occurred" (p. 265). Samelson pointed out that it is tempting to see this as an example of the progress of empirical science—the triumph of objective data over prejudices, misconceptions, and speculation. However, this seems to be a myth: "Empirical data certainly did not settle the issue, one way or the other, as the current controversy over the heritability of intelligence between respected psychologists at Harvard, Berkeley, and Princeton shows" (Samelson, 1978, p. 270).

This change in thinking seems more feasibly interpreted as a response to important social events and circumstances. Milner (1983) noted two important historical developments after World War I that were instrumental in stimulating a new approach. First, a black civil rights movement emerged in the United States during the 1920s; second, movements emerged that challenged the legitimacy of European colonial rule and white domination of colonial peoples. Both movements gained a good deal of sympathy in the United States. Samelson (1978) mentioned several other factors that, he argued, also influenced this shift in thinking. First, he suggested that the restriction of immigration in the early 1920s shifted attention from justifying the exclusion of certain peoples to resolving conflict within the country. Second, he noted an influx of ethnics, particularly Jewish persons, into the profession of psychology; third, a leftward shift among psychologists during the depression; and, finally, a desire "to unite the country against a dangerous enemy proclaiming racial superiority" (p. 265).

Overall, these historical developments seem to have influenced a rapid shift, at least among intellectuals and social scientists, away from beliefs in white racial superiority and the inferiority of other races. This, however, raised a crucial question: If other races were not inferior, how could their deprivations, and particularly their stigmatization by whites, be explained? According to Milner, Floyd Allport in 1924 was the first social psychologist to explicitly pose this issue with the statement that "the discrepancy in mental ability is not great enough to account for the problem which centers around the American Negro or to explain fully *the ostracism to which he is subjected*" (cited in Milner, 1975, p. 21; italics in the original).

In order to answer this question and to explain the stigmatization and "ostracism" of blacks, psychologists shifted their attention to white racial attitudes. With the belief in racial equality came the idea that negative and derogatory white racial attitudes were essentially unjustified and unfair. This resulted in the emergence of the concept of prejudice as a basically unjustified, irrational, or in some way faulty negative intergroup attitude. Thus, the social problem of race relations was redefined as a problem of white prejudice, rather than one of black inferiority.

Most research on prejudice during this period was concerned with its measurement and description in various groups. In 1925, for example, Bogardus published his classic work using the social distance scale to assess the acceptance or rejection of outgroups in situations of varying intimacy. In the next few decades, literally hundreds of studies were reported, describing the social distance patterns of different groups and subgroups. Katz and Braly's (1933) stereotype checklist had a similar impact, as did the use of Thurstone and later Likert scaling to measure interracial attitudes (e.g., Guilford, 1931).

Summing up, important historical processes after the World War I made a belief in racial inferiority untenable, at least for social scientists and intellectuals. The crucial social scientific question therefore became that of explaining the stigmatization of blacks and other minorities. The idea of racial prejudice as a serious social problem became the dominant paradigm for answering this question. Initially, research focused mainly on measuring prejudice and describing its patterning in various groups and settings. However, this paradigm also raised a new problem—that of how prejudice itself was to be explained. During the 1930s social psychologists began to turn their attention to this issue.

## Psychodynamic Processes: The 1930s and 1940s

Early attempts to explain prejudice occurred within the social context of white racism and black-white relations in the United States. For example, Bogardus's book, published in 1928, opened with the assertion that the single greatest issue confronting America was that of race relations (noted in Samelson, 1978, p. 271). If prejudice was a fundamentally irrational and unjustified response, as most psychologists (and other intellectuals) had come to believe, how then could the pervasiveness and ubiquity of white racism in the United States be explained? This appears to have been the crucial social scientific question made salient by these social and historical circumstances.

Psychodynamic theory seemed to provide a particularly appropriate framework for answering this question. From this perspective, prejudice could be seen as the result of the operation of universal psychological processes such as defense mechanisms. These processes operated unconsciously, channeling tensions and problems arising either within the personality or from environmental stresses, threats, and frustrations into prejudice against minorities. The universality of these processes thus accounted for the ubiquity of prejudice and their unconscious defensive function accounted for its fundamental irrationality.

A variety of psychodynamic processes were implicated in prejudice. These included projection (Ackerman & Jahoda, 1950; McClean, 1946), frustration (MacCrone, 1937), scapegoating, and the displacement of hostility (Dollard, Doob, Miller, Mowrer, & Sears, 1939). A number of these processes could be integrated into a coherent explanation of prejudice in terms of aggression, originating from chronic social frustrations, which is displaced onto minorities as scapegoats (Dollard et al., 1939; MacCrone, 1937). Approaches such as these seemed to provide a reasonably plausible explanation for the ubiquity of racism in the United States and for some of its more disturbing expressions, such as lynching (Hovland & Sears, 1940; Raper, 1933). It was also used to explain another important and disturbing historical event—the rise of Nazism and the spread of virulent anti-Semitism in Germany. This was attributed to the displacement of hostility generated by the political humiliations and economic frustrations of the German people after World War I (Dollard et al., 1939).

This explanatory paradigm stimulated research that used a variety of strategies, such as case studies, as well as historical and correlational research (e.g., Allport & Kramer, 1946; Morse & Allport, 1952). The most appropriate orientation to the investigation of universalistic causal processes of this kind, however, would tend to be experimental research, in which the presumption of cause and effect can be directly tested. A number of such studies were conducted during the late 1940s and early 1950s (e.g., Miller & Bugelski, 1948) with somewhat inconclusive results (see Chapter 5).

To sum up, social issues, such as that of white racism in the United States and the rise of Nazism and anti-Semitism in Germany, confronted psychologists with the problem of explaining how a fundamentally irrational and unjustified attitude could be so pervasive and ubiquitous. This explanatory problem helped condition the emergence of explanations of prejudice in terms of universal psychodynamic processes. As a paradigm, it was associated with an image of prejudice as an expression of unconscious psychological defenses diverting inner conflicts and hostilities, which were often seen as originating from externally induced frustrations and deprivations, against innocent outgroups and minorities. The assessment of causal relationships of this nature encouraged an emphasis on experimental research.

Although this research, which is reviewed in detail in Chapter 5, failed to produce clearly supportive findings, the psychodynamic approach was not rejected. In fact, theories in terms of the displacement of frustration were still being favorably noted in reviews of the literature decades later (Ashmore, 1970; Ashmore & DelBoca, 1976; Harding et al., 1969; Simpson & Yinger, 1985; Westie, 1964). Disappointing empirical findings may have helped influence a shift away from this paradigm, but the effect of certain historical events seemed to be more directly responsible.

## The Prejudiced Personality: The 1950s

An important shift in the dominant paradigm for explaining prejudice occurred after World War II and toward the end of the 1940s. Although, initially at least, the new formulations were still psychodynamically based, there was a crucial difference: The emphasis was no longer on process but on structure. Instead of explaining prejudice in terms of the operation of universal intrapsychic processes, the new paradigm viewed prejudice as the outcome of particular personality structures that conditioned the adoption of prejudiced attitudes.

The impact of an important and extremely disturbing historical event seems to have played a major role in precipitating this shift. This was the shock and revulsion inspired by the culmination of Nazi racial ideology and anti-Semitism in massive genocide. Such phenomena did not seem comfortably explicable in terms of universal and essentially normal psychological processes characteristic of all persons. As Milner (1981) pointed out, "the very obscenity of the holocaust connoted a kind of mass pathology, a collective madness. Explanations were therefore sought in the disturbed personality, for it was hardly conceivable that these could be the actions of normal men" (p. 106). The Nazis and their leaders, or at least an image of them as sharing a certain kind of disturbed personality structure, were originally seen as prototypal in this respect.

Prejudice was therefore seen as the expression of an inner need generated by basically pathological personality structures. Individuals characterized by such personality structures would tend to be particularly prone or susceptible to prejudice. This meshed with the well-established empirical finding that prejudice tended to be a generalized characteristic of individuals. Thus, persons who were anti-Semitic would be more likely to be antiblack or, for that matter, less favorable toward any other minority or outgroup (see Chapter 8). Consequently, the crucial social scientific question became that of identifying and describing the personality structures and characteristics that make individuals prone to prejudice and ethnocentrism.

The most influential answer to this question was the theory of the authoritarian personality (Adorno et al., 1950), which described a basic personality dimension that determines the degree to which individuals would be generally prone to prejudice. This theory was formulated partly in psychodynamic terms and concepts, whereas other approaches to the same issue were not; examples are Rokeach's dogmatism (Rokeach et al., 1960), Smith and Rosen's worldmindedness (1958), and Martin and Westie's (1959) work on "the tolerant personality." The dominant paradigm during this period was therefore not a psychodynamic one per se. Instead, it seems more appropriately described as an individual-differences orientation to the explanation of prejudice. This meant an emphasis on correlational research. An enormous amount of research investigating the personality, cognitive, and attitudinal correlates of prejudice, or related constructs such as authoritarianism, was generated by this paradigm.

It has been noted that an individual-differences orientation to the explanation of prejudice was particularly well suited to the spirit of the times. Thus, according to Fairchild and Gurin (1978):

The nearly exclusive concern with intraindividual causes of discrimination was supported by the mood of postwar America. The war had been won. Commitment to superordinate goals and faith in democracy was at no time greater than in the immediate postwar period. It was not a time when social scientists were prompted to question the social system or look to institutional explanations of prejudice and discrimination. (p. 760)

To sum up, therefore, during the late 1940s and the 1950s the fundamental explanatory problem that confronted psychologists appeared to be that of identifying the prejudice-prone personality, or bigot. The dominant image of prejudice was in terms of the expression of an inner need that stemmed from underlying pathology in the personality. This was stimulated initially by the revulsion engendered by the holocaust and the feeling that such acts could not be attributed to normal persons or processes. The individual-differences orientation to prejudice may also have been reinforced by the social stability and optimism of postwar America. Certain serious limitations of this approach, however, became apparent later when the problem of racism in the American South became the salient issue.

## Culture and Society: The 1960s and 1970s

At the end of the 1950s the emphasis in explaining prejudice moved away from individual-level psychological factors to broad social and cultural influences. This sociocultural perspective was clearly dominant during the 1960s and extended into the 1970s. It was associated with a marked decline in psychological interest in the causes of prejudice, particularly in contrast to the enthusiasm of the 1950s. This decline was especially notable by the late 1960s and 1970s, as the issue of explaining prejudice came to be regarded as a primarily sociological enterprise. A revival of psychological interest only occurred at the end of the 1970s with the emergence of a new and distinctively psychological paradigm, the cognitive perspective.

Two distinct phases can be distinguished within this overall period of sociocultural emphasis. These can be seen as representing different responses to the distinctive historical contexts and explanatory problems generated by American race relations, first in the early 1960s and then later in the 1970s. The general lack of psychological interest during this period as a whole, and the fact that these two phases share basically similar sociocultural assumptions, means that the difference between them is easily obscured. Nevertheless, two quite different questions about the causation of prejudice can be distinguished, which, it will be pointed out later in this chapter, are of crucial analytic significance for the development of an overall integrative framework for explaining prejudice. For this reason, the differences between these two phases rather than the similarities will be accentuated, and they will be treated as two distinct stages. The distinction between these two phases is similar to one made by Ashmore and DelBoca (1981) between consensus and conflict versions of the sociocultural perspective. Here the essential distinction between the two periods is seen as an emphasis on normative influence during the early 1960s as opposed to a preoccupation with intergroup dynamics and conflicts of interest during the 1970s.

The shift away from an individual-differences paradigm for explaining prejudice is usually attributed to the limitations of this approach, particularly its inability to account for the extremely high levels of prejudice in social settings such as the American South or South Africa (Pettigrew, 1958, 1959). These limitations, however, had been empirically demonstrated long before this shift occurred (e.g., Prothro, 1952; Prothro & Jensen, 1950; cf. also Minard, 1952). What appears to have happened is that the campaign for civil rights in the U.S. South exploded into public awareness in the late 1950s. This made salient the social problem of institutionalized racism and segregation in the South (Blackwell, 1982).

Prejudice in the American South could not be plausibly explained as an expression of underlying pathology or individual-difference constructs. This was empirically confirmed in several classic studies by Pettigrew (1958, 1959, 1960), who showed that the high levels of racial prejudice in South Africa and the American South were not due to persons from these societies being any higher in authoritarianism. In such settings an entire society was racist, and so was the "good citizen" (Ashmore & DelBoca, 1981, p. 23). This focused attention on the normative character of prejudice in highly prejudiced societies specifically and also, by extension, in all settings where prejudice was socially widespread. It came to be accepted, as Turner and Giles (1981) noted, that "prejudice is to be understood as a social or cultural norm, and that, furthermore, where this is not the case, it is unlikely to be of social significance" (p. 12).

The dominant image of prejudice, therefore, was that of a norm embedded in the social environment. The crucial psychological question then becomes that of how such norms influence and determine the prejudiced attitudes held by individuals. What causal mechanisms are operative in transmitting these social or normative influences to individuals? Two mechanisms have been most emphasized in the literature—socialization and conformity (Pettigrew, 1958; Proshansky, 1966; Westie, 1964). The research generated by this perspective tended to be observational research of childhood socialization (see, e.g., the studies reviewed by Proshansky, 1966) and correlational studies of conformity or perceived social pressure and prejudice (e.g., DeFriese & Ford, 1969; Ewens & Ehrlich, 1972; Fendrich, 1967; Hamblin, 1962; Pettigrew, 1958).

The normative approach to prejudice involved a basically optimistic view of the future of race relations. Prejudice was essentially a matter of social conformity to traditional norms and institutionalized patterns of interracial behavior and segregation. Change should therefore follow effective desegregation. The "problem" South could become like the "liberal" North. Fairchild and Gurin (1978), for example, suggested that up to the mid-1960s psychologists implicitly or explicitly accepted a "consensus model" of race relations. This model assumed that:

Black/white relations could be expected to be harmonious. The primary cause of disharmony was whites' lack of acceptance of blacks. Harmony could be achieved if whites were to change their prejudiced beliefs (inferiority of blacks) and accepted blacks in "their" schools, jobs, and neighborhood. Equal status contact was viewed as primarily responsible for creating this shift in whites' attitudes. Racial integration was the goal and no one much questioned whether it was viable. Conflict, power, and domination relations were nearly totally neglected in the social psychology of intergroup relations. (p. 767)

These optimistic assumptions began to fade rapidly in the later 1960s with "the urban revolts of the mid-to-late 1960s and the hardening of resistance to the civil rights movement, as its targets changed from public accommodations to voting rights, jobs, and income inequalities" (Fairchild & Gurin, 1978, p. 767). It became clear that the problem of race relations in the United States was not just a problem of Southern prejudice and segregation:

The alternative conditional segregation of the industrial and urban North was left virtually untouched by the civil rights movement and the 1964 Civil Rights Bill. In fact, conditional segregation began to gradually replace the overt and internationally embarrassing caste system in the South. Conditional segregation was untouched by the civil rights movement and legislation because it was impersonal, informally executed, and occasionally allowed mobility. (Bowser, 1985, p. 311)

Racism and discrimination, it seemed, were far more deeply rooted in American society than had been assumed previously. Socially shared and normative patterns of prejudice and discrimination could no longer be credibly viewed as just cultural and institutional traditions. Instead, they seemed to be maintained by more basic intergroup conflicts and social structural conditions. The salient question during the 1970s, the second phase of this period of sociocultural emphasis, therefore, was that of identifying and explaining those intergroup conflicts of interest and social structural conditions that underlie racist and discriminatory social systems.

Answers to this question were proposed in terms of factors such as internal colonialism (Blauner, 1972), a split labor market (Bonacich, 1972), institutionalized racism (Carmichael and Hamilton, 1967), and the socioeconomic advantages for whites of maintaining a stable black underclass (Thurow, 1969). The dominant image of prejudice was that it was an expression of group interests. White American racism, for example, was described as "a consequence of elite group self-interest and the desire to maintain historic privilege" (Bowser, 1985, p. 318). The theory and research that emerged from this perspective was almost entirely sociological and historical, and psychologists showed relatively little interest and involvement. The lack of interest by psychologists in the intergroup dynamics and social conditions that underlie normative patterns of prejudice seems puzzling. Two decades previously Sherif and Sherif (1953) had conducted a series of influential social psychological studies and formulated a theoretical perspective, realistic conflict theory (RCT), which was directly relevant to this issue.

Two factors may account for psychologists' lack of interest in the social and intergroup dynamics of prejudice during this period. First, there was a general lack of interest in group-related phenomena and an emphasis on the individual as the appropriate unit of analysis in American social psychology at the time (Steiner, 1974). Second, following Wicker's conclusion in 1969 that attitudes and behavior were only very weakly related, it was widely accepted that prejudiced attitudes might have little relevance for explaining discriminatory behavior or discriminatory social systems (see, e.g., Bowser, 1985). This seemed to be reinforced by surveys that showed large declines in racial prejudice but little apparent decline in racial discrimination (Campbell, 1971; Pettigrew, 1975). Consequently, there was a shift in attention away from the psychological concept of prejudice toward an emphasis on explaining and understanding discrimination, particularly social and institutional patterns of discrimination. This was viewed as a task for sociologists, and psychological interest in causal factors underlying intergroup relations only revived at the end of the 1970s.

To sum up, therefore, during the 1960s and 1970s social and cultural influences were seen as the most important causal processes underlying and determining prejudice. This period can be divided into two distinct phases. During the first, social circumstances made salient the problem of racism and institutionalized segregation in the American South. Explanations of prejudice in terms of individual differences or disturbed personalities were not particularly feasible in a setting such as this, where an entire society seemed to be racist. Instead, prejudice appeared to be more feasibly viewed as the expression of a sociocultural norm. The scientific question that this posed was how such norms operated to determine the prejudiced attitudes held by individuals.

By about 1970, however, it had become apparent that American racism was not just a problem of the South. Racism and discrimination seemed to be deeply embedded in American society as a whole, despite integration and surveys reporting marked declines in the acceptance of prejudiced beliefs. The perception of racism in terms of social conformity to traditional norms and institutionalized segregation no longer seemed as feasible as it once had. The crucial question now appeared to be that of explaining how racism and discrimination were rooted in the American social structure and basic conflicts of group interests. This tended to be seen as an issue for sociologists and historians rather than psychologists, and the approaches and theories that emerged in response typically viewed prejudice as an expression of group interests.

## Psychological Fundamentals: The 1980s and 1990s

During the 1970s several important empirical findings suggested that the persistence and pervasiveness of prejudice might not be fully explicable in terms of group interests and social structure. It became apparent that other, perhaps more fundamental, psychological processes might also be operative. One set of findings that may have influenced this conclusion emerged from the issue of symbolic racism (McConahay & Hough, 1976). As noted in the previous chapter, this research seemed to demonstrate that, contrary to what social surveys indicated, racism in the United States had not really declined, it had merely changed its form to a "more subtle, complex, and perhaps more insidious type of racial bigotry (Frey & Gaertner, 1986, p. 1083).

This research also indicated that racist actions, such as voting against a black mayor, opposition to affirmative action, and opposition to busing, were strongly correlated with symbolic racism, but not with the degree to which whites perceived blacks as threatening their interests (Kinder & Sears, 1981; Kleugel & Smith, 1983; McConahay, 1982; McConahay & Hough, 1976; Sears et al., 1979). Certain of these conclusions, particularly those concerning the role of perceived threat, were later challenged (Bobo, 1983; Sniderman & Tetlock, 1986a, 1986b). Nevertheless, these findings did help to demonstrate the continuing relevance of psychological constructs in determining racist behavior, and thus for understanding American racism.

An even more influential set of findings emerged from research using the minimal intergroup paradigm (Tajfel, 1970; Tajfel, Flament, Billig, & Bundy, 1971). In this research individuals were divided into groups on a completely arbitrary basis. There was no contact or interaction between groups, and there was no question of any conflict of interest or realistic social basis for antagonism. Yet individuals, when divided into such minimal groups, still showed bias, discrimination, and a competitive orientation in favor of the ingroup and against the outgroup. These findings had very fundamental implications. They indicated, as Tajfel and Turner (1979) pointed out, that:

The mere perception of belonging to two distinct groups—that is, social categorization per se—is sufficient to trigger intergroup discrimination favoring the in-group. In other words, the mere awareness of the presence of an out-group is sufficient to provoke intergroup competitive or discriminatory responses on the part of the in-group. (p. 38)

Intergroup bias and discrimination were therefore seen as inevitable outcomes of a normal, natural, and universal cognitive process that functioned to simplify and make more manageable the complexity of the social world (Ashmore & DelBoca, 1981; Hamilton, 1981c). This would explain why prejudice and discrimination were such ubiquitous, intractable, and almost universal social phenomena. It provided a new, powerful, and distinctively psychological perspective for understanding important social problems, such as the persistence of racism in America and an upsurge of neofascism, anti-Semitism, and anti-immigrant sentiment in Western Europe in the 1970s (Blackwell, 1982; Schönbach, Gollwitzer, Stiepel, & Wagner, 1981).

There are several different approaches to the issue of how such basic cognitive processes as categorization can influence prejudice and discrimination. Pure cognitive approaches have focused on the concept of stereotype as a cognitive structure that is directly determined by categorization, which organizes and represents information about social categories (e.g., Bar-Tal, Graumann, Kruglanski, & Stroebe, 1989; Hamilton, 1981a; Stephan, 1985, 1989; Tajfel, 1969). The social cognitive perspective has generated a great deal of experimental research, much of which has investigated the role of cognitive structures, such as stereotype, in biasing information processing and social behavior, particularly discriminatory behavior (e.g., Hamilton & Trolier, 1986; Lilli & Rehm, 1988). It has been widely accepted that much of prejudice and discrimination can be accounted for in such terms. A closely related perspective has proposed that motivational factors may be involved as well. This cognitive motivational approach views social categorization as triggering a basic motivational process, specifically a need to evaluate one's ingroup positively relative to outgroups (Hogg & Abrams, 1988; Tajfel & Turner, 1979; Turner, 1975). The research emerging from this cognitive motivational approach has also been predominantly experimental. Much of this research has focused on testing predictions derived from social identity theory concerning effects on ingroup bias, favoritism, and discrimination in minimal intergroup situations (Brewer, 1979; Brewer & Kramer, 1985; Messick & Mackie, 1989; Tajfel, 1982a).

The social cognitive and cognitive motivational perspectives together still constitute the dominant psychological approach to explaining and understanding prejudice and intergroup relations (Messick & Mackie, 1989). Despite its dominance, however, this approach does have serious limitations. One problem is the neglect by the social cognitive perspective of motivational and affective factors. As Hamilton (1981c) pointed out:

If there is any domain of human interaction that history tells us is laden with strong, even passionate, feelings, it is in the area of intergroup relations. And this point makes clear the fact that the cognitive approach, despite the rich and varied advances that it has made in recent years, is by itself incomplete. (p. 347)

A second problem is more pertinent to the cognitive motivational perspective. It is not at all clear that the kind of bias and favoritism observed in minimal intergroup situations is the same as the intergroup prejudice and hostility observed in natural social contexts. For example, bias in minimal intergroup situations seems to reflect ingroup favoritism rather than outgroup dislike (Brewer, 1979; Brewer & Kramer, 1985; Condor & Brown, 1988; Dion, 1979; Messick & Mackie, 1989). This suggests that this ingroup bias may be only a precursor of prejudice, which can become elaborated into prejudice under particular social conditions (see Chapter 5).

Finally, the broadly cognitive paradigm that has dominated the past few decades provides a seriously incomplete approach to explaining the phenomenon of prejudice in a number of important respects. For example, it has made little if any contribution to explaining individual differences in intergroup attitudes and behavior (Condor & Brown, 1988; Pettigrew, 1981). Nor has it shown any relevance for explaining how individuals are socialized in the intergroup attitudes and beliefs of their groups and culture (Condor & Brown, 1988). In contrast to the social cognitive perspective, social identity theory has shown relevance for understanding some of the macrosocial and intergroup dynamics that seem to be involved in prejudice and intergroup relations as group phenomena (cf. Hogg & Abrams, 1988; Tajfel & Turner, 1979). However, even at this level there are important gaps. Conflicts of interest between groups are dealt with only peripherally, and only as a factor that influences the salience of social categorization and not as a determinant of intergroup attitudes and perceptions in their own right. Yet it has been demonstrated empirically that, in certain circumstances at least, important group interests can completely overrule the effects on intergroup phenomena predicted by social identity theory (van Knippenberg, 1978). As a result, Tajfel and Turner (1979) emphasized that social identity theory "is intended not to replace RCT, but to supplement it" (p. 34).

Clearly, therefore, the broadly cognitive paradigm of the past few decades has been only a partial approach and has not provided a complete explanation of prejudice and intergroup relations. For this, its integration with other perspectives and approaches would be necessary. On occasion others have also made this point (see, e.g., Ashmore & DelBoca, 1981; Condor & Brown, 1988; Hamilton, 1981c; Stroebe & Insko, 1989). However, few, if any, attempts have been made to formulate an explanatory framework that integrates different perspectives and approaches to provide a comprehensive overall explanation of intergroup phenomena such as prejudice. Such an integrative framework is proposed in the following section.

To sum up, it became apparent during the 1970s that the intractability and persistence of racism and intergroup conflict might involve factors other than social structure and group interests. Thus, explanations were formulated in terms of basic, universal, and essentially normal cognitive processes. From this perspective, prejudice could be seen as an inevitable outcome of cognitive processes such as social categorization. The crucial question, therefore, became that of how normal cognitive processes determined intergroup phenomena such as conflict, discrimination, stereotyping, and prejudice. However, despite its contemporary dominance, this paradigm does have important limitations and does not provide a complete explanation of prejudice.

## AN INTEGRATIVE FRAMEWORK

The historical analysis described seven important shifts and stages in the way in which prejudice has been understood by psychologists. Each stage was characterized by a distinctive theoretical orientation and research emphasis, which seemed to emerge in response to particular historical circumstances. These historical circumstances appeared to make particular questions about the nature or causation of prejudice salient for social scientists. The different theoretical orientations can therefore be seen as attempts to answer these questions.

The first two periods described are basically concerned with the nature and conceptualization of prejudice; the remaining five pertain to its causation. These five periods involve four fundamentally different and equally valid questions about the causation of prejudice. One particular question—that concerning universal psychological processes that underlie prejudice—was addressed in two different periods. These four questions seem to correspond to four basic and qualitatively different causal processes in the determination of prejudice.

First, certain universal psychological processes build in an inherently human potentiality or propensity for prejudice. Second, social and intergroup dynamics describe the conditions and circumstances of contact and interaction between groups that elaborate this potentiality into normative and socially shared patterns of prejudice. Third, mechanisms of transmission explain how these intergroup dynamics and shared patterns of prejudice are socially transmitted to individual members of these groups. Fourth and finally, individual-difference dimensions determine individual susceptibility to prejudice, and so operate to modulate the impact of these social transmission mechanisms on individuals.

Each of these causal processes provides a partial but essential contribution to the explanation of prejudice. Together they provide a rudimentary integrative framework that involves four complementary processes and which gives a reasonably complete overall explanation of prejudice as both a group and an individual phenomenon. This framework is summarized in Table 4.2, which shows how existing theories and approaches to the causation of prejudice are logically and coherently subsumed within it. Thus, all existing theories of prejudice can be seen as proposing specific mechanisms to account for at least one of these four basic causal processes.

For example, universal psychological processes underlying an inherently human propensity or potentiality for prejudice have been ac-

**Table 4.2**
**Integrative Framework for Conceptualizing the Causation of Prejudice**

| | Psychological process | Social group | Interpersonal | Individual |
|---|---|---|---|---|
| Level of analysis | | | | |
| Causal process | Psychological fundamentals of prejudice | Social and inter-group dynamics | Social transmission of prejudice | Individual differences |
| Nature of the process | Universal psychological processes underlying an inherently human potential for prejudice | Conditions of intergroup contact and interaction which elaborate this potentiality into normative patterns of prejudice | Transmission of normative influences to the individual in the form of prejudiced attitudes | Modulation of social influence by individual differences in susceptibility to prejudice |
| Theories | Projection Displacement Universal color bias Belief similarity Social categorization Social identification | Realistic conflict Social competition Domination Intergroup differences in status, power, roles Convergent group boundaries | Socialization Conformity pressure Interpersonal contact Social perception and attributions | Frustration Adjustment Self-esteem Political ideology Cognitive factors Authoritarianism |

counted for in terms of psychodynamic mechanisms such as projection or the displacement of aggression. More recently, cognitively based processes, such as social categorization and its mobilization of basic motivational processes to evaluate ingroups positively relative to outgroups, have been emphasized. Alternative approaches to this issue have also been suggested in terms of a universal tendency to dislike outgroups with dissimilar values and beliefs (Rokeach et al., 1960) and, in the case of racism specifically, a basic bias against the color black (Williams & Morland, 1976). Each of these theories locates the roots of prejudice in certain inherent fundamentals of human psychological functioning. Thus, they describe basic perceptual, cognitive, or motivational mechanisms common to all persons that could account for the pervasiveness of prejudice and its near universality as a feature of human social behavior.

While certain fundamental psychological processes seem to determine an inherent human readiness or propensity for ethnocentrism and prejudice, these processes do not appear to operate in an automatic and inevitable fashion. All persons are not prejudiced against all outgroups. Some outgroups may be liked, others regarded with indifference, and still others disliked or even hated. Moreover, these intergroup attitudes are typically not just manifestations of individual idiosyncrasy but tend to be socially shared patterns that vary systematically with individual group memberships. Thus, certain social and intergroup dynamics seem to be necessary to elicit, elaborate, and direct these universal psychological propensities for prejudice into socially normative patterns of intergroup hostility. These include intergroup conflicts of interest such as direct competition (Sherif & Sherif, 1953) or domination and exploitation (Blauner, 1972; Bonacich, 1972; Cox, 1948; van den Berghe, 1967). Certain other conditions of intergroup contact and interaction that might also have this effect have been specified by social identity theory or other approaches. They include social competition, convergent group boundaries, differential treatment of groups, status differentials between groups (Brewer & Miller, 1984), and intergroup differentiation in social roles (LeVine & Campbell, 1972).

While prejudice as a group phenomenon can be explained in terms of the social and intergroup dynamics of contact and interaction between the groups, prejudice as an attitude is, of course, experienced and held by individuals. This raises the question of how normative group patterns of prejudice are acquired by or transmitted to the individual members of groups. The social transmission of normative patterns of prejudice from groups to individual group members has been explained in terms of conformity (Pettigrew, 1959) or childhood socialization (Proshansky, 1966). Alternative mechanisms are also possible. These include the social structuring of individual contact experiences with outgroup members, and their attributional responses to perceived intergroup differences on socially valued dimensions.

Finally, prejudice in individuals does not seem to be only a function of social influence. Individuals who are exposed to the same social influences may nevertheless differ in the degree to which they come to hold prejudiced attitudes. Certain individual-difference dimensions seem to be important in determining individual susceptibility to these social influences. These individual-difference dimensions can be seen as modulating the degree to which individuals absorb prejudice from the social environment, thus forming a generalized readiness or predisposition for prejudice. A number of theories have focused on individual-difference dimensions of this kind that might influence susceptibility to prejudice. Examples are authoritarianism (Adorno et al., 1950), self-esteem and psychological adjustment (Ehrlich, 1973), frustration (Dollard et al., 1939), cognitive factors (Frenkel-Brunswick, 1949), and political belief systems (Adorno et al., 1950).

To sum up, therefore, a historical analysis identified a number of systematic shifts that have occurred in the understanding of prejudice. These shifts suggest that at least four basic and complementary processes are involved in the causation of prejudice and are necessary for its explanation. Together, these four processes seem to provide a reasonably coherent framework that integrates the bewildering variety of theories and approaches attempting to elucidate the causes of prejudice. This framework is used and elaborated in the next four chapters, which focus on each of the four causal processes in turn, describing and evaluating the major theories proposed in each case. These four chapters (Chapters 5–8) thus deal successively with those theories that attempt to account for the psychological fundamentals of prejudice (Chapter 5), the social and intergroup dynamics of prejudice, (Chapter 6), mechanisms involved in the transmission of prejudice from group to the individual (Chapter 7), and individual differences in prejudice (Chapter 8).

# 5

# Psychological Fundamentals of Prejudice

A variety of theories have focused on the psychological fundamentals of prejudice. These theories seek to identify universal psychological processes, characteristic of all persons, that underlie or build in the potential for prejudice. As such, they suggest that prejudice, or at least the potential for prejudice, is a ubiquitous and an inherently human phenomenon.

An extremely influential exposition of this idea was the concept of ethnocentrism, as originally formulated by Sumner in 1906. Sumner viewed ethnocentrism as an interrelated set of values, attitudes, and behaviors involving both ingroup identification and outgroup hostility. He believed it was an inevitable and universal concomitant of the division of the social world into discrete groups. It involved "loyalty to the group, sacrifice for it, hatred and contempt for outsiders, brotherhood within, warlikeness without—all grow together, common products of the same situation" (Sumner, 1906, p. 13).

However, the universality of an ethnocentric syndrome of ingroup acceptance and outgroup rejection has been questioned. Three important criticisms may be noted. First, in the case of preindustrial societies, LeVine and Campbell (1972) pointed out that, contrary to the nationalistic assumptions of nineteenth-century anthropologists, social groupings are seldom clearly defined and demarcated. They cited evidence to indicate that group boundaries were often vague, diffuse, and shifting. Consequently, they argued that ethnocentrism, as Sumner conceptualized it, may be more characteristic of recently developed societies, specifically of the modern nation-state with its sharp and stable boundaries.

Second, membership and identification groups are not always synonymous. LeVine and Campbell (1972), for example, noted "documented cases of peoples who are territorially, economically, and politically autonomous, but who have taken another people as their positive reference group" (1972, p. 63). This is even more dramatically illustrated by the phenomenon of negative group identity (Tajfel, 1981), in which individuals and even entire social groups evaluate their membership groups negatively and identify with other groups.

Third, Brewer (1981), discussing findings from a series of cross-cultural studies of ethnocentrism, mentioned several findings that contradict Sumner's thesis. For example, different indices of intergroup differentiation, instead of being unidimensional, were often not very strongly related. Ingroup and outgroup attitudes, instead of being closely interrelated, could also be relatively independent of each other. Moreover, ingroup-outgroup differentiations were often not very stable and tended to be highly context-dependent and fluid. In other words, ingroup-outgroup differentiations seemed to be powerfully influenced by situational cues that made one group categorization salient rather than another. Such findings suggested that the concept of ethnocentrism, at least in its strong Sumnerian form, was not tenable. However, Brewer (1981) also noted that while outgroup hostility might not be universal, affective preference for one's ingroup, at least in the sense of the group with which individuals identify, and bias in its favor as opposed to outgroups, did seem to occur universally in the research reviewed.

The latter point suggests that a weaker form of the ethnocentrism hypothesis may be viable. This would involve a universal tendency toward preference for and bias in favor of situationally salient ingroups or identification groups, rather than attachment to a fixed membership group with hostility toward fixed outgroups. Besides the ethnographic evidence mentioned by Brewer (1981), a great deal of experimental evidence in favor of this proposition has emerged relatively recently.

This evidence derives from two quite different experimental paradigms: (a) that involving the evaluation of group products or performance and (b) the minimal intergroup paradigm pioneered by Tajfel and his coworkers (Tajfel, 1970; Tajfel et al., 1971). In the first case, arbitrarily created experimental groups perform tasks involving the creation of collective products. Even when such groups are not in competition, a tendency for the members of each to overvalue their group's product in relation to those of other groups has been found consistently (Hinkle & Schopler, 1979).

In the second case, the minimal intergroup paradigm, subjects are simply divided into completely arbitrary groups. These groups are truly minimal, involving no group activity or interaction of any kind. Yet when these subjects are asked to allocate rewards (or punishments) between ingroup and outgroup members, they do so in a manner that maximizes the differential between ingroup and outgroup, even though this may reduce the absolute benefits to the experimental subjects or even to the ingroup (Brewer, 1979; Tajfel, 1981). Moreover, the more salient the intergroup categorization is made, the stronger the tendency to show bias and discrimination in favor of the ingroup. A similar pattern is also found for other response measures. For example, ingroup members are rated more favorably than outgroup members on evaluative trait ratings.

These studies demonstrate that merely forming people into groups seems to inevitably engender bias in favor of the ingroup as opposed to the outgroup. In conjunction with the ethnographic evidence noted earlier, these findings support a weaker form of the ethnocentrism hypothesis. Contrary to the strong Sumnerian version, this concept of ethnocentrism does not see prejudice and hostility toward outgroups as inevitable. Ingroup favoritism and bias do not necessarily involve outgroup dislike or antipathy and there is clear evidence that this is so. Brewer (1981) pointed to the ethnographic finding that ingroup and outgroup attitudes are often relatively independent of each other. Evidence also derives from experimental studies using the minimal intergroup paradigm and the evaluation of the group products paradigm. In the former case, most studies reported that ingroup bias is expressed in the form of enhanced ingroup evaluations rather than tendencies to deprecate the outgroup (Brewer, 1979). In the latter case, studies found that biased evaluations of group performance or products derive from an overvaluation of the ingroup's product and not from undervaluing the outgroup's (Hinkle & Schopler, 1979).

All this evidence suggests that ethnocentrism, in the sense of a universal tendency to ingroup bias and discrimination, does not necessarily involve outgroup prejudice per se. Under certain circumstances, however, such as intergroup competition, ingroup bias does appear to be readily elaborated into active outgroup prejudice or hostility. Thus, ingroup bias can be seen as building in a basic human potentiality for prejudice. There is a great deal of evidence indicating how easily intergroup prejudice can be elicited under particular social circumstances and conditions. Sherif (1967), for example, took normal, well-adjusted, middle-class American boys attending a summer camp and formed them into quite arbitrary groups, which then competed in a tournament of games. This rapidly induced intense intergroup hostility and antagonism. The effect has been extensively replicated in different samples and settings (e.g., Blake & Mouton, 1979).

Summing up, therefore, it would seem that Sumner's assumption that outgroup hostility and prejudice are natural and inevitable concomitants of the existence of human groups is not tenable. However, whenever a group identification is made salient, a tendency toward preference and bias in favor of the ingroup seems to emerge. This ingroup preference does not necessarily involve outgroup derogation, and it does seem to be a universal characteristic of human social existence. Under certain social conditions, however, this basic ethnocentric bias can be easily and readily elaborated into active intergroup prejudice. Thus, a fundamental potentiality or predisposition for prejudice seems to be an inherent and universal attribute of human social life.

A number of theories of prejudice focus on basic and universal psychological processes characteristic of all persons that might underlie or build in the potential for prejudice. As such, they can be seen as general theories concerned with the psychological fundamentals of prejudice. This chapter will review these theories and propose some general conclusions.

## PROJECTION

The term *projection* refers to a defense mechanism that seeks to resolve an inner conflict by ascribing unacceptable and repressed impulses or attributes of one's own to others (Freud, 1946). This process may be used to explain how a particular individual's personal image of an outgroup may have been colored. Since it can be argued that inner conflict and the repression of unacceptable impulses may be a universal aspect of human social life (as psychoanaltyic theory, for example, assumes), projection may also be viewed as a universal mechanism underlying a tendency to acquire unfavorable stereotypes of outgroups and therefore dislike them. This approach explains the tendency for stereotypes to be shared, or consensual, images held by particular groups, not in terms of the actual traits of the outgroup, but by those needs or attributes that are unacceptable and taboo to the ingroup.

LeVine and Campbell (1972), for example, suggested that groups which disapprove of the open expression of aggression could, through projection, see outgroups as aggressive; and groups that emphasize the necessity for interpersonal generosity and sharing would see outgroups as stingy. Ashmore and DelBoca (1976) pointed out that projection theory has often been applied to the explanation of antiblack prejudice. Thus, it has been suggested that important aspects of racial prejudice, such as the belief that blacks are sexually uninhibited and insatiable, may derive from white society's repression and projection of "natural yet tabooed sexual drives onto blacks" (Ashmore & DelBoca, 1976, p. 78).

Bettelheim and Janowitz (1964) also noted that projection need not be independent of the actual characteristics of the outgroup. Thus, a group of low social status, such as American blacks, could be selected as id projections and represent repressed sexual desires. On the other hand, high-achieving groups, such as Jews, could be selected as superego projections. In this case, anti-Semitism would express resentment at a failure to live up to superego demands for success and achievement.

Although LeVine and Campbell (1972) listed a number of interesting and testable hypotheses derived from projection theory, very little empirical work has been done in this area. Moreover, the few studies that have been conducted have not clearly or consistently supported the theory. Thus, although Bettelheim and Janowitz (1964) interpreted some of the findings from their research on prejudice among American war veterans in terms of projection, these interpretations were post hoc in character. Ackerman and Jahoda (1950) studied the records of neurotic patients undergoing psychoanalytic therapy and found that they did seem to project impulses onto Jews. However, Ashmore (1970) pointed out that this could well have been due to a tendency for neurotics to generally use projection very extensively.

A methodologically sounder study of projection was conducted by Pompilo in 1957 (cited in Ashmore, 1970). He tested the hypothesis that persons who had undesirable traits, but denied having them, would ascribe them to minority groups. His subjects were rated by their peers and rated themselves on five undesirable traits often used to describe blacks or Jews: irresponsible, uninhibited, suspicious, hostile, and self-centered. There was no tendency for those subjects whose peers rated them as having such traits, but who themselves denied this, to be more likely to attribute them to blacks and Jews.

In conclusion, it is apparent that there has been very little empirical work on projection and prejudice. Moreover, the research that has been done seems to be methodologically weak, inconclusive, and badly dated. In 1970 Ashmore concluded his discussion of this literature by stating that "we are therefore forced to conclude that although projection does play some part in the development of prejudice at the individual level, the part is probably not a major one" (p. 272). This assessment which, if anything, seems on the optimistic side, appears to reflect the general consensus of expert opinion (e.g., Ashmore & DelBoca, 1976; Simpson & Yinger, 1985).

## FRUSTRATION-AGGRESSION-DISPLACEMENT THEORY

The frustration-aggression-displacement theory of prejudice proposes that aggression which cannot be expressed directly against a source of frustration may be inhibited and displaced onto a convenient substitute or scapegoat (Dollard et al., 1939; LeVine & Campbell, 1972; MacCrone, 1937). If it is assumed that organized social life inevitably involves at least some frustration of basic human needs, the idea that individuals would accumulate an underlying reservoir of "free floating" hostility, which could be displaced onto outgroups and minorities, follows quite logically. MacCrone (1937) stated this very succinctly:

Although the individual may submit freely enough to the restrictions placed upon him by group laws, customs, conventions, and the like, he nevertheless feels these restrictions as a constant strain to be endured, though not without reactions of revolt and hostility, either latent or overt. These privations of everyday life which give rise to the "discontents of civilization" may readily enough find expression in hostility directed against an "out-group"—hostility that would otherwise vent itself at the expense of the "in-group." (p. 250)

This is not a complete theory of prejudice. Zawadzki (1948) pointed out that it does not indicate why certain outgroups may be selected as scapegoats and others not. As Berkowitz (1962) noted in his reformulation of frustration-aggression theory, social factors need to be considered in order to explain the selection of scapegoats. Nevertheless, the theory does provide a powerful general approach to prejudice that seems capable of explaining its pervasiveness as an almost universal feature of human social life. It can also account for individual differences in prejudice. Thus, persons who are chronically more frustrated should be generally more prejudiced.

The theory has been extremely influential and is widely and respectfully cited in standard texts on prejudice. In addition to its power and generality, part of its appeal may also derive from its apparent applicability to important social phenomena. For example, it has been applied speculatively, though with seeming plausibility, to explain the rise of anti-Semitism in Germany after World War I (Dollard et al, 1939) and the historical correlation of periods of economic hardship with the increased lynching of blacks in the American South (Hovland & Sears, 1940).

More recently, the theory has been severely criticized as being too individualistic to adequately account for intergroup phenomena (Billig, 1976; Brown & Turner, 1981; Tajfel, 1981). This argument asserts that the theory is implausible "because it implies that collective aggression against some outgroup represents the simultaneous aggregation and convergence of individual motivational states" (Brown & Turner, 1981, p. 45). However, this criticism seems to miss an important point. The theory locates the origin of prejudice not in a transient motivational state but, rather, in the assumption that organized human social life is inherently frustrating as an ongoing process and that this creates an underlying reservoir of free-floating hostility within individuals. According to the theory, therefore, the actual origin of prejudice is social rather than individual, and these omnipresent social frustrations are merely mediated through individual motivational mechanisms.

Many reviews of the empirical research testing the frustration theory of prejudice have concluded that the research seems to be broadly supportive of the theory (e.g., Harding et al., 1969; Levin & Levin, 1982;

Simpson & Yinger, 1985). A close examination of this research, however, indicates that it is plagued by serious methodological problems, and the findings are so ambiguous that far more pessimistic conclusions seem appropriate.

A good deal of this research has been correlational in nature, seeking to demonstrate that persons experiencing higher levels of frustration will tend to be higher in prejudice. Such research does not permit clear causal conclusions and also seems to be more relevant to the issue of individual differences in prejudice rather than to that of frustration as a general cause of prejudice. Consequently, this research will be reviewed in some detail in Chapter 8 when the issue of explaining individual differences in prejudice is considered. Here, however, it may be noted that the findings from this correlational research tend to be extremely inconsistent, with some studies indicating that more prejudiced persons tend to be more frustrated (e.g., Allport & Kramer, 1946; Bettelheim & Janowitz, 1964; Campbell, 1947) and others finding no association (e.g., Hodge & Treiman, 1966; Patchen, Davidson, Hoffman, & Brown, 1977; Seeman, 1977).

A number of experimental studies are directly relevant to the issue of frustration as a general cause of prejudice. These studies have attempted to show that frustrating individuals increases their prejudice against outgroups and minorities. Although most of these studies report significant effects of frustration on prejudice (Cowen, Landes, & Schaet, 1959; Feshbach & Singer, 1957; Miller & Bugelski, 1948; Stricker, 1963), some have not (Lever, 1976; Stagner & Congdon, 1955). Even those studies with positive findings have not been unambiguous; for example, they may report significant results for certain measures but not for others. In the "classic" study by Miller and Bugelski (1948) experimentally induced frustration resulted in a significant tendency for subjects to use fewer favorable terms to describe outgroups. They did not, however, employ significantly more unfavorable terms in describing the outgroups—a finding that does not seem consistent with frustration-prejudice theory.

Studies showing increased prejudice after frustration also involve a serious methodological problem. This emerges from an important, though rarely cited, study by Silverman and Kleinman (1967), who found that while experimentally frustrated subjects scored higher on measures of prejudice, they also scored significantly higher on measures indicating a tendency to respond in a socially deviant manner. For example, these subjects were more likely to agree with cheating in examinations, to question the value of education, to support sexual promiscuity, and to decry democratic government. Moreover, prejudice and response deviance correlated .86 in the frustrated group and only .01 in the nonfrustrated group. These findings suggest that higher scores on prejudice scales by experimentally frustrated subjects may not reflect increased prejudice as such but, rather, a tendency to respond in a socially deviant manner to the frustration, possibly as an expression of aggression to the experimenter. Although this was not done by Silverman and Kleinman (1967), it seems highly likely that controlling for the effects of response deviance would have eliminated any association between frustration and prejudice.

A number of experimental studies have also tried to show that frustration would increase tendencies to act out prejudice against disliked groups, but the results have almost invariably failed to support the theory. For example, a study by Lindzey (1950) found that, after being frustrated, subjects high and low in prejudice did not differ in the amount of displaced aggression they indicated on projective and semiprojective measures. Although several other studies using direct indices of aggressive behavior have reported that highly prejudiced subjects do act more aggressively under frustrating conditions, these subjects seem to do so indiscriminately to all possible targets, and not selectively to the groups against whom they are prejudiced (Berkowitz, 1959; Genthner & Taylor, 1973). A study by Weatherley (1961) did report that when anti-Semitic subjects were frustrated, they were more negative to Jews than were nonprejudiced subjects. However, the difference between high and low-prejudice subjects was due to low-prejudice subjects decreasing hostility when frustrated and not to high-prejudice subjects increasing hostility—a finding that is not consistent with frustration-prejudice theory.

In general, as Konecni (1979) pointed out, most of the research on the frustration theory of prejudice tends to be badly dated and seriously flawed methodologically. This makes definitive conclusions rather difficult. It does seem reasonably clear, however, that virtually none of the experimental research unambiguously supports the idea that frustration and displaced hostility may be a general cause of prejudice. In addition, frustration does not appear to have much relevance to the ingroup/outgroup bias and discrimination revealed by Tajfel (1981) and others in the minimal intergroup paradigm and in studies concerning the evaluation of group products (Hinkle & Schopler, 1979). Both these paradigms show that the ethnocentric bias observed seems to arise from heightened evaluations of the ingroup (Brewer, 1979; Hinkle & Schopler, 1979), and not outgroup deprecation as frustration theory would predict.

The correlational research reviewed in Chapter 8 does suggest, however, that frustration and prejudice may be related at least under certain circumstances. It is possible, therefore, that frustration may contribute to the explanation of individual differences in prejudice. This is considered in detail in Chapter 8.

## UNIVERSAL COLOR BIAS

It has been proposed that a basic and universal evaluative orientation to the colors white and black underlies the development of racial prejudice through generalizing to social categories designated by the same color names (Williams & Morland, 1976). In support of this, a number of studies have found that adults and children show a clear evaluative preference for the color white over that of black (Williams, 1964; Williams, Boswell, & Best, 1975; Williams & Morland, 1976). This effect has been replicated in a variety of cultures, demonstrating that it is not just specific to North American or Western society but seems to be culturally universal (Adams & Osgood, 1973; Iwawaki, Sonoo, Williams, & Best, 1978; Williams & Morland, 1976).

Evidence for a direct link between this color preference and racial attitudes comes from two main sources. First, significant correlations have been obtained between the degree of color bias shown and racial attitudes for both adults (Williams, 1969) and children (Best, Naylor, & Williams, 1975; Boswell & Williams, 1975). Thus, the more negatively persons rated the color black, the less favorably they evaluated blacks. Second, the functional nature of this relationship has been confirmed by studies demonstrating that these color preferences could be readily modified in children, using operant conditioning techniques, and that these modifications would generalize to racial attitudes (Elliot & Tyson, 1983; Spencer & Horowitz, 1973; Traynham & Witte, 1976; Williams, Boswell, & Best, 1975).

Thus, it seems to have been reasonably conclusively established that a culturally widespread preference for the color white over the color black exists and that this color preference influences racial prejudice. What could be the basis for this color preference? One possibility is that it could be learned from cultures in which white is used to symbolize goodness and black badness. However, a cultural socialization hypothesis has usually been discounted for several reasons. First, Williams and Morland (1976) argued that this hypothesis does not account for the cross-cultural generality of this color preference and its presence in very young preschool children. Second, although most culturally acquired concepts tend to show an age progression during the preschool years with more intelligent children acquiring cultural influences more rapidly, this color bias does not seem to correlate with either chronological age or IQ in young children (Williams et al., 1975).

Williams and Morland (1976) therefore proposed an alternative explanation, which attributes this white-black color bias to the diurnal nature of human beings. Because need satisfaction and effective functioning tend to occur during daylight hours, "the early experience of the young child with the light of day and the dark of night may cause him to develop a preference for light over darkness, which may then generalize to the colors white and black" (Williams et al., 1975, p. 506). They speculated that the basic color preference set up in this manner may also be reinforced by an "innate aversion to darkness, perhaps based on an evolutionary history in which avoidance of the dark was an adaptive characteristic" (Williams & Morland, 1976, p. 262). In their approach, then, color preference is the psychological basis and cause of cultural color symbolism and not an effect of it. This provides an evaluative basis for racial preferences and prejudice through the systematic association of color terms with categories of people designated by similar color names.

The proposition that the roots of racial prejudice might rest in such basic experiences, and perhaps even be reinforced by innate biological dispositions, has occasioned some disquiet (cf. Milner, 1981, pp. 130–131). Nevertheless, because of its apparently strong and consistent empirical support, the theory has not been seriously challenged. Two important studies, however, have reported findings that seem to question the theory (May & May, 1979, 1981). These have been the only controlled studies thus far to use very young children and infants as subjects and to use nonverbal rather than verbal color preference tests. Children ranging in age from six months to four years were presented with a series of pairs of toys. The toys were identical, except that one was white and the other black. The findings did not indicate a tendency to choose the white toy preferentially. In fact, six-month-old children showed a significant bias in favor of black, which gradually decreased with age until a slight bias in favor of white was evident in the older children.

These findings seem to contradict the thesis that bias in favor of the color white could be due to very early experiences with light and dark or, for that matter, to innate dispositions. Instead, they appear to support an explanation in terms of socialization. On this basis, it is possible to speculate that color symbolism, being embedded in language, may be acquired during language learning. The cross-cultural generality of the phenomenon might simply reflect a global distribution of wealth, status, and power along racial and color lines. As such, white-black color bias might be a historical rather than a truly universal phenomenon and an effect rather than a cause of prejudice. In the case of individuals, learned color symbolism and racial attitudes would therefore tend to be mutually reinforcing.

The idea that black-white color bias is acquired in the course of socialization and language learning seems consistent with the relative ease with which color preferences in children can be modified by very limited experimental interventions and the facility with which these effects generalize to racial attitudes. If color symbolism were caused by very early and basic experiences, and even innate biological predispositions, as

Williams and Morland (1976) argued, it should surely be much more resistant to change.

In concluding, it can be emphasized that prejudice is not necessarily associated with color or race. Antipathies based on criteria completely unrelated to color—such as religion, nationality, and language—have historically proved no less severe or intractable than prejudice based on skin color. This suggests that color bias cannot be attributed any primary causal role in racial prejudice. It could, however, play a secondary reinforcing role during the socialization of racism, and as Milner (1975) noted, it may also "provide an *evaluative context* into which prejudices about people's colour can be easily fitted, and which gives them credence" (p. 67; italics in the original). Thus, color bias helps explain the finding that racial awareness and prejudice seem to emerge earlier than other kinds of prejudice and intergroup differentiations (Aboud & Skerry, 1984).

## BELIEF CONGRUENCE AND SIMILARITY

A consistently positive relationship has been observed between attitudinal similarity and interindividual attraction (Byrne, 1971; Newcomb, 1961). Thus, people seek out and are attracted to those who are similar to themselves and tend to dislike those who are dissimilar. Not surprisingly, it has been suggested that this basic principle might also apply to intergroup attraction and rejection. The best-known and most systematic application of this principle to the understanding of prejudice is the theory of belief congruence formulated by Rokeach et al. (1960).

Belief congruence theory proposes that perceived dissimilarity in group attitudes, values, and beliefs is the basic psychological mechanism that underlies prejudice. Thus, outgroups would tend to be less favorably evaluated to the extent that they are perceived as holding beliefs different from one's own. On this basis, Rokeach et al. (1960) predicted that "*insofar as psychological processes are involved*, belief is more important than ethnic or racial membership as a determinant of social discrimination" (p. 135; italics in the original). They tested this by having research subjects indicate whether they could or could not be friends with persons who were similar or different in race and belief, for example, "A Negro who believes in God" or "A white person who is an atheist." The results showed that subjects discriminated on the basis of both race and belief but that the belief effect was larger. These findings were replicated by a number of later studies, which showed that belief similarity overrides racial differences in determining interpersonal liking and acceptance in situations involving little social pressure and no intergroup competition (e.g., Byrne & Wong, 1962; Insko, Nacoste, & Moe,

1983; Rokeach & Mezei, 1966; Smith, Williams, & Willis, 1967; Stein, 1966).

Belief congruence theory has engendered a good deal of controversy, however, and despite its empirical support, it has often been regarded rather dismissively. Some commentators have felt that the principle of belief dissimilarity might be too logical, too simplistic, and too superficial to account credibly for the affective intensity, intractability, and irrationality with which racial prejudice may be manifest. Harding et al. (1969), for example, concluded their discussion of belief congruence theory by stating that "perhaps the ethnic attitudes so vividly described by Goodman . . . and by Wright . . . are mainly the result of assumed belief dissimilarity, but it seems scarcely possible that this is really true" (p. 36). Others have criticized the theory as an attempt "to explain away racism by calling it belief prejudice" (Fairchild & Gurin, 1978, p. 766).

A more compelling objection to belief congruence theory was made by Triandis (1961). He suggested that belief might outweigh race effects only in the case of rather trivial, nonintimate interracial behaviors that involve little social distance, such as liking or casual friendliness. A good deal of research has investigated this by assessing the relative strength of race versus belief effects for different criterion behaviors in varying conditions. The findings have shown that, in fact, racial dissimilarity did tend to outweigh belief dissimilarity in determining more intimate interracial behaviors, such as "marriage," "dating," and "acceptance as kin" (Insko et al., 1983; Mezei, 1971; Stein, Hardyck, & Smith, 1965; Triandis & Davis, 1965). These findings seemed to substantiate Triandis's (1961) argument. As a result, it has been suggested that they provide "a nontrivial complication for the belief theory of prejudice" (Ashmore & DelBoca, 1976, p. 93).

However, it can be argued that Triandis's and similar findings are not necessarily inconsistent with Rokeach et al.'s theory (Insko et al., 1983). In their original formulation of the theory, Rokeach et al. stated that because belief congruence was the *psychological process* underlying prejudice, its effects could be counteracted by external social influences, such as powerful institutionalized norms. Thus, Insko et al. (1983) pointed out that the findings indicating that race effects were stronger than belief effects for more intimate interracial behaviors could have been due to powerful social norms overriding belief effects.

The research of others supports Insko et al.'s suggestion (Goldstein & Davis, 1972; Mezei, 1971; Moe, Nacoste, & Insko, 1981; Silverman, 1974; Silverman & Cochrane, 1972). These studies indicated that the relative importance of race or belief effects is directly related to the strength of the social norms regulating these interracial behaviors. Thus, where normative pressures governing interracial behavior were stronger, race effects were stronger, and where normative pressures were weaker, belief effects were stronger. This means, as Insko et al. (1983) emphasized, that the findings that race effects were stronger than belief effects for certain more intimate interracial behaviors are not really contrary to Rokeach's theory.

An additional problem for belief congruence theory is that it is not entirely clear whether it is dissimilarity in belief only that leads to prejudice, or whether other kinds of dissimilarity may have the same effect. Kidder and Stewart (1975), for example, suggested that any kind of intergroup dissimilarity could generate dislike. It is difficult to assess their argument, however, because perceived dissimilarities that are ostensibly unrelated to beliefs could nevertheless result in the inference that differences in belief exist. On the other hand, some of the findings reported by Tajfel and his associates, using the minimal intergroup paradigm, suggest that any perceived differences can create intergroup bias. Tajfel's research indicated that almost any criterion for dividing or categorizing persons into ingroup and outgroup will induce bias and discrimination in favor of the ingroup and against the outgroup (Brewer, 1979; Tajfel, 1981). It is not possible to conclusively rule out the idea that such divisions affect bias only through inducing the assumption that such minimal groups differ in beliefs. However, this does not seem very convincing in cases such as those where people are divided into completely arbitrary groups using a throw of the dice.

As a result of such findings, it has been argued that belief similarity in itself may not be a necessary psychological condition for prejudice. Instead, it might simply be a special case of social categorization, as such, and exert its primary effect on prejudice in its role as a cue for categorization. Brown and Turner (1981), for example, asserted that "belief incongruence may in fact only be important in so far as it functions as a cue to group membership and not otherwise" (p. 51).

This has been supported by a study by Allen and Wilder (1975), which assessed the degree to which experimental subjects behaved in a discriminatory fashion when the similarity of ingroup and outgroups was systematically varied. Their findings indicated that the perceived similarity and dissimilarity of outgroups did not alter the extent to which behavioral discrimination occurred against these outgroups. However, later studies, which also used the minimal intergroup paradigm, have not obtained such clear-cut findings. Sometimes outgroup similarity has reduced bias against the outgroup (Brown, 1984a; Brown & Abrams, 1986; Diehl, 1988) as belief congruence theory would expect. In other cases, a directly opposite effect has been reported. The more similar the outgroup, the more discrimination there has been against it (Diehl, 1988; Moghaddam & Stringer, 1988).

There have been several attempts to explain these conflicting findings. Brown (1984b) suggested that similarity of the outgroup might decrease bias under intergroup cooperation but increase it under competitive intergroup conditions; however, this hypothesis was not clearly supported in two experimental studies (Brown, 1984a; Brown & Abrams, 1986). An alternative explanation was proposed by Diehl (1988), who argued that belief congruence theory might hold when subjects are reacting to an individual ingroup or outgroup member about whose personal similarity or dissimilarity they have information. On the other hand, when subjects react to an individual not on the basis of personal similarity but on the basis of the similarity or dissimilarity of the group to which that individual belongs, the opposite might happen. These subjects, it is suggested, will discriminate more against a person from a similar group than from a dissimilar group.

Diehl (1988) reported findings supporting this hypothesis. However, his research used only one outcome measure in the crucial experiment— behavioral discrimination—and did not include a measure of liking. This is an important omission, as Brown (1984b) noted some evidence suggesting that outgroup similarity may have different effects for different outcome measures. One implication of this is that belief congruence theory might hold when outcome measures of attraction or liking are used. Thus, similar outgroups may be liked more. On the other hand, when the outcome measure is behavioral discrimination (allocating rewards between ingroup and outgroup members), similarity may induce more discrimination (e.g., Brown, 1984a; Brown & Abrams, 1986; Diehl, 1988; Moghaddam & Stringer, 1988). Post hoc examination of several studies that used one or both of these outcome measures does seem broadly consistent with this (e.g., Brown, 1984a; Brown & Abrams, 1986; Diehl, 1988; Moghaddam & Stringer, 1988). However, the possibility has not yet been systematically tested.

Overall, therefore, belief congruence theory enunciates a universal and parsimonious general principle, which is capable of explaining the pervasiveness of prejudice as a distinctively human phenomenon. Despite the criticisms of this theory, there is a great deal of empirical evidence that supports it. In addition to the evidence already noted, a number of ethnographic and cross-cultural studies have consistently shown a close association between intergroup dissimilarity and rejection (e.g., Brewer, 1968; LeVine & Campbell, 1972, pp. 177–188).

Several issues concerning belief congruence theory, however, have not yet been adequately clarified. For example, it is not clear to what extent dissimilarity of belief specifically, as opposed to dissimilarity in general, is related to prejudice. Moreover, it seems well established that dissimilarity exerts an important effect on intergroup bias and liking as a cue for categorizing persons into ingroup and outgroup. Dissimilarity also seems to have effects over and above group categorization. Thus, once group categorization has occurred, the degree to which outgroups are similar or dissimilar does affect intergroup liking and discrimination. However, these effects appear to be more complex than belief congruence theory would expect and are not yet well understood.

## COGNITIVE CATEGORIZATION

The idea that basic cognitive processes used by all humans to simplify, structure, and give meaning to their social environment might be involved in prejudice, and particularly stereotyping, has long been acknowledged. For example, both Allport (1954) and Lippman (1922) discussed the role of cognitive processes in stereotyping. However, it has been only fairly recently, since the publication of Henri Tajfel's seminal paper, "Cognitive Aspects of Prejudice," in 1969, that the full implications of this proposition have been developed.

The basic cognitive mechanism implicated in prejudice is social categorization—that is, the perceptual classification of individuals into discrete categories or groups. One effect of categorization, readily demonstrated with physical objects, is the accentuation of intracategory similarities and intercategory differences (Tajfel & Wilkes, 1963). In his 1969 paper, Tajfel argued that, in the case of social categorization, these effects could adequately account for the phenomenon of social stereotyping.

A large number of studies have subsequently confirmed that dividing persons into discrete categories does result in this accentuation effect. Individuals who are categorized into groups will exaggerate their similarity to fellow ingroup members and the dissimilarity of ingroup members to outgroup members, and this will occur on dimensions other than the criterion for categorization as well (Allen & Wilder, 1975; Lilli & Rehm, 1988; Wilder, 1986). They will also tend to view outgroups as relatively less complex, less variable, and less individuated than their ingroups (Hamilton & Troiler, 1986; Judd & Park, 1988; Wilder, 1986). Tajfel's view that these effects of social categorization account for stereotyping as a social phenomenon has been widely accepted. Hogg and Abrams (1988), for example, asserted that "just as categorization causes accentuation effects in physical perception, so it does in social perception, where the effects are indistinguishable from stereotyping. Categorization can thus be considered to be the process underlying and responsible for stereotyping" (p. 73).

This view of stereotyping as a purely cognitive process, and the concept of stereotype as a cognitive structure organizing and representing information about social categories, has been central to a great deal of research and theorizing during the past decade (cf. Bar-Tal et al., 1989; Brewer & Kramer, 1985; Hamilton, 1981a; Hamilton & Troiler, 1986; Messick & Mackie, 1989; Stephan, 1985, 1989). This social cognitive approach to intergroup processes has focused on a number of issues, including (a) the nature of the cognitive biases directly determined by social categorization, such as the accentuation and outgroup homogeneity effects, which appear to contribute to stereotyping (cf. Wilder, 1986); (b) how stereotypical information about social categories may be cognitively structured (cf. Messick & Mackie, 1989); (c) how illusory correlations under certain very specific conditions influence the content of stereotypes, particularly about highly distinctive minority group members (cf. Hamilton, 1981b; Hamilton & Sherman, 1989); and, most prominently, (d) the way in which stereotypes once established influence information processing and interpersonal behavior (cf. Stephan, 1989). The most important and well-established conclusion from this research is that stereotypes appear to bias information processing in a number of ways. Moreover, most of these biases have essentially the same effect: They operate to maintain and preserve the stereotype.

The social cognitive approach to intergroup processes has been enormously productive within a relatively short period. The crucial question here, however, is whether stereotyping as a purely cognitive process can adequately account for a fundamental human predisposition to prejudice. It has been well established that stereotyping in the sense described here is a universally human process. Furthermore, it is entirely feasible that negative stereotypes could underlie and determine prejudiced attitudes. Nevertheless, there are important reasons why stereotyping as a purely cognitive process does not adequately resolve this issue.

One reason is that stereotyping as a cognitively determined perceptual distortion should be essentially neutral in an evaluative sense. Thus, stereotyping as a cognitive process should not itself determine or influence the content of stereotypes. The only qualification here would be the case of certain highly specific and probably uncommon circumstances that are conducive to the formation of illusory correlations. In general, stereotyping as a purely cognitive and perceptual process would merely operate to represent and accentuate real differences between social categories, irrespective of whether these were evaluatively positive, negative, or neutral. These real differences would tend to be socially determined, and, when they were such that their cognitive accentuation generated negative stereotypes about certain social categories, these differences could well contribute to prejudiced attitudes toward the social categories. In such cases, the actual cause of the prejudice would seem more appropriately viewed as the social circumstances that determine these real inequities and differences. Stereotyping, in this case, would be the mechanism operating to translate these social inequities into prejudice. The role of stereotyping in generating prejudiced attitudes in this way will be discussed in detail in Chapter 7.

In practice, however, stereotypes are not evaluatively neutral. Stereotyping tends to be ethnocentric. Thus, stereotypes of the ingroup will be evaluatively more positive and those of outgroups evaluatively more negative than would be expected on the basis of the purely cognitive biases and processes involved in stereotyping (Hogg & Abrams, 1988; Tajfel, 1982b). This suggests the operation of a further process responsible for this ethnocentrism. Research by Tajfel and his colleagues (Tajfel, 1970; Tajfel et al., 1971), after his initial work on categorization and its accentuation of intracategory similarity and intercategory differentiation, demonstrated that social categorization seemed to have other effects as well, which could account for this ethnocentric tendency. This research has primarily used the minimal intergroup paradigm, described in the introduction to this chapter, which demonstrated that the mere act of dividing individuals into groups inevitably sets up an evaluative bias and discriminatory behavior in group members in favor of the ingroup and against the outgroup.

This effect has been extensively replicated and found to be robust under a variety of conditions and for a variety of outcomes. Outcome measures have included evaluative trait ratings, evaluation of group products, and allocation of rewards or penalties (Brewer, 1979; Brewer & Silver, 1978; Brown & Turner, 1979; Doise, 1978; Locksley, Ortiz, & Hepburn, 1980; Moghaddam & Stringer, 1986). Moreover, the more salient the categorization, irrespective of how trivial or arbitrary it might be in itself, the stronger the resulting intergroup bias. As a result, it has been concluded that social categorization, in the form of any ingroup/ outgroup distinction, will generate intergroup bias, competition, and even prejudice in the complete absence of any functional conflict of interests or "realistic competition" between groups (Tajfel, 1981).

This conclusion could indicate that social categorization itself is the direct causal mechanism underlying prejudice, discrimination, and ethnocentrism. Doise (1978), for example, argued that the cognitive differentiation, which individuals make between ingroup and outgroup as a direct result of categorization, adequately accounts for the ensuing intergroup bias and discriminatory behavior. However, others (e.g., Brewer, 1979; Brewer & Kramer, 1985; Tajfel & Turner, 1979; Turner, 1975) noted fundamental asymmetries in these phenomena, which are not easily accounted for in terms of purely cognitive processes. Thus, whereas the categorization of objects always accentuates intercategory differences, social categorization does not necessarily do this. In social categorization, differences are only accentuated when they are favorable to the ingroup and tend to be minimized if they are favorable to the outgroup (Brewer & Kramer, 1985; Tajfel, 1981; Turner, 1981).

Such asymmetries do not seem to be adequately explained in terms of cognitive factors alone, and they suggest that motivational factors must also be operative to generate this ingroup bias. Brewer (1979), for example, on the basis of an extensive review of the evidence concluded that "in-group bias results from a motivated search to represent the differences between groups along dimensions that favor the in-group" (p. 320). The most important attempt to elucidate these motivational factors has been social identity theory (Tajfel & Turner, 1979; Turner, 1975), which is discussed in the following section.

## SOCIAL IDENTITY THEORY

Social identity theory proposes that social categorization generates basic motivational processes in individuals, which directly induce intergroup social competition. The theory proceeds from the assumption that the individual's social category and group memberships collectively determine his or her social identity, an important component of the overall sense of identity. The evaluations of these social category and group memberships thus contribute to the individual's personal self-evaluation and self-esteem. Given a basic human desire to establish and maintain positive self-esteem, individuals will try to view their own social category memberships as positively as possible. This stimulates a motivated search for intercategory social comparisons that would be favorable to the social categories or groups with which the self is identified.

These processes are assumed to be activated when a particular social categorization becomes salient. To the extent that this occurs, individuals will respond to others—no longer in terms of their personal characteristics, but in terms of their category or group identities. Intergroup behavior is therefore switched on whenever a group identity becomes salient, and social interactions become primarily regulated by individual group memberships and identities. Thus, intergroup behavior is viewed as qualitatively distinct from interpersonal behavior, where social interactions are governed by the unique personal characteristics and personal identities of individuals. When a particular social categorization is cued, the need for a positive social identity creates a competitive intergroup orientation, which engenders perceptual biases and discriminatory behavioral strategies in attempts to differentiate ingroup from outgroup in a manner favoring the ingroup. Thus, differences favorable to the ingroup will be emphasized and exaggerated, while differences favorable to the outgroup may be ignored or minimized. Individuals would consequently tend to behave in ways that maximize the relative advantage for the ingroup over the outgroup.

Social identity theory accounts for the ethnocentric evaluative biases and behavioral discrimination observed in minimal intergroup experimental situations: an ingroup favoritism that is accentuated by increasing the salience of group membership. It also accounts for the observation that distinctions unfavorable to the ingroup are minimized rather than accentuated—a finding, as previously noted, that is not easily explained in terms of the purely cognitive processes involved in categorization (Brewer, 1979; Tajfel, 1982b). In addition, the theory explains the strategy, observed in these experiments, for group members to seek maximum relative advantage for the ingroup over the outgroup, even when this interferes with the achievement of maximum absolute outcomes for the subjects (Brewer, 1979; Brewer & Kramer, 1985).

Finally, as Brewer (1981) noted, the theory is consistent with two important observations from ethnographic and cross-cultural research: First, intergroup differentiations are often fluid and shift readily in response to situational cues; second, a generalized tendency to favor the ingroup (at least in the sense of identification group) seems to be almost universally evident. Social identity theory also accounts for those exceptional but theoretically important cases in which "negative social identities" exist—that is, where individuals evaluate their own membership groups negatively and identify with outgroups (Tajfel, 1981). In these cases, certain specific circumstances are presumed to have made it impossible for individuals to evade the psychological consequences of salient social identities in which the ingroup occupies a consensually inferior social status relative to the outgroup.

Social identity theory has stimulated a great deal of research during the past two decades. Surprisingly few studies, however, have attempted to test its central proposition, which relates intergroup bias and discrimination to the need for self-esteem; moreover, these studies have not always been clearly or unambiguously supportive of the theory. Two important confirmatory studies showed that if subjects, who are categorized into minimal groups, are given the opportunity to discriminate, they do show increased self-esteem (Lemyre & Smith, 1985; Oakes & Turner, 1980). Another study found that an experimental devaluation of the ingroup did have negative effects on group members' self-esteem (Wagner, Lampen, & Syllwasschy, 1986); contrary to expectation, however, devaluation of the ingroup relative to one outgroup in this same study did not result in ingroup members devaluing a second outgroup. Finally, Meindl and Lerner (1984) found that after a self-esteem lowering experience, ingroup members showed more extreme reactions to outgroup members, in both aggressive and benevolent directions. They argued that the findings were not inconsistent with social identity theory because the highly benevolent responses in their study could have expressed a paternalistic attitude and an emphasis on the relative superiority of the ingroup.

Although it has been assumed that social identity theory expects persons with low self-esteem to be more motivated to show intergroup bias and discrimination (e.g., Abrams & Hogg, 1988), this assumption has not been empirically supported. Several studies have found no relationship between self-esteem and bias or discrimination in minimal intergroup situations (Crocker & Schwartz, 1985; Crocker, Thompson, McGraw, & Ingerman, 1987; Thompson & Crocker, 1990); others have found exactly the opposite of this prediction (Abrams, 1982, 1983, cited in Abrams & Hogg, 1988). In studies in which subjects' self-esteem is threatened—for example, by informing them that they have failed on a task—before placing them in minimal intergroup situations, subjects who were higher in self-esteem responded with greater intergroup bias and discrimination (Crocker et al., 1987; Crocker & Luhtanen, 1990; Thompson & Crocker, 1990).

Although these findings have been viewed as disconfirming social identity theory's "self-esteem hypothesis," it can be argued that they may not have been appropriate tests of the hypothesis. Strictly speaking, the theory relates intergroup bias and discrimination to the need for self-esteem. The stronger the need for self-esteem, the greater the intergroup bias that should be shown in minimal intergroup situations. It is therefore differences in the individual *need* for rather than in the manifestation of self-esteem that should be related to discrimination in minimal intergroup situations. Individual differences in the need for self-esteem and in manifest self-esteem may not be very strongly associated. In fact, to the extent that there is an association, instead of persons with lower self-esteem having a higher need for self-esteem, it seems more likely that persons who have a stronger need for self-esteem may be generally higher in manifest self-esteem, simply because they usually try harder. Thus, the findings from most of the above studies showing that high self-esteem persons tend to show more intergroup bias may be consistent rather than inconsistent with the theory. It is surprising that no research has yet been reported directly examining the association between individual differences in need for self-esteem and intergroup bias in the minimal intergroup situation. Such research would seem to provide a much more direct test of the presumed link between self-esteem and ethnocentric tendencies to favor ingroups over outgroups than has been conducted thus far, and it might help to finally resolve this issue.

The theory has also been extended to analyses of specific intergroup circumstances (e.g., Hogg & Abrams, 1988; Tajfel & Turner, 1979). One issue has been that of how intergroup similarity should affect intergroup behavior. The prediction from social identity theory is that greater similarity between groups will usually stimulate more discrimination and bias as the groups strive to establish positive distinctiveness from each other (Tajfel, 1982b)—a prediction that is diametrically the opposite of that from belief congruence theory. Research bearing on this issue was discussed in the previous section, and it seems apparent that the issue has not yet been resolved and that it may be even more complex than is indicated by either of the two theories.

Because social identity theory postulates a basic and universal need for positive social identity, social and intergroup circumstances that confront the individual with a negative social identity are of particular interest. These are situations in which the individual's salient categorization is into an ingroup that is of consensually low status in a social stratification system. In this case, the theory predicts that the individual will seek to leave the group. If this is not feasible, the individual will tend to adopt what social identity theorists have termed a social change orientation.

A social change orientation involves trying to change the status position of the ingroup as a whole. Two possible strategies to accomplish this are proposed: (a) a strategy of social competition, which involves actions aimed at effecting real changes in the group's relative status (e.g., political activism) and (b) a strategy of social creativity, which involves primarily cognitive tactics that will result in a more positive evaluation of the ingroup. Tajfel and Turner (1979) suggested three primary ways in which the strategy of social creativity can be used to evade negative social identities. First, individuals may find new dimensions on which to compare ingroup and outgroup that are more favorable to the ingroup. Second, the values attached to the existing dimension of comparison can be changed in order to favor the ingroup (e.g., the slogan "black is beautiful"). Third, new outgroups may be selected for intergroup comparisons.

The kind of strategy—social competition or social creativity—which the individual confronted with a negative social identity will use to try and establish a more positive group identity is presumed to depend on the nature of the intergroup status differential—specifically, the degree to which it is perceived to be stable (i.e., not capable of being changed) and legitimate. A variety of predictions have been derived and tested about how individuals will pursue positive social identities and will try to avoid negative identities under various permutations of stability and legitimacy. Because these propositions pertain primarily to the macrosocial aspects of social identity theory (that is, the kind of macrosocial conditions of intergroup contact and interaction that influence intergroup attitudes and behavior), they will be discussed in more detail in the following chapter.

A great deal of research has been conducted in the past decade and a half to test predictions from the theory in these and a variety of other areas (e.g., Brown, 1978; Commins & Lockwood, 1979; Ellemers, van Knippenberg, de Vries, & Wilkie, 1988; Finchilescu, 1986; Sachdev & Bourhis, 1987; Skevington, 1981; Tajfel, 1982b, pp. 16–20). This research will not be reviewed in detail here, but some general conclusions may be noted. Many of the findings seem broadly supportive of the theory. With one exception, which will be discussed shortly, there are no conclusively established findings that clearly and directly contradict obvious predictions from the theory. However, findings that were not predicted or seemed inconsistent with particular predictions have been reported quite frequently (e.g., Brown, Condor, Matthews, Wade, & Williams, 1986). Often these apparently nonsupportive findings have been capable of some kind of post hoc reinterpretation, which does not seem totally inconsistent with the theory. As a result, a definitive assessment of the theory is not easy at this stage, and assessments of the overall performance of the theory have varied. For example, recent reviews by Brewer and Kramer (1985) and by Hogg and Abrams (1988) concluded in favor of the theory, whereas those by Messick and Mackie (1989) and by Taylor and Moghaddam (1987) were much less positive.

This situation may be largely due to the breadth and complexity of the theory, particularly in its application to natural social situations. Taylor and Moghaddam (1967) noted that field studies using natural groups have often generated problematic findings. For example, Brown and his colleagues (Brown & Williams, 1984; Oaker & Brown, 1986) did not find consistent support for the expected positive association between ingroup identification and intergroup differentiation among various occupational groups, whereas other studies did (e.g., Hinkle, Taylor, & Fox-Cardamone, 1989; Kelly, 1988). Condor and Brown (1988) pointed out that a problem with studies using natural social groups is that they have often tested predictions abstractly derived from the theory without an adequate understanding of the actual social circumstances of these groups and the historical status differences between them. They argued that when such differences exist and are deeply rooted in the social structure, experimental manipulations may not have enough impact to test such hypotheses. In addition, studies of natural social groups have often ignored variables such as power that were not originally incorporated in the theoretical analysis. Yet, as Ng (1982) demonstrated, the nature of power differentials between social groups also seems to be an important factor that influences how individuals will strive to maintain or enhance positive social identities.

In certain cases, however, nonsupportive findings seem to illuminate important limitations of the theory. For example, several studies have found that low-status groups have exaggerated differences favorable to a higher status outgroup and minimized differences favorable to itself (Bourhis & Hill, 1982; van Knippenberg, 1978; van Knippenberg & van Oers, 1984). Conversely, the high-status group exaggerated differences favorable to the low-status group and minimized differences favorable to itself. These effects, which are directly opposite to those predicted by social identity theory, have been reported for polytechnic versus uni-

& Schopler, 1979; Lalonde, Moghaddam, & Taylor, 1987; Purdue, Dovidio, Gurtman, & Taylor, 1990). However, it would appear that under
certain social circumstances and intergroup conditions, this basic ethnocentric tendency to ingroup favoritism may be readily elaborated into
overt outgroup hostilities and dislike. These social and intergroup dynamics of prejudice are discussed in the next chapter.

# 6

# Social Dynamics of Prejudice

Although certain fundamental psychological processes, considered in the previous chapter, seem to determine an inherent human propensity for ethnocentrism and prejudice, these processes do not operate in an automatic or inevitable fashion. Instead, certain cues or stimuli from the social environment appear to be necessary to elicit, elaborate, and direct these processes.

Thus, all persons are not prejudiced against all outgroups. Some outgroups may be liked and others may elicit indifference; while still others may be disliked and even hated. Moreover, the particular pattern of intergroup attitudes and prejudice held by individuals tends not to be just a product of individual idiosyncrasy. Typically, these are socially shared patterns, varying systematically with individuals' group memberships. As Sherif (1967) pointed out:

The problem of group prejudice and stereotyped images of other groups is not a problem of the idiosyncratic hates and unfounded beliefs of a few separated individuals. It is the problem of hostilities and images shared, in varying degrees, by large numbers of persons belonging to the same human grouping. (p. 24)

Three features of prejudice illustrate its nature as a social or group phenomenon: (a) Social groups tend to be characterized by normative or consensual patterns of prejudice; (b) different groups may have very different patterns of prejudice; (c) these patterns of prejudice may shift historically as groups' circumstances change.

The socially consensual or normative nature of prejudice has been well documented. For example, the American pattern of prejudice has been described by repeated social distance and stereotype surveys over the past half century (cf. the review by Owen, Eisner, & McFaul, 1981).

At the top of this hierarchy of social distance are the fair-skinned North European peoples, followed by Eastern and South Europeans, then Asian, and finally African peoples at the bottom. This pattern is widely diffused and accepted in the United States, and its general pattern has remained remarkably stable over the past fifty years. The consensual nature of social distance or prejudice hierarchies is illustrated by the way in which they are also accepted by those minority groups who occupy a very low ranking on them, with only one exception—they rate their own group high (Ashmore & DelBoca, 1976; Levin & Levin, 1982; Simpson & Yinger, 1985).

The socially consensual nature of such attitudes was clearly demonstrated in an early American study by Horowitz (1936, cited in Harding et al., 1969). He found that white children living in quite different geopolitical areas in the United States—New York City, urban Tennessee, and rural Georgia—developed essentially similar attitudes toward black people. He concluded that racial attitudes are determined not "by contact with Negroes but by contact with the prevalent attitude toward Negroes" (p. 35).

That different groups may have quite different normative patterns of prejudice is equally well established. Ashmore and DelBoca (1976), for example, noted

consistent and rather lasting differences among cultural groups with respect to ethnic attitudes. As one moves from one society to the next, there is wide variety in the groups against which prejudice is directed, but there is much consistency through time in the pattern of intergroup relations within a particular society. (p. 94)

Thus, racial prejudice is extremely high in certain societies, such as South Africa, the mainland United States, and Australia, while it is very much lower in other societies, such as Mexico, Brazil, and Hawaii (Bonacich, 1972). Dramatic differences in level of racial prejudice have been demonstrated in highly proximate societies, such as Britain and Holland (Bagley et al., 1979), in similar cultural groups, such as English-speaking white South Africans and British (Hampel & Krupp, 1977), and even for different regions within the same country, such as South and North in the U.S. (Middleton, 1976; Pettigrew, 1959).

Finally, while the normative pattern of prejudice characteristic of a particular society is often quite stable over time, changing historical circumstances may produce systematic and very substantial changes. Simpson and Yinger (1985) described numerous examples of such shifts. Some of the more dramatic of these are the shifts that have occurred in the attitudes of nations and other groups toward each other as they have moved between states of war, peace, and alliance. A prime example is the relatively positive American attitude toward Japanese earlier in the twentieth century; then the extremely negative attitudes toward Japanese and Germans during World War II accompanied by more positive attitudes toward Russians, which then, in the postwar period, changed to more positive attitudes toward Germans and Japanese and negative attitudes toward Russians. In South Africa a study of successive student cohorts by Nieuwoudt and Plug (1983) suggested that antiblack attitudes among whites became significantly more negative after the eruption of open black rebellion during 1976 (the "Soweto riots").

The observation that social groups have normative or consensual patterns of prejudice toward outgroups, that these vary between groups and shift with changing historical circumstances, raises important questions. What are the social and intergroup dynamics that generate these consensual patterns? And how do these dynamics elaborate the basic human tendency to favor the ingroup into enduring patterns of hostility and prejudice against particular outgroups?

These questions have usually been answered in terms of the nature of the relationship between the groups concerned. Thus, the state of intergroup attitudes is viewed as reflecting the state of intergroup relations. The study of intergroup relations, of course, involves issues and problems that are often viewed as located at a level of analysis that is not appropriate for social psychological investigation. As a result, the study of the social and intergroup dynamics of prejudice has been often treated as a rather peripheral area by social psychologists. They seem to have considered it best left to sociologists, historians, and anthropologists. Yet, in the past, social psychologists have done some extremely important work in this area, particularly in small group contexts (cf. Blake & Mouton, 1979; Sherif, 1967). Explanatory principles of considerable generality can be derived from this research, suggesting that the essential social dynamics of prejudice may be basically similar for small face-to-face and large sociocultural groups. A similar conclusion flows from social identity theory, which, during the past decade, has focused attention on how certain intergroup circumstances, relevant to both small minimal groups and large-scale natural groups, influence intergroup behavior, perception, and attitudes.

In general, therefore, social psychological theory and research suggest that certain features of the relationship between social groups may be crucial in determining intergroup attitudes at a macrosocial level. One set of factors appears to be the degree to which the interests of the groups converge or conflict. The most prominent perspective here has traditionally been realistic conflict theory (RCT), which has viewed intergroup attitudes as a product of intergroup competition. This approach will be discussed in some detail in the next section, and it will be suggested that it can be profitably broadened to cover a much wider range of situations. Social identity theory, however, has argued that two kinds of intergroup competition can be distinguished: realistic competition over real physical resources and power (which is treated by RCT) and social competition over the purely psychological resource of status or prestige. Because social identity theory proposes a universal motivational tendency to strive for positive social identity, it has viewed the latter as the more fundamental determinant of intergroup attitudes and behavior. From this perspective, certain macrosocial intergroup conditions, specifically the existence and nature of status differentials between social groups, should be particularly important. These are discussed in a second section of this chapter. The third section in this chapter considers certain other macrosocial conditions of intergroup contact and interaction that do not necessarily involve conflict or competition but which also seem conducive to the emergence of intergroup patterns of prejudice.

## REALISTIC CONFLICT THEORY

Realistic conflict theory (RCT) may be viewed as a broad social psychological perspective or framework expressing very general principles. It is a term rarely used by sociologists and other social scientists, who have generally formulated far more specific and elaborate theories, many of which, however, are essentially consistent with RCT.

RCT has been most frequently linked with the name of Muzafer Sherif, the social psychologist who formulated the basic propositions of the approach in a form applicable to small group behavior (Sherif, 1967). He also demonstrated the validity of these propositions in a series of dramatic and influential field experiments. Sherif focused specifically on one kind of conflicting intergroup relationship—competition between groups that are relatively similar in power and status. These groups pursue incompatible goals, such that each group in striving to attain its goals directly threatens the probability of the other realizing its goals. Following this perspective, RCT has been typically limited to situations in which each group is perceived as posing a real threat to the other (cf. LeVine & Campbell, 1972, pp. 29–42).

It is possible, however, to identify several other forms of intergroup conflict of interest, where the concept of "real threat" is not particularly relevant. Although these forms of conflicting intergroup interests have been noted in the literature, their implications for RCT have not been systematically elaborated. For example, intergroup domination and exploitation clearly involve a conflict of interests between groups. In this case, negative attitudes toward the dominated and exploited group need not necessarily involve a response to threat. In fact, it has been aptly pointed out that this conflict of interests seems to involve the "hope of gain rather than fear of loss" as the underlying motive (Harding et al.,

1969, p. 116). Finally, intergroup scapegoating seems to constitute a third kind of intergroup conflict of interest that is distinct from both direct intergroup competition and domination. In this case, intergroup hostility, and sometimes persecution, does not arise from either real threat or cupidity. Instead, it seems to involve the attribution of blame to an outgroup for problems afflicting the ingroup in a manner that is functional for the ingroup.

At least three basic forms of intergroup conflict of interest can therefore be distinguished. In each case, prejudice is functional for the ingroup. However, each of these three forms generates distinctive patterns of prejudice, which may also differ depending on the structural location of groups within these conflict systems. For example, the patterns of prejudice of dominant and subordinate groups toward each other will naturally differ. The following section will attempt to elaborate RCT by describing these different forms of intergroup conflict of interest and the distinctive patterns of prejudice elicited by each. It will be suggested that each of these patterns of prejudice appears to involve a distinctive image of the outgroup, demonstrates a particular kind of affective and behavioral response to it, and serves particular functions for the ingroup.

### Intergroup Competition

According to Sherif and Sherif (1979):

When groups engaged in reciprocally competitive and frustrating activities, such that the gain of desired goals by one results in loss for the other, unfavorable stereotypes of the out-group and its members come into use. In time, these unfavorable attitudes are standardized in a group, and the out-group is placed at a prejudicial distance, even to the point that group members want nothing whatever to do with members of the other group. (p. 10)

LeVine and Campbell (1972) noted that the competing groups constitute a "real threat" to each other, and it is this threat that elicits "hostility to the source of threat" (p. 30) proportional to its magnitude.

A great deal of historical evidence can be cited in support of this proposition (cf. Simpson & Yinger, 1985, Ch. 3). For example, direct competition between nations over political, economic, or, indeed, any other issue, invariably elicits markedly hostile intergroup attitudes and perceptions. This tends to be particularly dramatic when conflict takes the form of open warfare. A neatly documented example is that of the China-India border dispute of 1959. Sinha and Upadhyaya (1960) measured Indian students' attitudes to the Chinese before the border dispute in February of that year. They found a generally favorable image: Chinese were viewed as friendly, progressive, honest, brave, and cultured. In December, after the border dispute had erupted, the study was repeated. The Indian students now described the Chinese as aggressive, dishonest, cruel, and stupid.

Sherif's (1967) own research provided an important validation of this perspective in small groups. He conducted three field experiments during the late 1940s and early 1950s, which for their realism, care, and dramatic impact have deservedly acquired the status of social psychological classics. The subjects were normal, healthy, well-adjusted American boys from stable middle-class backgrounds who were attending summer camps. These summer camps were organized in such a way that a number of hypotheses concerning the effects of intergroup competition and cooperation on intergroup attitudes and behavior could be tested.

Three kinds of intergroup contact or interaction were experimentally created. First, during the initial stages of a camp, individuals were allocated to groups which were kept apart, with each cooperating in its own activities. Each group developed a distinct group structure during this phase characterized by status hierarchies, norms, and definite ingroup feeling. Second, groups were placed into competition with each other by means of a series of tournaments and by organizing camp activities on a competitive basis. There were a number of effects, but the most salient were an arousal of intense intergroup hostility coupled with increased intragroup cohesion and solidarity. Finally, in a third stage, successive situations were created in which the groups had to cooperate to achieve mutually desired goals. The cooperative activity toward these superordinate goals was accompanied by a marked decrease in intergroup hostility and tension.

The two most basic conclusions were that competitive group goals cause conflict and intergroup hostility, while superordinate group goals result in cooperation and more positive intergroup attitudes. These conclusions have been well replicated subsequently by further field studies using quite different samples and situations (e.g., Blake & Mouton, 1979), as well as by experimental studies (see Turner, 1981, pp. 67–75). However, as Turner (1981) pointed out, an important qualification of the Sherifs' conclusions has emerged from the experimental research. There seem to be certain conditions of intergroup contact under which cooperation does not improve intergroup-attitudes and may even result in cooperating groups showing more intergroup bias than competing groups. These findings will be discussed in more detail later in this chapter. They do illustrate, however, the point made in the introduction to this chapter, that the existence of conflicting versus cooperative group goals is not the only social dynamic that governs intergroup attitudes.

The manner in which groups experience contact with each other and the institutionalized roles that they occupy in relation to each other are also important and can create intergroup antagonism even when the groups might be cooperatively rather than competitively interdependent.

A number of sociological and historical theories have elaborated explanations of racial antagonism based on direct intergroup competition. Two of these have relevance to South African racial attitudes. These are MacCrone's (1937) frontier hypothesis and Bonacich's (1972) split labor market theory. Although MacCrone's thesis has not escaped criticism (cf. du Preez, 1977), it does illustrate how competitive intergroup processes within a particular social and historical context may come to be translated into powerful intergroup antipathies. MacCrone argued that it was the frontier situation in South African history which crucially conditioned the emergence and form of racial prejudice in South Africa, as well as certain features of Afrikaner society. Once the Dutch colonists had spread from the original settlement at the Cape to the interior, the frontier situation and an enduring conflict with the indigenous black peoples developed. The essential characteristics of the frontier situation were its isolation (physical, social and political) and an extreme insecurity in the struggle for existence. This created a society characterized by an intense group consciousness, emphasis on group cohesion, and pervasive ethnocentrism. In an atmosphere of war and threat, religious attitudes fused with racial distinctions. The dichotomy between Christian and heathen became a dichotomy between white and black. Thus, Christianity and skin color became the criteria of group consciousness and exclusivity, and they formed the basis of an intense and deeply embedded racial prejudice that eventually acquired caste-like properties.

Bonacich's (1972) theory shows how racial or ethnic antagonism arises from the situation of a split labor market. She described this as a market in which there is a large differential in the price of labor for the same occupation between two ethnic groups. As a result, a conflict of interests develops between three key groups: business, higher-paid labor, and cheaper labor. Business seeks to displace higher-paid by cheaper labor. Higher-paid labor responds to the threat with hostility to the lower-paid group and struggles to protect and entrench its position. If the higher-paid group is strong enough, it may try to exclude cheaper labor from the market (e.g., by restricting or stopping immigration). This may not be possible because the cheaper labor group is already present and cannot be excluded. In this case, a caste arrangement may arise with an elaborate battery of laws, customs, and beliefs designed to prevent the cheaper labor group from competing and also from gaining political or other resources that might enable it to change the situation.

The applicability of this model to South Africa is obvious. A substantial wage differential arose historically between the white settlers and the indigenous blacks—du Preez (1977) noted that the ratio of white to black wages was 13.4 : 1 in 1917 and still virtually the same in 1970 at 12.9 : 1. The three-way conflict between capital, white labor, and black labor came to a head in 1922 when attempts to replace white by cheaper black labor in the gold mines resulted in the 1922 white workers "Rand revolt." Although the revolt was put down, an alliance of white labor and the National party supported by rural Afrikaners won the 1924 election and, as de Kiewiet (1957) pointed out, "committed South Africa to policies conceived more resolutely than ever before in the interests of white society" (p. 224). This process ultimately culminated in the Apartheid state.

To sum up, therefore, considerable evidence indicates that direct competition between social groups is invariably associated with the emergence of prejudiced intergroup attitudes. The experience of intergroup competition seems to elicit an image of the outgroup as threatening. This generates hostility and antagonism to the outgroup, a response which would typically function to mobilize the ingroup to enable it to compete most effectively.

### Intergroup Domination and Exploitation

In the previous section it was noted that when groups are in direct competition, the threat posed by each to the other elicits intergroup antagonism. This hostility may involve a view of the competing group as inferior, but this is not necessarily so. Competing groups not infrequently view each other as particularly able, powerful, and menacing adversaries. Examples are the Allied view of Nazi Germany during World War II and the American view of the Soviet Union during the cold war period.

Sometimes competitive interaction between groups may culminate in a victory for one group, such that it is able to establish and institutionalize power over the other group and use this power to maintain economic advantages for itself at the other's cost. Once this occurs, a belief in the oppressed group's inferiority seems to arise almost inevitably. It would seem that the establishment of an intergroup relationship of domination and exploitation makes the development of justifying and rationalizing beliefs about the oppressed group a psychological necessity for the dominant group. Invariably, this involves derogation of the subordinate group and a firm belief in its inferiority.

Although dominated and exploited groups are viewed as inferior, it is interesting that they are not necessarily disliked or viewed with hostility. This was shown in van den Berghe's (1967) classic comparison of paternalistic versus competitive racism. In the case of the paternalistic system, racial domination is so entrenched and institutionalized that it is unquestioningly accepted as right and natural by all concerned. In such cases, although the subordinate group is viewed as inferior, the attitude of the dominant group may be paternalistic and not involve overt dislike and hostility. In fact, to the extent that members of the subordinate group accept their inferiority and respectfully acquiesce in their oppression, members of the dominant group may experience positive affect toward them.

Numerous historical examples confirm the correlation of intergroup domination and exploitation with a belief in the inferiority of the oppressed group (cf. Simpson & Yinger, 1985, Ch. 3). Perhaps the most direct case of domination and exploitation in human history has been that of slavery—a system that has been inevitably accompanied by a firm belief on the part of the slave owners in the natural inferiority of their slaves fitting them ideally for their lot. For example, Newby (1968, cited in Ashmore, 1970) noted that "only after Negroes were enslaved did white Americans conclude that slavery was the natural status of the race" (pp. 19–20). In the case of South Africa, racial prejudice may have been important in justifying white political domination of the black majority and the existence of numerous social and legal arrangements that operate to the economic advantage of whites and the disadvantage of blacks.

Several theories have elaborated more complex explanations of racism in terms of domination and exploitation. For example, Marxist variants were proposed by Cox (1948) and Reich (1972), who argued that racism is created and maintained by capitalists in order to promote competition and division between white and black workers and to intensify exploitation. In direct contrast to Bonacich, these theorists saw white business rather than white workers as the villain of the piece. Thus, Cox asserted that "race prejudice is a social attitude propagated among the public by an exploiting class for the purpose of stigmatizing some group as inferior so that exploitation of either the group itself or its resources may both be justified" (1948, p. 343). This argument could be applied to both South Africa and the United States. However, it has been usually viewed rather skeptically as little evidence can be cited for it (cf. Ashmore & DelBoca, 1976). The theory also seems to suggest that whites of higher socioeconomic status should express more prejudice than those of lower socioeconomic status, whereas the opposite has generally emerged empirically (Harding et al., 1969; Hyman & Wright, 1979; Simpson & Yinger, 1985). Thus, white workers usually seem to express more racial prejudice than do white capitalists.

In general, little experimental evidence seems to be available on the role of domination and exploitation in the emergence of prejudice, probably because there are clear practical difficulties involved in designing and conducting such research. However, one classic social psychological study, although it was done with different objectives, seems highly relevant. This study, conducted by Haney and Zimbardo (1976), simulated a prison environment on the campus of Stanford University in order to demonstrate the effect of deindividuated roles on behavior in institutional settings.

Students were recruited and paid to act as either guards or prisoners for a two-week period. Subjects were normal, intelligent, middle-class young people with no history of antisocial behavior, and were randomly allocated to their roles. The behavior of the subjects was intensively observed during the study, and the experimenters were not supposed to intervene in any way. However, the outcome of the study was so disturbing that the experiment had to be terminated after only six days. From the very beginning, the "guards" began to attach abusive and denigrating labels to the "prisoners," and extremely derogatory stereotypes rapidly emerged. Over time, the "guards" showed increasingly brutal, sadistic, and dehumanizing behavior to the "prisoners," half of whom were reported to have experienced emotional breakdowns by the time the experiment had to be called off. Conventionally this study has been interpreted as showing the power of social situations and roles to structure behavior. However, it also shows dramatically how domination of one group by another creates powerful psychological pressures to justify the situation by the emergence of derogatory beliefs and hostile affect directed at the subordinate group.

Summing up, therefore, it would seem that domination and exploitation create prejudiced intergroup attitudes as inevitably as direct competition does. However, the pattern of prejudice differs. The subordinate group is not inevitably seen as threatening, and it is not even necessarily disliked. It is, however, invariably viewed as inferior and derogated. This image of the dominated group seems to involve the process of psychological rationalization, which functions to justify oppression and exploitation.

### Intergroup Scapegoating

Psychologists have usually understood scapegoating in terms of frustration-aggression-displacement theory (cf. LeVine & Campbell, 1972). However, as Tajfel (1981) pointed out, social scapegoating can be seen in broader terms than simply the displacement of aggression. He suggested it can also be viewed in terms of attributions of social causality that are functional for groups. Thus, he pointed out, intergroup circumstances may be such that it may be functional for a group to seek the "causes of distressful social events . . . in the characteristics, intentions or behavior of outgroups" (p. 155). Stephan (1983) described intergroup scapegoating in similar terms as:

a process by which other individuals or groups are held to be the cause of one's own problems. Typically it involves members of a higher-status group blaming a less powerful group for a particular problem. . . . In this defensive maneuver the individual avoids blaming himself and redirects the blame towards others. To the extent that he blames these groups for his problems, he is likely to be prejudiced towards them. (p. 425)

The studies by Blake and Mouton (1979) demonstrated how task failure by a group can lead to a loss of cohesion, rejection of the leadership, and even disintegration of the group. If failure or other problems that groups may encounter can instead be attributed to the malicious actions of deviants, minorities, or outgroups, then these dysfunctional consequences might be avoided and cohesion maintained, or even solidified. In fact, Babad et al. (1983) suggested ironically that a useful rule for group functioning might be that "when there is tension and social problems seem insurmountable, find an innocent, weak, and distinctive group to blame and victimize" (p. 103).

Historical accounts suggest that intergroup scapegoating has been an important factor in anti-Semitism (cf. Simpson & Yinger, 1972, Ch. 10). This was exemplified in the pogroms in Eastern Europe and in the persecution that culminated in the holocaust in Nazi Germany. In the latter case, it has been pointed out that "the Jews were widely viewed by the members of German society as being directly responsible for the severe economic problems that plagued them" (Levin & Levin, 1982, p. 184). In a broader context, Billig (1978) noted the role that contemporary anti-Semitism plays in providing an elaborate ideology capable of explaining an enormous variety of social ills. Thus:

Crude anti-Semitism is based upon a belief that Jews have immense powers of evil in the world. Modern anti-Semitic dogma asserts that Jews control both communism and capitalism and that they aim to dominate the world in a regime which will destroy Western civilization. All facts are explained in terms of this pervasive and perverse belief. (p. 132)

Some interesting experimental demonstrations of scapegoating as a social process have been reported. In a particularly elegant study, for example, Lauderdale, Smith-Cunnien, Parker, and Inverarity (1984) showed that an external threat to a group (not involving frustration) may result in some group members being labeled deviant and rejected. Moreover, the group's level of solidarity tended to increase to the extent to which deviants were labeled and rejected.

Summing up, therefore, intergroup scapegoating is associated with

prejudice toward the scapegoated group. The pattern of prejudice, however, differs from that characteristic of intergroup competition or domination. In this case, the attribution of difficulties or problems
experienced by the ingroup to the scapegoated group typically results
in the perception of that group as malicious, often in a particularly sly,
underhand, and cunning manner. Blaming the scapegoated group helps
maintain ingroup cohesion and results in punitive hostility to that group,
perhaps even its episodic or systematic persecution. As Berkowitz and
Green (1962) pointed out, scapegoated groups are usually socially distinctive groups who may be already disliked or resented. They also tend
to be much weaker than the ingroup as their persecution might otherwise
arouse a real threat to it.

## Responses to Oppression or Persecution

The discussion thus far has not yet considered the response of dominated and scapegoated groups to their oppression or persecution. Tajfel
(1981) pointed out that it has usually been assumed that the logical
response of oppressed and persecuted groups would be one of hostility
to their oppressors and persecutors, a reaction that Allport (1954) termed
an extrapunitive response pattern. However, this does not necessarily
occur. Frequently, an oppressed group accepts the superiority of the
dominant group and its own inferiority, in certain cases even to the
extent of what has been termed "self-hatred" (Lewin, 1948). Allport
(1954) labeled this an intropunitive response pattern in which the individual tends, "if not actually to blame himself, at least to take the
responsibility upon himself for adjusting to the situation" (p. 160).

This intropunitive response pattern has been well documented in
many studies of minorities (cf. the reviews by Milner, 1983, and Tajfel,
1981). An example is the classic work of the Clarks in the 1940s on
outgroup preference and own-group rejection in black American children. The response has also been documented in high-status minorities
whose combination of social privilege and political vulnerability makes
them actual or potential social scapegoats. Examples are Jews in Western
Europe (Simpson & Yinger, 1985) and Chinese in Southeast Asia (Hewstone & Ward, 1985). In the case of an intropunitive pattern, members
of an oppressed or subordinate group reject their own group and prefer
the outgroup. They may even adopt and experience the prejudice directed toward them. This is often associated with self-blaming attributions that involve attribution of the ingroup's experience of social
subordination and discrimination to its own characteristics or inferiority
(Hewstone & Ward, 1985). Thus, ingroup members view the dominant

outgroup as superior, respond to it with submission, and exhibit an orientation of admiration and abasement toward it.

Superficially, an intropunitive response to oppression may seem to be dysfunctional for a group in that it would tend to induce helplessness and resignation so that members of an oppressed group thereby collaborate in their own oppression. In fact, under certain circumstances it should be highly functional. These circumstances exist when the balance of power between groups is such that an oppressive system cannot realistically be changed—when the oppressed group is too weak to liberate itself. Under these circumstances, an intropunitive response should ensure passive acquiescence to injustice instead of actions that might provoke an intensification of oppression and perhaps even genocidal policies. In this situation, an intropunitive response pattern would have survival value for an oppressed group.

One crucial question is what determines the nature of a subordinate group's response, whether it accepts its own inferiority in intropunitive fashion, or responds extrapunitively with hostility toward the oppressor. Tajfel (1981) suggested that, at a psychological level, ingroup inferiority and negative social identity will be accepted to the extent that the intergroup power and status differential is perceived as being stable (i.e., it cannot realistically be changed) and legitimate. If, on the other hand, the existing power and status system comes to be seen as unstable and illegitimate, the subordinated group will reject it, and may shift to an extrapunitive response pattern.

What could cause such changes in perception and belief? RCT would imply that changes in such perceptions would tend to follow real historical changes in the balance of forces between groups. That is, as social, political, and economic changes occur, which begin to create the potential for real changes in previously stable systems of oppression, the oppressed will begin to perceive the social system as unstable and illegitimate, and so change from an intropunitive response pattern to an extrapunitive pattern. This will be associated with an important shift in the kinds of social attributions that members of the subordinate group make. Self-blaming attributions involving the attribution of the ingroup's social subordination to its own inferiority are replaced by "system blame," or the attribution of their subordination to the actions of the dominant group (Guimond, Begin, & Palmer, 1989; Hewstone, 1988).

Changing attributions in this way seems to be an important component of revolutionary "consciousness raising" and in creating what Billig (1976) referred to as an "ideology of discontent." As a result of these processes, the oppressed group shifts from an image of the dominant outgroup as superior to a view of it as oppressive and discriminatory. This engenders an attitudinal orientation of resentment and antagonism toward the oppressor and a response of rebellion. This attitude functions to help mobilize the subordinate group for the struggle to change the intergroup power relationship—in political terms, a struggle for its liberation.

### Reactions to Rebellion

What effect do these processes have on a dominant group? When a subordinate group challenges its oppression, perhaps even to the extent of open rebellion, all the material advantages of domination, as well as a social identity of natural superiority, are threatened for the dominant group. The perception of this threat changes the dominant group's attitudes and perceptions of the subordinate group. In essence, the perceptual and attitudinal pattern characteristic of intergroup competition superimposes itself upon that characteristic of intergroup domination. Thus, the subordinate group is no longer merely seen as inferior, but as both inferior and threatening. The dominant group therefore responds not only with superiority and derogation, but also with hostility and antagonism. This pattern functions both to justify oppression and to mobilize the dominant group for the struggle to maintain its dominance.

Van den Berghe (1967) described and documented this transition in the context of race relations—that is, the shift from paternalistic to competitive racism in the historical experience of Brazil, South Africa, and the United States. In each case there was a transition from a relatively secure and stable system of racial domination to increasingly challenged and competitive systems. With this shift came a change in the image of the subordinate group: "Stereotypes of the subordinate group changed from the humble, happy-go-lucky 'good' Negro or 'Native who knew his place' to the cheeky, uppity, insolent, treacherous, sly, violent, 'new Negro' or 'detribalized scum' who threatens the status quo" (p. 128).

A second, quite different, reaction by a dominant group to a subordinate group that challenges its subordination can also occur. This reaction can be described as one of conciliation and is associated with a very different pattern of prejudice. It appears to arise when the balance of forces between a dominant and subordinate group is such that the struggle of the subordinate group can no longer be legitimately denied. Often this may be because the power relationship between dominant and subordinate group has changed so completely and dramatically that the subordinate group has become, or may easily become, the more powerful. If open conflict occurs, the dominant group cannot prevail. This makes a policy of repression and attitudes of open hostility and derogation toward the subordinate group extremely dangerous for the dominant group, inviting open conflict and a possibly catastrophic defeat. The perception of the subordinate group as powerful, too powerful to risk a trial of strength with, therefore generates an attitude of superficial or ambivalent tolerance in members of the dominant group and a response of conciliation or appeasement. The response is clearly functional for the ingroup, in the final analysis serving the function of self-preservation and survival.

Such a pattern, or one very similar, may describe the contemporary attitudes of many white Americans to blacks. This pattern appears to have arisen with the perception by many whites that the black struggle is one that cannot legitimately be denied on the basis of important social values such as democracy and equality of opportunity. The shift in the intergroup power relationship here seems fundamentally an ideological one, involving the social legitimation of its struggle by a cohesive determined minority (cf. Moscovici's [1976] experimental demonstrations of effects that may be analogous), rather than shifts in political, economic, or military power.

This ambivalent attitude of superficial tolerance superimposed on an underlying, covert negative affect has been well documented in research in the United States. It seems to be characterized by a commitment to very general principles of racial equality but a resistance to their practical implementation (Jackman & Muha, 1984). Overt racist beliefs are rejected, while a much more subtle "symbolic racism" (McConahay & Hough, 1976) or "modern racial prejudice" (Pettigrew & Martin, 1987) is espoused. Superficially liberal egalitarian beliefs coexist with subtly discriminatory behavior (Crosby et al., 1980; Gaertner, 1973), except in public and visible situations where reverse discrimination may occur (McConahay, 1983). When individuals are emotionally aroused or angered, however, there may be a regression to blatantly overt racism and discriminatory behavior (Rogers & Prentice-Dunn, 1981).

A similar pattern seems to exist for many white English-speaking South Africans. A number of studies have shown that English speakers tend to be much less racially prejudiced than Afrikaners (Duckitt, 1988; Hampel & Krupp, 1977; Mynhardt, 1980). However, much of this tolerance may be relatively superficial. Empirical studies have shown the coexistence of liberal attitudes in English South Africans with the maintenance of strict social distance from blacks (Preston-Whyte, 1976) and paternalistic reverse discrimination (Tyson, Schlachter, & Cooper, 1988).

Some interesting findings also support the idea that the more tolerant racial attitudes of English speakers may involve a measure of appeasement and anxiety about the increasing power of black resistance to white rule. For example, a large-scale survey of white South Africans found that anxiety about the future correlated negatively with racial prejudice for English speakers, but not for Afrikaans speakers (Hampel & Krupp, 1977). Essentially similar findings were reported from a survey that was in progress when the "Soweto riots"—a black uprising that posed a major challenge to white rule—erupted in 1976 (Nieuwoudt, Plug, & Mynhardt, 1977). The researchers were able to compare the attitudes of whites surveyed immediately before the "riots" began and those surveyed during the uprising. This comparison suggested that the onset of the riots resulted in Afrikaners' racial attitudes becoming more negative while English speakers' racial attitudes became more positive. Interestingly, a further survey a year later when the "riots" had been forcibly repressed suggested that English speakers' attitudes to blacks had now become significantly less positive, possibly because the threat of change had receded.

To summarize, therefore, when a dominant group is challenged by a subordinate group, two basic patterns of response by the dominant group seem to occur. In one case, the old pattern of secure paternalism is infused with hostility and dislike and, in certain circumstances, may be expressed through a strategy of violent repression. Alternatively, if members of the dominant group come to believe that the claims of the subordinate group cannot be denied and its struggle cannot be suppressed, the response will be one of conciliation, expressed in an attitude of superficial and ambivalent tolerance.

### Realistic Conflict Theory: Conclusions

RCT attributes prejudice to relationships between groups that involve real conflicts of interest. Thus, prejudice is viewed as functional for the groups that express it. From the preceding discussion it is apparent that a great deal of evidence, historical and experimental, supports the proposition that intergroup conflicts of interest do induce prejudiced intergroup attitudes.

RCT has typically been viewed only in terms of direct competition between groups that are relatively similar in power and status. It was argued, however, that at least two other forms of intergroup conflicts of interest can be identified, both of which are relevant to the determination of prejudice. While negative intergroup attitudes arise under each of these conditions, the different forms that the conflict of interests takes, and the structural location of each group within the conflict system, seem to generate qualitatively different patterns of prejudice. These patterns vary in terms of the image of the outgroup, the nature of the affective and behavioral responses elicited by this image, and the functions served for the ingroup. The essentials of this analysis are summarized in Table 6.1.

However, this does not mean that prejudice must always be caused by intergroup conflicts of interest. It has been noted already that much research, particularly those studies using the minimal intergroup paradigm, has shown that intergroup bias and discrimination can emerge between groups where no conflict of interests is involved. Thus, Tajfel

**Table 6.1**
**Nature of Realistic Conflict and Patterns of Intergroup Prejudice**

| Nature of conflict | Image of outgroup | Response of ingroup | Orientation to outgroup | Function for ingroup |
|---|---|---|---|---|
| Competition | Threatening | Antagonistic | Hostility | Mobilization for conflict |
| Domination (Stable) | Inferior | Rationalizing | Derogation | Justifies oppression |
| Scapegoating | Malicious | Blaming | Punitive | Maintains cohesion |
| Oppression (Stable) | Superior | Submission | Intropunitive: abasement | Avoids conflict |
| Oppression (Unstable) | Oppressive | Rebellion | Extrapunitive: hostile | Mobilization for struggle |
| Challenged dominance 1 | Inferior and threatening | Repression | Hostility and derogation | Justification & mobilization |
| Challenged dominance 2 | Powerful | Conciliation | Superficial tolerance | Avoids conflict |

(1981) and other protagonists of social identity theory distinguished "social competition," which involves competition over purely psychological issues—such as positive identity at the individual level and relative status at the group level—from realistic conflicts over "real" issues—such as power and physical resources. The macrosocial intergroup conditions that elicit and influence social competition are therefore discussed in the next section.

## INTERGROUP SOCIAL COMPETITION

As in the case of small groups, social identity theory proposes that, in any macrosocial situation where an intergroup distinction is salient, the basic human tendency to seek a positive social identity will inevitably result in "social competition" (Hogg & Abrams, 1988; Tajfel & Turner, 1979). Thus, groups will tend to adopt a competitive orientation to each other and compete for status or prestige in the complete absence of any "realistic" conflict of interests. However, as was noted in the previous chapter, there is a good deal of evidence that the ingroup bias and favoritism in minimal intergroup situations of social competition generally involve an enhancement of the attitude to the ingroup and not necessarily a more negative outgroup attitude (Brewer, 1979; Gaertner et al., 1989; Hinkle et al., 1989; Hinkle & Schopler, 1979; Lalonde et al., 1987; Purdue et al. 1990). Thus, while the mere existence of a salient intergroup categorization may inevitably engender ingroup favoritism, attitudes toward outgroups are not always negative, and, as noted in the introduction to this chapter, they may often be neutral or even positive. This raises the question of what intergroup conditions, according to social identity theory, could operate to intensify this competitive intergroup orientation to produce prejudiced attitudes. Unfortunately, the theory has not dealt with this issue directly. In fact, it has shown little interest in the concept of prejudice as such, often seeming to make the rather dubious assumption that the ingroup bias and discrimination observed in minimal intergroup situations can be viewed as essentially equivalent to prejudice. The theory does, however, specify two sets of factors that affect the intensity of social competition: first, social cues or circumstances that influence the salience of an intergroup distinction and, second, the existence and nature of status differentials between ingroup and outgroup.

Precisely what makes certain intergroup distinctions (the first set of factors) more salient than others in natural social contexts is clearly an important factor in prejudice. As Brewer and Kramer (1985) noted, "large complex societies are categorized by multiple cross-cutting systems of social categorization, and individuals have corresponding multiple social identities, any one of which may be activated in a given social situation" (p. 283). Unfortunately, social identity theory has had little to say about what factors determine social category salience, although Turner (1985) proposed some very broad principles in his elaboration of self-categorization theory. Brewer and Kramer (1985), however, suggested several macrosocial features of intergroup contact and interaction which could create and maintain prejudice by influencing the salience of intergroup distinctions. In most cases, these factors seem likely to affect prejudice in other ways as well. They are therefore discussed in the third section of this chapter together with other macrosocial conditions of intergroup contact and interaction that tend to be associated with social patterns of prejudice.

Because social competition is over status and prestige, the existence of intergroup status differentials should influence the way in which the groups compete and, consequently, their intergroup attitudes and behavior. Precisely how this happens is presumed to be governed by two sets of factors: first, the permeability of group boundaries—that is, how easy or difficult it is for individuals to leave the ingroup and become a member of the outgroup—and, second, the legitimacy and stability of the intergroup status differential (Hogg & Abrams, 1988; Tajfel & Turner, 1979; van Knippenberg, 1989).

The permeability of group boundaries is regarded as a particularly important factor governing the response of low-status groups because intergroup social mobility would be the obvious strategy for members of these groups to enhance their social identity. Permeable group boundaries are therefore viewed as conducive to a social mobility orientation, and when this is the case it is hypothesized that members of the low-status group will show less bias and discrimination against the higher status outgroup, as well as a tendency to outgroup identification. Some support for this derives from laboratory studies that have experimentally manipulated both group status and intergroup permeability. Thus, it has been shown that members of low-status groups identify less with their own group and more with a higher status outgroup when group boundaries are permeable as opposed to when they are impermeable (Ellemers et al., 1988; Ellemers, van Knippenberg, & Wilkie, 1990).

Consequently, as Hogg and Abrams (1988) pointed out, "it may be to the advantage of high status groups to foster social mobility belief systems (or 'false consciousness', in Marxist terms) among low status groups" (p. 56). The role of permeability in natural social groups does not seem to have been systematically researched yet, but this proposition does seem plausible. Certainly the most seriously problematic manifestations of intergroup conflict seem to occur when group boundaries are relatively impermeable—that is, between racial, cultural, and national groups. In contrast, irrespective of the degree to which group boundaries are or are not permeable in reality, the existence of social mobility beliefs, as is typically the case for social classes and occupational groups, seems to defuse a conflict orientation and intergroup hostility in lower status groups. Social identity theorists do not appear to have extended their analysis to the effects of permeability on the intergroup orientation of high status groups. However, it does appear as though extremely prejudiced attitudes against persons trying to move from lower to higher status groups may not be uncommon. The history of anti-immigrant prejudice in the United States and Western Europe during this century is an example, and others are not difficult to find. Presumably, social identity theory could account for this in terms of the high-status group's perception that mobility, particularly large-scale mobility, would progressively erode its positive distinctiveness from the low-status group.

The second set of social factors that influences intergroup attitudes and behavior when groups differ in status is the stability and legitimacy of the intergroup status differential. These two factors are regarded as particularly important when intergroup boundaries are relatively impermeable and social mobility is not perceived as a significant option. It was noted in the previous section on RCT that these concepts can also be applied to realistic conflicts between groups differing in power—specifically in determining the response of subordinated groups to their oppressors (illustrated by van den Berghe's 1967 classic comparison of paternalistic versus competitive racism). Social identity theory suggests an essentially similar analysis for groups differing only in status. If the intergroup status differential is perceived to be stable and legitimate ("secure"), both higher and lower status groups should show little bias and discrimination against each other. Neither group is able to conceive of "cognitive alternatives" to the existing status relationship. Thus, members of the low-status group may even tend to identify with the higher status outgroup. On the other hand, when this differential is perceived to be unstable and illegitimate ("insecure"), both groups are expected to show much more bias and discrimination. This arises out of the attempts of the high-status group to defend its threatened positive identity and the lower status group's attempt to improve its relative status position.

Even more refined predictions about the way in which groups differing in status will respond to various permutations of stability and legitimacy have been derived from the theory. For example, Turner and Brown (1978) conducted an experiment that manipulated the degree to which status differences between groups were seen as legitimate and stable. They found that members of the high-status group showed more intergroup bias and discrimination when they regarded their superiority as legitimate but unstable, or as stable though illegitimate. Members of the lower status group, on the other hand, discriminated more when their inferiority was perceived to be illegitimate, particularly when it was also seen as unstable. These findings seem broadly consistent with the theory, though it should be noted the effects in this study were rather weak and not always statistically significant. Moreover, contrary to expectation, instability on its own did not have a clear effect on discrimination.

A number of other studies have tested predictions from the theory about the effects of intergroup status differences (e.g., Brown, 1978; Commins & Lockwood, 1979; Ellemers et al., 1988; Finchilescu, 1986; Sachdev & Bourhis, 1987; Skevington, 1981; Tajfel, 1982b, pp. 16–20). Although most of the findings have seemed broadly supportive, inconsistent findings have also been reported quite often (cf. Messick & Mackie, 1989). Thus, some studies have found that high-status groups discriminate more (e.g., Commins & Lockwood, 1979; Doise & Sinclair, 1973; Sachdev & Bourhis, 1987); others have found that low-status groups discriminate more (e.g., Branthwaite, Doyle, & Lightbown, 1979; Finchilescu, 1986), and others have found no effect for differential status (e.g., Ng, 1985; Tajfel et al., 1971). Taylor and Moghaddam (1987) also noted that the findings of laboratory and field studies have not always been in agreement. For example, experimental laboratory studies have generally confirmed that illegitimacy of intergroup status differentials increases bias and discrimination, whereas certain field studies have not confirmed this.

A number of methodological reasons could account for these inconsistencies. Thus, some studies have not considered the perceived stability or legitimacy of the status differentials (e.g., Sachdev & Bourhis, 1987), while others have not checked whether their attempts to experimentally create status differences were successful (e.g., Commins & Lockwood, 1979). Possibly relevant variables such as power have been neglected (Ng, 1982), and the social and historical status circumstances of natural groups in field studies may not have been given sufficient consideration (Condor & Brown, 1988). The breadth and complexity of social identity theory's potential applications to specific social phenomena also make its predictions somewhat slippery at times. Thus, findings that were not predicted, or which were even contrary to prediction, can often be reinterpreted as not entirely inconsistent with the theory. As it was noted in the previous chapter, this makes a definitive assessment of the theory difficult at this stage.

In natural social situations, intergroup status differentials are often correlated with differential power and involve intergroup power relationships or conflicts of interest. In these cases, it is very difficult, if not impossible, to disentangle the effect of status differences on prejudice from these other factors. However, situations do exist in which status differences between groups or social categories do seem to be relatively uncontaminated by direct conflicts of interest. Examples are differences between urban and rural persons, occupational groups, men and women in situations where power differences are not a factor, and different academic tracks in schools. In such situations, there seems to be a pervasive tendency for the emergence of negative stereotypes and prejudiced attitudes against the low-status group. Such effects have also been documented in the literature on interpersonal contact between members of different social groups and prejudice. Unequal status contact—particularly when the contact is between majority and minority group members of higher and lower status, respectively—has been consistently found to be associated with intergroup prejudice and negative stereotyping against the lower status group (Amir, 1976; Brewer & Kramer, 1985; Stephan, 1987). This appears to be the case for any kind of intergroup inequity on socially valued dimensions. Thus, when groups differ or appear to differ on dimensions such as wealth, sophistication, education, living circumstances, appearance, skill, achievement, and so forth, a powerful and pervasive tendency seems to result for negative evaluations of and prejudice toward the lower ranking group.

It is not at all clear that social identity theory can account adequately for such effects, particularly because many of these status differentials seem more likely to be viewed as stable and legitimate rather than the reverse. Moreover, there is evidence that the negative stereotypes and prejudice against low-status groups emerge not only for members of the relevant groups but also for totally disinterested observers (e.g. Lerner, 1980; Lerner & Miller, 1978; Ryan, 1971) for whom considerations of intergroup social identity and positive distinctiveness would presumably not be considerations. It has been demonstrated that this effect seems to reflect a basic tendency for low status or, indeed, any other inequity or misfortune to be blamed on the victim through the attribution of inferiority or other negative traits. These attributional tendencies, which will be discussed in detail in the next chapter, seem to provide a more plausible explanation for the sheer pervasiveness of prejudice against low-status groups.

To sum up, therefore, the mere division of individuals into groups stimulates intergroup competition over relative status and prestige, creating bias and discrimination in favor of the ingroup. This does not necessarily, however, involve outgroup derogation. Social identity theory suggests two sets of factors that crucially influence this social competition and could intensify these biases into hostile and prejudiced outgroup attitudes. These are, first, social cues and circumstances that make certain intergroup distinctions particularly salient and, second, intergroup status differentials. The former have been largely ignored by social identity theory and will be discussed in the following section. The effect of status differentials on intergroup behavior and attitudes is presumed to vary, depending on factors such as the permeability of group boundaries and the stability and legitimacy of the intergroup status differential. Although there is a good deal of supportive experimental evidence, this evidence is marred by inconsistencies and is by no means conclusive. In addition, when status differences are found in natural social groups, they seem to be invariably associated with prejudice against the low-status group. The pervasiveness of prejudice against low-status and not high-status groups seems better explained in terms of the operation of attributional processes such as victim blaming rather than by tendencies to seek positive social identities. Social identity effects may moderate this such that the pervasive prejudice against low-status groups becomes intensified when the high-status group's advantage is threatened ("insecure"), and such that the low-status group comes to express prejudice against the high-status group when its advantage is seen as illegitimate and unstable.

It would seem that much more systematic research is necessary to confirm and clarify the effects predicted by social identity theory for intergroup status differentials under varying conditions of permeability, stability, and legitimacy on intergroup attitudes and behavior. A second research priority would be to establish when these effects actually involve outgroup prejudice and not just ingroup favoritism. A third important objective would be to elucidate the interrelationship between realistic intergroup conflicts of interest and social competition over status alone in affecting intergroup attitudes and behavior. If the two approaches are indeed complementary, as Tajfel (1982a) suggested, their integration into a broader framework may be feasible. It may be that social competition is decisive when realistic conflicts are absent or weak, but overridden when they are strong. Thus, the few research studies that have compared the influence of realistic conflicts and social competition in natural settings have usually found that realistic conflicts were the stronger predictors of intergroup attitudes and behavior (e.g., Brown et al., 1986; Brown & Williams, 1984; Kelly, 1988).

## INTERGROUP CONTACT CONDITIONS

It was noted toward the end of the previous section that, when groups differing in status are in contact, prejudice against the low-status group can arise through attributional processes. Thus, conflict or competition, whether realistic or over relative status, does not appear to be a necessary condition for the emergence of socially consensual patterns of prejudiced intergroup attitudes. Other macrosocial conditions of intergroup contact seem able to elicit and maintain prejudice without any kind of conflict being involved.

Psychologists have typically viewed the issue of intergroup contact in terms of the kind of interpersonal contact between individuals of different groups that reduces prejudice. A very substantial research literature has emerged around this question of the "contact hypothesis." Here, however, the issue is not that of the effects of interpersonal contact on prejudice in individuals—a problem that will be treated in the following chapter. Instead, the issue concerns the kinds of macrosocial conditions of contact and interaction between social groups that would tend to create normative patterns of prejudice in these groups.

Traditionally, social psychologists have not shown much interest in identifying such macrosocial conditions of intergroup interaction. Brewer and Miller (1984), however, recently examined this issue. Noting that social identity theory has largely neglected the crucial issue of what makes particular intergroup categorizations and distinctions salient, they set out to explicate "what factors make particular social categories more salient than others across a wide range of social occasions and settings" (p. 283). Two of the factors they mention—real intergroup conflicts and intergroup status differences—have already been discussed in this chapter. In addition to their effects on prejudice already noted, it is apparent that the existence of intergroup conflict or competition would also have the effect of making intergroup distinctions highly salient. This heightened salience in itself would have the effect of triggering categorical, deindividuated, and stereotypical responding conducive to prejudice. Other factors mentioned by them are the existence of convergent group boundaries, differential treatment of the groups by external authorities or agents, and the relative size of the interacting groups.

Two further macrosocial conditions of intergroup contact or interaction that appear relevant to the development of intergroup prejudice can also be identified. One seems to arise when groups are associated with different social or economic roles, particularly when this occurs within the same social structure. This situation was discussed by LeVine and Campbell (1972), who showed that it appears to be highly conducive to stereotyping and intergroup prejudice. Finally, an intergroup contact condition of considerable significance for prejudice is the degree of institutionalized segregation between groups, such as that involved in Apartheid in South Africa. The effects of each of these macrosocial conditions of intergroup interaction will be considered in more detail below.

## Convergent Boundaries

The more groups are characterized by convergent boundaries—the coincidence of many possible distinctions, such as religious, social class, linguistic, political orientation, and so forth—the more likely it seems to be that intergroup contact will result in prejudice between them, and the less likely it is that contact will reduce prejudice. Brewer and Miller (1984) argued that this occurs because "when social category membership is so multiply determined, the probability is high that at least one cue to category identity will be relevant in almost any social situation" (p. 283).

There is a good deal of evidence that convergent boundaries or dissimilarity at the intergroup level are important determinants of intergroup attitudes. Most of this evidence consists of correlations between intergroup attitudes and the perceived similarity of outgroups. These findings were broadly reviewed in the previous chapter in dealing with belief congruence theory. A problem with this evidence, as far as inferring causality is concerned, is its correlational nature. It is as feasible that dislike causes perceived dissimilarity as is the reverse (cf. Brewer, 1968). However, there are several more adequate studies in which the similarity of groups was rated by objective observers. Thus, Brewer and Campbell (1976), in a study of thirty East African tribes, found that the degree to which independent judges rated groups as culturally and linguistically similar was strongly associated with the degree to which these groups liked each other. This was also found in a study of twelve Kenyan ethnic groups, where the similarity of groups to each other was rated by anthropologists on the basis of standardized criteria of linguistic similarity, beliefs about common descent, and cultural pattern (LeVine & Campbell, 1972).

Findings such as these support the proposition that intergroup prejudice should be facilitated when the boundaries of naturalistic groups, such as racial and ethnic groups, covary with other socially significant distinctions, such as social class, urbanicity, language, and lifestyle, even in the absence of any real conflict of interests. It is a depressing reality that such convergent group boundaries are extremely common—often arising naturally, for example, when language differences create barriers to contact and communication, which may ultimately lead to further differences in culture, lifestyle, norms, and values. They may also, however, be artificially imposed by legal constraints or customary practices that effectively constrain the geographical or socioeconomic mobility of groups. This tends to be a major consequence of segregationist social systems. These systems create and reinforce convergent group boundaries, which may not be easily eliminated by formal integration, as experience in the United States demonstrates.

When group boundaries are not convergent, individuals should find themselves belonging to one group on one criterion and different groups on other criteria. This cross-cutting of category and group memberships should reduce the perceived salience and importance of any one particular group membership. Anthropological evidence indicates that cross-cutting group loyalties of this kind may have been an important mechanism reducing intergroup conflicts and maintaining social integration in tribal societies (LeVine & Campbell, 1972). Experimentally created cross-cutting group categorizations have also been shown to reduce intergroup bias and discrimination (Brown & Turner, 1979; Deschamps & Doise, 1978; Rehm, Lilli, & Eimeren, 1988; Vanbeselaere, 1987).

### Differential Treatment

The extent to which different categories or groups of persons are subjected to differential treatment by outside agents, such as social or organizational systems, seems to be a significant factor in creating and reinforcing group identities and accentuating intergroup differentiation and bias. Brewer and Miller (1984) pointed out that this is supported by studies using the minimal intergroup situation where the action of an external authority (the experimenter) in merely assigning individual subjects to different groups tends to induce intergroup bias and discrimination. Rabbie and Horwitz (1969) took this a step further to demonstrate more clearly the effects of differential group treatment. In their study, simply classifying individuals into groups with different labels did not produce intergroup bias. However, after one group was arbitrarily awarded a prize and the other group was not, subjects in both groups began to show significant bias in favor of their group.

In naturalistic groups differential treatment seems to be a potent factor in generating a perception of "common fate" and accentuating perceived intergroup differentiation and prejudice. Schwarzwald (1984), drawing on the Israeli experience, noted that academic tracking in integrated schools often disproportionately allocated Western and Middle Eastern Jews to different tracks, with the effect of reinforcing and sharpening stereotypic and prejudiced intergroup attitudes.

This effect of differential treatment seems particularly powerful when one group receives more favorable treatment than the other, as occurs overtly in caste or segregationist systems such as Apartheid, and covertly in what has been termed institutional discrimination. In the latter case, ostensibly fair rules actually operate to the advantage of one group. Thus, Chesler (1976) argued that institutional racism in America "no longer requires conscious or even overtly racist acts to sustain it" (p. 42). He suggested that this institutional racism may be the primary factor maintaining and reinforcing racial stereotyping and prejudice in American society.

If the differential treatment of groups tends to stimulate bias and prejudice, could prejudice be reduced or inhibited by explicitly treating groups in an egalitarian manner? In fact, there is a good deal of evidence to this effect. Both Allport (1954) and Amir (1976), in their influential reviews of the literature, noted that a strong commitment to the equal and nondiscriminatory treatment of minority members by institutional authorities has been an important determinant of favorable change in intergroup attitudes in contact situations.

## Relative Group Size

It has been suggested that the relative size of interacting groups may influence intergroup attitudes. For example, Amir (1976) mentioned speculative suggestions that an approximate 40 percent black composition in desegregated classrooms in the United States might be an optimum level for facilitating intergroup acceptance. However, he noted that little direct evidence relevant to this issue has been reported.

More recently, Brewer and Kramer (1985) argued that "a relatively equal representation of two social categories will make category distinctions less salient, whereas the presence of a clear minority will enhance category salience" (p. 285). In support of this, experimental studies have demonstrated that a distinct minority, as opposed to equal representation, does accentuate intergroup differentiation (Mullen, 1983) and increases bias in favor of the ingroup (Sachdev & Bourhis, 1984). A good deal of evidence also exists that "solo status" (e.g., a single black in a group of whites) is particularly conducive to stereotyping and prejudice. Pettigrew and Martin (1989) noted that such situations are likely to be common when one group is a small minority, as black Americans may often be in organizations, and so contribute to prejudice against them.

On the other hand, Longshore and Prager (1985) found that intergroup attitudes were least favorable when whites and blacks were fairly evenly divided in desegregated schools, so that neither group clearly controlled the territory. These views seem contradictory, but they could be reconciled if the effect of group size depended on the degree to which intergroup relations were competitive or noncompetitive. If intergroup relations are competitive or conflictual, equal representation could stimulate an open struggle for supremacy and so intensify conflict and prejudice. In such a situation, if one group were clearly smaller and weaker, this might not occur. On the other hand, when intergroup relations are cooperative or noncompetitive, equal representation might make the intergroup differentiation less salient than a clear minority situation would. Consequently, there would be more prejudice and stereotyping in the latter situation.

The relative status and power of the two groups may also be important. For example, Moscovici and Paicheler (1978) found that numerical majorities of low status and minorities of high status exhibited much more overt outgroup discrimination than majorities of high status and minorities of low status. The best conclusion at this stage would therefore appear to be that while the relative size of groups does seem to influence prejudiced intergroup attitudes, its effects are complex and almost certainly moderated by other variables, such as the degree of competition or conflict between the groups and their relative power and status.

## Differences in Social and Economic Roles

The differential distribution of groups into social and economic roles in relation to each other can powerfully influence the manner in which they view each other. LeVine and Campbell (1972) reviewed a good deal of anthropological evidence to indicate that intergroup role relationships, which have become institutionalized within social structures, often influence the content of the stereotypes which groups hold of each other. They pointed out that:

Institutionalized role relations constitute the most repeated and socially reinforced context for interaction and observation between groups varying in degree of urbanization and occupation. This context acts to *sensitize* persons to the role relevant attributes of those groups, thus limiting the basis for stereotype content. This makes it possible to predict the stereotyped images that will develop when there are ethnic groups occupying particular positions in the socioeconomic system. (p. 158; italics in the original)

Two processes may be operative here. First, if the interaction of individuals from one group with those of another consistently involves each engaging in particular role-related activities, each may come to believe that the abilities and personality attributes required to carry out that activity are typical of the other group. Second, social identity theory would suggest that the more interaction between members of different groups was structured by group differences in social roles, to that extent contact would accentuate and reinforce intergroup differentiation.

Within social systems LeVine and Campbell (1972) suggested that group differences in occupational roles and roles associated with urban and rural residence may be particularly important. Other examples would be groups interacting largely as master and servant, peasant and townsman, employer and employee, trader and customer. Racial stereotypes and prejudice in both South Africa and the United States appear to be influenced by a number of such polarities. In both countries, blacks were traditionally rural dwellers, and rural persons have typically been stereotyped by urbanites as "unsophisticated, guileless, gullible and ignorant" (Stephan, 1983, p. 420). Likewise, blacks' overrepresentation at lower socioeconomic levels has resulted in the common stereotype of the manual laborer or lower class person, as "ignorant, lazy, loud, dirty, and happy-go-lucky" (Stephan, 1983, p. 420), being incorporated in racial stereotypes.

In the case of anti-Semitism, LeVine and Campbell (1972) noted that the trader or businessman is typically stereotyped as "grasping, haughty, cunning, exclusive, and domineering" (p. 157) and that "the stereotype of the Jew in Europe appears to recur for ethnic groups specializing in trade anywhere: the Indians in East Africa, the Chinese in Southeast Asia, the Syrians in the Middle East, the Arabs in Ethiopia, and the Lebanese in West Africa" (p. 158). Research indicates a similar stereotype of Indian South Africans, which may also be influenced by this group's visibility in trade and business (Kinloch, 1977; MacCrone, 1937).

## Apartheid and Prejudice

An extremely extensive literature has been concerned with the effects of intergroup contact on intergroup attitudes (e.g., Allport, 1954; Amir, 1976; Stephan, 1987). Most work on contact effects has been explicitly or implicitly concerned with movement from segregated or noncontact situations to desegregated or contact situations. This work has clearly refuted the early simplistic idea that contact would necessarily improve intergroup attitudes over the noncontact situation (Allport, 1954; Amir, 1976; Stephan, 1987). Thus, the implementation of racial integration in previously segregated situations may leave racial attitudes unchanged or even make them worse.

The reverse of this—moving from an integrated to a segregated situation—has rarely been considered, theoretically or empirically. It is not difficult to find reasons for this. Segregation has been a serious social problem in the United States and almost universally abhorred by social scientists. The implicit assumption appears to have been that its effects on intergroup attitudes must be bad or, if this could not be assumed, that segregation represented such an undesirable state of affairs that one would prefer not to even contemplate the possibility that its effects might not always be negative. However, the argument that segregation might have positive effects on intergroup attitudes has been presented very seriously. It has also been tested and implemented in a massive feat of coercive social engineering—the implementation of Apartheid in South Africa, particularly by the ruling National Party after 1948. For this reason alone, it seems important for social scientists to confront and assess Apartheid's rationale. Foster and Finchilescu (1986) recently clarified this. Quoting extensively from the principal architects of the Apartheid policy, they concluded that:

The guiding principal of Apartheid may thus be presented in the form of a negative contact hypothesis: that if contact between blacks and whites could be reduced to the absolute minimum, conflict and racial problems would disappear, or would be reduced to a minimum, while simultaneously "civilization" and "peace" would be maintained. (p. 120)

Foster and Finchilescu (1986) set out to evaluate this hypothesis empirically against the sparse and rather inconclusive literature on contact effects in South Africa. Another way of approaching this issue, which will be adopted here, would be to examine Apartheid's actual impact on interracial contact against the empirically established effects of different kinds of intergroup contact on intergroup attitudes in general. Because a number of basic principles concerning contact effects have been well-established by a very substantial research literature (cf. Amir, 1976; Stephan, 1987), deducing the probable effects of Apartheid measures on attitudes is not difficult.

Although the ostensible objective of apartheid was the reduction of interracial contact, Foster and Finchilescu's (1986) analysis of the effects of Apartheid laws makes it clear that only certain kinds of contact were reduced while others continued or increased. The kinds of interracial contact that were prohibited are precisely those equal-status, interpersonal contacts that have been found to be important conditions for positive changes in interracial attitudes. Thus, Foster and Finchilescu (1986) concluded that Apartheid "therefore precludes most activities satisfying the contact hypothesis criterion of cooperation in the achievement of a joint goal" (p. 7). Yet they also pointed out that there is more interracial contact in South Africa than in the United States. Pettigrew in 1971 made exactly the same observation. This contact generally involves formal economic roles of superior and inferior. Thus, most interracial contact in South Africa occurs within the context of relationships such as master and servant, employer and employee, supervisor and worker, businessman and client, administrator and applicant.

The kind of contact permitted, if not encouraged, under Apartheid, is therefore unequal-status contact. Instead of describing Apartheid society as a noncontact society, it would be more appropriately described as an unequal-status contact society. Because equal-status contact is an important condition for the reduction of prejudice, and because unequal-status contact tends to strengthen and reinforce prejudice, there seems to be a basic contradiction between the stated intention of Apartheid and its probable effects on interracial attitudes and conflict.

In trying to account for this, it is possible to argue that the "negative contact hypothesis" might simply be an empty rationalization for a policy that has quite different goals. This is certainly possible. However, a consideration of the intergroup social dynamics discussed in this chapter does suggest that Apartheid's negative contact hypothesis might well have a fundamental psychological rationality.

This emerges as soon as the social psychological implications of unequal-status interracial contact are considered *in the context of white political domination*. The discussion of oppressed groups' responses to domination in the section on RCT earlier in this chapter noted that an intropunitive response pattern occurs when the intergroup power and status relationships are perceived as stable and legitimate (Tajfel, 1981). That is, both the oppressed and dominant groups unquestioningly accept the inferiority of the oppressed group and its unfitness to hold or share power equitably. Such beliefs require that interpersonal contact between members of such groups be almost exclusively on the basis of unequal status. As soon as equal-status interpersonal contact begins to occur on a large scale, the assumption of superiority/inferiority starts to break down, particularly for the oppressed or lower status group. Thus, as the legitimacy and perceived stability of the intergroup power relationship erodes, the oppressed group will shift to an extrapunitive orientation toward the oppressing group, will openly challenge the power relationship, and will mobilize against it.

In the case of the oppressor or higher status group, equal-status contact with a supposedly inferior group on a large scale should reduce prejudice and weaken the assumption of the subordinate group's inferiority. This could create conflicts of values for members of the dominant group and reduce their readiness to accept the use of highly coercive measures to maintain an oppressive social system.

A study by Finchilescu (1988) documents exactly these reactions in response to equal-status interracial contact in South Africa. This study examined the effects of participating in integrated versus segregated training programs on the attitudes of black and white trainee nurses in several South African private hospitals. Not unexpectedly, all groups who had participated in the integrated training programs favored integrated over segregated training. More interestingly, however, after integrated training, the white group tended to reduce ingroup bias— that is, rated blacks relatively more favorably. In contrast, blacks after integrated training showed more ingroup bias, as well as a greater awareness of race as a factor determining the inequitable treatment of nurses in the hospitals in general. Thus, the black nurses' experience of equal-status contact in the training program increased their awareness and resentment of discrimination against them.

This argument and these findings suggest that from the point of view of the social psychological dynamics involved, Apartheid does have a basic rationality. That is, it represents an attempt to entrench and maintain the psychological legitimacy of white domination in the minds of members of both the dominant white group and the subordinated black group. In one particular sense, therefore, it does attempt to do what its architects claimed for it: It seeks to reduce intergroup conflict, though not in the form of prejudice and discrimination, but in the form of black rejection of white rule and resistance to it. Apartheid in this sense can be seen as an attempt to maintain the psychological conditions for a stable system of racial oppression.

This is, of course, not to say that Apartheid has not had other goals and functions. Clearly it has. The argument here focuses on only one such function, the attempt to reinforce the eroding psychological legitimacy of a caste system by preventing equal-status contact between members of the dominant and subordinate groups. For a time, Apartheid may have succeeded in this, but its failure to entrench the legitimacy of white domination in the minds of the black majority became increasingly apparent after 1976, which heralded the onset of massive and sustained internal resistance to the Apartheid state. This, together with the international sanctions campaign, ultimately made Apartheid untenable, at least in its traditional form. Whether the transition that is now under way in South Africa involves an abandonment of Apartheid and white rule, or merely a change from a crude, old-fashioned, and traditional form of Apartheid to a newer, more subtle, and modernized version in which white political control will continue, still appears to be in the balance.

### Conclusions

In conclusion, it seems that direct conflicts of interest between groups or social competition over status are not the only social factors that create intergroup hostility. Certain conditions of contact and interaction between groups also facilitate intergroup stereotyping and prejudice in the absence of any conflict of interest, and even when groups are cooperatively interdependent (Turner, 1981). These conditions include convergent group boundaries, differential treatment of groups, the relative size of the groups (although the operation of this effect is not yet well understood), and the extent to which groups occupy different social roles in relation to each other. The primary mechanisms through which these intergroup social circumstances influence prejudice seem to be by making intergroup distinctions highly salient and by triggering the attribution of negative traits or inferiority to outgroups. Besides their more direct effects, intergroup conflicts of interest and intergroup status differentials also seem to have such effects.

Finally, Apartheid was briefly considered as a special case of segregation. Apartheid has been rationalized in terms of a noncontact hypothesis with the object of reducing intergroup conflict and hostility. However, it prevents only certain kinds of contact—equal-status contact—which normally operates to reduce prejudice and discrimination. It was argued that this apparent contradiction can be resolved if Apartheid is seen as having had the objective of attempting to preserve the psychological legitimacy of an oppressive caste system.

## SOCIAL DYNAMICS OF PREJUDICE: GENERAL CONCLUSIONS

The existence of socially consensual or normative patterns of prejudice has been well documented. While the explanation of such phenomena has been often viewed as primarily a problem for sociologists and anthropologists, a good deal of social psychological theory and research suggests that the basic social dynamics involved may be essentially similar in both small groups and in large sociocultural groups.

Most of this work has focused on the degree of conflict or harmony in the interests and objectives of groups, with a good deal of evidence indicating that intergroup conflicts of interests consistently generate intergroup hostility and prejudice. Moreover, particular patterns of conflicting intergroup interests—such as direct intergroup competition, domination, and exploitation, as well as intergroup scapegoating—seem to induce distinctive forms of prejudiced intergroup attitudes. Social identity theory, however, has suggested that intergroup competition and consequent negative attitudes do not necessarily arise from real conflicts of group interests. They can arise from the mere existence of group divisions, which will tend to trigger intergroup competition over relative status and prestige. Status differences between groups will tend to intensify this intergroup competition, particularly when group boundaries are impermeable and the status differential is insecure, and so impact on intergroup attitudes and behavior.

Finally, certain macrosocial conditions of intergroup contact and interaction also seem to be conducive to normative patterns of intergroup prejudice, even though they do not necessarily involve conflict or competition. These intergroup conditions seem to generate or reinforce prejudice between groups in several ways. Thus, they appear to influence the salience of group identities and intergroup distinctions; they structure the nature of interpersonal contact that members of different groups typically experience with each other; and they stimulate the attribution of negative traits and inferiority to outgroup members. In certain cases, the effects of such conditions in creating prejudice, such as the existence of convergent group boundaries, differential group treatment, and the role of status differences and associated inequities on socially valued dimensions such as wealth, sophistication, and education between groups seem reasonably well documented. The effect of other factors, such as the relative size of interacting groups, is less well understood.

To sum up, there seem to be a number of ways in which social structures contribute to intergroup patterns of prejudice. The most prominent appear to involve intergroup conflicts of interest, intergroup social competition, threats to ingroup cohesion that can be conveniently blamed on outgroups or minorities, inequity between social groups on highly valued dimensions, and social circumstances that make particularly intergroup distinctions highly salient. Finally, while prejudice as a group or social phenomenon can be explained in terms of the social structural characteristics of groups and the nature of the relationships between them, prejudice as an attitude is ultimately, of course, experienced and held by individuals. This raises the crucial question of how group patterns of prejudice, as determined by social and intergroup dynamics, are acquired or transmitted to the individual members of groups. These mechanisms of transmission are discussed in the next chapter.

# 7

# The Social Transmission of Prejudice to Individuals

The perspectives discussed in the previous chapter explain social patterns of prejudice by directly relating them to particular social and intergroup dynamics, such as intergroup conflicts of interest or the nature of intergroup role and status relations. Such explanations account for prejudice as a societal, institutional, and group phenomenon. They do not, however, specify how individuals within social groups and contexts come to acquire their shared prejudices. The basic theoretical question here is that of how the normative patterns of prejudice characteristic of social groupings are transmitted to and acquired by individual members of these groups in the form of attitudes and beliefs. This requires theories that focus on the individual in a social and interpersonal context as the unit of analysis.

Socially shared patterns of prejudice have frequently been conceptualized as social or cultural norms. From this perspective, commonly termed the cultural norm theory of prejudice, the social and intergroup dynamics described in the previous chapter set up particular patterns of prejudice in social groups, which then acquire normative properties. As such, two processes—socialization and conformity pressures—should be particularly important in the transmission of norms of prejudice to individuals. Both provide powerful accounts of how groups transmit normative standards or beliefs to their individual members. Consequently, the overwhelming importance of these processes as determinants of prejudice in individuals has been widely assumed (cf. Ashmore & DelBoca, 1976; Harding et al., 1969; Simpson & Yinger, 1985).

Perhaps because socialization and conformity seem such obvious and powerful explanations of how individuals come to acquire shared prejudices by virtue of their group membership, other processes that may also be operative have been neglected. Two such processes seem particularly relevant. First, being a member of a social group may generate certain common perceptions of and attributions about outgroups whose interests conflict with the ingroup's, or which differ in role or status from the ingroup. Second, the mere fact of group membership could also condition certain kinds of interpersonal contact experiences with outgroup members. Some kinds of interpersonal contact with outgroup members tend to reduce prejudice, whereas other kinds may create or reinforce prejudice (Allport, 1954; Amir, 1976; Stephan, 1987). Consequently, if being a member of a particular group caused individuals to have disproportionately more "unfavorable" contact experiences with outgroup members, then a socially shared pattern of prejudice against that outgroup could emerge without any other factors having to be operative.

These two factors—perceptual-attributional processes and interpersonal contact experiences—complement socialization and conformity in explaining the social transmission of prejudice in an important respect. While socialization and conformity explain how individuals acquire existing patterns of prejudice from their social groups, they do not explain how these patterns of prejudice might have arisen in the first place. That is, before a particular prejudiced attitude becomes a social norm, it must have come to be widely adopted by the individuals who comprise a social group. This means that processes other than socialization and conformity must also be operative. Perceptual and attributional processes and shared interpersonal contact experiences resulting from the mere fact of membership in a particular group could generate shared patterns of prejudice in situations where social or cultural norms did not yet exist.

Four processes—socialization, conformity, socially structured interpersonal contact experiences, and social perception and attribution—could therefore account for the generation of socially shared patterns of prejudice in the individual members of social groups. These four processes are discussed and evaluated in the remainder of this chapter, and some general conclusions are proposed.

## SOCIALIZATION AND THE LEARNING OF PREJUDICE

It is generally accepted that the basic social attitudes of a society or culture are acquired in childhood as part of the process of socialization (Katz, 1976; Milner, 1981). The concept of socialization itself is one that is often used in a very broad sense. Thus, it may denote the effects on the developing individual of the totality of his or her social and cultural experience. As Milner (1983) noted, "What is this reality, this construction of the world which is absorbed by the child? It is the aggregate of experience, the experience of perceiving people, objects and events, discriminating between them, understanding them, evaluating them and reacting to them" (p. 54).

The very breadth of this conception, involving a variety of processes and mechanisms through which attitudes may be acquired, makes it too imprecise to be particularly useful. Consequently, in considering the acquisition of social attitudes such as prejudice, socialization is often limited to social learning from significant others, whether they be individuals, groups, or institutions. It is in this somewhat more restricted sense that the concept will be used here. Thus, processes such as contact experiences with outgroup members, social perception and attribution, and conformity, which seem to involve different psychological mechanisms will be treated separately, although they could be viewed as aspects of a broad socialization process.

Intergroup attitudes appear to be learned in essentially the same way that other social attitudes are acquired. However, the ease and the rapidity with which the young child learns particular intergroup attitudes does seem to depend on the visibility and the social salience of group differences. Tyson (1985) noted that there is evidence that skin color seems to be a particularly distinctive cue for children and is learned even more quickly than other physical cues such as physiognomy and hair type. As a result, racial preferences and the awareness of racial differences seem to develop at a much earlier age, typically between the ages of three and five years, than the awareness of religious and national differences, which occurs around the age of ten years or later (Katz, 1976; Tyson, 1985). In discussing the particular sensitivity of children to conspicuous physical differences between ethnic groups, Aboud and Skerry (1984) suggested that:

Lacking a set of elaborated and organized cognitions about people, children rely more than adults on overt perceptual information. . . . Such information is what conveys group differences (for instance, skin color). Not till the age of 10 or 11 do children refer to internal attributes such as beliefs and feelings, which would be more useful for differentiating between individuals. This pattern of development seems to be a general one and affects self-descriptions as well as ethnic group descriptions. (p. 25)

It should also be emphasized, as Milner (1983) pointed out, that the process by which the child is socialized into the racial and intergroup attitudes of his or her milieu or culture is not a passive process of indoctrination. On the contrary, "the child is a very active participant, at first eager for information from the available sources, and later seeking out independent sources. . . . The child is striving to attain an understanding of the world and this is a positive constructional task, not merely an inert absorption of parental ideas" (p. 55). How precisely does this learning and socialization occur? Three issues in particular seem to merit consideration. First, what mechanisms or processes of learning are involved in the acquisition of racial attitudes? Second, how does this learning proceed developmentally? Third, what are the most important agents of socialization and learning involved? Each of these three issues will be considered briefly in turn.


## Mechanisms of Socialization

There seems to be relatively little concrete evidence describing precisely how prejudice comes to be learned (Katz, 1976; Milner, 1983). However, a dichotomy often noted in the research literature is that of direct versus indirect processes of acquisition. For example, prejudice may be directly and intentionally taught and reinforced. Alternatively, it may be transmitted indirectly, without conscious intention on the part of socialization agents, and acquired through processes such as observation and imitation.

In the case of the direct tuition of prejudice, Milner (1983) commented that "it seems intuitively likely that parents provide a good deal of direct instruction about values and attitudes. Most people can recall occasions from their own childhood when their parents declared their own beliefs about a particular issue and encouraged them to feel likewise" (p. 55). Some research evidence indicating that direct instruction can be important in the learning of prejudice has been reported. For example, Horowitz and Horowitz (1938) found that direct instruction, reward, and punishment were important mechanisms by which parents in a rural community in Tennessee transmitted racial attitudes to their children. Thus, the transgression for which children were most frequently punished was that of playing with black children. Similarly, Bird, Monachesi, and Burdick (1952) found that in a Northern city in the United States almost half the white families sampled had definite rules against playing with black children. Moreover, those children who were directly prohibited from playing with blacks tended to be the more prejudiced.

Katz (1976), however, concluded that the evidence that prejudice is learned through direct tuition, particularly from parents, is very scanty. Certainly, Allport (1954) had raised the possibility that prejudice might be "caught" rather than "taught" (p. 300). Several important ways in which prejudice could be indirectly learned and unintentionally transmitted—that is, "caught"—include observation, modeling, and identification. Thus, the child would model the way in which significant others behaved toward outgroup members, their statements and comments about them, and the kind of ethnic labels and terms they used. In addition, the broader process of identification with admired and loved figures may result in entire value and belief systems being adopted and internalized (Bagley et al., 1979; Milner, 1981).

Once again, however, little direct evidence of the operation of processes such as modeling and identification on the learning of prejudice has been reported. Nevertheless, the operation of such mechanisms can often be easily inferred from the kind of comments made by children in intergroup contexts. Milner (1983), for example, citing an unpublished study by Pushkin, reported a six-year-old white boy refusing to invite black doll figures to his home for a "tea party" with the words, "If I have to sit next to one of these I'll have a nervous breakdown" (p. 60).

Allport (1954) discussed the importance of children learning derogatory ethnic labels such as "nigger," "goy," "kike," and "dago" with their intense affective significance ("power words"). The degree to which negative ethnic labels, and implicitly or explicitly derogatory ethnic jokes and stereotypes, are commonly used in the child's social environment, and the response of significant others to the child's use of them, may be a particularly potent transmitter of prejudice. It is surprising that hardly any attention has been given to such factors in the research literature.

Finally, prejudice can be socialized in even less direct fashion. This could occur, for example, through the learning of social values and beliefs, which did not themselves involve prejudice, but which could be generalized to facilitate or reinforce the acquisition of prejudice. Thus, the social transmission of cultural values and beliefs such as an intolerance of differences, distrust of strangers and their ways, and excessive pride in ingroup identity and customs could generalize to facilitate intergroup prejudice (cf. Allport, 1954, pp. 298–300). Another example would be the learning of color-meaning concepts.

It has been well established that color terms have definite connotative meanings—particularly in the case of white connoting "good" and black "bad"—and that these evaluative connotations are related to attitudes toward groups designated by the terms "white" and "black." This has been most effectively demonstrated in studies that have used reinforcement procedures to modify this evaluative color bias (preference for white and antipathy to black) in children, and which have found that these effects generalize to subjects' attitudes toward black people (e.g., Elliot & Tyson, 1983; Spencer & Horowitz, 1973).

This phenomenon was discussed in some detail in Chapter 5, where Williams and Morland's (1976) theory that this color bias develops in young children as a result of early experiences with darkness and light was considered. However, it was noted that important evidence, showing that young infants at six months of age prefer and choose black objects over white objects (May & May, 1979, 1981) does not support this theory. It was therefore argued that the evaluative connotations of

these color names and the cross-cultural generality of this color symbolism may be a social and historical product reflecting centuries of
European and North American global economic, political, and cultural
dominance. This color symbolism embedded in the hegemonic culture
and language is then learned by children in the course of socialization,
particularly during language learning. These color evaluations, that
white is good and black bad, then generalize to social groups identified
with these color names, so helping to establish and reinforce racial prejudice against darker skinned persons.

Overall, therefore, societies may transmit prejudice to new generations directly, by openly teaching and reinforcing prejudiced attitudes
and beliefs, indirectly through children observing and modeling the
utterances and actions of significant others, and even less directly
through cultural values, such as color symbolism, which may generalize
to influence the evaluation of outgroups differentiated on the basis of
skin color. The issue of whether direct or indirect ways of learning racial
prejudice is more important has been frequently discussed (e.g., Katz,
1976; Milner, 1983). This might not, however, be a particularly useful
question. It seems reasonably self-evident that both can be important,
and evidence indicating a role for both mechanisms has been reported.

A more interesting and useful question might be that of under what
conditions direct as opposed to indirect methods of socializing prejudice
are more important. Here certain tentative hypotheses could be formulated. For example, when groups are formally segregated and when
overtly prejudiced sentiments are normatively accepted, as has been the
case in South Africa, then the direct tuition of prejudice might be more
important. This may also be the case under conditions of direct intergroup competition and overt hostility. However, when groups are formally integrated, when the overt expression of prejudiced beliefs is not
socially approved, and when ostensibly egalitarian beliefs are normative,
then the direct tuition of prejudice may be rare and indirect methods of
socialization may be more important.

## Stages of Development

Several outlines of how racial attitudes emerge and are formed developmentally in children have been proposed. Goodman (1952), for
example, identified three consecutive stages. First, at about the ages of
three and four years, the child acquires racial awareness, recognizing
group differences and becoming able to differentiate races. Second, between the ages of about four and seven, racial awareness becomes associated with positive or negative feelings toward racial groups, forming
a racial orientation. Third, as the child grows older, this orientation

becomes more differentiated and elaborated, gradually coming to approximate a fully developed adult attitude.

Katz (1976), although broadly concurring with this sequence, proposed a much more complex and elaborate developmental pattern. She identified at least eight overlapping stages, beginning with the development of the capacity to discriminate racial cues, such as skin color, followed by the formation of rudimentary concepts of black people which often already involve evaluative components. Learning to differentiate that concept from others, and the recognition that racial cues are irrevocable and immutable, then follows. Around the age of five, the concept of black persons is consolidated, as the perceptual, belief, and evaluative aspects become functionally interrelated. As this concept is consolidated, differences between groups come to be accentuated and intragroup differences are diminished, at least for outgroup members. Finally, two stages, termed cognitive elaboration and attitude crystallization, describe the increasing elaboration, differentiation, integration, and stabilization of these attitudes as a result of experience and the influence of peers, school, and others.

Evaluating such developmental models is not easy. In broad outline these schemas do seem reasonably consistent with what is known of racial attitude development. Nevertheless, little research is available on the specifics of these models. It is not at all clear, therefore, if the complexity of Katz's model is really justified. It is also possible that these models may underemphasize affective as opposed to cognitive and perceptual factors. Thus, most theorists suggest that racial awareness precedes evaluation. This is very notable in Goodman's (1952) theory. It is also formally specified in Katz's model, though she does caution that awareness and evaluation can develop together. A good deal of evidence, however, suggests that evaluation *typically* accompanies awareness and is learned at the same time (cf. Katz, 1976, pp. 149–150). In fact, Allport (1954, pp. 304–308) pointed out that derogatory labels and statements concerning a group may be learned before the capacity to identify and discriminate members of that group is acquired—a phenomenon that he termed pregeneralized learning. Bagley et al. (1979) also reviewed a good deal of evidence indicating that children first acquire prejudices of an affective or emotional kind that may precede the capacity to differentiate ethnic groups accurately.

### Agents of Socialization

Ashmore (1970) suggested that the four primary agents involved in the socialization of prejudice and intergroup attitudes are parents, peers, schools, and the mass media. The influence of parents has been investigated in a number of studies examining the degree to which children adopt the racial attitudes of their parents. Contrary to the expectation that parents would be very important, these studies have indicated that although parent-child attitudes were positively related, the correlation was typically not a very powerful one. Some studies have reported a moderate positive relationship (Bagley et al., 1979; Edwards, 1972; Epstein & Komorita, 1966), and others rather a weak one (Bird et al., 1952; Davey, 1983; Frenkel-Brunswick & Havel, 1953).

The magnitude of this relationship seems to depend on a number of factors, some of which are methodological. For example, Branch and Newcombe (1986) found a much stronger association between interview-based ratings of parent-child prejudice than was obtained for questionnaire data. One possibility raised by this finding is that the problem of equivalence in the questionnaire measures administered to parents and children may influence the correlations obtained. In other words, the same questionnaire item may not always have the same meaning for parents and children.

A number of other factors also seem to influence these correlations. Thus, Carlson and Iovini (1985) found that parent-child correlations were moderately strong for whites but nonsignificant for blacks in a U.S. sample. Spencer (1983) found a much higher correspondence between parent-child attitudes when black parents in the U.S. had actively intervened to teach pro-black beliefs. Parent-child correlations have also been stronger for younger than for older children (Branch & Newcombe, 1986; Foster, 1986). A possible interpretation for these findings could be that the degree of parent-child association in racial attitude may depend on the degree to which the parental attitudes which the child initially has contact with are later confirmed or contradicted by peers and broader social influences. Where considerable divergence exists, parental influences may be substantially overridden, unless the parents had taken a very active and directive role in teaching attitudes.

It seems self-evident and is generally accepted that, as the child grows older, the influence of peers on racial attitudes will grow stronger (Ashmore, 1970; Ashmore & DelBoca, 1976; Katz, 1976). A number of studies have been conducted that report significant correlations between adolescents' racial attitudes and the attitudes of their peers (e.g., Bagley & Verma, 1979; Patchen, 1982). However, because these data are purely correlational, their interpretation tends to be rather problematic. Thus, these correlations could reflect tendencies to select friends with similar beliefs, values, and backgrounds, rather than a causal effect of friends' attitudes on one's own. A study by Cohen (1977), for example, found that much of the similarity in his adolescent subjects' attitudes and the attitudes of their friendship groups was due to homophilic selection. There also has been very little research on exactly how peers influence prejudice. Thus, the relative importance of processes such as direct tuition, providing information, conformity, reinforcement, modeling, and identification is not known. Consequently, although there is general agreement that peers probably are strong influences on children's and adolescents' prejudiced attitudes, little is known about the manner and magnitude of this influence.

The effect of schools and the educational system on racial prejudice is likely to be complex and to depend on factors such as the racial composition of the school, the quality of race relations, the nature and opportunities for interracial contact, and peer group and teacher norms (Katz, 1976; Milner, 1983; Patchen, 1982). There seems to be little direct research on the transmission of racial attitudes by teachers. Although there can be little doubt that this does occur, its importance is not clear. More work has been done on the role of the content of school textbooks. Du Preez (1983), for example, surveyed a large number of textbooks prescribed for use in South African schools and noted that a number of underlying assumptions ("master symbols") were evident throughout these texts. These included the assumptions that whites are superior, that blacks are inferior, and that South Africa rightfully belongs to the white Afrikaner. MacCrone (1937) also reported that a common reason given by his white South African subjects for their dislike of blacks consisted of references to the history they had learned at school—a history emphasizing black-white conflict and atrocities committed by blacks.

Finally, it is widely accepted that the mass media play an important role in transmitting and reinforcing the normative values, beliefs, and attitudes of a culture or society. Literature, particularly children's literature, comics, the press, and television have received attention as transmitters of racial prejudice (cf. Milner, 1983). A number of ways in which prejudice can be communicated by the media have been noted:

1. Omission—a tendency to ignore the existence of black people—has been extensively documented in children's books, comics, and on television in both Britain and the United States (Bagley et al, 1979; Milner, 1983). This, as Milner (1983) notes, implies their lack of worth and deprives black children of identification figures.

2. Blacks are presented in stereotyped terms. This teaches and reinforces negative stereotypes and, even when the stereotypes are not negative, tends to emphasize how different "they" are from "us" (Bagley et al., 1979).

3. Black persons occupy a disproportionate number of "bad" or low-status roles in literature and television. For example, reviewing research on how black persons are depicted in children's comics in the United Kingdom, Foster-Carter (1984) points out that "the few non-white characters who do appear are usually portrayed as criminal, savage, treacherous, stupid, exotic, child-like or subordinate" (p. 1).

4. Negative characteristics are attributed to outgroup members simply because they are members of a particular racial or national group (Milner, 1983).

5. Ethnocentric norms are communicated, in which the customs and beliefs of the majority group are presented as good and natural and deviations from them are depicted as inferior, alien, and unnatural.

6. A widespread tendency has been noted in the British media to present blacks as "symbols or embodiments of a problem" (Foster-Carter, 1984, p. 1). Milner (1983) points out that this "began with immigration as a problem (despite the net outflow of population) and has continued through every conceivable social problem of the inner-city which predated black immigration . . . to more recent racial disturbances, even when these were provoked by white extremists" (p. 98).

7. An important bias in news reporting arises because bad news makes good copy. As a result, reports of racial conflict and the negative behavior of minorities far outweigh reports of harmonious race relations or the positive achievements of minorities (Milner, 1983).

8. Finally, the media may transmit cultural values and beliefs that may create prejudice indirectly. Color symbolism where white connotes good and black bad is an example. However, any values that happen to be unequally distributed between groups could also subtly generate prejudice. Thus, the media and literature might promote social values involving the desirability of wealth, success, high status, education, being expensively dressed and groomed, having a luxurious house, and so forth. To the extent that blacks are perceived to be lower on these values, and represented as such in the media, prejudice could be generated or reinforced.

While there has been a good deal of research documenting racial bias in literature, television, and films, once again there has been very little research estimating its actual impact on individuals. Some correlational research does exist. For example, Zuckerman, Singer, and Singer (1980) found that children's racial attitudes were correlated with the type of television program they watched. However, it is possible that such correlations might at least partially reflect individuals' tendencies to select material that supports preexisting attitudes. Nevertheless, despite the lack of specific evidence, it is generally assumed that the power and scope of the media make them extremely potent vehicles for the transmission of socially normative intergroup attitudes and beliefs (cf. Bagley et al., 1979; Milner, 1983).

## Conclusions

The idea that socially normative intergroup prejudices are acquired by new generations through social learning from significant others is an intuitively compelling one, and one that is backed by a good deal of evidence. Moreover, it is widely accepted that the more established and consensual particular prejudiced beliefs are in a culture or society, the more important social learning will be. As Milner (1983) pointed out:

When racism has taken root in the majority culture, has pervaded its institutions, language, its social intercourse, and its cultural productions, has entered the very fabric of the culture, then the simple process by which a culture is transmitted from generation to generation—the socialization process—becomes the most important determinant of prejudice. (p. 75)

Le Roux (1986) illustrated this in a semi-autobiographical account of growing up as a white Afrikaner in South Africa:

Young Afrikaners of the 1950s and 1960s grew up in an atmosphere of pervasive and unquestioned racism. Racial stereotypes which we acquired at home were mostly reinforced at school. Our history books . . . , our literature . . . , and the attitudes of teachers, preachers, parents and friends left us in no doubt that Africans were very different from whites and had to be treated as a separate, inferior group. (p. 198)

The influence of early socialization on adult racial attitudes has been emphasized by the theory of symbolic (Kinder & Sears, 1981) or modern racism (McConahay et al., 1981). This perspective, formulated partly to explain the persistence of racism in the United States, suggests that the basic affective component of racial prejudice is acquired during early childhood socialization and thereafter remains very resistant to change. Thus, more egalitarian norms have resulted in cognitions about blacks changing, specifically in the rejection of crude, old-fashioned racist stereotypes, but not the underlying affective attitude, which has merely become attached to far more subtly racist beliefs.

However, it should be noted that the actual importance of socialization for determining adult racial attitudes has never been directly assessed. While it seems intuitively plausible that early social learning may be of overwhelming importance for the very young child, it is possible that its influence may decrease with age. Ashmore and DelBoca (1976), for example, pointed out that conformity, as a process distinct from social learning, becomes more important as the child has more contact with peers, and may be particularly important during adolescence. Certainly, there is no doubt that very substantial changes in intergroup attitudes or other important social attitudes have been demonstrated during adolescence and adulthood. Newcomb's (1943) classic Bennington College study indicated a substantial liberalization of social attitudes in students who had been conservatively socialized as a result of their college experience.

Tyson and Duckitt (1990), in a longitudinal study of British immigrants to South Africa, also demonstrated a substantial increase in racial prejudice soon after their subjects settled in South Africa (cf. also Foley, 1976; Pearlin, 1954). There is also a good deal of evidence that when the nature of the relationship between groups changes, particularly from cooperation or neutrality to competition or conflict, previously socialized attitudes can shift suddenly and very dramatically (e.g., Sinha & Upadhyaya, 1960).

Such findings suggest that social learning from significant others may be much more important during early childhood, reflecting the child's dependence on others in material, emotional, and informational senses, than at later ages. Thus, as the child matures, other influences, such as personal contact experiences, conformity to peer and other group pressures, perception of group interests, and perception of the relative status and circumstances of groups, come to be increasingly important influences on intergroup attitudes, possibly capable of overriding earlier social learning.

## CONFORMITY AND SOCIAL PRESSURE

In concluding the previous section it was suggested that the influence of early socialization on behavior and beliefs may be limited or even overridden by other influences during later life stages. This argument can be taken a good deal further. Hoffman (1977), for example, argued that internalized beliefs and standards acquired during early socialization may not be nearly as important in later life as has been commonly supposed. He noted four major sources of evidence in support of this.

First, extensive shifts in behavioral norms from one generation to the next are not uncommon—a phenomenon that is well illustrated by those studies noted in the previous section, which have found weak parent-child correlations in racial attitude. Second, surveys have found that individuals can accept with equanimity gross breaches of supposedly basic internalized values, such as lying, stealing, and deceit, in themselves and others as long as these transgressions are undetected. Third, a number of cases have been reported of large-scale collapses of morality when social policing agencies have been removed. For example, a strike by the Montreal police in 1966 resulted in the outbreak of widespread looting in the city. Finally, studies of obedience and conformity, such as those of Milgram (1963), have shown how seemingly minor situational pressures (in this instance, requests from respectable authority figures) result in persons behaving in ways that directly contradict important internalized norms concerning the harming of others (cf. also Altemeyer, 1981, pp. 273–276; Haney & Zimbardo, 1976). Hoffman (1977) suggested, therefore, that internalized standards, norms, and beliefs can be highly vulnerable to external pressures and may rarely persist unchanged through life without consistent social support and reinforcement.

One process through which internalized beliefs and norms are rein-forced and maintained is that of normative conformity pressure, exerted by groups or significant others on individuals. Normative conformity can be seen as controlling the behavior and beliefs of individuals in at least three ways. First, social pressures directly induce conforming be-havior in the individual, who risks sanctions, disapproval, or even re-jection by not complying and gains rewards, approval, and acceptance by complying. Second, with repeated compliance, these norms may become internalized over time and so gain the power to influence be-havior and belief in the absence of sanctions or surveillance. Third, continuing social conformity pressures will provide a general social sup-port system of normative contingencies, which, as Hoffman (1977) noted, may be crucially necessary to reinforce, firm up, and maintain internalized norms and beliefs.

The concept of conformity is a complex one, and, as Kiesler (1969) pointed out, it has occasioned a good deal of confusion in the research literature. This has been largely because the concept has been used in quite different ways that have involved very different assumptions, which have not typically been made explicit. At times, the term has been used in the sense of an individual difference or personality trait dimen-sion; at other times, it denotes a psychological process. The discussion in this section is concerned with conformity in the latter sense—that is, with conformity as a process through which social norms of prejudice become expressed in the behavior and beliefs of individuals. As a social and psychological process, the term conformity has also been used to refer to two distinct social influence phenomena, which seem to involve quite different causal processes. This has been a more serious source of confusion in the literature (Kiesler, 1969), and it is important that the distinction be clarified.

In one case, group influence may result both in a person's actions or expressed views moving toward agreement with the group (public com-pliance) and in private beliefs being influenced accordingly (private ac-ceptance). This has been termed "true conformity" (Worchel & Cooper, 1976), conversion (Darley & Darley, 1976), internalization (Kelman, 1961), private acceptance (Kiesler, 1969), and informational social influ-ence (Deutsch & Gerard, 1955). The essential element here is that of private acceptance (Kiesler, 1969). Public compliance often occurs, but not necessarily always. Maass and Clark (1984), for example, noted that private acceptance without public compliance is often reported in studies of minority influence (cf. also Moscovici, 1976). In their classic paper, Deutsch and Gerard (1955) pointed out that this kind of group or social influence typically involves an informational component. The mecha-nism through which change occurs, therefore, seems to consist of a cognitive validation process with the individual generating and considering arguments and counterarguments (Maass & Clark, 1984). Group influence of this kind is therefore usually viewed in terms of an attitude change paradigm, and not a normative conformity one (Kiesler, 1969).

The second case can be seen as the normative conformity paradigm proper (Kiesler, 1969). It has also been termed "expedient conformity" (Worchel & Cooper, 1976) and identification or compliance (Kelman, 1961). In this case, group influence leads to public compliance and may or may not result in private acceptance. The essential component, therefore, is public compliance, which is induced by the perception of "real or imagined group pressure" (Kiesler, 1969). The mechanism is thus an interpersonal rather than a cognitive one (Maass & Clark, 1984). Private acceptance or internalization may follow public compliance because of dissonance reduction (Festinger, 1957) or self-attributional processes (Bem, 1972). Mowrer (1960) also suggested that this may occur through conditioned anxiety eventually coming to be aroused by the mere perception of normative expectations in the absence of surveillance, and being reduced by conforming behavior.

It is widely accepted that normative conformity pressure is an important mechanism of social influence and control. The power of group pressure to influence the behavior and even beliefs of individuals has been dramatically demonstrated in experimental situations, notably by Asch (1952) and Milgram (1963). A great deal of field research also seems to show the effects of conformity on attitudes and beliefs in naturalistic social situations (cf. the review by Singer, 1981, pp. 69–72).

Social pressure and conformity provide a potentially powerful explanation of how prejudiced beliefs and attitudes may be created and maintained in the members of groups and cultures where prejudice has become normative. Harding et al. (1969), for example, stated that:

The normative character of ethnic prejudice involves far more than the fact that attitudes are shared by members of a majority or minority group. Each member is expected to hold such attitudes, and on those who fail to conform in this regard, pressures in a variety of forms are brought to bear (for example, loss of status, verbal condemnation, group rejection). These pressures toward conformity are often subtle, but they are very real. They become far less subtle in the experience of the individual when he deviates in what he says or does from the established ethnic norms of his own group. (p. 27)

A great deal of evidence is typically cited as supporting the importance of conformity as a determinant of prejudice. Much of this evidence, however, tends to be rather indirect and speculative with conformity effects being inferred rather than demonstrated. For example, Allport (1954) noted that wartime surveys of United States armed forces personnel indicated that about 50 percent more persons supported segregationist working arrangements than did persons who indicated personal objections to working with blacks. He therefore speculated that "about a half of all prejudiced attitudes are based only on the need to conform to custom, to let well enough alone, to maintain the cultural pattern" (p. 286). Studies ruling out alternative explanations of prejudice have been also cited as supporting a normative conformity explanation. Thus, although Southerners in the United States were shown to be much higher than Northerners in antiblack prejudice, they were not higher in authoritarianism, anomie, or prejudice toward other target groups (Middleton, 1976; Pettigrew, 1959). Consequently, it was suggested that prejudice in the American South was a subcultural or normative phenomenon and would therefore be powerfully determined by social pressures and conformity to group norms.

A study by Minard (1952) of a coal mining town in the United States is also frequently cited as an illustration of the importance of conformity to situational norms in regulating interracial behavior and attitudes. Minard observed that although most white miners accepted blacks as equals in the mine and union hall, they maintained strict segregation and racial discrimination in their residential communities. The influence of normative conformity has also been inferred from numerous findings that desegregation implemented with strong institutional support can be remarkably successful in modifying both attitudes and behavior in apparently unfavorable situations. For example, the integration of American military units during World War II was readily accepted and was followed by appreciable reductions in the amount of racial prejudice expressed by whites serving in those units (Westie, 1964).

Research that has investigated the role of normative conformity in determining prejudice more directly can be broadly divided into three categories. The first group includes studies that examine the relationship between prejudice and conformity proneness. A number of these studies have been conducted with white South Africans, a group in which racism would seem to be normative. These studies have reported strong positive correlations between indices of racial prejudice and Pettigrew's well-known conformity scale (e.g., Heaven, 1983a; Kinloch, 1974; Nieuwoudt & Nel, 1975; Orpen, 1971b, 1975; Pettigrew, 1958). A second group of studies has looked at the relationship between individual racial attitudes and the normative attitudes of significant others, such as family, friends, peers, and so forth. These studies have consistently reported strong positive correlations between racial prejudice and either perceived social pressures for prejudice from significant others (DeFriese & Ford, 1969; Ewens & Ehrlich, 1972; Fendrich, 1967; Goldstein & Davis, 1972; Hamblin, 1962; Mezei, 1971; Silverman, 1974; Silverman & Cochrane, 1972) or, more rarely, the actual racial attitudes of important reference groups or others (Bagley & Verma, 1979).

A third group of studies has indicated that when individuals shift to new social groups with different norms, their attitudes change in the direction of these norms. Newcomb's (1943) classic Bennington College study has been extensively cited in the psychological literature as demonstrating this effect on social attitudes. Thus, a substantial liberalization of students' attitudes following their college experience seemed to be explicable in terms of the adoption of their college as a positive reference group that mobilized conformity to its liberal norms. A similar study, in this instance of attitudes toward blacks, was conducted by Pearlin (1954) among white students at a university in the U.S. South. His findings paralleled those from the Bennington College study in suggesting that students adopted less-prejudiced attitudes in line with the norms of their university.

Middleton (1976) compared persons living in the United States North and South and found that persons who had spent most of their childhood in one region and later moved to the other had racial attitudes intermediate to those characteristic of the two regions. This change was not found for other kinds of prejudice, such as anti-Semitism. It seemed, therefore, that migrants had changed their racial attitudes toward the new subcultural racial norms that they encountered. Watson (1950) also found that persons moving to New York become more anti-Semitic, presumably due to exposure to anti-Semitic norms there. Finally, Foley (1976) assessed the racial attitudes of prisoners before and then three weeks after their admission to different living areas in a United States maximum security prison. A prior survey had found marked differences in the normative racial attitudes in the different living areas. The pre- and post-admission assessments of racial attitude indicated a highly significant tendency for new inmates' attitudes to shift toward the normative racial attitude of the living areas that they had joined.

Although the evidence that normative conformity is an important determinant of prejudice seems convincing and has been widely accepted, it does not stand up well to close examination. The studies mentioned are open to a number of serious criticisms, and their interpretation in terms of conformity can be questioned. First, the studies correlating conformity and prejudice have typically used a measure of conformity—Pettigrew's scale—that has never been validated as an index of conformity and which may merely measure social conservatism (see Chapter 9). Second, studies correlating prejudice with social pressures to hold prejudiced beliefs do not justify the causal conclusion that pressure causes prejudice. They could as readily reflect tendencies to select reference groups and others who support previously internalized prejudices, or they might reflect long-term social learning.

Third, studies indicating attitude change after shifts in reference groups have not shown that the changes were actually determined by exposure to social pressures to comply with new norms. It is quite possible that these changes could have been caused by other factors associated with the shifts in reference groups, such as changes in group interests or conditions of intergroup contact. For example, Foley (1976) interpreted the shifts in prejudice observed in her study as caused by pressures to conform to the norms of prejudice characteristic of the living areas in which inmates had been placed. However, in her report of this study she noted that the lower prejudice living areas were racially integrated with reasonably amicable race relations, while the high-prejudice areas were characterized by "much interracial conflict" (p. 853). Thus, it is possible that the changes that occurred in new inmates' racial attitudes could have been a direct reaction to the kind of interracial contact prevailing in the different areas, and not a response to conformity pressure per se.

Consequently, despite its apparent plausibility, the thesis that normative conformity pressures may be important determinants of prejudice has not yet received conclusive empirical support. Nevertheless, this proposition has been widely accepted in the literature (cf. Ashmore & DelBoca, 1976; Bagley et al., 1979; Harding et al., 1969; Pettigrew, 1975), particularly for groups or societies that are highly prejudiced against specific outgroups. For example, normative conformity has been regarded as a particularly important determinant, if not the dominant one, of racial prejudice in South Africa (cf. Orpen, 1975; Pettigrew, 1975; van den Berghe, 1967). As such, the perspective has powerfully influenced research and thinking on racial attitudes in South Africa. This work will be reviewed in depth in Chapter 9.

## INTERPERSONAL CONTACT

Certain macrosocial conditions of intergroup contact and interaction that seemed to facilitate intergroup prejudice were reviewed in Chapter 6. These macrosocial conditions included convergent group boundaries, group status differentials, differential treatment of the groups, groups occupying different social or economic roles within social structures, and the degree of institutionalized segregation between the groups. In such circumstances one of the mechanisms by which prejudice could be created in members of the interacting groups would be through these macrosocial conditions tending to structure the kinds of interpersonal contact that typically occurs with outgroup members.

In social structures such as South Africa, and to a certain extent the United States, where whites are usually of higher and blacks of lower socioeconomic status and where formal or informal social segregation exists, personal contact between white and black individuals would typically be between white superiors and black inferiors. Socially structured

interpersonal contact experiences of this nature might generate prejudice—in this example, an image of blacks as inferior—in the absence of
any other causal influences from the social environment, such as socialization experiences or conformity pressures.

The idea that direct personal contact with members of disliked outgroups should reduce prejudice toward those outgroups in individuals
is commonly known as the contact hypothesis. This hypothesis has
generated a substantial body of research during the past thirty years.
In its naive form the contact hypothesis expected that the more interpersonal contact members of different groups experienced with each
other, the less prejudiced they would be toward those groups. Thus,
segregation should foster prejudice and integration should eliminate it.
However, as Allport pointed out in 1954, this expectation was soon
refuted. Early studies demonstrated that interpersonal contact between
the members of different groups did not always reduce prejudice. In
1954, Allport summarized these findings by suggesting that only certain
kinds of contact would reduce prejudice, specifically:

equal status contact between majority and minority groups in the pursuit of
common goals. The effect is greatly enhanced if this contact is sanctioned by
institutional supports . . . , and provided it is of a sort that leads to the perception
of common interests and common humanity between members of the two
groups. (p. 281)

During the almost four decades following this statement, research on
the contact hypothesis has grown enormously. The conclusion that only
certain kinds of contact actually reduce prejudice has been clearly confirmed. In fact, it has become increasingly apparent that contact does
not reduce prejudice nearly as easily as had been hoped. Thus, while
conclusions concerning the core conditions that should characterize contact situations in order for prejudice reduction to occur have remained
basically similar to Allport's original statement, their formulation has
tended to become more rigorous and qualified (cf. Amir, 1976). For
example, Cook, summing up the literature in 1978, stated that:

Attitude change favorable to a disliked group will result from equal status contact
with stereotype-disconfirming persons from that group, provided that the contact is cooperative and of such a nature as to reveal the individual characteristics
of the person contacted, and that it takes place in a situation characterized by
social norms favoring equality and egalitarian association among the participating groups. (pp. 97–98)

This research literature also indicates that certain contact conditions
will tend to increase or reinforce prejudice. More specifically, a number
of characteristics of unfavorable contact situations can be identified.

These have been listed, for example, by Amir (1976) and Stephan and Stephan (1984). Thus, prejudice will be increased when the contact is between persons of unequal status (particularly when the person from the disliked group is of lower status); when there is institutional opposition to or lack of support for contact; when the contact situation involves competition, reveals opposing interests and values, is unpleasant, tense, or frustrating, and involves superficial rather than intimate contact; and when the contact tends to confirm rather than disconfirm negative stereotypes.

Amir (1976) pointed out that for those contact studies conducted under natural social conditions—that is, when "social situations seem to be more typical of 'average' everyday life" (p. 285)—outcomes have generally not been positive and have frequently been negative. This has certainly been the case for research on school desegregation in the United States, where only a minority of studies have reported decreases in prejudice following desegregation (Longshore & Prager, 1985). In discussing these findings, Amir noted that opportunities for direct personal intergroup contact can be very limited under natural social conditions. In addition, he pointed out that individuals generally prefer contact with ingroup members rather than outgroup members. Consequently, "making individuals interact across ethnic lines seems to be a major difficulty" (p. 287).

It would appear, therefore, that the degree to which broader macrosocial circumstances generate opportunities for and facilitate personal contact across group boundaries will powerfully determine the degree to which such contacts will occur. To the extent that contact does occur, change in prejudice may be expected, with the direction of the change contingent on the nature of the situations in which contact typically occurs. Moreover, the degree to which these contact situations will typically tend to be favorable or unfavorable will also be largely determined by the broader social structure and circumstances of group interaction. From this perspective, personal intergroup contact can be viewed as an intervening variable that transmits broader social structural influences on the intergroup attitudes of individuals. Table 7.1 illustrates this by successively showing: first, relevant conditions of intergroup contact at the macrosocial level; second, individuals' opportunities for personal contact with outgroup members that arise out of these macrosocial conditions; third, the corresponding kinds of personal contact that individuals will have with outgroup members; and fourth, the effect of this personal contact in either facilitating or inhibiting prejudice.

Finally, it can be noted that many of the conclusions drawn from the literature on the contact hypothesis represent very broad generalizations from a research literature that has tended to produce findings of increasing complexity as it has grown. Thus, although a contact situation

**Table 7.1**
**Summary of How Intergroup Contact Conditions at the Macrosocial Level
Structure Individuals' Opportunities for Contact and Their Personal Contact
Conditions So That Prejudice Is Either Facilitated or Inhibited**

**Groups:**

| | |
|---|---|
| Segregated | Integrated |
| Have conflicting interests | Have compatible interests |
| Sharply demarcated by convergent boundaries | Group boundaries are blurred by multiple cross-cutting categories |
| Differentially treated | Receive same treatment |
| Characterized by different social roles and statuses | Not systematically differentiated in social role and status |

**Individuals:**

| | |
|---|---|
| Can easily avoid contact situations in natural social settings, and when contact occurs, it tends to be in unfavorable situations: as listed below | Have frequent opportunities for personal contact with outgroup members, and when contact occurs, it tends to be in generally favorable situations: as listed below |

**Personal contact conditions:**

| | |
|---|---|
| Between persons of unequal status | Between persons of equal status |
| Against institutional opposition | With institutional support |
| Competitive | Cooperative |
| Reveal opposing interests, values | Reveal common interests, values |
| Unpleasant, tense, frustrating | Pleasant, rewarding |
| Confirm negative stereotypes | Disconfirm negative stereotypes |
| Superficial and casual | Intimate |

**Contact results in prejudice being:**

| | |
|---|---|
| Facilitated or increased | Inhibited or reduced |

involving cooperative activity generally reduces prejudice, the degree
to which it does so can be quite markedly influenced by a number of
other situational contingencies. Stephan (1987) recently summarized
these as follows:

Cooperation is most effective when it is successful . . . , when measures are taken
to avoid the negative effects of different levels of task ability . . . , when the ingroup and out-group are similar in attitudes . . . , when the in-group and outgroup are numerically balanced . . . , when assignment to groups does not make
social categories salient . . . , when both in-group and out-group members are
well represented among the authority figures sanctioning the conduct . . . , and
when the interaction is socially oriented rather than task oriented. (p. 21)

It is generally accepted that a major problem with the literature on the contact hypothesis has been its atheoretical nature (cf. Longshore & Prager, 1985). This has resulted in a progressive accumulation of empirical findings, underpinning essentially similar but increasingly complex and qualified generalizations. As Stephan (1987) noted, "the list of conditions considered important in creating contact situations that have positive outcomes continues to grow and grow" (p. 31). It would seem that any really significant advance in our understanding in this area might require a shift toward serious attempts to understand the basic mechanisms through which contact experiences actually affect prejudice, rather than the examination of increasingly complex and refined situational contingencies.

Two potentially important theoretical statements in this direction have been made recently. First, Brewer and Miller (1984) argued that cues in the contact situation might influence prejudice through their effects on social categorization. Second, Rothbart and John (1985) elaborated the idea that contact affects prejudice through confirming or disconfirming social stereotypes. Both these theories seem able to account for a mass of relatively unrelated contact findings and integrate them into broader explanatory frameworks. The testing and refinement of theories such as these may be crucial for the effective future development of knowledge on the contact hypothesis.

## PERCEPTUAL AND ATTRIBUTIONAL PROCESSES

Merely being a member of a social group may generate certain common perceptions of and attributions about outgroups such that individual ingroup members come to share prejudiced attitudes toward those outgroups. Two fairly distinct perceptual processes can be identified. The first involves the perception of common ingroup interests that conflict with an outgroup's interests. It will be argued that the mere perception of such interests by individual ingroup members will result in the emergence of shared prejudice toward the outgroup. The second involves the perception of certain differences between groups that are explained by attributing traits or characteristics to the outgroup that explicitly or implicitly have the effect of derogating them.

This is not to say that socializing or normative influences will not also be involved in the generation of prejudice under such conditions. Generally they will. The point is, however, that these perceptual-attributional processes can and will occur independently of any contact or interaction with other group members. Thus, as in minimal intergroup situations, they are stimulated by the mere fact of membership in a group that is perceived to be related in particular ways to certain outgroups.

## Perceived Interests

Realistic conflict theory, which was discussed in Chapter 6, relates conflicts of interest between groups to intergroup patterns of prejudice. The example most commonly mentioned in the social psychological literature is that of direct competition between groups where, as LeVine and Campbell (1972) pointed out, each group poses a "direct threat" to the other. In addition, they noted a further proposition that realistic conflict theorists usually leave implicit—that is, "real threat causes perception of threat" (p. 30) among individual ingroup members—and that it is this perception of threat which elicits hostility to the perceived source of the threat in group members. Thus, by simply becoming members of a particular ingroup, individuals may become aware of shared group interests that are threatened by an outgroup. This awareness could then generate a shared prejudice against that outgroup among ingroup members, in the absence of any socializing or normative influences.

A question that has attracted very little attention is that of precisely how perceived threat results in prejudice. Typically, a simple frustration-aggression model seems to be assumed (cf. LeVine & Campbell, 1972). Thus, the perception that an outgroup's actions frustrate, or might frustrate, ingroup members' goals elicits their hostility to that outgroup. It is possible, however, that the processes involved may be more complex and less mechanistic than this.

Cooper and Fazio (1979) outlined a cognitive model that seems to have considerable heuristic value. They pointed out that under conditions of intergroup conflict, intergroup attitudes and perceptions may manifest an extreme degree of virulence and irrational intensity with "people inventing the most outrageous logic to convince themselves of the evil inherent in the outgroup member" (p. 150). Such beliefs and perceptions are often not easily explicable in terms of a simple and basically rational perception and calculation of realistic threat.

Cooper and Fazio noted that, according to attribution theory, certain biases occur in the otherwise rational process by which individuals assess others' intentions and dispositions from their behavior. One of these biases is that the more another's behavior has hedonic relevance for an individual (i.e., promotes or interferes with his or her values), the more that behavior will be seen as reflecting the other's intentions and basic dispositions—and the more extreme will become judgments of the other. This attributional bias, Cooper and Fazio suggested, will also occur and, in fact, will be magnified under intergroup conditions.

Thus, if ingroup and outgroup have discordant goals, any action by the outgroup to promote its goals will interfere with the ingroup's goal achievement. To the extent that this harms the ingroup's interests, it will have hedonic relevance for ingroup members. This will bias the attributions of ingroup members so that they will attribute the out-group's actions not to the pursuit of its own goals, but to an intention to harm the ingroup's interests. Thus, Cooper and Fazio (1979) pointed out that the perception by ingroup members that the outgroup's actions are intended to injure them ("vicarious personalism") results in:

an evaluation of outgroup members that is more negative than a dispassionate inference process would predict and one that is held with an extreme degree of certainty. A simplistic correspondent inference about the evil nature of the out-group members is made. Negatively valued dispositions are ascribed to the members of the goal-discordant group, and negative attitudes toward them are formed. (pp. 151–152)

Although Cooper and Fazio's model was cogently illustrated by ref-erence to the 1974 racial rioting precipitated by the busing issue in Bos-ton, it has not yet been subject to direct empirical testing. Nevertheless, it does seem to provide a plausible account of how intergroup compe-tition and the perception of outgroups as threats to ingroup interests can create prejudiced attitudes and beliefs in individuals of extreme and seemingly irrational intensity.

As noted in Chapter 6, conflicts of interest between groups can take forms other than that of direct competition. In the case of intergroup domination, for example, the subordinate group does not necessarily pose a threat to the dominant group. Here the crucial psychological task for members of the dominant group appears to be the rationalization and justification of inequality, domination, and their social advantages.

An important mechanism through which this can be accomplished is what Ryan (1971) termed victim-blaming attributions. The essence of Ryan's argument is that the privileged in inequitable societies are able to live comfortably with poverty, exploitation, and discrimination by blaming these phenomena on their victims. This is typically done by attributing to them traits of inferiority and inadequacy. Their possession of these failings and deficiencies, therefore, causes their misfortunes, and not oppression, exploitation, or social circumstances that deny them opportunities. For example, the poverty of blacks in the United States may be attributed to a natural, biological inferiority or, according to more liberal and sophisticated ideologies, to traits acquired from living in a culture of poverty. Thus, "blaming the victim is a rationalization for those who seek to justify the status quo with respect to majority-minority relations" (Levin & Levin, 1982, p. 43).

A somewhat different attributional process seems to be characteristic of intergroup scapegoating. Tajfel (1981) and others (e.g., Stephan, 1983) suggested that intergroup scapegoating is more appropriately concep-tualized in terms of attributions of social causality that are functional for social groups, rather than the more mechanistic frustration-aggression-displacement approach. Thus, scapegoating occurs when ingroup members misattribute the cause of difficulties or failures being experienced by the ingroup to the intentions of an outgroup. Why does this misattribution of causality occur among ingroup members? Generally, it would function to divert blame from the ingroup itself or its leaders, an outcome that would have the effect of weakening ingroup cohesion. Thus, a strong commitment to ingroup identity and to maintaining its cohesion would motivate ingroup members to shift the blame for failure and other ingroup problems from the ingroup itself to an appropriate outgroup. Moreover, as Cooper and Fazio's (1979) model indicates, these ingroup problems would tend to be seen as intentionally caused by the outgroup, resulting in extremely negative and hostile evaluations of the outgroup and its possible persecution.

In order to plausibly attribute serious ingroup strains and failures to the intentional actions of a scapegoated group, that group will tend to be seen as relatively powerful. This creates the paradox that groups which in actuality are usually numerically and politically weak can be seen as extremely powerful and menacing. For example, Coser (1956) noted the anti-Semites' perception of "the Jew's power, aggression, and vengefulness' (p. 107). Billig (1978), as previously noted, also pointed out how contemporary anti-Semitism "is based upon a belief that Jews have immense powers of evil in the world . . . that Jews control both communism and capitalism and that they aim to dominate the world in a regime that will destroy Western civilization" (p. 132).

Another issue involved in intergroup scapegoating is that of how ingroup members come to select the scapegoated group. The psychological literature cites three characteristics of groups that are believed to facilitate their selection as social scapegoats. First, scapegoated outgroups should be relatively weak, or at least not powerful enough for their persecution to arouse a real threat to the ingroup (Ashmore, 1970; Levin & Levin, 1982). Second, the outgroup should be visible or conspicuous enough to be a highly salient social cue for ingroup members (Ashmore, 1970). Third, the outgroup should already be disliked or resented by ingroup members (Berkowitz & Green, 1962; Coser, 1956).

Historical evidence suggests that groups that have been subject to systematic scapegoating and persecution do seem to fit these criteria well. For example, cultural or ethnic minorities heavily engaged in trade and commerce seem to have been frequently scapegoated. Examples are the Jews in Western Europe, the Indians in East Africa (and to a certain extent South Africa), and the Chinese in Southeast Asia (LeVine and Campbell, 1972). These groups are politically and numerically weak. Their relative wealth, their cultural or ethnic differences, and their dispersal through the host society necessitated by their commercial activities make them highly distinctive socially. These attributes, together with the inevitable tension arising from the conflict of interests between buyers and sellers, may also result in such groups being resented and disliked.

The operation of perceptual and attributional processes in intergroup scapegoating can therefore be summarized as follows. The attribution of ingroup failure and strains to deficiencies of the ingroup or its leadership could seriously impair group cohesion. Consequently, this motivates ingroup members, who are highly committed to their group, to attribute these difficulties to the actions and intentions of highly salient, disliked, and weak scapegoat groups.

Finally, the issue of research on the degree to which perceived interests affect the prejudiced intergroup attitudes of individuals in naturalistic social contexts may be considered. Surprisingly little research has been done in this area, and most of what has been pertains to the effects of perceived threat. The evidence, indicating that perceived threat influences racial prejudice in the United States, was reviewed by Ashmore and DelBoca (1976). They noted studies that indicated a shift in the white stereotype of blacks from one of blacks as inferior to one of blacks as violent and threatening. They suggested that this could be caused by black militancy during the 1960s and 1970s. Several other kinds of evidence were also discussed. First, several studies were noted, indicating that survey items tapping perceived racial threat in areas such as housing, employment, economic resources, and personal safety correlated well with each other, suggesting that a coherent "perceived racial threat" syndrome seemed to exist among American whites. Second, these measures of perceived racial threat correlated highly with evaluative ratings of blacks and behavioral indices of prejudice (cf. Feagin, 1970). Third, surveys had shown that those who seemed more directly in competition with blacks, such as city dwellers as opposed to suburbanities, were lower in sympathy for black protest (Campbell, 1971).

More recent research in the United States, largely done by researchers exploring the concept of symbolic racism, has produced contrary findings, which suggest that racial threat might not be a significant influence on racial attitudes and actions. For instance, Kinder and Sears (1981) found that direct racial threats to white suburbanites' private lives (to their jobs, their neighborhoods, their children's schooling, and their families' safety) had little if any relation to voting for a black mayoral candidate and a measure of symbolic racism. Sears and Allen (1984) also reviewed a number of studies indicating that opposition to racial busing by American whites was not correlated with the personal difficulties and disruptions that busing would actually involve for them. White Americans' support for racial equality was also found to be generally unaffected by tangible racial threats (Kinder & Rhodebeck, 1982). And, finally, several studies found that whites' economic self-interest seemed to be only very weakly correlated with their support of or opposition to affirmative action in the United States (Jacobson, 1985; Kleugel & Smith, 1983).

These more recent findings, however, have proved somewhat controversial, and two important criticisms have been leveled against them. First, Bobo (1983) has pointed out that these studies have frequently relied on "objective" indices of the vulnerability of whites to threat from blacks. Examples are having children in public schools that participate in public busing programs and the objective probability that one's child might be bused. Bobo argues that these "objective" threats might, in fact, not always be perceived as threatening by individuals. Thus, it would have been more appropriate if these studies had assessed subjectively perceived threats. Second, these studies have used a conception of self-interest in terms of "gains or losses to the individual's tangible private well-being" (Sears et al., 1979, p. 371). As Sniderman and Tetlock (1986a) argued, however:

This may sound like a reasonable conception, yet it is actually a very restrictive way to think of self-interest. An example will make clear why. Consider blacks over 30, who favor affirmative action quotas for college admissions. They will not themselves benefit from such a quota. . . . The calculus of self-interest in politics is a calculus of group, not individual, benefits. (p. 141)

Overall, therefore, the influence of perceived racial threat on white racial attitudes in the United States seems to be an unresolved issue. A major impediment to research in this area may have been the failure to adequately conceptualize the idea of perceived group interests (as opposed to the more limited concept of personal interests) and to develop adequate measures of this construct.

In South Africa, a good deal of sociological and historical work suggests that intergroup conflicts of interest may have been particularly important in determining racial attitudes (e.g., Rex, 1970; van den Berghe, 1967). Although very little social psychological research has examined this issue, and then only relatively obliquely, the results do seem supportive. For example, Heaven (1983a) found that a scale measuring support for the protection of white workers' economic interest was a stronger predictor of racial prejudice in a sample of white Afrikaners than were a variety of psychological variables, such as measures of authoritarianism and conformity. In addition, research that assessed the racial attitudes of successive annual cohorts of students from 1973 to 1978 (Nieuwoudt & Plug, 1983) suggested that white hostility to blacks was influenced by the degree of threat perceived to white interests from black resistance and political activism. This research indicated that white students' attitudes to blacks became markedly more negative immediately after the "Soweto riots" in 1976. Finally, Furnham (1985) compared just-world beliefs in matched white South African and British samples. The belief in a "just world" was significantly higher in the South African sample. This, it was argued, would serve to justify the status quo in an unjust society and "to condemn or devalue the innocent victims of apartheid" (p. 365).

Summing up, therefore, it has been argued that merely being a member of a social group may generate shared patterns of prejudice in group members through their coming to perceive common interests that conflict with an outgroup's interests. This seems to motivate and trigger certain attributional biases and processes. These may result in outgroups coming to be viewed as inferior or unworthy in some way or other, thereby justifying their oppression and exploitation. Alternatively, in the case of competing or scapegoated groups, these attributions result in a belief in the basically evil and malevolent nature of the outgroup. Finally, research on the degree to which perceived interests seemed to actually influence racial prejudice was briefly reviewed. While findings have been inconclusive in the United States, several studies suggest that both perceived threat to white privilege and the need to justify racial oppression may be important determinants of racial prejudice among white South Africans.

## Social Perception and Trait Attribution

Ryan (1971) viewed victim-blaming attributions as stemming directly from the motive in those who benefit from social inequality to justify and rationalize their advantages. However, there is evidence that victim-blaming attributions will also be made as part of a more general process, by persons without any direct stake in preserving the social status quo. Thus, anyone who merely observes others suffering the effects of discrimination or any other personal or social disadvantage may tend to derogate and blame them for this, frequently by attributing negative characteristics to them to explain their misfortunes.

An important theory explaining why such inferences or victim-blaming attributions may be a universal tendency has been proposed by Lerner (1980). He suggested that individuals have a basic need to believe that they live in a world that is a just and orderly place where people generally get what they deserve and "deserve what they get." Becoming aware of an innocent victim threatens the belief in a just world and motivates strategies to protect this belief. Lerner and his colleagues (Lerner & Miller, 1978) conducted a great deal of research demonstrating that when this occurs, an important strategy used is that of derogating the victim and seeing the suffering as deserved.

This principle can be readily generalized to the perception of social groups. In this case, in order to maintain the belief in a just world, the mere perception that a particular group was disadvantaged, oppressed, exploited, or discriminated against could generate a tendency, even in totally disinterested observers, to derogate it and attribute to it characteristics causing its misfortunes.

A second process may also be operative in such situations. The phenomenon of attributing characteristics to individuals (or groups) to explain their circumstances or behavior seems to occur as a perceptual cognitive process without involving the need to maintain a belief in a just world or any other motivational component. This has been termed the fundamental attribution error. It involves a basic bias in the way others are perceived, consisting of a tendency to underestimate the impact of situational factors in producing another's behavior and to overestimate the role of dispositional or personality factors. As Jones (1982) pointed out, "we are likely to judge the behavior of someone who behaves differently, as someone from a different cultural or ethnic background might well do, as revealing that person's stable dispositions" (p. 63). This attributional bias seems to stem largely from how individuals allot their attention when observing persons in situations (Ross, 1977).

This principle seems directly relevant to the perception of group differences and the formation of stereotypes. Stereotypes may be purely descriptive, as in the stereotype of a particular group as "tall" or "wealthy." However, stereotypes often contain an inferential component by which an observed group difference is attributed to a stable group disposition—usually a personality trait. Thus, the stereotype of a group as "lazy," for example, consists first of an observation of a group difference (real or imagined), possibly in achievement or work orientation. Second, it involves the attribution of this observed difference to the trait of "laziness." Eagly and Steffin (1984), in describing how stereotypes are socially generated, illustrated this very clearly:

If perceivers often observe a particular group of people engaging in a particular activity, they are likely to believe that the abilities and personality attributes required to carry out that activity are typical of that group of people. For example, if perceivers consistently observe women caring for children, they are likely to believe that characteristics thought to be necessary for child care, such as nurturance and warmth, are typical of women. (p. 735)

Stereotypes therefore generally explain perceived group differences by attributing them to stable group traits or dispositions, rather than to social influences, such as roles or circumstances. This can be viewed as an instance of the fundamental attribution error, since there will rarely be any empirical reason why a particular group difference is any more likely to be due to a group's traits rather than to its social circumstances. For example, a group stereotyped as "lazy" might well be lower in occupational achievement than the ingroup. However, in many cases, such a difference could be as feasibly attributed to the social opportunities and barriers that the group experiences as to its traits or dispositions.

Because stereotyping involves a basic attributional bias of explaining perceived group differences in terms of a group's traits, rather than its social circumstances, groups considered inferior on any socially valued dimensions will tend to be attributed negative traits that indicate inferiority. In this way, negative stereotypes and prejudice against a group could arise merely from the perception that the group was lower on certain socially valued dimensions—that is, poorer, of lower status, occupying manual economic roles, being less educated, living in slum conditions, and so forth. This means that attributing traits of inferiority to a socially disadvantaged group need not always involve a motivational process such as victim-blaming. It can occur as part of the more general process of social stereotyping as a perceptual cognitive phenomenon involving the attribution of traits inferred from and explaining perceived group differences. This process could therefore be nonmotivational and not involve needs to maintain the belief in a just world, or a vested interest in maintaining an inequitable social status quo. In practice, of course, both the perceptual attributional process involved in stereotyping and the motivational processes involved in victim-blaming would tend to occur together and reinforce each other.

One final comment seems merited. The argument above does appear to have an important implication for the old debate over the extent to which stereotypes have a kernel of truth. As LeVine and Campbell (1972) pointed out in their influential review of this issue, psychologists had traditionally assumed that stereotypes are invariably false and distorted. LeVine and Campbell themselves argued very plausibly, citing sociological and anthropological evidence, that stereotypes may often reflect real social differences between groups.

Subsequently, this argument has been taken a good deal further, most notably in important papers by Brigham (1971a) and McCauley et al. (1980). In these papers the argument that stereotypes inevitably involve certain biases and errors, which tend to make them false and distorted, is carefully examined and refuted. Thus, it is shown that stereotypes are not necessarily "illogical in origin, resistant to new information, and obviously invalid" (McCauley et al., 1980, p. 195). Other arguments commonly made against stereotypes, such as their "ethnocentrism, genetic implications, projected hostility, and exaggeration of real group differences" (p. 195), are shown to apply only to particular stereotypes, typically negative ones, and not to stereotypes in general. As a result, it has been concluded that stereotypes are basically no different from any other "concepts" (McCauley et al., 1980) or "generalizations" (Brigham, 1971a). According to Babad et al. (1983), "stereotypes are universal, used by every human being in processing information about the social environment [and] are not only inevitable but also are usually quite functional for effective social interaction" (p. 75).

While this debate as a whole is beyond the scope of the present discussion, two points made here seem directly relevant. First, the assertion that stereotypes are simply cognitive generalizations is misleading. While stereotypes may be purely descriptive, they generally contain an inferential component attributing a perceived group difference to a particular personal disposition or trait regarded as being characteristic of a group. This is so general that stereotypes are often defined as beliefs about the "personal attributes" (Ashmore & DelBoca, 1981) or "traits" (Brigham, 1971a) of groups. Second, the attribution of perceived group differences to personal dispositions rather than to the social environment of the group does constitute a basic error or bias in stereotyping that is directly equivalent to the fundamental attribution error in the case of individual behavior.

This bias of trait stereotypes seems to have profound implications for attitudes and behavior toward outgroups. Apostle et al. (1983), for example, reported research indicating that prejudice and discrimination result when perceived group differences unfavorable to an outgroup are attributed to the character of the group, but not when they are attributed to social environmental factors. Stereotypic trait attributions are also fundamentally conservative—socially and politically. That is, they negate policies to assist disadvantaged groups by social change and reform. The only remedial actions they may countenance focus on changing the disadvantaged individual (cf. Ryan, 1971, who discusses the conservative policy implications of victim-blaming attributions). It is possible that part of the political staying power of conservatism may result from this basic attributional bias involved in trait stereotyping.

This argument does not only apply to negative stereotypes. Even positive trait stereotypes, by emphasizing that groups differ in their nature rather than in their circumstances, may facilitate prejudice, or at least create cognitive conditions suitable for its growth. Wilder (1986), for example, noted that "dispositional attributions to the behavior of outgroup members . . . encourages deindividuation of outgroup members, thereby nurturing the likelihood of bias. By contrast developing a more Galilean view of outgroups (i.e., attention directed to the context of behavior) should promote a more supportive, self-like response to them" (pp. 340–341). Miller (1982) also pointed out that the dehumanization of outgroup members will be facilitated "when members of one group think about members of another as intrinsically different" (p. 478).

This may help explain how an initially positive outgroup stereotype can shift rapidly and easily to become extremely negative with a change in circumstances. For example, Sinha and Upadhyaya (1960) showed how an extremely positive stereotype of Chinese people held by Indian students was transformed into an extremely hostile and derogatory one in a matter of a few months at the time of the China-India border dispute of 1959. In such situations the prior existence of the positive stereotype, as opposed to the attribution of group differences to environmental factors, may have the seemingly paradoxical effect of facilitating the later emergence of negative stereotypes and intergroup hostility.

To sum up, therefore, it has been argued that socially shared patterns of prejudice may arise from the mere perception that outgroups differ from the ingroup in particular ways. This tends to occur when outgroups are perceived to be lower on socially valued dimensions or criteria— that is, they are lower in status, power, wealth, education, sophistication, socioeconomic role, and so forth. In that case, the perception of differences results in ingroup members explaining such differences by attributing stereotypic traits indicative of inferiority and inadequacy to the outgroup and derogating it. The crucial assumption involved in these trait attributions is that group differences are due not to situational or environmental factors but to stable dispositional attributes of the group. It was suggested that this bias can be viewed as a fundamental error inherent in stereotyping and that it has important negative implications for intergroup attitudes and behavior, even when stereotypes are positive ones.

A somewhat different process from those discussed in this chapter is that termed the "ultimate attribution error" by Pettigrew (1979). In essence, this involves ingroup members attributing positive behavior by members of a disliked outgroup to circumstances, luck, or some other exceptional factors, and negative behavior by these outgroup members to stable traits or dispositions. Several empirical studies have reported findings broadly supporting these propositions (e.g., Greenberg & Rosenfield, 1979; Whitehead, Smith, & Eichhorn, 1982). These attributional biases, however, do not explain the creation or emergence of prejudice against outgroups. They provide a mechanism that maintains and reinforces prejudice and intergroup dislike which already exists. Consequently, this approach will only be noted here and not discussed in more detail.

## CONCLUSIONS

Each of the theories discussed in this chapter concerns the social transmission of prejudice to the individual: Each therefore proposes answers to the basic question of how individuals acquire the pattern of prejudice that is characteristic of their particular culture or social group.

This has been typically viewed as occurring through socialization, particularly in the sense of social learning from significant others in early life, and normative conformity. Together, these two processes provide powerful explanations of how individuals acquire and internalize prejudiced attitudes from significant others and their social groups. A good deal of evidence was reviewed, indicating that early learning powerfully influences the intergroup attitudes of children, though its actual importance in the case of adults' attitudes is difficult to gauge. Normative conformity pressures may directly induce compliance with prejudiced norms, which can result in their internalization, and, in addition, provide a set of social contingencies and sanctions that shore up, maintain, and reinforce such internalized beliefs.

The plausibility of conformity as a cause of prejudice has been supported by dramatic experimental demonstrations of the power of group pressure to influence individual behavior. However, although extensive field research on the influence of conformity on social attitudes can be cited, this research has serious methodological shortcomings. These, it was argued, seem to preclude definitive conclusions about conformity as a major determinant of prejudice. Systematic research on conformity and prejudice is necessary in order to evaluate this perspective more adequately. This seems particularly important in societies that are very high in prejudice, where conformity has been thought to be of particular importance. Such research is discussed in Chapter 9.

Two further perspectives have received very little attention in the literature as far as explaining the social transmission of prejudice is concerned. First, personal contact with outgroup members has been generally discussed in the context of prejudice reduction. However, ample evidence exists indicating that certain kinds of personal contact experiences with outgroup members will create, reinforce, or intensify prejudice against those groups. It was argued that the kind of personal contact encounters that would be experienced with outgroup members would be largely determined by the macrosocial conditions of interaction and contact between the groups. Thus, these broader social structural conditions would influence prejudice in individuals through structuring the personal contact situations in which members of the different groups encounter each other.

Second, it was argued that merely being a member of a particular social group could generate certain perceptions and attributions about outgroups, resulting in prejudice against them. Thus, ingroup members could share a perception of certain common interests that might be threatened by an outgroup. Alternatively, ingroup members could perceive outgroups as lower on socially valued dimensions. As a result, they would attribute traits and dispositions to these groups to account for their "inferiority." This can be viewed as an expression in the intergroup situation of the fundamental attribution error. In addition, whenever perceived group differences of this kind involve some kind of inequity or injustice to an outgroup, derogation and victim-blaming attributions could also result from a basic need to maintain a belief in a just world where people get what they deserve.

Finally, it was noted in Chapter 4 that prejudice in individuals is not simply a function of social influences. Individuals who are exposed to the same social influences conducive to prejudice may nevertheless differ in the degree to which they come to hold these prejudiced beliefs. Psychological factors seem to be important in determining individual susceptibility to such social influences. These individual-difference dimensions can be seen as modulating the degree to which individuals absorb prejudice from their social environment, forming a generalized predisposition or readiness for prejudice. These psychological dimensions are dealt with in the next chapter.

# 8

# Individual Differences
# and Prejudice

A number of theories are based on the idea that prejudice is not simply absorbed from the social environment but is also influenced by attributes of the individual. Prejudiced attitudes can therefore, at least in part, be explained in terms of factors within the prejudiced individual. Milner (1981) pointed out that this perspective seemed particularly compelling in the aftermath of World War II. Anti-Semitism in Nazi Germany and the nature of the holocaust had not been easily explicable in terms of rational self-interest and realistic social conflicts: "Explanations were therefore sought in the disturbed personality, for it was hardly conceivable that these could be the actions of normal men" (Milner, 1981, p. 106). The classic example is the theory of the authoritarian personality, which was probably the dominant psychological approach to prejudice during the 1950s.

The idea that prejudice may be influenced by factors within the individual has an important empirical basis. This is the finding that prejudice tends to be a generalized attitude. Thus, persons who report favorable attitudes toward some outgroups seem more likely to be favorable toward others. Conversely, persons who are hostile or prejudiced toward one outgroup tend also to have less favorable attitudes toward other outgroups or minorities. Empirically this has been documented by high positive correlations between attitudes to different outgroups. Such findings have been consistently reported in a number of studies using a wide diversity of samples and target groups (see, e.g., the studies reviewed by Harding et al., 1969, pp. 15–17).

Some early studies, such as Adorno et al.'s (1950) classic investigation of authoritarianism, found extremely high intercorrelations of prejudice toward different minority groups. For example, they reported a correlation of .74 between anti-Semitism and anti-black prejudice. However, their correlations, as Altemeyer (1981, pp. 117–146) elegantly demonstrated, were almost certainly inflated by the use of prejudice scales that were not balanced against acquiescence. Nevertheless, when psychometrically adequate measures of prejudice are used, the intercorrelation of attitudes toward different target groups, though reduced in magnitude, still remains a powerful one—typically around .50 (e.g., Bierly, 1985; Glock, Wuthnow, Piliavin, & Spencer, 1975; Prothro & Jensen, 1950; Prothro & Miles, 1952; Ray & Lovejoy, 1986).

Similar findings are evident from studies that use social distance scales. The social distance reported by individuals toward large numbers of other ethnic and national groups tends to be strongly intercorrelated (Fink, 1971; Hartley, 1946; Murphey & Likert, 1938). Hartley (1946) even used fictitious groups ("Danireans," "Pireneans," and "Wallonians") and found significant positive correlations between attitudes to real groups and these fictitious groups. Although Fink (1971) later reported that these correlations are very much attenuated when subjects can use a neutral category in rating fictitious groups, this does not really invalidate the significance of the original findings as far as the generality of prejudice is concerned. The point is that when subjects are not allowed to use neutral ratings and are forced to choose, generality emerges clearly.

The degree of covariation between attitudes to quite different groups is strong enough for it to be feasible to measure prejudice as a generalized disposition. For example, scales can be constructed with items referring to feelings about a variety of different outgroups or minorities which show excellent internal consistency. A number of such scales have been developed and used. Of these, Adorno's antiminorities scale (Adorno et al., 1950) and the "xenophobia" scale of Campbell and McCandless (1951) are probably the best known. A more recent generalized prejudice scale was developed by Altemeyer (1988a, pp. 108–110). The twenty items of this scale, which refer to a number of ethnic groups such as Jews, Chinese, native Canadian Indians, West Indians, Filipinos, Asians, blacks, Metis, Pakistanis, Arabs, and Sikhs, show an average interitem correlation of about .25. This indicates a very high degree of generality over an extremely diverse collection of outgroups.

Certain empirical findings seem to complicate or even refute the idea that prejudice may be generalized, however. Prothro (1952), for example, in a study in the U.S. South, used his data to show that many of his subjects were very antiblack yet not at all anti-Semitic. In fact, a number of his subjects were both antiblack and quite positive toward Jews. This finding, which has been confirmed in a number of other studies, has often been interpreted as contrary to the idea that prejudice tends to be generalized (Ehrlich, 1973; Rhyne, 1962; Seeman, 1981).

In one sense, this criticism clearly holds. Prothro's findings do refute the idea of "generalized negativity" in an absolute sense—that is, in the sense that someone who is negative to one group would tend to be negative toward other groups. This interpretation of the idea of the generality of prejudice is one that has been commonly presented in the literature. Gordon Allport (1954), for example, asserted that "one of the facts of which we are most certain is that people who reject one out-group will tend to reject other out-groups. If a person is anti-Jewish, he is likely to be anti-Catholic, anti-Negro, anti any out-group" (p. 68).

The idea of the generality of prejudice can be interpreted differently, however, in a relative rather than in an absolute sense. In this sense it is not at all inconsistent with Prothro's findings. According to this interpretation, individuals do not tend to be literally negative (or positive) to all outgroups, but they do tend to be negative (or positive) relative to the prevailing attitude in their social environment. Thus, more "negative" persons would not necessarily be negative to any specific group, but would tend to be less favorable toward it than are most of their compatriots. Consequently, if the normative attitude to an outgroup was very positive, such persons would be moderately positive; if the normative attitude was one of indifference, they would be somewhat negative; and if the norm was one of dislike, they might be virulently hostile. In essence, this interpretation means, not that individuals would have the same attitude to different outgroups, but that the rank ordering of individual attitudes toward different outgroups would be similar. Thus, as Prothro's findings show, it is possible for most subjects in a sample to be antiblack and pro-Jewish, yet for there to be a strong positive correlation between the two attitudes. The point is that in a sample that was generally very antiblack and fairly pro-Jewish, those persons who were more antiblack would tend to be less pro-Jewish.

The distinction between these two interpretations of the idea of the generality of prejudice has important implications about the kind of process that might underlie and cause this generality. For example, the idea of generalized negativity in an absolute sense implies some kind of inner need or disposition to dislike or be hostile to outgroups, which is relatively independent of the social environment. On the other hand, a generalized tendency to be less (or more) favorable to outgroups in a relative sense suggests a conceptualization in terms of susceptibility or vulnerability.

Consistent individual differences in a generalized susceptibility to prejudice would result in persons being differentially receptive to the prejudiced attitudes that they encounter in their social environment. More precisely, such a susceptibility could be seen as modulating the impact of social cues or influences toward prejudice (as described in Chapter 7) on the individual in any particular social setting. Thus, the social cues for prejudice in a particular environment could be very low (resulting in a generally favorable attitude toward a particular outgroup) or very high (resulting in a generally negative attitude toward that outgroup). Whatever the nature of these cues in any setting, however, highly susceptible persons will be more receptive to them than are less susceptible persons. Thus, consistent with Prothro's findings, persons highly susceptible to prejudice may be quite favorable to groups to whom the feeling in their milieu is generally very positive. However, they would tend to be less positive than persons with a low susceptibility to prejudice.

The existence of reasonably stable and consistent individual differences in susceptibility to prejudice has often been explained in purely psychological terms using concepts such as traits or personality. This interpretation has been particularly common when the findings indicating that prejudice tends to be generalized have been interpreted in an absolute sense, as reflecting some kind of inner need or disposition to be specifically hostile or negative to outgroups. Thus, according to Seeman (1981):

No theory of prejudice that depends on contact experience and its generalization can account for these results demonstrating high cross-group intolerance.... such a range of cross-group negativisms can hardly be either experiential or rational, hence one must look to deep-lying personality for their source: what binds together these illogical antagonisms is their psycho-logic. (p. 382)

The inference that personality dynamics creating a need for prejudice must underlie the generality of prejudice has been widely accepted (Adorno et al., 1950; Ashmore, 1970; Babad et al., 1983; Bagley et al., 1979; Harding et al., 1969; Simpson & Yinger, 1985). However, as soon as the generality of prejudice is no longer viewed in absolute terms, it becomes apparent that this inference may be an overly restrictive one. There is no reason why any stable individual-difference dimension might not underlie a generalized susceptibility to prejudice. Such a susceptibility could be acquired as a result of exposure to particular social contexts or experiences (Hyman & Sheatsley, 1954; Rhyne, 1962). Hyman and Sheatsley (1954), for example, have stated that "certainly, consistency must be explained, not in terms of the specific objects of prejudice, but as a generalized disposition within the person—but the organizing factor behind this generalized disposition may very well be societal" (p. 112). Thus, social factors indexing stable individual differences—such as social status, social mobility, occupation, education, urbanicity, and so forth—might also underlie generalized tendencies to tolerance or intolerance of outgroups (Brown, 1965; Hyman & Sheatsley, 1954).

A number of specific social and psychological individual difference dimensions have been identified as possible influences on individual susceptibility to prejudice. These include frustration (Dollard et al., 1939), poor psychological adjustment and low self-esteem (Ehrlich, 1973), political and religious belief systems (Allport, 1954; Glock et al., 1975), status (Sherif, 1967) and other social or experiential factors (Hyman & Wright, 1979), cognitive factors (Rokeach et al., 1960), and authoritarianism (Adorno et al., 1950). The nature of these factors, their presumed role in affecting prejudice, and the evidence pertaining to their effects will be reviewed in the remainder of this chapter.

## FRUSTRATION

Hostility stemming from the ubiquitous frustrations of social life, which is then displaced onto outgroups, has been viewed as a general causal mechanism or process underlying prejudice. This theory was discussed in Chapter 5. A review of experimental research indicated that this proposition had not been unambiguously supported (Cowen et al., 1959; Feshbach & Singer, 1957; Lever, 1976; Lindzey, 1950; Miller & Bugelski, 1948; Silverman & Kleinman, 1967; Stagner & Congdon, 1955; Stricker, 1963; Weatherley, 1961). However, besides providing a general theory to account for the seeming universality of prejudice, or at least its potential in all social groups, this theory can also account for individual differences in prejudice. Thus, persons who are chronically high in frustration should be more susceptible to prejudice than are those who typically experience little frustration.

A good deal of correlational research can be cited which has relevance to this issue. The findings are not entirely consistent, however, and the measures of frustration used are often very indirect. For example, several frequently cited studies concern the response of victims of prejudice to other minority groups. Thus, Catholics in the United States who felt they had been victims of discrimination expressed more prejudice against Jews and blacks (Allport & Kramer, 1946; Rosenblith, 1949). Similarly, Gordon in 1943 found that Jewish subjects who reported they had experienced anti-Semitic prejudice tended to be more prejudiced against blacks. Although these studies seem confirmatory, the extent to which the experience of prejudice or discrimination can be regarded as indicative of frustration is rather problematic. Certainly other responses, such as anxiety, depression, or reduced self-esteem, seem as likely. Moreover, Ashmore and DelBoca (1976) pointed out that Jews in the United States, despite experiencing more prejudice than Protestants or Catholics, nevertheless show less prejudice overall against blacks.

A number of other findings can be mentioned. An American survey by Campbell (1947) found that those who were dissatisfied with their economic condition were higher in anti-Semitism. Glock et al. (1975) in their study of U.S. adolescents in three communities found that socioeconomic and academic deprivation was significantly associated with antiblack and anti-Semitic prejudice. Unfortunately, their study did not include more direct measures of experienced frustration. Two other studies used a variety of indices of general dissatisfaction, deprivation, and angry feelings but reported inconsistent findings. Although some of these measures did correlate with prejudice, most did not (Marx, 1967; Morse & Allport, 1952). A large-scale study of students attending eleven racially mixed schools in a U.S. city found little association between racial prejudice and black and white students' satisfaction with their home and school life. However, this study did find strong correlations between prejudice and aggressiveness in both racial groups (Patchen et al., 1977).

Downward social mobility can be regarded as a chronically frustrating experience. Bettelheim and Janowitz (1964), in their study of U.S. veterans of World War II, concluded that:

The highest degree of association established in this study [was that] between intolerance on the one hand and feelings of deprivation and downward social mobility on the other. The deprivations so highly associated with intolerance were . . . ones very closely related to adverse economic experiences, or a fear of their recurrence. (p. 278)

Seven other American studies conducted between 1950 and 1964, which were reviewed by Bettelheim and Janowitz, produced a fairly consistent pattern of findings that indicated an association between downward mobility and prejudice. More recently, Bagley and Verma (1979) have also obtained supportive findings from a British study. However, there have been some contrary findings. Hodge and Treiman (1966) in the United States; Seeman, Rohan, and Argeriou (1966) in Sweden; and Seeman (1977) in France and the United States found no association between downward mobility and increased prejudice.

The concept of relative deprivation refers to dissatisfaction due not to deprivation in any absolute sense but to the perception of deprivation relative to some comparison person or group (cf. Gurr, 1970). Thus, relative deprivation can also be viewed as inducing frustration. In fact, many of the findings pertaining to downward mobility, dissatisfaction, feelings of deprivation, or discrimination could be interpreted in terms of relative deprivation. Several studies have used more direct measures of relative deprivation and found associations with prejudice (Appelgryn & Nieuwoudt, 1988; Tripathi & Srivastava, 1981; Vanneman & Pettigrew, 1972). However, these findings are not very clear-cut or consistent. For example, there are indications that fraternal relative deprivation (relative to an outgroup) may be more important in determining intergroup attitudes and prejudice than is egoistic relative deprivation (relative to other ingroup members) (cf. Guimond & Dube-Simard, 1983; Vanneman & Pettigrew, 1972). It has been argued, therefore, that any effects of relative deprivation on prejudice are probably mediated by cognitive social comparison processes, rather than by frustration per se, as egoistic relative deprivation should create as much frustration as that created by fraternal relative deprivation (Guimond & Dube-Simard, 1983). Taylor (1980) has also challenged Vanneman and Pettigrew's (1972) conclusion that there is a link between fraternal relative deprivation and antiblack prejudice in American blue-collar workers after a reanalysis of their data. Moreover, the South African study by Appelgryn and Nieuwoudt (1988) indicated that relative deprivation was related to the antiwhite attitudes of black subjects, but not to the outgroup attitudes (toward blacks, Indians, Coloureds, or English-speaking whites) of their white Afrikaans-speaking subjects.

Finally, there has been a fairly consistent finding that aggressiveness and hostility are associated with prejudice. For example, a number of laboratory studies of aggression have found that highly prejudiced subjects behave in a generally more aggressive manner (irrespective of whether their targets are members of the disliked group or not) than less prejudiced subjects (Donnerstein, Donnerstein, Simon, & Ditrichs, 1972; Leonard & Taylor, 1981; Rogers, 1983). Studies using self-report measures of aggressiveness have shown a similar relationship (Genthner & Taylor, 1973). However, aggressiveness need not necessarily have been induced by frustration. The tendency for more prejudiced persons to be more aggressive and hostile could quite easily be due to factors other than frustration. For example, Altemeyer (1988a) has shown that the heightened aggression and hostility characterizing the authoritarian personality syndrome seems to reflect a generalized perception of the world as a dangerous and threatening place that is learned in the course of socialization and is not due to frustration. Since authoritarianism is related to prejudice (Adorno et al., 1950; Altemeyer, 1981, 1988a; Meloen, 1983; Meloen, Hagendoorn, Raaijmakers, & Visser, 1988), this could account for an association between aggressiveness and prejudice without the concept of frustration having to be invoked at all.

Overall, therefore, it is not easy to draw definitive conclusions from this research. Not only are the findings often inconsistent, but also a number of methodological weaknesses characterize the studies. The most important would appear to be that frustration, as indicated by angry and resentful affect, has rarely been measured directly. In addition, the scales and items used to measure concepts such as deprivation and dissatisfaction are themselves often of uncertain reliability and validity (cf. Taylor, 1980).

In general, however, there does appear to be a tendency for individuals who are deprived, downwardly mobile, and dissatisfied to be higher in prejudice, at least in North America and Britain. It is not at all clear, though, that this is because these individuals are frustrated. These findings could just as well indicate the effects of other factors, such as anxiety, depression, low self-esteem, alienation, or a generalized negativity and pessimism. Finally, this tendency does not appear consistently. This could be due to the methodological weaknesses of the studies. It is also possible that the relationship of these factors and prejudice may be a complex one that is moderated by other variables: That is, frustration or dissatisfaction might predispose individuals to greater prejudice under certain conditions but not under others. For example, Ashmore and DelBoca (1976) argued that frustration may affect intergroup behavior only when clear social norms legitimize a scapegoat group.

This suggests that there could be a strong relationship between frustration and racial prejudice among white South Africans. However, this relationship has not emerged from the research. For example, several South African studies have found nonsignificant correlations between whites' racial attitudes and measures of frustration, dissatisfaction, or relative deprivation (Appelgryn & Nieuwoudt, 1988; Duckitt, 1988; Lever, 1976). Two explanations have been proposed. One, by Orpen (1975), is that when prejudice is normative in a society, as racism has been among white South Africans, these prejudiced attitudes will be largely determined by conformity to these norms of prejudice and will show little if any relationship with psychological factors, such as frustration or authoritarianism. This issue will be considered in detail in Chapter 9. The second possible explanation is that frustration (and other negative feelings, such as low self-esteem) may influence prejudice only when individuals experience some degree of direct equal-status interpersonal contact with outgroup members under either competitive conditions or conditions that make intergroup distinctions highly salient (Duckitt, 1988). In this situation, individuals can easily direct their negative feelings at outgroup members. By structuring an unequal-status contact society in South Africa (cf. Chapter 6), Apartheid has largely precluded such situations. In general, therefore, it would seem that more research of a methodologically sounder nature is needed to resolve issues such as these.

## PSYCHOLOGICAL ADJUSTMENT

It has frequently been argued that poor psychological adjustment, as manifest in anxiety, insecurity, low self-esteem, alienation, and neuroticism, might predispose individuals to prejudice (Allport, 1954; Bagley et al., 1979; Ehrlich, 1973; Levin & Levin, 1982; LeVine & Campbell, 1972). If so, this could provide an alternative account for many of the findings noted in the previous section. Bettelheim and Janowitz (1964), for example, suggested that downward mobility and deprivation could have affected prejudice through creating anxiety and insecurity.

Several theoretical frameworks propose a relationship between psychological adjustment and prejudice. The most prominent are Ehrlich's (1973) "principle of self-congruity," social comparison theory, and psychoanalytically based accounts in terms of ego defense. The principle of self-congruity (Ehrlich, 1973) proposes that individuals have a generalized attitude to self and others: "Positive self attitudes provide the basis for the acceptance of others; negative self attitudes for the rejection of others" (Ehrlich, 1973, p. 130). Low self-esteem thus predisposes the individual to generally negative attitudes toward others, one aspect of which would be prejudice against outgroups and minorities.

The most direct application of social comparison theory to the issue of how self-esteem might influence prejudice has been Wills's (1981) principle of downward comparison. This suggests that persons experiencing negative affect "can increase their subjective well-being through comparison with a less fortunate other" (p. 245). Downward social comparisons can also be effected by derogating an outgroup relative to the ingroup or by focusing on an outgroup that is relatively much worse off than the ingroup. Thus, individuals who are experiencing ego threat, negative affect, and lowered self-esteem can try to enhance their well-being through prejudice. Almost exactly the same idea has been proposed by psychoanalytically orientated theorists. For example, Jahoda (1960) argued that prejudice is ego defensive and functions to defend the individual against underlying anxiety or psychopathology.

An interesting problem is what correlations these approaches would predict between prejudice and well-being or self-esteem. In the case of self-congruity theory, this is straightforward: Low self-esteem should be directly associated with prejudice. The issue is not quite as clear-cut in the case of the downward comparison and psychoanalytic approaches. On the one hand, it can be argued, as Jahoda (1960) has, that these approaches imply that adopting prejudiced attitudes will increase well-being and self-esteem in ego-threatened persons. Therefore, prejudiced persons would not necessarily be higher in overt anxiety or neuroticism. On the other hand, it has been more commonly argued that persons who experience chronically low self-esteem or negative affect should be more motivated than others to engage in downward social comparisons or to defend their egos through prejudice (Bagley et al., 1979; Crocker et al., 1987; Wills, 1981). Thus, low self-esteem or well-being should be associated with higher prejudice.

### Experimental and Longitudinal Research

The downward comparison and psychoanalytic approaches are thus usually interpreted, as making exactly the same prediction about outgroup attitudes as Ehrlich's (1973) self-congruity theory. They expect persons with chronically low self-esteem or well-being to be more negative to outgroups. However, they make quite different predictions about ingroup attitudes. Self-congruity theory expects both attitudes to ingroup and outgroup to be negative. Downward comparison theory expects individuals to try and enhance their well-being by differentiating as much as possible between ingroup and outgroup in a manner that favors the ingroup. Thus outgroup derogation will not be accompanied by a similarly negative attitude to the ingroup. Several experimental studies have tested these predictions by allocating subjects high and low in self-esteem to arbitrary groups using Tajfel's (1981) minimal intergroup situation and comparing their evaluation of, or reaction to, ingroup and outgroup members (Crocker & Schwartz, 1985; Crocker et al., 1987). As expected, low self-esteem subjects were more negative to the minimal outgroup than were high self-esteem subjects. However, in support of the self-congruity perspective and contrary to downward comparison theory, the low self-esteem subjects tended to be more negative to their ingroups as well.

Some experimental research has also found downward comparison effects in response to experimental manipulations to reduce subjects' self-esteem and induce negative affect (usually involving some kind of failure feedback). However, these findings are complex. Only some subjects seem to react to failure by increasing ingroup favoritism (Crocker et al., 1987; Levin, 1969, cited in Levin & Levin, 1982). In addition, benevolent reactions of a paternalistic kind to outgroups are as likely to occur as is greater prejudice (Meindl & Lerner, 1984). It seems as though it may be persons with typically high levels of self-esteem who respond to failure with ingroup favoritism and not low self-esteem persons (Crocker et al., 1987). Presumably their high self-esteem stems at least partly from their successful use of such self-serving strategies. Moreover, ingroup favoritism in this research occurred through enhancing the ingroup rather than by derogating the outgroup, so that the reduced self-esteem did not necessarily increase prejudice per se.

The tendency for persons low in self-esteem to be more negative to outgroup members in minimal intergroup situations, therefore, does not seem to be caused by a downward comparison process. Instead, it appears to reflect a generalized negativity to others, irrespective of whether they are ingroup or outgroup members, stemming from chronic negative affect and low self-esteem. Although downward comparison effects do occur in response to ego threat, they appear to be complex and do not create the tendency for low self-esteem to be associated with prejudice, at least in these minimal intergroup situations.

Several longitudinal studies have also reported findings that indicate a link between self-esteem or negative affect and prejudice. Stephan and

Rosenfield (1978) found that increases in the self-esteem of high school students at desegregated schools over a two-year period were strongly correlated with positive change in racial attitudes. Bagley et al. (1979) used a counseling intervention designed to raise self-esteem in a sample of British high school students. They found that increases in self-esteem were significantly correlated with positive changes in these students' racial attitudes. Rubin (1967) similarly conducted sensitivity training with groups of adult Americans (mainly white-collar persons) and found that changes in self-acceptance were significantly correlated with decreases in prejudice. These findings do provide some corroboration in naturalistic contexts for the minimal intergroup experimental studies.

### Correlational Research

Many more studies have used purely correlational designs. A number of these studies have found significant tendencies for indices of anxiety, alienation, generalized maladjustment, and low self-esteem to be associated with higher prejudice. In contrast to the experimental and longitudinal research, however, these findings are not very consistent. A number of studies have found no association, and some, mainly in South Africa, have even reported significant correlations in the opposite direction—that is, tendencies for better psychological adjustment to be associated with greater prejudice.

Thus, several early studies found strong associations between anti-Semitic or antiblack prejudice and what was termed a threat-competition orientation or a "jungle weltanschauung" (Allport & Kramer, 1946; Martin, 1964; Martin & Westie, 1959; Rosenblith, 1949). The items assessing this "orientation" seem to describe a generalized cynicism, suspiciousness, pessimism, distrust, and hostility to others. Srole's (1956) anomia scale appears to measure a similar construct, described by Seeman (1975) as "alienation conceived as generalized unhappiness, negativism, or despair" (p. 5). A number of studies have reported positive correlations between this anomia scale and prejudice of around .40 or greater (Hamblin, 1962; McDill, 1961; Mulford, 1968; Roberts & Rokeach, 1956; Srole, 1956). In a few studies, however, the correlation was much weaker (e.g., around .20 in Lutterman & Middleton, 1970) or even nonsignificant (Knapp, 1976). Maykovich (1975) also did not find a significant association between antiblack prejudice and a short scale containing items written to assess distrust in people and general dissatisfaction. Middleton (1976), on the other hand, found consistent significant correlations between anomia and a number of indices of prejudice against a variety of target groups in a nationwide survey of nearly 2000 American adults. Although these correlations were rather weak, a three-item scale of unknown reliability was used to measure anomia.

Overall therefore, there does seem to be a tendency for alienation, as Srole has used the term, and prejudice to go together, at least in North America. The concept of anomia clearly has a good deal of correspondence with Ehrlich's (1973) idea of generalized negativity to others. It also corresponds with at least one of the components of Adorno et al.'s (1950) authoritarian personality syndrome ("destructiveness and cynicism"), as well as with Altemeyer's (1988a) recent finding that a generalized hostility stemming from a view of the world as a dangerous and threatening place underlies authoritarianism.

A number of other studies in the United States have examined the association between prejudice and various indices of psychic distress, with rather mixed findings. Ehrlich (1973) reviews three studies of children indicating that satisfaction with self was associated with more positive ethnic attitudes (Gough, Harris, Martin, & Edwards, 1950; Tabachnick, 1962; Trent, 1957). A number of studies of adults have similarly found significant correlations between either antiblack or anti-Semitic prejudice and measures of insecurity (Morse & Allport, 1952), anxiety (Cheson, Stricker, & Fry, 1970), morale (Marx, 1967), and self-esteem (Rubin, 1967). However, there have also been a number of contrary findings. Thus, although Prentice (1961) found consistently positive correlations between ethnocentrism and anxiety in three samples, these were mostly nonsignificant. Nonsignificant correlations have also been reported by Glock et al. (1975); Middleton (1976), in a large community sample; Moore, Hauk, and Denne (1984); and Serum and Myers (1970).

Evaluating these inconsistent American findings is not easy. Measures and samples differ and few studies control for potentially confounding variables such as social class, education, or intelligence. Moreover, the most common methodological problems of using small student samples, short ad hoc measures of uncertain validity (cf. Middleton, 1976), or failure to control other relevant variables seem fairly evenly distributed over supportive and nonsupportive studies. Unfortunately, the dearth of studies that use large community samples together with reasonably valid measures and adequate controls makes it difficult to explain these inconsistent findings.

There does, however, seem to be a slight trend in the American data for more recent studies to obtain weaker and nonsignificant correlations. If so, this might be related to the shift during the 1960s and 1970s in the United States toward overt public norms that strongly favor nondiscrimination, at least in the case of Jews and blacks (Schuman, Steeh, & Bobo, 1985). Cook (1972) had earlier shown in a classic experimental study that when highly prejudiced whites were placed in a very favorable interracial contact situation with strong social pressures to nondiscrimination, subjects with low self-esteem showed more positive racial attitude change, probably as a result of conforming more to the new norms of nondiscrimination. Perhaps low self-esteem persons have been more ready to conform to the changed public interracial norms in the United States (at least on self-report measures). If so, this could well obscure a more basic psychological tendency for low self-esteem persons to be more susceptible to prejudice in general, particularly if such a tendency was not a very powerful one.

In Britain, Bagley et al. (1979) reported an impressive series of seven studies using well-validated measures of racial prejudice, self-esteem, and neuroticism. Although the subjects were mainly high school students (and in one case polytechnic students), several reasonably large community samples were also used. Results indicated a consistent tendency for racist attitudes to be associated with neuroticism and low self-esteem. These correlations ranged from .17 to .41, with the average being around .30, indicating a weak to moderate association. A number of studies have been reported in the very different cultural context of India. Once again, although correlations have tended to be in the weak-to-moderate range, they have been impressively consistent. Religious prejudice (Hindu versus Moslem), caste prejudice, and prejudice against women have shown significant correlations with anxiety, poor self-image, and general maladjustment (Hassan, 1975, 1976, 1978; Sharan & Karan, 1974; Sinha & Hassan, 1975).

In the case of South Africa, a rather different pattern of findings has emerged. Elsewhere, correlations between prejudice and maladjustment have been either positive or on occasion nonsignificant. Among white South Africans, however, low self-esteem or poorer adjustment has consistently not been associated with racial prejudice (Duckitt, 1985a; Heaven, 1983b; Orpen, 1972a; Ray, 1988b). The two possible explanations that have been proposed for this finding were noted at the end of the previous section on frustration. First, Orpen (1972a, 1975) suggested that, because of its normative nature, racial prejudice among white South Africans would be determined primarily by conformity and would not be much influenced by psychological factors such as low self-esteem or frustration, an explanation that will be considered in more detail in the next chapter. Second, it has also been suggested that individuals who experience chronic negative affect would be more likely to direct that affect toward outgroup members under conditions of either direct equal-status interpersonal contact of a competitive nature or conditions in which intergroup distinctions were made highly salient, conditions that would exist in the multiracial British schools studied by Bagley et al. (1979) but not in South Africa (Duckitt, 1988).

### Conclusions

Overall, there is a good deal of evidence that low self-esteem, anxiety, alienation, and other indicators of negative affect and psychological maladjustment might predispose individuals to prejudice. The strongest evidence for this derives from longitudinal studies showing that changes in self-esteem are accompanied by changes in prejudice and from experimental studies using minimal intergroup situations. The latter studies also suggest that the increased susceptibility of persons with chronically low self-esteem to prejudice is part of a syndrome of generalized negativity to self and others, as Ehrlich (1973) proposed.

Correlational research, of which there has been a great deal, has not been quite so consistent. Most of these studies have shown weak to moderate correlations between indicators of maladjustment and prejudice. However, a number of studies, particularly more recent research in the United States, have reported nonsignificant findings. In addition, studies of white South Africans have also found no association between low self-esteem or various indices of psychological maladjustment and racial prejudice. It seems possible that superficial conformity to change in social norms in the United States and adjustment to long-established and entrenched norms of prejudice in South Africa might account for some of these discrepancies in the correlational literature. Research using large community samples, well-validated measures, and controls for other relevant variables, which could also examine the role of potential moderators such as the nature of the prevailing conditions of intergroup contact or the degree to which prejudice is normatively entrenched in a group, seems necessary to clarify these inconsistencies.

## POLITICAL AND RELIGIOUS BELIEFS

Religious and political belief systems may influence individuals' proneness to prejudice. A good deal of research suggests that religious involvement and activity might be related to prejudice. Similarly, the left-right dichotomy in politics, typically articulated in terms of liberalism and conservatism, also seems to be associated with attitudes to outgroups and minorities.

### Religion and Prejudice

Research on religion and prejudice has focused almost exclusively on Christian religions. Because most of this research has been conducted in North America, many studies have also included Jewish persons. However, very little systematic research appears to have been done on prejudice and other faiths such as Buddhism, Islam, and Hinduism, despite their global prominence. This means that whatever empirical generalizations can be made about religion and prejudice may well be applicable only to the Judeo-Christian religions.

A basic and quite consistent finding is that church members tend to be more prejudiced than nonmembers, irrespective of the target of prejudice (Argyle & Beit-Hallahmi, 1975; Gorsuch & Aleshire, 1974). Denominational differences in prejudice have also been reported, but the pattern has not been very consistent. Perhaps the most consistent findings in this respect have been for very strict and fundamentalist Protestant churches and sects to be most ethnocentric (e.g., Triandis & Triandis, 1960) and for Jewish persons to be least ethnocentric (e.g., Allport & Kramer, 1946). Even the latter finding is not entirely clear-cut, however, since some very conservative Jewish groups can also be highly ethnocentric (Triandis & Triandis, 1960). In addition, American Jews tend to score very low on all measures of religious activity and belief compared with other groups (Argyle & Beit-Hallahmi, 1975), a factor that might contribute to their low ethnocentrism. As far as Catholics and most larger Protestant churches are concerned, denominational differences in prejudice are not clear and tend to vary by region or the target of prejudice (Argyle & Beit-Hallahmi, 1975).

Although the tendency for church members to be more prejudiced than nonmembers has emerged consistently, the relationship between religious involvement and prejudice does not appear to be a simple linear one. Most studies suggest a curvilinear relationship, with those church members who are most religiously active and involved being less prejudiced than those who are relatively uninvolved or only moderately involved. For example, of the twenty-five studies reviewed by Gorsuch and Aleshire (1974), which reported data enabling a test of the curvilinear hypothesis, twenty conformed to this pattern, with both the nonreligious and most highly religious subjects being the least prejudiced. This pattern has also been reported for a sample of English-speaking white South African students by van den Berghe (1962).

One attempt to account for this apparently paradoxical finding has been in terms of the idea that there might be different kinds of religious attitude and involvement. The implication here is that those who are highly involved in their religion might differ from those who are less involved in terms of a basic religious orientation that would also result in their being less prejudiced. The most frequently invoked distinction in this respect has been that made by Gordon Allport (1966) between intrinsic and extrinsic religious orientations. An extrinsic orientation involves religious belief as a means to other primarily instrumental and utilitarian ends. Thus, extrinsics "find religion useful in a variety of ways to provide security and solace, sociability and distraction, status and self-justification" (Allport & Ross, 1967, p. 434). An intrinsic orientation, on the other hand, involves religion as an end in itself, the "master motive" in life, a creed that the individual has fully internalized and lives by. Initially, the intrinsic and extrinsic distinction was viewed as a single bipolar continuum with the superficial adherent at the extrinsic pole and the "true believer" at the intrinsic pole. Allport (1966) felt that "one of these orientations (the extrinsic) is entirely compatible with prejudice; the other (the intrinsic) rules out enmity, contempt, and bigotry" (p. 456).

These expectations were not all confirmed by later research, which has used self-report scales to measure extrinsic and intrinsic orientations, most notably those of Feagin (1964) and Allport and Ross (1967). First, extrinsic and intrinsic orientations have been shown not to be two opposite poles of a single dimension but seem to represent two separate and largely independent dimensions. Donahue (1985) thus noted that the mean correlation between intrinsic and extrinsic subscales over thirty-four published studies was only − .06. Second, while scores on the extrinsic scale tend to be positively related to various indices of prejudice, intrinsic scores seem to be unrelated to prejudice. Thus, Donahue's (1985) meta-analysis indicated mean correlations with prejudice of .34 for extrinsic measures and − .05 for intrinsic measures.

Contrary to Allport's expectation, therefore, a tendency for persons who are high in intrinsic religious orientation to be less prejudiced than those low in intrinsic orientation, which could help account for the curvilinear relationship between religious involvement and prejudice, does not seem to hold. On the other hand, the tendency for persons high on extrinsic orientation to be more prejudiced does fit, since such persons would probably not be the most deeply involved and active in their religion. However, the validity of these conclusions has not yet been definitively established; certain problems with the research on intrinsic and extrinsic religious orientations and prejudice need to be mentioned.

First, these scales are typically not balanced against acquiescence, and this could quite conceivably influence their correlations with other variables. Second, the reliability of the scales, particularly the very widely used extrinsic scale of Allport and Ross (1967), has been found to be very low (Altemeyer, 1988a). Third, these studies—and, indeed, almost all studies on religion and prejudice—have used rather crude, obvious, and traditional self-report measures of prejudice. McConahay and Hough (1976) used a more subtle and covert measure of prejudice (the symbolic racism scale) and found a positive correlation with the intrinsic scale. Subjects higher in intrinsic religious orientation were more prejudiced. This effect was not clearly replicated in two other studies using covert or behavioral measures of prejudice, although these studies did find that persons higher on the intrinsic scale and those most religiously involved and active appear to be strongly motivated to seem unprejudiced to others (Batson, Flink, Schoenrade, Fultz, & Pych, 1986; Batson, Naifeh, & Pate, 1978). If so, the curvilinear relationship between prejudice and religious involvement might be artifactual and not appear when more sophisticated and subtle indicators of prejudice are used.

Another dimension of religious orientation is that of religious orthodoxy or fundamentalism, which appears to be relatively independent of both the intrinsic and extrinsic dimensions (Donahue, 1985; Feagin, 1964). Orthodoxy or fundamentalism has consistently been found to be associated with prejudice (Donahue, 1985; Gorsuch & Aleshire, 1974; Webster & Stewart, 1973). That is, the more orthodox tend to be more prejudiced.

Overall, therefore, it is not yet clear whether religion in general or only certain kinds of religious orientation are associated with prejudice. On the basis of the evidence thus far, the latter proposition seems more likely and is certainly more widely accepted in the literature. Attempts to explain why religious adherence, or certain kinds of religious adherence, are associated with prejudice can be broadly divided into three categories: First, religious adherence may directly or indirectly cause a generalized proneness to prejudice; second, religion may attract persons who are already predisposed to prejudice; and third, the association of religion and prejudice may merely reflect conformity to two different and causally unrelated belief systems, which both happen to be socially normative.

In the first case, several ways in which religious belief or socialization could cause prejudice have been suggested. For example, Argyle and Beit-Hallahmi (1975) noted religion's role in "unifying the community of believers around a consensus of values, while at the same time making in-group and out-group distinctions which contribute to social divisions" (pp. 115–116). Altemeyer (1988a) pointed out that religious training may emphasize obedience to supernatural (and ecclesiastical) authority, encourage conventionalism, and inculcate self-righteousness and superiority toward nonbelievers—factors that are directly linked to authoritarianism. An emphasis on the exclusive access to divine truth and the importance of unquestioning faith similarly relates to dogmatism. These explanations therefore see religion as either causing prejudice directly or influencing it indirectly by causing authoritarianism or dogmatism.

In the second case, it may be argued that religion does not cause prejudice directly or indirectly but attracts persons who are already prone to prejudice. Thus, authoritarian personalities and dogmatic or rigid cognitive styles could predispose individuals to both prejudice and religion (Adorno et al., 1950; Allen & Spilka, 1967; Rokeach et al., 1960), particularly to more fundamentalist and extrinsic religious orientations. Both the above two explanations see religious persons as being more susceptible to prejudice. The difference rests in the causalities involved.

In the first case, religion causes the susceptibility to prejudice (either directly or by causing authoritarianism or dogmatism). In the second case, cognitive or personality factors such as authoritarianism or dogmatism cause both religious adherence and prejudice.

In the third case, it may be argued that religious adherents may be no more prone to prejudice than anyone else. Both religious adherence and prejudice may be expressions of conformity to social norms (Ehrlich, 1973; Gorsuch & Aleshire, 1974; Orpen, 1975). That is, since religious adherence is socially conventional, more conforming persons, or persons who are more socially integrated and therefore have greater exposure to conformity pressures, will tend to be more religious. In societies where prejudice is also normative, such persons would be more prejudiced as well. This implies the prediction that the more normatively entrenched prejudice is in a society, the stronger should be the association between conventional religious adherence and prejudice. Evidence on this point is not consistent. For example, in comparisons of less prejudiced Northern and more prejudiced Southern communities in the United States, Pettigrew (1959) reported supportive findings, whereas Middleton (1976) did not. Thus, it is not yet clear whether religion or certain religious orientations involve a generalized susceptibility to prejudice or whether the covariation between religion and prejudice is caused by conformity to social norms. This question will be considered in more detail in Chapter 9 in terms of the broader issue of how social and psychological factors interrelate in the determination of prejudice.

## Sociopolitical Beliefs and Prejudice

It is widely accepted that social, political, and economic beliefs and attitudes tend to be organized into reasonably coherent clusters or patterns. Attitudes toward outgroups and minorities also form part of this patterning. The degree to which sociopolitical beliefs are ideologically organized and the way in which they are actually structured has, however, occasioned some disagreement. One view, perhaps the majority one, is that sociopolitical beliefs cluster into one basic bipolar left-right dimension with one pole usually labeled conservatism and the other liberalism or radicalism (Comrey & Newmeyer, 1965; McClosky, 1958; Wilson, 1973). A good deal of research based on factor or cluster analyses of large numbers of social belief and attitude items seems to support this position. These studies typically generate a number of first-order factors or clusters which then factor into a single second-order dimension (Comrey & Newmeyer, 1965; Wilson, 1973). Thus, Comrey and Newmeyer (1965), using American data, found:

At the radical end of the continuum we have belief in the welfare state, powerful federal government, pacifism, world government, racial tolerance, and rapid social change. On the conservative end of the continuum, we have belief in severe treatment of criminals, capital punishment, religion, moral censorship, and service to country. (p. 367)

The idea that sociopolitical attitudes are unidimensionally structured has been questioned, however. Some research, for example, has found relatively little ideological consistency in individuals' sociopolitical attitudes and beliefs, particularly among persons who are low in education and political awareness (Converse, 1964). It has also been argued, once again on the basis of factor-analytic findings, that social-political attitudes may be better viewed as multi- rather than unidimensional. Three views have been particularly prominent in this respect, with each proposing that social attitudes are organized in terms of two independent dimensions.

First, Eysenck (1954) suggested a two-factor approach with a radicalism-conservatism dimension superimposed on an orthogonal personality-based dimension of tough- versus tendermindedness. The evidence that Eysenck originally cited in support of this view has been very severely criticized (for reviews see Altemeyer, 1981, pp. 80–89; Brown, 1965, pp. 526–541). However, some more recent research has supported a similar two-factor approach (Goertzel, 1987). Second, economic liberalism-conservatism has been distinguished from noneconomic or social liberalism-conservatism (Campbell, Converse, Miller, & Stokes, 1960: Lipset, 1963). Third, Kerlinger (1984) reported factor analytic evidence indicating that liberalism (consisting of egalitarian and humanitarian attitudes) and conservatism (consisting of economic conservatism and traditional beliefs about authority and religion) may be two quite separate and independent dimensions.

It seems clear, therefore, that the degree and nature of structuring in social attitudes has not yet been definitively established. One possibility is that the degree to which social attitudes are structured might be a function of the samples being investigated (Mann, 1970; Tygart, 1984). While subjects low in political awareness and activity might show little ideological consistency, the social attitudes and beliefs of those who are more politically aware and active might fit a unidimensional model. Some evidence consistent with this has been reported by Tygart (1984), who demonstrated unidimensionality of political liberalism and conservatism in a sample of persons highly interested and active in politics.

To the extent that social attitudes tend to be ideologically organized or patterned, attitudes toward outgroups and minorities seem to form part of this patterning. Thus, racial tolerance, low ethnocentrism, support for integration, opposition to segregation, belief in the equality of women, tolerance of homosexuals, and so forth tend to be associated with liberalism and radicalism rather than with conservatism. Less favorable attitudes toward minorities and outgroups, on the other hand, are usually associated with conservatism (Adorno et al., 1950; Comrey & Newmeyer, 1965; Kerlinger, 1984; McClosky, 1958; Wilson, 1973). The evidence in this respect is literally overwhelming. A number of studies in South Africa have also found positive correlations between sociopolitical conservatism and prejudice (Mynhardt, 1980; Orpen, 1972a; Spangenberg & Nel, 1983).

This is not to say that there are no ambiguities in the literature. There are, and these seem particularly likely when separate facets of liberalism and conservatism are examined. For example, among white Afrikaners in South Africa certain socialist beliefs (economic radicalism) seem to be associated with greater antiblack prejudice (Heaven, 1983a). Some studies have also found patriotism to be uncorrelated with prejudice (Forbes, 1985; Ray & Lovejoy, 1986). Such anomalous findings may stem from the multidimensionality of conservatism or from a lack of ideological consistency in the samples studied.

An important issue that has not yet been clarified is that of why conservatism and prejudice should be associated. Clearly, this requires a theory of conservatism that elucidates the nature of the organizing principle underlying this ideological organization of attitudes and beliefs. There have been surprisingly few attempts to tackle this issue. Wilson's (1973) theory proposes that a basic orientation to change underlies the liberalism-conservatism dimension and provides it with its ideological cohesion. This is seen as stemming from a personality trait reflecting fear of uncertainty. On this basis, the tendency for conservatives to be more ethnocentric can be attributed to a fear of people who are different (Wilson, 1973; Wilson & Shutte, 1973). Another possibility is that a basic attitude to others underlies the liberalism-conservatism organization of attitudes. A number of characterizations of this dimension (cf. McClosky, 1958; Tomkins, 1963) imply that it may arise from basically positive versus negative beliefs about the nature of man. As Ray (1974) pointed out, liberalism sees man as inherently good, while conservatism involves a fundamentally "cynical or hardened view of mankind" (p. xxiv). Such a generally negative view of others could account for the tendency for conservatism to be associated with greater negativity to outgroups and minorities.

In general, therefore, it seems well established that prejudice is related to sociopolitical ideology. To the extent that social attitudes are structured along a left-right or liberal-conservative dimension, greater prejudice and ethnocentrism appear to be associated with the conservative rather than the liberal pole. However, while conservatism does seem to predispose persons to more prejudiced attitudes to outgroups, the reason why this should be so and the nature of the causalities involved have not yet been definitively clarified. Thus, it is not clear that it is conservative ideology itself which predisposes to prejudice, or whether some other underlying or associated factor, such as generalized cynicism and a negative attitude toward others, determines both conservatism and prejudice.

## STATUS, EDUCATION, AND OTHER SOCIAL CHARACTERISTICS

A number of social or sociodemographic characteristics seem to be related to prejudice. The most prominent of these are education, socioeconomic status, social mobility, urbanicity, and geographic mobility. These factors can be viewed as affecting prejudice by influencing individual susceptibility to prejudice—hence their inclusion in this chapter—though other interpretations are also possible. In this section, the emphasis will be on reviewing the evidence linking these social variables with prejudice and on noting the various mechanisms that have been proposed to account for these relationships.

### Status and Prejudice

The concept of status is usually defined in terms of prestige or social ranking. In modern industrial societies it is typically measured as socioeconomic status (SES), a compound of educational level, occupational prestige, and income. In general, research has found SES to be negatively correlated with prejudice against outgroups and minorities (Bagley & Verma, 1979; Harding et al., 1969; Simpson & Yinger, 1985; Wuthnow, 1982). Thus, persons of higher SES tend to be less prejudiced. Effects reported for occupational prestige and income, when these were examined separately, have been similar though weaker and less consistent (Harding et al., 1969; Simpson & Yinger, 1985; Wuthnow, 1982). However, these effects often disappear or are very substantially reduced when level of education is controlled (Harding et al., 1969; Seeman, 1981; Wuthnow, 1982). Thus, most if not all the effect of SES as a compound variable, or of occupational prestige and income assessed separately on prejudice, may be due to the effect of education.

There are two reasons, however, why it may be premature to dismiss the correlations between SES and prejudice as solely due to education. First, the intercorrelations between education, income, and occupation are usually quite substantial. This means that partialing out effects due to education tends to remove a great deal of variance from variables such as income and occupational status that would lessen their capacity to show clear relationships with variables such as prejudice. Second, neither occupational prestige nor income is a pure measure of social status. While each provides some index of status, each also reflects a variety of other influences. It is interesting, therefore, that several studies that assessed status more directly, as an individual's rank in small-group contexts, have found significant relationships with prejudice.

Sherif and Sherif (1953), for example, in their classic research on intergroup relations using groups of boys attending summer camp, found that boys of lower status within their groups were more hostile to the outgroup than were those of higher status. Rabbie and Wilkens (1971) also found that low-status group members were more biased in favor of the ingroup, particularly under conditions of intergroup competition. These results are interesting and suggestive. However, they are based on only two studies, and the failure to obtain more convincing effects from macrosocial studies using indicators such as SES has not yet been clarified. As such, the best conclusion seems to be that the relationship between status and prejudice has not yet been definitively resolved. If such a relationship is indeed demonstrated, it may reflect a tendency for higher status persons to be more secure and confident and to have higher self-esteem, and therefore to have generally more positive attitudes toward others (Bagley & Verma, 1979). Alternatively, it could be because low status involves at least some degree of chronic frustration.

## Education and Prejudice

A number of empirical studies have shown that higher levels of formal education are associated with lower prejudice. This relationship has usually held up when potentially confounding factors such as occupational status or income are controlled. Most of the evidence reported in the literature comes from the United States and concerns antiblack and anti-Semitic attitudes (e.g., Hyman & Sheatsley, 1964; Marx, 1967; Middleton, 1976; Quinley & Glock, 1979; Selznick & Steinberg, 1969). This has been reinforced by findings on other target groups in other countries, such as Britain (Bagley & Verma, 1979), Germany (Schönbach et al., 1981; Wagner & Schönbach, 1984), Australia (Beswick & Hills, 1972), Holland (Bagley & Verma, 1979), and South Africa (Hampel & Krupp, 1977; Lever, 1980).

These findings, however, have been criticized. Questions have been raised over, first, the magnitude and consistency of the relationship between education and prejudice and, second, the meaning and significance of this relationship. In the former case, a comprehensive review of the relationship between education and prejudice in twenty-six American social surveys between 1948 and 1959 was published in 1961 (Stember, 1961). This review has been extremely influential and very widely cited. It generally supported a link between education and prejudice, particularly in respect of negative stereotypes, discriminatory policies, and nonintimate social contact. On the other hand, the findings were often weak and tended not to be entirely consistent. In certain instances, Stember noted that the highly educated even seemed more prejudiced. For example, they appeared more likely to "hold certain highly charged and derogatory stereotypes, favor informal discrimination in some areas of behavior, [and] reject intimate contacts with minority-group members" (p. 168).

Stember's review has been largely responsible for a widely accepted conclusion. This is the conclusion that while education is generally related to prejudice, the effects of education on prejudice are often weak, limited, inconsistent, or complex (cf. Ehrlich, 1973; Harding et al., 1969; Seeman, 1981; Simpson & Yinger, 1985). However, there are several reasons why Stember's conclusions may have been overstated. First, the survey findings that he cited often used single or only a few ad hoc items to measure prejudice, rather than reliable and validated scales. The limited variance and uncertain reliability of such indices could have contributed to weak and inconsistent findings. Second, most research following Stember has reported rather clearer and more consistent relationships between education and prejudice (e.g., Apostle et al., 1983; Bagley & Verma, 1979; Hyman & Wright, 1979; Quinley & Glock, 1979; Surgeon, Mayo, & Bogue, 1976; Wilson, 1986; Wuthnow, 1982). The few exceptions to this once again used single survey items (cf. Jackman & Muha, 1984). Studies using reliable and valid scales to measure prejudice have typically reported quite consistent correlations with education, usually in the region of .30 (e.g., Bagley & Verma, 1979). This has been even more clear-cut when generalized measures of prejudice over a number of outgroups and minorities were used (e.g., Beswick & Hills, 1972). Moreover, contrary to Stember's conclusions, no dimensions of prejudice have been reliably identified where higher education is consistently associated with greater prejudice.

Another attack on the conclusion that education influences prejudice has questioned the meaning and significance of this relationship. It has been argued that education does not produce a real and deeply rooted change in intergroup attitudes but merely a superficial commitment to democratic norms and principles (Jackman, 1978; Jackman & Muha, 1984). Thus: "The educated may show greater support for abstract democratic principles, but be no more willing to apply these principles to specific situations. Education merely 'polishes' and qualifies a person's negative attitude expressions" (Jackman & Muha, 1984, p. 753). In support of this, Jackman (1978) reported a significant relationship between education and two survey items that indicated support for the general principle of racial integration, but little or no association between education and two items that endorsed specific policies aimed at implementing these principles.

Jackman's (1978) study has been criticized, however. First, the assumption that the implementation items imply genuine commitment to integration whereas the principle items do not has been questioned (Schuman & Bobo, 1988; Schuman et al., 1985). Second, Schuman et al. (1985) noted that other studies did not find weaker effects for education on implementation items than on principle items. Once again the problem seems to involve undue reliance being placed on single survey items of limited variance and unknown reliability. A more recent paper by Bobo (1988) also does not support Jackman's argument. This study used nationally representative U.S. survey data and reported correlations between education and a series of short prejudice-related scales. Two of these scales assessed traditional racism (segregationism and affective differentiation between black and white) and produced correlations of $-.19$ and $-.32$ with education. Two other scales assessed implementation or action-relevant issues (attitudes to the black political movement and disapproval of social protest). The correlation for these two action-relevant scales and education were $-.30$ and $.26$, respectively, which are quite similar to those obtained for the two general prejudice scales. Thus, a clear trend for education to be less strongly related to beliefs about the implementation of racial integration than the principle has not yet been demonstrated.

A closely related issue is that of the nature of the relationship between education and prejudice. That is, if education does affect prejudice, how does it do so? A number of mechanisms have been proposed. First, education could reduce prejudice by providing information about minorities or outgroups. Stephan and Stephan (1984) reviewed evidence indicating that ignorance may facilitate prejudice and that this can be reduced by the provision of appropriate information. Second, following their argument that education has only a superficial effect on prejudice, Jackman and Muha (1984) suggested that this effect occurs through education making individuals more ideologically sophisticated. Thus, when subordinate groups challenge their domination, the better educated among the dominant group lead the way in "developing interracial beliefs, feelings, and personal predispositions that pull back from making sharp categorical distinctions while maintaining critical racial boundaries." In this way "group distinctions are minimized, and dominant groups develop a commitment to individual rights both as a diversion from subordinate-group demands and as a principled basis for the rejection of such demands" (p. 765).

It is possible that both these explanations, in terms of information about the outgroup or ideological sophistication, may be factors in the effect of education on prejudice and be very important in certain contexts. Nevertheless, neither seems to be widely regarded as having the range and breadth to account adequately for the phenomenon. Two other explanations have been much more widely cited in the literature:

first, in terms of cognitive sophistication (which will be discussed in more detail later in this chapter) and, second, in terms of normative exposure.

In the first case, education is seen as developing a real breadth of perspective and cognitive flexibility, which engenders a genuine capacity for tolerance toward those who are different (Glock et al., 1975; Kelman & Barclay, 1963; Selznick & Steinberg, 1969). An important implication of this is that not all education facilitates tolerance. Only "liberal" education, which aims at such objectives as the development of broader and more enlightened perspectives and exposes individuals to a diversity of ideas, should reduce prejudice. This means that education may have little if any effect on prejudice in authoritarian and conservative cultures, where education aims primarily at the preservation and inculcation of traditional norms and mores.

In the second case, education is seen as influencing prejudice through regulating exposure to social norms. Thus, higher education may expose individuals to more liberal and egalitarian norms, particularly with regard to attitudes and behavior toward minorities. Conversely, higher education may reduce individual exposure to the traditional and normative prejudices characteristic of their societies. In this sense, it has been suggested that educational mobility "lessens social integration and increases the likelihood of a marginal perspective" (Ehrlich, 1973, p. 147; cf. also Jones, 1972; Orpen, 1975). An important implication of this is that education should be more important in reducing prejudice in societies with strong traditions and norms of prejudice than in those without (cf. Orpen, 1975). This issue is discussed in more depth in the next chapter.

Overall, therefore, there is a good deal of evidence that higher levels of education are associated with less prejudice toward outgroups and minorities. However, the strength, consistency, and significance of this effect have been questioned. Not all these issues have been definitively resolved. Nevertheless, it would appear that early assessments, such as that of Stember (1961), may have been overly cautious. Education does seem to have a consistent and at least moderate association with prejudice. The most important unresolved issue is that of explaining this effect. The two mechanisms that have been most commonly proposed are that education affects prejudice through cognitive sophistication or exposure to social norms of prejudice or nonprejudice.

## Other Social Variables and Prejudice

Several other social variables, such as age, urbanicity, and mobility, have shown reasonably consistent associations with prejudice. In the case of age, a number of studies have reported quite substantial inverse correlations with anti-Semitic prejudice in North America and Western Europe (Bagley & Verma, 1979; Firebaugh & Davis, 1988; Selznick &

Steinberg, 1969; Wilson, 1986). This effect remains clearly significant when the tendency for younger persons to be better educated is controlled (Bagley & Verma, 1979; Selznick & Steinberg, 1969; Wuthnow, 1982). Generally, the tendency for younger persons to be less prejudiced than older persons is attributed to the historical trend for indices of prejudice and social distance to decline during most of the twentieth century (Firebaugh & Davis, 1988; Selznick & Steinberg, 1969; Wuthnow, 1982).

A number of studies have shown that urbanicity is related to prejudice, with those living in rural areas or smaller towns being more prejudiced than those living in large cities (Beswick & Hills, 1972; Marx, 1967; Middleton, 1976). A related concept is that of "localism," referring to the degree to which individuals are oriented toward their family, immediate friends, and local community as opposed to cosmopolitan interests of national or international scope. More locally oriented individuals have been shown to be higher in anti-Semitism and racial prejudice, even when differences in education were controlled (Roof, 1978). Geographic mobility (both within and between countries) has also been shown to predict prejudice, with more mobile persons being generally less ethnocentric and prejudiced (Hills, 1976; Kalin & Berry, 1980).

The direction of causality is not always clear in these relationships. For example, in the case of geographic mobility exposure to diversity could cause a generalized tolerance of diversity. On the other hand, it is possible that less-prejudiced persons may be more mobile because they are less rigid and dogmatic or more interested in novel experiences (Kalin & Berry, 1980). The assumption that urbanicity and localism affect prejudice seems somewhat less problematic. If this kind of causal assumption can be made, then the two kinds of mechanisms noted in the case of education may be operative. First, mobility, urbanism, and localism could influence prejudice through helping to engender cognitive sophistication or breadth of perspective. Second, these factors could indicate the degree to which individuals are exposed to pressures to conform with the traditional prejudices of their culture. Thus, persons who are more local, who live in smaller communities, and who are less geographically mobile should experience greater pressures to conform to such normative prejudices (cf. Ehrlich, 1973).

### Conclusions

Evidence linking a number of social variables to prejudice has been reviewed. In the case of certain variables, such as that of status, the evidence is not clear. Variables such as occupation and income, while usually related to prejudice, may largely indicate the effects of education. Although age is often related to prejudice, it seems to reflect the influence of historical change over time with successive age cohorts being less ethnocentric, at least in twentieth-century North America and Western Europe. Such factors as education, urbanicity, localism, and geographic mobility do seem to relate independently to prejudice. However, the significance of the effects of education on prejudice has been questioned, and, as in the case of factors such as geographic mobility, the direction of causality is not always clear.

A common interpretation of the effect of such variables has been that they might determine a generalized susceptibility to prejudice through individual-difference constructs such as breadth of perspective (Kelman & Barclay, 1963) or cognitive sophistication (Glock et al., 1975). It has also been argued that these social variables might index the degree to which individuals have been differentially exposed to social influences favoring or not favoring prejudice. Thus, social variables could influence prejudice by regulating the degree to which individuals are exposed to pressures to conform to prejudiced social norms, rather than by influencing their susceptibility to prejudice (Orpen, 1975). This issue will be discussed in more detail in the next chapter.

## COGNITIVE FACTORS

Traditional conceptions of prejudice have frequently invoked the idea of a failure of rationality (Harding et al., 1969). Thus, prejudice has been viewed as involving faulty generalization (Allport, 1954), undifferentiated and simplistic categorization (Allport, 1954), judgments based on insufficient evidence (Ashmore, 1970), rigidity (Simpson & Yinger, 1985), inflexibility (Krech et al., 1962), and imperviousness to corrective influences (Ashmore, 1970). This implies that persons who are disposed to faulty thinking and to more rigid, concrete, and categorical habits of thought should be more prone to prejudice.

More recently, the idea that prejudice is necessarily based on faulty or abnormal processes has been challenged. Tajfel (1981), for example, pointed out that the cognitive process of social categorization underlies both stereotyping and prejudice. This is viewed as an essentially normal and generally adaptive process that operates to systematize and simplify information from the social world (cf. Brewer & Kramer, 1985; Hamilton, 1981a). Neither prejudice nor stereotyping, therefore, necessarily involve cognitive abnormalities or faults. Nevertheless, it remains possible that individual differences in cognitive abilities and style could affect the operation of a process such as categorization. Thus, individual differences in the readiness with which individuals form, maintain, and generalize social categories could influence a generalized readiness or susceptibility for prejudice.

These considerations have provided the rationale for a link between cognitive constructs and prejudice. Thus, an association between general intelligence as measured by formal IQ tests and prejudice has frequently been proposed. A broader construct that has received attention is that of cognitive sophistication, a compound of formal intelligence and social experience. In addition, a number of more specific cognitive styles have been related to prejudice, such as rigidity, intolerance of ambiguity, cognitive complexity, and dogmatism. These concepts and the evidence linking them to prejudice will be discussed in the following sections.

## Cognitive Style and Prejudice

The concepts of intolerance of ambiguity and rigidity have been treated as essentially equivalent (cf. Adorno et al., 1950). There are, however, important differences between them. Altemeyer (1981), for example, differentiated them as follows:

Rigidity refers to a tendency to maintain a perceptual or problem-solving set when such maintenance is inappropriate; intolerance of ambiguity refers to a tendency to form such a set when the cues do not warrant it. For example, a person can be intolerant of ambiguity but not rigid, or tolerant but rigid once the set is formed. (p. 49)

Intolerance of ambiguity could influence prejudice by facilitating simplistic "us-them" categorizations and a tendency to disregard complex individuating and stereotype-inconsistent information. Rigidity, on the other hand, could result in the maintenance and overgeneralization of such categorizations over diverse situations and be responsible for the inflexibility and resistance to change that seem to characterize stereotypes and prejudice.

While there is evidence relating both rigidity and intolerance of ambiguity to prejudice, it is seriously inconsistent. Several studies have reported that persons high in prejudice or ethnocentrism were less able to shift problem-solving strategies or perceptual set on tasks in a manner suggesting rigidity. The best known of these is Rokeach's (1948) "Einstellung" water jar problem. However, subsequent attempts to replicate these findings have failed to do so unambiguously (Applezweig, 1954; Brown, 1953). Block and Block (1951) found that ethnocentric subjects stabilized their judgment of light position more quickly when confronted with the autokinetic phenomenon, a finding that was interpreted as indicating intolerance of ambiguity. Most other studies, however, have failed to replicate either apparent intolerance of ambiguity or rigidity (i.e., changes in judgment of movement) in ethnocentric subjects using the autokinetic phenomenon (cf. Altemeyer, 1981, pp. 49–53).

Studies using questionnaire measures of these two constructs have also been inconclusive. Thus, measures of intolerance of ambiguity, such as Budner's scale, have shown weak significant correlations with prejudice on some occasions but not on others (cf. Ray, 1988a; Sidanius, 1988). This could be due to the poor reliability (and dubious validity) of these measures (Ray, 1988a; Ward, 1988). Several studies on rigidity, for example, have found significant correlations between prejudice and the flexibility scale of the California Personality Inventory (Glock et al., 1975; Gough, 1957; Rokeach & Fruchter, 1956). However, the items of this measure seem to reflect one's willingness to entertain new and complicated ideas and would therefore load quite heavily on social conventionality and conservatism, which could account for the correlation with prejudice.

In general, therefore, the evidence on the relation between prejudice and both cognitive rigidity and intolerance of ambiguity is not at all clear. The major problem appears to be the absence of adequately valid and reliable measures of these two constructs. In fact, their viability as individual-difference constructs (as opposed to situationally determined responses) has yet to be conclusively demonstrated (Ray, 1988a). Both Brown (1965) and Altemeyer (1981) concluded earlier overviews of this research with essentially this verdict, and very little has happened subsequently to alter it.

The concept of cognitive complexity assumes stable individual differences in the capacity to differentiate and integrate information (MacNeil, 1974). Persons who are low on complexity would tend to handle complex information by relying on only a few simple categories, thereby obscuring subtle differences and similarities among stimuli. This could make less complex persons more prone to stereotyped thinking and prejudice. Few studies have investigated this, and these have usually found significant though rather weak associations with prejudice (Gardiner, 1972; Sidanius, 1985; Tetlock, 1983; Wagner & Schönbach, 1984).

There is a general problem with research relating cognitive styles such as rigidity, intolerance of ambiguity, and cognitive complexity to prejudice. Although the tasks and measures that have been used to assess these constructs do not always correlate with general intelligence (cf. Ehrlich, 1973, p. 143), they sometimes do (Ray, 1988a). That means that any correlation with prejudice could reflect an association with general intelligence rather than with the cognitive style specifically. Only one study has attempted to control for this. Interestingly, this study found that although the correlation between cognitive complexity and prejudice was substantially reduced when general intelligence was controlled, it did remain significant (Wagner & Schönbach, 1984).

Rokeach (1954) defined the concept of dogmatism as "(a) a relatively closed cognitive organization of beliefs and disbeliefs about reality, (b) organized around a central set of beliefs about absolute authority which, in turn (c) provides a framework for patterns of intolerance and qualified tolerance towards others" (p. 195). Dogmatism, therefore, refers to the degree to which new ideas will be resisted and all new information evaluated in terms of preexisting standards. This particular style of cognitive functioning is presumed to underlie prejudice and intolerance. The more dogmatic the structure of an individual's beliefs, the more disposed he or she will be to reject and dislike those persons and outgroups who do not share these beliefs.

The questionnaire measure of dogmatism developed by Rokeach has shown consistent positive correlations with measures of prejudice and ethnocentrism. However, although his theory of dogmatism has often been viewed as interesting and potentially important, the validity of his dogmatism (D) scale has been severely criticized (Altemeyer, 1981; Ray, 1979a; Wylie, 1979). It has been shown to be multidimensional without a stable and intelligible factor structure and to have an unacceptably low internal consistency. The items are vague and ambiguous and are not balanced against acquiescence. Billig (1976) showed that, although the D scale was supposed to represent the structure rather than the content of belief systems, its items appear to be heavily biased ideologically. Even though the D scale was intended to assess general authoritarianism, and, therefore, to be applicable to both the political right and left, it has been found to correlate with authoritarianism of the right only (Hanson, 1983; Stone, 1980). The D scale has also correlated so highly with authoritarianism as measured by Adorno et al.'s (1950) F scale (Kerlinger & Rokeach, 1966) that its independence from that concept has been seriously questioned (e.g., Kirscht & Dillehay, 1967). As a result, it seems doubtful whether the D scale has much validity as a measure of cognitive style. The correlations with prejudice could simply reflect its association with authoritarianism (as measured by the F scale) and political conservatism.

Overall, it seems that the research relating particular cognitive styles, such as rigidity, intolerance of ambiguity, cognitive complexity, and dogmatism, to prejudice has been inconclusive. Although a rationale for an association with prejudice exists, serious problems in the operationalization and measurement of these concepts have been important obstacles to an adequate assessment. The development of reliable and valid measures, and more systematic research that controls for potentially confounding factors (particularly general intelligence) would seem to be indicated.

## Intelligence, Cognitive Sophistication, and Prejudice

It has been noted that correlations between particular cognitive styles and prejudice could reflect a correlation between prejudice and general intelligence. However, as Ehrlich (1973) pointed out, relatively few studies have used formal measures of intelligence along with measures of ethnic prejudice, probably because intelligence testing is so time consuming. His review of these studies indicated that most had found that higher intelligence was associated with lower prejudice. Only two of nine studies reported nonsignificant correlations. The degree of association, however, was not very powerful, with the typical correlation being around .30.

More recent studies have reported similar findings. Thus, significant correlations between formal tests of intelligence and various indices of prejudice have been reported for high school students in Britain (Bagley et al., 1979) and Germany (Wagner & Schönbach, 1984) and for general population samples in Britain and Holland (Bagley et al., 1979). In the United States, Moore et al. (1984) obtained a significant correlation for black high school students but not for whites. Overall, therefore, the evidence suggests a relationship between general intelligence and prejudice. It does not seem to be a very powerful relationship, however, and the extent to which it holds in non-Western cultures is not clear.

A broader concept, termed cognitive sophistication (Glock et al., 1975; Wuthnow, 1982), simplism (Selznick & Steinberg, 1969), or breadth of perspective (Kelman & Barclay, 1963), has also aroused interest. This concept is usually described in rather vague terms. It seems to incorporate both dispositional and experiential attributes. Kelman and Barclay (1963), for example, described two components: (a) psychological capacity, which refers to both intelligence and traits of authoritarianism and rigidity, and (b) opportunity, which refers to the variety and breadth of the individuals' environmentally determined social experience. In the latter case, such factors as residence in urban and cosmopolitan areas, higher education, exposure to social and cultural heterogeneity, skilled employment, geographical mobility, and social mobility would be seen as broadening experiences that contribute to cognitive sophistication.

An interesting point has been made concerning the way in which cognitive sophistication is presumed to increase resistance to prejudice. Besides reducing the readiness with which simplistic social categorizations may be formed, maintained, and generalized, cognitive sophistication may also affect prejudice through the kind of attributions that are made about group differences. Thus, cognitive sophistication may sensitize individuals to the possibility that perceived group differences (negative to the outgroup) may not be due to deficiencies inherent to the outgroup but could be due to complex historical, cultural, and social factors. As Glock et al. (1975) pointed out:

Explanations that are sensitive to the historical circumstances which gave rise to group differences and that recognize the cultural, social, and psychological forces which sustain them guard against relative differences being made absolute. More importantly, such reasoning makes it clear that the group itself is not at fault. (p. 167)

In the absence of validated measures, researchers have used a variety of ad hoc indices to assess cognitive sophistication. Selznick and Steinberg (1969) used a scale with items indicating tendencies to reduce complex social problems to simple solutions. Glock et al. (1975) used indices of interest in intellectual pursuits, a flexibility scale (Gough, 1957), and agreement with simplistic views of human nature. These presumed indices of cognitive sophistication proved to be the strongest predictors of anti-Semitic and racial prejudice in these two studies. Cognitive sophistication as a global cognitive-experiential construct could account for the correlations that have been obtained between prejudice and various cognitive styles, as well as with general intelligence. Cognitive sophistication could also explain the correlations obtained between prejudice and sociodemographic variables, such as education, occupation, urbanicity, and geographical mobility.

## Conclusions

Because basic cognitive processes such as categorization seem to be involved in prejudice (Tajfel, 1969, 1981), it is plausible that stable individual differences in cognitive factors could influence a generalized susceptibility to prejudice. A number of specific cognitive styles have been linked to prejudice, but, for the most part, the evidence has been rather inconsistent. A major problem has been ambiguity over the conceptualization and measurement of these styles as stable individual-difference dimensions. In the case of general intelligence, most of the research evidence suggests a significant tendency for higher intelligence to be associated with lower prejudice. However, these correlations have not been very powerful, and the cross-cultural generality of the association has not yet been demonstrated.

A more global cognitive-experiential construct that has received attention is that of cognitive sophistication. This construct seems to effectively integrate a variety of concepts and findings within a broader conceptual edifice that provides a plausible rationale for individual differences in susceptibility to prejudice. Although relatively little research has been done, the findings seem promising. The main problem appears to be that the concept has been used in a rather vague manner. Conceptual clarification and its effective operationalization and measurement appear to be necessary before more definitive research will be possible.

## AUTHORITARIANISM

### Introduction and Background

The theory of the authoritarian personality (Adorno et al., 1950) has been the most ambitious and influential attempt to understand the psychology of prejudice. It goes beyond approaches that have linked isolated traits or attributes to prejudice and proposes instead that a number of traits, needs, and cognitive and behavioral dispositions covary in order to form a more general syndrome of personality. This syndrome, then, determines a susceptibility not only to prejudice but also to broader patterns of belief and ideology. It could be seen as essentially similar to the kind of second-order personality dimensions described by Cattell and his associates (Cattell, Eber, & Tatsuoka, 1970), such as extraversion and neuroticism, which integrate a number of distinct primary traits, and so have a major impact on the coherence and presentation of the personality.

Before publication of *The Authoritarian Personality* (Adorno et al., 1950), the rise of fascism in Europe during the 1920s and 1930s had stimulated a number of attempts to understand the psychology of fascism. These had usually involved descriptions of a personality type considered to be particularly attracted to fascist ideology and likely to be involved in fascist movements. In rudimentary form, these were very similar to the picture later presented by Adorno and his associates in their book. Both the early descriptions and Adorno et al.'s theory were strongly influenced by psychoanalytic theory, and often by Marxism as well. Reich (1975), for example, argued that capitalist social structures used authoritarian families and child-rearing practices involving extensive sexual repression to create authoritarian personality types who would be unlikely to rebel against exploitative social conditions. This authoritarian character structure was described as conservative, afraid of freedom, submissive to authority, obedient, yet with "natural aggression distorted into brutal sadism" (p. 66). Such persons are acquiescent subjects in authoritarian societies and are strongly attracted to authoritarian and fascist ideology. Maslow (1943) and Fromm (1941) produced quite similar accounts.

These descriptions of an authoritarian personality type were presented from social perspectives that were basically opposed to fascist and ethnocentric ideology. It is interesting to note, therefore, that the Nazi psychologist, Jaensch, produced a description of the ideal Nazi, the J-type, which was quite similar to the authoritarian personality. According to Brown (1965), Jaensch depicted the J-type as the kind of person who:

made definite, unambiguous perceptual judgments and persisted in them. He would recognize that human behavior is fixed by blood, soil, and national tradition. He would be tough, masculine, firm; a man you could rely on. His ancestors would have lived from time immemorial in the North German space and within the North German population; it would be these ancestors which had bequeathed him his admirable qualities. (p. 478)

Finally, a similar personality pattern was also described by MacCrone (1937) in accounting for the evolution of racial prejudice in South Africa. He suggested that the nature and exigencies of frontier life in South Africa before the twentieth century had molded what he termed a Calvinist-puritanical personality type. This personality was intropunitive, extrapunitive, ethnocentric, conservative, religious, and racist.

## The Theory of the Authoritarian Personality

Two important differences between the views of Adorno and his colleagues and the earlier views largely accounted for the much greater impact of the Adorno theory. First, their theory of the authoritarian personality was far more detailed, comprehensive, and sophisticated than its predecessors. Second, their theory was based on an extensive empirical investigation using generally accepted methods of empirical social science. Thus, they produced psychometric measures of their central constructs and demonstrated their intercorrelation. They also validated the theory by comparing empirically generated criterion groups of persons high and low in ethnocentrism on a large number of indices and ratings scored blind from interview and TAT protocols.

Their investigation began with the objective of explaining the psychological bases of anti-Semitism. This was shown to be part of a much broader ethnocentric pattern that involved a generalized dislike of outgroups and minorities, as well as an excessive and uncritical patriotism. Anti-Semitism and ethnocentrism were also strongly related to political and economic conservatism. These attitudes and beliefs appeared to cluster together to form a coherent pattern, and this patterning seemed best explained as an expression of basic needs within the personality. Thus, it was suggested "that the political, economic, and social convictions of an individual often form a broad and coherent pattern, as if bound together by a 'mentality' or 'spirit,' and that this pattern is an expression of deeplying trends in the personality" (p. 1).

Evidence from a number of sources and particularly their own interview data suggested a constellation of nine traits that seemed to covary to constitute this personality syndrome. Questionnaire items were developed to assess each trait and this culminated in the F scale as a measure of this "authoritarian personality." These nine traits and an example of an item written to assess each trait are shown in Table 8.1.

In fact, the term authoritarian may not have been the most appropriate

Table 8.1
Definitions and Illustrative F-scale Items for Adorno et al.'s Nine Traits of the
Authoritarian Personality Syndrome

---

1.  CONVENTIONALISM:  Rigid adherence to conventional middle-class values
    "A person who has bad manners, habits, and breeding can hardly expect to
    get along with decent people."

2.  AUTHORITARIAN SUBMISSION: A submissive, uncritical attitude toward idealized moral
    authorities of the ingroup
    "Obedience and respect for authority are the most important virtues children
    should learn."

3.  AUTHORITARIAN AGGRESSION: A tendency to be on the lookout for, and to condemn,
    reject, and punish people who violate conventional values
    "Homosexuals are hardly better than criminals, and ought to be severely
    punished."

4.  ANTI-INTRACEPTION: An opposition to the subjective, the imaginative, the tender-minded.
    "Nowadays more and more people are prying into matters that should remain
    personal and private."

5.  SUPERSTITION AND STEREOTYPY: The belief in mystical determinants of the individual's
    fate; the disposition to think in rigid categories
    "Some day it will probably be shown that astrology can explain a lot of
    things."

6.  POWER AND TOUGHNESS: A preoccupation with the dominance-submission, strong-weak,
    leader-follower dimension; identification with power figures; exaggerated assertion of strength
    and toughness
    "People can be divided into two distinct classes, the weak and the strong."

7.  DESTRUCTIVENESS AND CYNICISM: Generalized hostility, vilification of the human
    "Human nature being what it is, there will always be war and conflict."

8.  PROJECTIVITY: The disposition to believe that wild and dangerous things go on in the
    world; the projection outwards of unconscious emotional impulses
    "Most people don't realize how much our lives are controlled by plots hatched
    in secret places."

9.  SEX: Exaggerated concern with sexual "goings-on"
    "The wild sex life of the old Greeks and Romans was tame compared to some
    of the 'goings-on' in this country, even in places where people might least
    expect it."

---

label for this personality syndrome. Adorno et al. (1950) did not report
any real evidence indicating that the F scale's items or the nine traits
identified by them were related to fascist or authoritarian tendencies.
Both the traits comprising the syndrome and the F-scale items were
primarily derived from the interview data comparing groups high and
low in ethnocentrism. Item selections for the F scale were also based on
each item's capacity to correlate highly with the anti-Semitism scale.

This personality syndrome might therefore have been more aptly labeled an "ethnocentric" rather than an "authoritarian" personality. The latter was really just a seemingly plausible inference from the image of an individual who was conservative, ethnocentric, and anti-Semitic and, perhaps, from its apparent similarity to the earlier speculations of Fromm (1941), Maslow (1943), and Reich (1975).

Overall, the theory sketched out by Adorno et al. (1950) can be seen as relating together phenomena at four different levels. This is summarized in Table 8.2. Thus, strict and punitive parental socialization sets up an enduring conflict within the individual. Resentment and hostility toward parental authority, and by extension all authority, is repressed and displaced because of a fear of and a need to submit to that authority. These psychodynamics are given expression at the surface of personality in a syndrome of nine covarying traits. It is this constellation of traits that constitutes the authoritarian personality per se. Finally, these traits are expressed in certain social beliefs, attitudes, and behaviors, most notably in those implicitly antidemocratic beliefs sampled by the F scale.

This theory inspired a great deal of enthusiasm. It seemed to effectively tie together concepts over an extremely broad range—from individual psychodynamics to sociological phenomena of immense significance for human society and history. However, the theory and the investigation on which it was based also elicited a great deal of serious criticism.

### The Critical Response

The critical response to *The Authoritarian Personality* raised methodological, conceptual, and psychometric issues. For example, a number of serious methodological flaws were outlined by Hyman and Sheatsley (1954) shortly after the book's publication. They noted that the samples used were not representative and that the correlations obtained thus might not have general validity. The correlations between the questionnaire measures could have reflected overlapping item content, and, in certain cases, they were at least partly built in through the item-selection procedures. For example, items were selected for the F scale not only on the basis of internal consistency but also because they correlated highly with the anti-Semitism scale. In the comparative study, interviewers were aware of subjects' research classification, so that the differences between the interview and TAT responses of high and low ethnocentric groups could have been influenced by interviewer bias. Such potentially important confounding variables as education were also not controlled. Thus, obtained group differences in beliefs, personality, childhood experiences, and cognitive style might have reflected educational or socioeconomic differences between the groups.

As a result of these and other flaws, Hyman and Sheatsley (1954) felt

**Table 8.2**
**The Theory of the Authoritarian Personality**

| Family structure and interrelationships | Depth personality: Intrapsychic conflict | Surface personality: Traits | Social beliefs and behavior |
|---|---|---|---|
| Values— rigid, conventional, status orientated | Resentment and hostility toward parental discipline | Conventionalism<br>Authoritarian submission<br>Authoritarian aggression | Implicitly anti-democratic beliefs (e.g., F-scale items) |
| Interrelationships— role determined, emotionally distant, dominant-subordinate | Repressed and displaced because of fear of and need to submit to parental authority | Anti-intraception<br>Projectivity<br>Superstition and stereotypy | Ethnocentrism, prejudice, chauvinism, discriminatory behavior to out-groups and minorities |
| Socialization— strict, punitive, arbitrary discipline; intolerance of nonconformity | Weak ego, punitive and unintegrated superego | Power and toughness<br>Destructiveness and cynicism<br>Overconcern with sexual "goings on" | Politico-economic conservatism, fascist ideology, right-wing political activity |

*Source:* "Prejudice and Racism." J. Duckitt, in *Social Psychology in South Africa* (p. 177), by D. Foster & J. Louw-Potgieter (Eds.), 1991, Isando, South Africa: Lexicon. Copyright © 1991 by Lexicon. Reprinted by permission.

that the conclusions of *The Authoritarian Personality* had not been proven. The failure to control for variables such as education and socioeconomic status also left important alternative explanations of the findings open, most notably in terms of constructs such as "lower class norms" (Brown, 1965), breadth of perspective (Kelman & Barclay, 1963), and cognitive sophistication (Glock et al., 1975).

A major conceptual criticism was that *The Authoritarian Personality* represented only authoritarianism of the right and not authoritarianism of the left. Shills (1954), for example, argued that while both fascism and communism were authoritarian, communists seemed to score low rather than high on the F scale. Thus, he suggested, the F scale could not be a measure of authoritarianism per se. This criticism was extremely influential in leading to the development of alternative conceptualizations to assess authoritarianism of both left and right. Two important examples are the concepts of dogmatism (Rokeach et al., 1960) and toughmindedness (Eysenck 1954). In general, however, this criticism has lost force over time, perhaps because, as Stone's (1980) review of the evidence shows, an authoritarian of the left was never clearly demonstrated scientifically. As a result, the idea that the F scale and other measures of authoritarianism assess only authoritarianism of the right has not seemed as great a problem as it did in the 1950s during the cold war (cf. Altemeyer, 1981).

A major psychometric criticism of the F scale was that all its items were worded so that agreement indicated authoritarianism (Bass, 1955; Brewster-Smith, 1965; Couch & Keniston, 1960). This raised the possibility that a response set, particularly a tendency to agree irrespective of item content, which Bass (1955) termed acquiescence, influenced F-scale scores. This also applied to Adorno et al.'s ethnocentrism (E) and anti-Semitism (A-S) scales. The issue of whether these scales were measuring acquiesence rather than constructs such as authoritarianism, and, if so, to what extent, stimulated a fierce debate that lasted for over a decade. A great deal of research was done that seemed to demonstrate the influence of acquiescence on F-scale scores. First, reversals of original F-scale items were constructed (for which disagreement implied authoritarianism), and it was shown that these reversed items did not correlate nearly as strongly as they should have with the original items (e.g., Bass, 1955; Christie, Havel, & Seidenberg, 1958; Jackson & Messick, 1957). Peabody (1961), in a similar vein, found a substantial rate of double agreement between original items and their supposedly opposite reversals. Second, independent measures of acquiescence, usually the number of "agree" responses to items that covered a very wide range of content, were shown to correlate with the F scale (e.g., Bass, 1956; Couch & Keniston, 1960; Gage, Leavitt, & Stone, 1957).

The conclusion that acquiescence substantially influenced F-scale scores was seriously questioned in two influential papers during the 1960's, however (Rorer, 1965; Samelson & Yates, 1967). It was carefully shown, particularly by Rorer (1965), that both the above kinds of findings could be due to the actual content of the measures or items used and, therefore, the results were not necessarily due to acquiescence. Nevertheless, a general conclusion in the literature on acquiescence and the F scale at that time seems to have been that, while the influence of acquiescence on F-scale scores had not been conclusively demonstrated, the use of questionnaires with all items formulated positively remained problematic (Brown, 1965; Kirscht & Dillehay, 1967). Several more recent psychological studies have supported the conclusion that acquiescence is indeed a problem undermining the validity of the F scale (Altemeyer, 1981; Duckitt, 1985b; Ray, 1983). Sociological research has also demonstrated that double agreements to original and reversed F-scale items increase dramatically with decreasing educational status (Campbell et al., 1960; Landsberger & Saavedra, 1967; Lenski & Leggett, 1960), a finding that strongly suggests acquiescence.

An important problem raised by the issue of acquiescence was that correlations between any two measures that consisted only of positively formulated items could be artificially inflated. Kirscht and Dillehay (1967) suggested that in such cases correlations "in the neighborhood of .40 could be generated on the basis of response bias alone" (p. 28). This means that the magnitude of the relationship between authoritarianism and ethnocentrism could have been significantly overestimated by Adorno et al. (1950) and others using their measures.

One response to the issue of acquiescence and the F scale was that a number of attempts were made to develop alternatives to the original F scale with equal numbers of positively and negatively worded items to rule out any possible contamination by acquiescence (cf. Altemeyer, 1981; Byrne & Bounds, 1964; Christie et al., 1958; Kohn, 1974; Ray, 1972). However, these attempts were not particularly successful. Because of the complexity of the original F-scale items, and uncertainty about how the opposite of authoritarianism should be defined, serious difficulty was found in producing effective negative items. As a result, the internal consistencies and reliabilities of these balanced F scales tended to be rather low (Altemeyer, 1981). Therefore, none of these scales became a serious rival to the original F scale.

Overall, then, the critical reaction to *The Authoritarian Personality* revealed a number of serious flaws and weaknesses in the investigation and its conclusions. As a result, even though the critics conceded that the theory and concept of the authoritarian personality was important, exciting, and plausible (cf. Hyman & Sheatsley, 1954), its propositions were regarded as essentially unproven. Moreover, important questions about the conceptualization of authoritarianism and the adequacy of its measurement by the F scale had been raised. As a result, a vast research literature emerged in response to issues such as these during the four decades following its publication. From the point of view of understanding the psychology of prejudice, two issues in this research seem particularly important. First, there is the issue of the validity of Adorno et al.'s theory of the structure, psychodynamics, and childhood origins of the authoritarian personality. Second, there is the issue of the validity of the construct of authoritarianism as it was operationalized in the F scale. The question here is whether this construct displays the pattern of covariation with related concepts such as prejudice and ethnocentrism, political conservatism, fascist authoritarianism, social attitudes, and behavior, which is implied in its conceptualization. Research pertaining to both these issues will therefore be discussed.

## Validity of the Theory

In assessing the validity of Adorno et al.'s theory, four issues corresponding to the four levels of their theory, as depicted in Table 8.2, can be identified: first, whether certain childhood experiences and socialization underlie authoritarianism; second, whether inner conflicts concerning authority and ego weakness are characteristic of authoritarian persons; third, whether the model of nine covarying traits appropriately represents authoritarianism at the surface of the personality; and, fourth, whether this model of nine covarying traits is adequately measured by the F scale.

The kind of early socialization that supposedly resulted in later authoritarianism and ethnocentrism was described as "a relatively harsh and more threatening type of home discipline which was experienced as arbitrary by the child. Related to this is a tendency . . . to base interrelationships on rather clearly defined roles of dominance and submission in contradistinction to equalitarian policies" (Adorno et al., 1950, p. 385). An adequate test of whether such childhood socialization actually causes later authoritarianism would require an ambitious and expensive longitudinal research design. No such study has been conducted, and a good deal of the research typically cited as bearing on this hypothesis does so rather indirectly. For example, a number of studies have indicated that more authoritarian or ethnocentric persons favor stricter and harsher child-rearing practices (Block, 1955; Bush, Gallagher, & Weiner, 1982; Hart, 1957; Levinson & Huffman, 1955; Thomas, 1987; Zuckerman, Barrett-Ribback, Monashkin, & Norton, 1958). Moreover, the authoritarianism of individuals and their parents seem to be positively correlated, although the relationship does not appear to be very powerful (Altemeyer, 1981; Byrne, 1965; Williams & Williams, 1963).

These findings—that authoritarian parents favor stricter child-rearing practices and that they tend to have authoritarian offspring—however, do not prove that the stricter child rearing is what makes these children authoritarian. A somewhat better test of this is provided by studies that directly examine the relationship between parental child-rearing attitudes and the authoritarianism or ethnocentrism of their children. Some of these studies have reported significant positive relationships, with stricter and more severe parental discipline being associated with off-springs' higher prejudice (Bagley et al., 1979; Dickens & Hobart, 1959; Kates & Diab, 1955) or authoritarianism (Lyle & Levitt, 1955). Most studies, however, have not found a clear tendency for stricter and more punitive parenting to be associated with greater offspring prejudice (Epstein & Komorita, 1965, 1966; Harris, Gough, & Martin, 1950; McCord, McCord, & Howard, 1960; Mosher & Scodel, 1960) or authoritarianism (Altemeyer, 1981; Richert, 1963).

Unfortunately, these studies have been characterized by quite serious methodological flaws (cf. Altemeyer, 1981), including the use of small and unrepresentative samples, the use of measures of unknown validity or poor reliability, failure to control potentially confounding factors such as education or socioeconomic status, and retrospective reports of parental behavior from either the parents themselves or their offspring. The dubious validity of retrospective reports is exemplified by a study by Altemeyer (1981) that found very weak correlations between parents' reports of how strict they had been with their children and their childrens' reports of how strict their parents had been.

The best of the studies correlating parental strictness with offspring ethnocentrism or authoritarianism are probably those of Altemeyer (1981), who used large samples and satisfactory measures, and McCord et al. (1960), who used a longitudinal design and independent interviewer ratings of parenting behavior. Both these studies found no relationship between parental punitiveness and offspring authoritarianism and prejudice. The minority of studies finding that punitive parenting was associated with ethnocentric and authoritarian offspring probably reflect the ethnocentric and authoritarian attitudes of the parents. Their children could have simply learned these attitudes directly from their parents—a more parsimonious explanation than one in terms of child-rearing practices causing prejudice and authoritarianism (Altemeyer, 1981; Harding et al., 1969).

It would seem, therefore, that research has not supported the proposition that certain childhood socialization experiences cause the acceptance of authoritarian and ethnocentric beliefs (cf. also Altemeyer, 1981; Ashmore & DelBoca, 1976; Harding et al., 1969; Katz, 1976; Proshansky, 1966). A second proposition, that inner conflicts concerning parental authority and later all authority, together with a weak ego and punitive but poorly integrated superego, are characteristic of authoritarian persons has received very little research attention. This could be due to both the difficulty of unambiguously operationalizing constructs of this nature and the relatively low regard in which psychoanalytic concepts and procedures have been held by social psychologists. One corollary that can be derived from this proposition is that authoritarians should be more anxious and generally lower in psychological adjustment than are nonauthoritarians. Although this inference was not made by Adorno et al. (1950), others have argued that it seems a reasonable deduction from the contention that the authoritarian has a "weak ego" (Byrne, 1966; Masling, 1954).

Some studies have found that persons high on authoritarianism were more anxious or less well adjusted than were persons low on authoritarianism (Friedman, Webster, & Sanford, 1956; Larson & Schwendiman, 1969). A number of other studies, however, have not found any difference in this respect (Crabbe, 1974; Duckitt, 1983b; Heaven, Conners, & Trevethan, 1987; Masling, 1954; Maykovich, 1975; Mehryar, 1970; Michael, 1967; Ray, 1981a). These studies cover a variety of societies and include several using large and representative community samples (e.g., Duckitt, 1983b; Maykovich, 1975). Overall, they suggest that authoritarianism does not necessarily imply anxiety or any other form of maladjustment. To the extent that this can be viewed as a concomitant of "ego weakness," Adorno et al.'s propositions concerning the underlying psychodynamics of authoritarianism do not seem to be supported.

At the next theoretical level is the assumption that these underlying psychodynamics are expressed at the surface of personality in a syndrome of nine covarying traits. Since groups of F-scale items were written to represent each of these nine traits, one way to validate this model would be to show empirically the existence of item clusters that correspond to these theoretical traits. These item clusters and, of course, items should also then covary sufficiently with each other to indicate an underlying general factor. A number of factor- or cluster-analytic studies of the F scale have been reported (Altemeyer, 1981; Aumack, 1955; Camilleri, 1959; Christie & Garcia, 1951; Kerlinger & Rokeach, 1966; Lever, Schlemmer, & Wagner, 1967). In almost all these studies the F scale has been shown to be multidimensional. However, the dimensions or item clusters that emerged have not been stable and have varied markedly from study to study. They have also not corresponded with the traits proposed by Adorno et al. (cf. also Altemeyer, 1981; Christie, 1954; Knapp, 1976).

Research has therefore failed to verify this model of the structure of the authoritarian personality or to show that the constellation of covarying traits proposed are represented in the F scale. These conclusions are consistent with those derived from research on the childhood origins and inner psychodynamics of authoritarianism. That is, Adorno et al.'s psychoanalytically orientated theory of the authoritarian personality has not been clearly supported by empirical research at any of its four levels (see Table 8.2). However, findings indicating that this theory does not seem to be valid do not necessarily mean that the construct of authoritarianism, as broadly described by Reich, Fromm, and Maslow, and operationalized by Adorno et al. in the F scale, is invalid. In fact, most of the literature on authoritarianism following Adorno et al.'s investigation never really relied on their psychodynamic model per se. Instead, as Kirscht and Dillehay (1967) pointed out, the F scale was adopted as "the working definition of authoritarianism" (p. 6). An important question, therefore, is whether this concept, as it was operationalized in the F scale, shows the expected pattern of covariation with such concepts as prejudice, nationalism, ethnocentrism, political conservatism, fascist authoritarianism, and other relevant social attitudes and behavior.

### Validity of the Construct

A central issue is that of the covariation between authoritarianism and prejudice. This has been the focus of a great deal of research. Although most studies have reported positive relationships, the findings have not been completely consistent. Thus, the obtained correlations have been extremely variable ranging from very weak, and even statistically nonsignificant in a few cases, to correlations as powerful, or almost as powerful, as those originally reported by Adorno et al. (1950). Several factors may account for this inconsistency. These are whether the original F and E scales were used, the use of unbalanced measures open to the effects of acquiescence, whether variables such as education or socioeconomic status (SES) were controlled, and the degree to which prejudice is regulated by group norms in the subjects studied.

For example, studies that used Adorno et al.'s (1950) original F and E scales generally replicated their very powerful correlations (e.g., Campbell & McCandless, 1951; Christie & Garcia, 1951; Gaier & Bass, 1959; Hoogvelt, 1969; Kates & Diab, 1955; Kaufman, 1957; McDill, 1961; Meloen et al., 1988; Roberts & Rokeach, 1956). However, as in the original study, these correlations could have been inflated by acquiescence, overlapping scale content, and the existence of built-in associations between these two scales. Not surprisingly, therefore, studies using independently derived measures of prejudice uncontaminated by acquiescence have usually reported lower, though still highly significant, correlations (Campbell & McCandless, 1951; Martin & Westie, 1959; Triandis, Davis, & Takezawa, 1965). For example, Campbell and McCandless (1951) reported a correlation of .73 between the original F and E scales, and correlations ranging between .42 and .57 between the F scale and their independently developed and balanced xenophobia scales. Studies in which both the measures of authoritarianism and prejudice were balanced against acquiescence have also reported lower correlations, usually in the region of .40–.50 (Kohn, 1974; Lee & Warr, 1969; Ray, 1980a, 1984).

A second issue left open by *The Authoritarian Personality* was that the relationship of authoritarianism and ethnocentrism could reflect the effects of education or SES. However, studies using samples of persons at the same educational level, such as college students, found correlations between the F scale and prejudice that were lower than those reported by Adorno et al., but not dramatically so (Christie & Garcia, 1951; Gaier & Bass, 1959; Kates & Diab, 1955). Other studies using nonstudent samples that controlled for education, SES, or related variables also found this relationship reduced, but still highly significant and reasonably substantial (Kaufman, 1957; McDill, 1961; Middleton, 1976; Pettigrew, 1959; Roberts & Rokeach, 1956).

Finally, a number of studies conducted in South Africa have produced results seriously at variance with those obtained elsewhere. These studies found nonsignificant correlations between the F scale and antiblack prejudice (Heaven, 1979; Orpen, 1971a; Orpen & Tsapogas, 1972). Other South African studies have reported significant but very weak correlations between authoritarianism and prejudice—no more than about .30 (Colman & Lambley, 1970; Heaven & Rajab, 1980; Lambley, 1973; Lambley & Gilbert, 1970; Orpen, 1973a, 1973b; Spangenberg & Nel, 1983). The one study that used a large community sample of 1884 white adults found correlations of only .17 (for Afrikaans speakers) and .32 (for English speakers) between the F scale and social distance to a number of outgroups (Lever, 1978). Somewhat higher correlations have been obtained in those South African studies using unbalanced measures of both authoritarianism and prejudice that are open to the effects of acquiescence (Nieuwoudt & Nel, 1975; Pettigrew, 1958). However, even these correlations have seemed lower than those typically obtained in studies outside South Africa when similarly unbalanced measures have been used.

In order to explain these seemingly anomalous findings, it has been argued that prejudice in very highly prejudiced societies such as South Africa is primarily determined by very powerful social norms. Because prejudice is normative and a product of conformity to these social pressures, psychological factors such as authoritarianism should have less influence on prejudice (Lever, 1978; Orpen, 1975; Pettigrew, 1958; van den Berghe, 1967). This argument will be considered in more detail and some of its implications will be elaborated in Chapter 9.

The findings on the relationship between authoritarianism and prejudice can be summed up as follows. Apart from the South African findings, the existence of this relationship seems well established. What is unclear seems to be the magnitude of the relationship, and perhaps its universality across social contexts. There can be no doubt that use of the original F and E scales seriously inflates the actual relationship. Studies using balanced measures of both authoritarianism and prejudice suggest that the relationship may be a moderate rather than a very powerful one. However, the poor psychometric qualities and, particularly, the very low internal consistencies of balanced F scales (Altemeyer, 1981) make this conclusion a tentative one. Finally, authoritarianism may only be very weakly related to prejudice in contexts such as South Africa where prejudice is socially normative.

A second issue that seems central to the construct validity of authoritarianism is its covariation with political conservatism and right-wing fascist extremism. It was noted earlier that Adorno et al. (1950) had never produced any evidence that authoritarianism indicated a susceptibility for fascism, despite their designation of the F (fascist) scale. A great deal of research subsequently set out to replicate their finding of an association with conservative political sentiment and activity. There have been several reviews of these studies (Altemeyer, 1981; Kirscht & Dillehay, 1967; Meloen, 1983; Meloen et al., 1988). The most extensive of these has been that of Meloen (1983), who conducted a meta-analysis of three decades of authoritarianism research involving some 30,000 American and 15,000 non-American subjects. Mean F-scale scores from these studies were standardized on a 1.00 to 7.00 scale with a neutral midpoint of 4.00. Means of over 4.50 were classified as high, and means of under 3.50 as low. There was a clear overall tendency for more politically conservative groups to obtain higher mean scores and more liberal or radical groups to obtain lower scores.

The mean scores of several right-wing extremist and fascist groups were included in the meta-analysis. These are of particular interest for assessing the capacity of the F scale to indicate susceptibility to fascism. In clear support of this, the standardized means for these groups were all extremely high: British fascists, 5.30; former members of the SS in Germany, 5.23; superpatriotic American members of an ultraconservative society, 5.08; supporters of a Dutch right-wing extremist party, 5.00.

In general, these findings support an association between authoritarianism, political conservatism, and susceptibility to fascism. However, in summing up his review of this literature, Altemeyer (1981) sounds a cautionary note. He points out that, despite the generally confirmatory pattern of findings, there have been a number of inconsistent and ambiguous findings (e.g., Mischel & Schopler, 1959; Schwendiman, Larson, & Cope, 1970; Wrightsman, Radloff, Horton, & Mecherikoff, 1961; Zippel & Norman, 1966). He also notes that the overall relationship indicated by the literature is not as powerful or clear-cut as the conceptualization of authoritarianism expects it to be, or as Adorno et al.'s original research suggested.

Research on the relationship between authoritarianism and nationalism seems to suggest similar conclusions. Once again, many studies can be cited demonstrating that authoritarianism, measured by either the original F or balanced F scales, is associated with nationalism or patriotism (Farris, 1960; Fensterwald, 1958; Heaven, Stones, & Bester, 1986; Hughes, 1975; Levinson, 1957; MacKinnon & Centers, 1957; Martin, 1964; Marx, 1967; Ray & Furnham, 1984; Smith & Rosen, 1958). This correlation has been also demonstrated for related constructs such as dogmatism and conservatism (Chesler & Schmuck, 1964; Heaven, 1981; McClosky, 1967; Ray & Furnham, 1984; Terhune, 1984). Findings are not entirely consistent, however. Several studies have reported little or no correlation between the F scale and indices of nationalist sentiment (e.g., Forbes, 1985). Moreover, the correlations in those studies reporting confirmatory findings have varied widely and sometimes been very low (e.g., Ray, 1981b). Most of these studies have been weak methodologically, using rather small student samples (e.g., Smith & Rosen, 1958), using dubious and unvalidated indices of nationalism (e.g., MacKinnon & Centers, 1957), or failing to control for education or SES, a correlate of both nationalism and the F scale (cf. Kirscht & Dillehay, 1967, pp. 66–67).

Evaluating these findings is also complicated by certain unresolved conceptual issues. The most important would seem to be that of whether there are different kinds of nationalism and patriotism. For example, Adorno et al. (1950) originally suggested that a healthy and nonethnocentric patriotic love for one's country does exist and should be distinguished from the ethnocentric and chauvinistic kind of nationalism that they focused on. Forbes (1985) recently elaborated this distinction, arguing that the nationalism of oppressed or minority groups would often be of the former kind (i.e., a healthy nonethnocentric patriotism) and so would tend not to be associated with authoritarianism. Doob (1964) also documented what seems to be a nonethnocentric form of patriotic sentiment that might not be associated with authoritarianism.

Despite these difficulties, the overall conclusion from this research seems essentially the same as those previously reached for the other theoretically vital associations of authoritarianism with prejudice and conservatism. In each of these cases, a correlation central to the validity of the construct has emerged, but it has not done so as consistently or as strongly as would be theoretically expected. A number of other behavioral and cognitive constructs, although not as central to the validity of authoritarianism as these, should nevertheless covary with it. These include conformity, hostility and aggression, rigidity, intolerance of ambiguity, and behavior in group contexts. Research investigating their correlation with the F scale was comprehensively reviewed by Altemeyer (1981). His conclusions are not dissimilar to those reached above. The findings are often inconsistent, with some studies reporting expected correlations and others nonsignificant findings. Moreover, when confirmatory findings are reported, the correlations tend to be less substantial than would be expected theoretically.

Overall, these findings, particularly those pertaining to covariation with the conceptually central constructs of prejudice, nationalism, conservatism, and right-wing extremism, do broadly suggest that the concept of authoritarianism as it has been operationalized in the F scale has validity. However, they do so in a manner that is neither conclusive nor convincing. Altemeyer (1981) argued that this could be due to serious psychometric limitations of the F scale and other measures of authoritarianism. These limitations, he suggested, make them extremely imperfect indices of authoritarianism and so result in the pattern of weak and inconsistent findings characterizing the research literature. This critique led Altemeyer to the development of an important new measure of authoritarianism and a refinement of the concept.

### Altemeyer's Approach

The traditional psychometric critique of the F scale had focused primarily on the all-positive phrasing of its items and the consequent possibility that tendencies to acquiesce could influence scale scores. Altemeyer (1981), however, suggested that the very low internal consistency of the F scale was an even more fundamental problem. Thus, the F scale's mean interitem correlation has been only around .13. This would also be inflated by acquiescence; hence the even lower internal consistencies of balanced F scales. A careful reexamination of factor analytic studies also revealed that, in addition to demonstrating an unstable multidimensionality, these studies had not shown a strong general factor underlying F-scale scores. Altemeyer therefore concluded that the F scale's items (and the nine traits they had been written to express) did not comprise a coherent and unitary syndrome or dimension. This could account for the pattern of weak, inconsistent, and conflicting findings characterizing the literature on F-scale validity.

Altemeyer (1981) did note that a small group of items of the original F scale covaried sufficiently to suggest that they might be measuring a common construct. These core items seemed to tap only three of the nine constructs listed by Adorno et al. (1950). These were conventionalism, authoritarian submission, and authoritarian aggression. This conclusion was confirmed by a series of item-testing studies using large item pools drawn from the F scale and other traditional measures of authoritarianism, as well as new specially written items. The conceptualization of authoritarianism was therefore refined to "the covariation of these three attitudinal clusters" (Altemeyer, 1981, pp. 147–148), and the RWA (right-wing authoritarianism) scale was developed to measure it. A series of validation studies revealed that the RWA scale had excellent psychometric properties. Despite being balanced against acquiescence, it showed a high level of internal consistency and was essentially unidimensional. Moreover, it substantially outperformed a number of traditional measures of authoritarianism in predicting a variety of validity criteria at a consistently high level.

Thus far, relatively little research has been done with the RWA scale. However, several important propositions concerning authoritarianism have been confirmed. An important finding, relevant to the understanding of prejudice, has been that the RWA scale shows consistent positive correlations with measures of generalized prejudice against outgroups and minorities, at least in the North American samples that have been studied (Altemeyer, 1981, 1988a). These findings show that the relationship between authoritarianism and prejudice is a moderate one (with correlations around .40) rather than the very powerful one indicated by Adorno et al. Consistent relationships with political orientation and activity have been also found. High-scoring subjects on the RWA scale readily accept unjust acts by governmental authorities, see law as the basis of morality, and are more punitive toward unconventional targets.

In fact, one of the most startling findings using the RWA scale has been the punitiveness and aggression of high scorers toward any target sanctioned by conventional authority. Summing up a series of studies in which subjects were asked to respond to situations in which governmental authorities had hypothetically proscribed various groups or organizations, Altemeyer (1988b) noted that:

High scorers are more likely than others not only to hunt down and kill Communists but to help persecute others, as well. One might expect low scorers to be more aggressive than highs toward, say, the Ku Klux Klan; yet when the Klan was hypothetically outlawed, high scorers remained the least reluctant . . . to accept and act on the edict. The same pattern held when Canada's Progressive Conservative Party—a party for which high scorers had, in other surveys, voiced strong support—was banned. Though reluctant to persecute such a respectable group, people with high RWA scores were once again more likely than others to accept the "necessity" of destroying the party. It seems, in short, that they would be the first to attack almost any target—left-wing or right-wing, respectable or unsavory—as long as their behavior was sanctioned by some established authority. (pp. 33–34)

A series of studies to try and explain the psychological bases of the authoritarian's aggression generated important new findings (Altemeyer, 1988a, 1988b). Consistent with prior findings using the F scale, little support emerged for Adorno et al.'s original psychoanalytic theory. Thus, the correlations between parental punitiveness and strictness in child rearing and the RWA scores of their offspring were not significant. Moreover, signs of repressed aggression in daydreams and fantasies were no more common among high than among low RWA scorers. However, two hypotheses derived from social learning theory were impressively supported: (a) fear resulting from the perception of the world as a dangerous place and (b) self-righteousness and the view of oneself as morally superior seemed to account for most of the covariation of authoritarianism and aggression toward a wide variety of targets. Altemeyer (1988b) pointed out that these two factors were essentially complementary with "fear of a dangerous world serving as the instigator that arouses the authoritarian's hostility and self-righteousness serving as the disinhibitor that unleashes it" (p. 37).

Altemeyer's refinement of the concept of authoritarianism and his development of the RWA scale as a reliable and valid measure of the construct would finally seem to have made it possible for the study of authoritarianism to move beyond the unresolved methodological controversies and inconclusive findings that have thus far plagued it. Research with the RWA scale, although still in its infancy, already appears to have generated a consistent pattern of associations that confirm the validity and relevance of the concept of authoritarianism for understanding important aspects of human social and interpersonal behavior. In addition, it seems to have generated crucial new insights into the origins and causes of authoritarian behavior. Altemeyer's work, however, has not resolved all extant questions about authoritarianism. It can be argued, for example, that a critical conceptual issue remains essentially unresolved. This is the issue of what basic underlying individual-difference construct is being measured by the RWA scale. A possible answer will be discussed in the next section.

### Reconceptualizing Authoritarianism

It was noted earlier that, on the basis of his empirical findings, Altemeyer (1981, 1988a) defined authoritarianism as the covariation of three attitudinal clusters: conventionalism, authoritarian submission, and authoritarian aggression. It has been suggested, however, that this definition really begs the question (Duckitt, 1989). The critical issue of conceptualization here can be seen as that of what constitutes this covariation. In other words, what underlying construct pulls these three together into a single unitary and coherent dimension?

I have suggested elsewhere that a single theme does underlie these three components (Duckitt, 1989, 1990a). Each can be seen as an expres-

**Figure 8.1**
**Reconceptualizing Authoritarianism**

sion of an intense (and insecure) identification with one or more important social groups (usually national, ethnic, tribal, or societal) and a
consequent emphasis on and demand for group cohesion. Authoritarianism can therefore be defined as a set of beliefs organized around the
normative expectation that the purely personal needs, inclinations, and
values of group members should be subordinated as completely as possible to the cohesion of the group and its requirements. Thus, conventionalism reflects an emphasis on behavioral and attitudinal conformity
with ingroup norms and rules of conduct; authoritarian submission reflects an emphasis on respect and unconditional obedience to ingroup
leaders and authorities; and authoritarian aggression reflects intolerance
and punitiveness toward persons not conforming to ingroup norms and
rules. In fact, this conception of authoritarianism not only subsumes
Altemeyer's three components, it also predicts a fourth covariate—an
emphasis on unconditional loyalty to the ingroup.

Broadly, therefore, authoritarianism is a set of normative beliefs held
by individuals (or social groups) about what the appropriate relationship
between ingroups and their individual members should be. The more
strongly individuals identify with their groups and the more threatened
and insecure these identifications are, the greater will be their emphasis
on the importance of group cohesion, and the greater the extent to which
their beliefs will specify that individuals should be subordinated to the
requirements of their ingroups. This conception is summarized sche-
matically in Figure 8.1.

This conceptualization has a number of implications for our understanding of authoritarianism (cf. Duckitt, 1989, 1990a). Three of these
implications will be briefly noted here in order to illustrate how the
approach helps clarify important theoretical issues or findings from the
psychological literature on authoritarianism. These concern the relationship of authoritarianism with fascist ideology, with the findings of research on authoritarianism in South Africa, and with the relationship
between authoritarianism and prejudice.

First, conceptualizing authoritarianism in terms of an intense group identification that creates a demand for the subordination of individual group members to the cohesion of the group helps clarify why fascist ideology is such a pure expression of authoritarianism. This is illustrated by the symbol of the fasces, from which the term fascism derives. The fasces were the ancient Roman symbol of authority and consisted of a bundle of sticks bound together. Singly each stick was easily broken; bound together they were unbreakable. Fascist ideology thus demanded the binding together of all classes, levels, and elements of the nation into a single organism with a single will.

Second, research in South Africa has found substantial differences in the mean F-scale scores of English- and Afrikaans-speaking whites (e.g., Duckitt, 1983a; Mynhardt, 1980). Despite both groups sharing political domination and common socioeconomic advantages over the black majority, English speakers do not obtain particularly high F-scale scores, whereas Afrikaners do. Discussion of these findings has often seen them as reflecting intrapsychically determined adjustment patterns and the stricter socialization practices of Afrikaners (e.g., Lambley, 1980; Mynhardt, 1980; van der Spuy & Shamley, 1978). These interpretations do not seem very feasible given the failure of research using either the F scale or Altemeyer's new RWA scale to find any clear relationship of ego weakness, adjustment problems, or punitive socialization with authoritarianism (see e.g., Altemeyer, 1981, 1988a; Duckitt, 1990b, pp. 175–179). On the other hand, the high levels of authoritarianism among Afrikaners becomes quite explicable if authoritarianism is viewed as an expression of a strong identification with a social group whose identity has been tightly bound up with the social and economic advantages obtained through political domination. The insecure and threatened nature of this identity would lead to a particularly intense emphasis on group cohesion with its concomitant demand for conformity to group norms, ingroup loyalty, unconditional submission to ingroup leaders, and rejection of nonconformers. In fact, these are all well-documented features of Afrikaner nationalist ideology (see, e.g., Foster, 1991, pp. 366–369).

Finally, a problem with traditional approaches to authoritarianism has been that although measures of authoritarianism are consistently related to prejudice, no satisfactory mechanism has been proposed to explain this relationship. Conceptualizing authoritarianism as the expression of a particular kind of social identification helps resolve this issue. Social identity theory provides a mechanism (the need to maintain a positive social identity) through which identification with a particular social group generates discrimination and bias against outgroups. The stronger or more salient this identification, and the more insecure and threatened it is, the more intense the resultant bias and discrimination (Brewer, 1979; Hogg & Abrams, 1988; Tajfel & Turner, 1979). In a sense, this view of authoritarianism can be seen as an extension of social identity theory to the problem of explaining individual differences in susceptibility to prejudice.

Although a good deal of evidence has been reviewed that is consistent with this conception (see Duckitt, 1989), very little empirical work has yet been done to test it directly. One recent finding, however, does support a central proposition of the approach. Thus, one of the most important social groups for most persons will be their societal or national group. The nature of their identification with this group would usually make an important contribution to their overall level of authoritarianism. In order to test this in a large sample of Canadian students, a balanced twenty-two–item "need for group cohesion" scale with reference to Canadian society was developed (e.g., "It is absolutely vital that all true Canadians forget their differences to form a truly united and cohesive nation" and "Differing and even conflicting opinions and ideologies are absolutely essential for a truly democratic Canadian society"). This scale was adequately reliable with an alpha coefficient of .82. More importantly, this scale correlated positively and strongly with Altemeyer's RWA scale ($r = .49$) (B. Altemeyer, personal communication, 11 November 1990). This "need for group cohesion" scale also correlated highly significantly with several indices of prejudice and attitudes toward minorities. Interestingly, these correlations were generally higher than those of the RWA scale with the same indices. This would be consistent with the proposition that authoritarianism is related to prejudice because it reflects a particular kind of group identification (intense and threatened) and a consequent demand for group cohesion.

To sum up, it has been argued that Altemeyer's conceptualization of authoritarianism as the covariation of three attitudinal clusters—conventionalism, authoritarian submission, and authoritarian aggression—is incomplete because it does not explain why these three components covary. A new approach sees these three components as expressing an intense and insecure identification with an important social group, which generates a set of beliefs demanding the subordination of the personal needs, interests, and values of group members to the cohesion of the group and its requirements. Thus, measures such as the F and RWA scales can be seen as measuring a relatively stable set of normative beliefs held by individuals (or groups) about the sort of relationship they believe should exist between the social group and its individual members. Although little research has yet been done to test this approach, some preliminary findings seem reasonably encouraging.

## Authoritarianism: Overview and Conclusions

The psychological construct of an authoritarian personality type has had a long history, beginning with Reich's and Fromm's works. The major impetus to research, however, came with Adorno et al.'s classic investigation in 1950, which saw authoritarianism as a dimension of personality that underlies a generalized tendency to prejudice and ethnocentrism. This work stimulated an enormous research interest in the psychology of authoritarianism. However, their investigation had been characterized by very fundamental methodological and conceptual problems. One expression of this was their measure of authoritarianism, the F scale, which was a seriously flawed instrument. As a result, the research literature that developed around this measure and conceptualization turned out to be largely inconclusive. Although the findings did broadly suggest that the concept of authoritarianism had some validity (cf. Meloen, 1983; Meloen et al., 1988), they tended to be weak and inconsistent.

One response to the inconclusiveness of this research literature was the development of alternative concepts and measures such as those of dogmatism (Rokeach et al., 1960), toughmindedness (Eysenck, 1954), or conservatism (Wilson, 1973). None of these, however, proved particularly successful (cf. Altemeyer, 1981, pp. 80–104). Certain alternatives, such as Ray's construct of directiveness (Ray, 1976), also diverged far too much from the original conceptualization of authoritarianism to be seen as relevant to it (cf. Duckitt, 1982, 1984). The result, therefore, was a progressive loss of interest in the concept of authoritarianism and the feeling that it might not be particularly useful for understanding human social behavior.

More recently, Altemeyer (1981, 1988a, 1988b) effectively refined the concept of authoritarianism and developed a valid and reliable new measure. Initial findings from this approach have strongly confirmed the validity and importance of the concept. It has been shown to be a stable individual-difference dimension with crucial relevance for the explanation of a wide range of social and interpersonal behaviors and beliefs. This includes consistent evidence that individual differences in authoritarianism do underlie a generalized susceptibility to prejudice and ethnocentrism. A further refinement has also been proposed viewing authoritarianism as arising from an intense and insecure identification with an important social group, which generates a set of normative beliefs demanding the subordination of individuals to the requirements of group cohesion (e.g., Duckitt, 1989). However, this conceptualization has not yet been subject to much empirical testing.

A number of empirical questions also remain unanswered or need clarification. One of these pertains to the possibility that the relationship between authoritarianism and prejudice may not be universal. For example, there are indications from research using the original or balanced versions of the F scale that, under certain conditions, this relationship may be severely attenuated. Specifically, it appears that this might be the case in social settings such as South Africa, where prejudice seems to be normative and regulated by powerful social pressures that may completely override individual psychological propensities (Lever, 1978; Orpen, 1975; Pettigrew, 1958; van den Berghe, 1967).

## INDIVIDUAL DIFFERENCES AND PREJUDICE: CONCLUSIONS

A good deal of research was reviewed indicating that prejudice tends to be a generalized attitude. Thus, intergroup attitudes toward diverse groups intercorrelate quite substantially. This suggests stable individual differences in susceptibility or proneness to prejudice. A number of psychological factors, and some social attributes, which seem relevant for an explanation of these individual differences, were considered in this chapter. These were frustration, self-esteem, cognitive attributes, political and religious beliefs, certain sociodemographic characteristics, and authoritarianism.

Although there is a great deal of evidence that these factors do differentiate persons more prone to prejudice from those less prone to prejudice, this evidence has often been difficult to evaluate because of certain conceptual and empirical problems. Empirically simple bivariate research designs that have not controlled for potentially confounding variables have characterized the research. As a result, it has often not been clear whether correlations express real relationships between the two variables considered or reflect the effect of other variables. The dimensions investigated have often been poorly conceptualized and inadequately measured. Examples are frustration, dogmatism, and cognitive sophistication. This was also a major problem in the case of Adorno et al.'s F scale, which dominated research on individual differences in prejudice for many years. It is possible that the mass of inconclusive findings and unresolved methodological controversies in which F-scale research ultimately became mired contributed significantly to the subsequent neglect of the entire issue of individual differences in prejudice.

These methodological problems could conceivably explain why the research findings have often been inconsistent. For example, they might account for those studies which on occasion have reported nonsignificant correlations of psychological factors such as frustration, self-esteem, and even authoritarianism with prejudice. There is, however, an alternative explanation for these inconsistencies. It has been argued that the relationship between psychological factors and prejudice might be moderated by environmental or contextual factors, most prominently by the intensity of social pressures toward prejudice. Thus, when social pressures to prejudice are powerful, psychological factors would tend to have little effect (Bagley et al., 1979; Orpen, 1975; Pettigrew, 1958; van den Berghe, 1967). Mischel (1977) has also suggested that "strong situations"—that is, situations in which strong behavioral norms are operative—would tend to wash out individual differences. This kind of argument has been applied to racial prejudice among white South Africans: that is, powerful conformity pressures for individuals to hold prejudiced racial attitudes would result in psychological factors not being particularly significant factors in determining racial prejudice (Orpen, 1975; Pettigrew, 1958; van den Berghe, 1967). This issue, which essentially concerns the nature of the interaction between psychological factors and social pressures in the determination of prejudice, is discussed in the following chapter.

# 9

## Social versus Psychological Determinants of Prejudice: The Case of Racism in South Africa

The framework outlined at the end of Chapter 4 and elaborated in Chapters 5 through 8 proposed that four basic processes are involved in the causation of prejudice and are therefore necessary for its explanation. First, certain universal psychological processes build in an inherently human potentiality for prejudice. Second, social and intergroup dynamics describe the conditions and circumstances of intergroup contact and interaction, which elaborate this potentiality into socially shared patterns of prejudice in these groups. Third, mechanisms of transmission explain how these intergroup dynamics and shared patterns of prejudice are socially transmitted to individual members of these groups. Fourth, individual-difference dimensions determine individual susceptibility to prejudice and so operate to modulate the impact of these social influence mechanisms on individuals.

These four causal processes are regarded as complementary. Each describes a qualitatively different aspect of the causation of prejudice and thus makes an essential contribution to its explanation. Two of these processes, the social transmission of prejudice and individual-difference dimensions governing susceptibility, are necessary to account for the formation of prejudiced attitudes in individuals. They therefore correspond broadly with the distinction made in the psychological literature between social determinants of prejudice on the one hand and psychological or personality determinants on the other hand.

The issue of how these two sets of causal influences interrelate in determining the prejudiced attitudes held by individuals has attracted a good deal of attention from psychologists. The general conclusion has been that this interrelationship is interactive in nature. Thus, when social factors are important, psychological factors will have little significance. Conversely, if social factors are less important, psychological factors become correspondingly more significant. As it will be shown later in this chapter, this conclusion has come to be widely held in the psychological literature on prejudice and is often regarded as a settled issue (cf. Bagley et al., 1979; Colman & Lambley, 1970; Kinloch, 1974; Lever, 1978; Orpen, 1971a, 1975; Segall, Dasen, Berry, & Poortinga, 1990; Turner & Giles, 1981; van den Berghe, 1967; Yinger, 1983). It is apparent, however, that this conclusion is not entirely consistent with the framework presented in this book, which suggests that social and psychological factors should be complementary rather than interactive, with both making different though equally essential contributions to the determination of prejudiced attitudes.

For this reason, the issue will be critically reexamined in this chapter. It will be shown that the evidence is actually inconclusive and certainly does not justify the view that this is a settled issue. Finally, new research will be described that shifts the weight of evidence decisively against the interactive hypothesis. First, however, it is necessary to describe the interactive hypothesis and its origin in Pettigrew's (1958, 1959, 1960) classic South African research in more detail. This hypothesis was also briefly noted at the end of the last chapter, where it was pointed out that it has been often used to explain why well-established psychological correlates of prejudice, such as authoritarianism, sometimes show no empirical association with particular prejudiced attitudes.

## NORMATIVE PREJUDICE AND THE INTERACTIVE HYPOTHESIS

The interactive hypothesis has been most frequently raised in the case of highly prejudiced societies or social groups. Antiblack prejudice in the American South and in South Africa are prominent examples. In such groups, it is argued, prejudice becomes a social norm. As a result, individuals experience powerful conformity pressures to hold these normative prejudices. Thus, the argument continues, the prejudiced attitudes held by individuals in such societies are primarily determined by conformity to social pressure. Under these circumstances, psychological factors such as authoritarianism should be less important as determinants of prejudice (Bagley et al., 1979; Orpen, 1975; Pettigrew, 1959; van den Berghe, 1967).

This does not mean that conformity would only be relevant to the determination of prejudice in very highly prejudiced societies. The role of conformity pressures in determining prejudice in general was discussed in Chapter 7. It was noted that, together with social learning, conformity to social pressure has been regarded as a ubiquitous mechanism through which individuals acquire and maintain the beliefs and prejudices of their social groups. Conformity can thus be viewed as a general process that determines prejudiced attitudes. However, it has also been argued that the more a prejudiced attitude is normative in a particular group or society, the more powerful and intense the pressures to conform to that belief should be in the group. As a result, conformity pressures have been seen as particularly important factors in highly prejudiced societies, such as South Africa and the American South. These highly prejudiced societies therefore seem to be particularly appropriate settings for studying both the role of social conformity pressures in affecting prejudice and their interaction with psychological individual difference factors.

Consequently, it is not surprising that several very influential early studies were conducted in these settings. Pettigrew (1958, 1959, 1960) set out to investigate whether the high levels of racial prejudice in South Africa and the American South could be due to psychological factors. He found that, although white South Africans and white American Southerners were generally much higher in racial prejudice than were comparable groups, they were not much higher in authoritarianism— and clearly not to an extent able to account for their high levels of racial prejudice. This finding has been well replicated in later studies. Examples are studies by Middleton (1976), who compared persons in the American South and North, and Kinloch (1974), who compared white college students in South Africa and Hawaii.

Pettigrew's findings in this respect have been much cited, and his studies have virtually acquired the status of classics. This may be because these studies were done at a time when psychological explanations of prejudice in terms of factors such as authoritarianism largely dominated social scientific inquiry in the area. Pettigrew's findings, however, indicated that the heightened levels of prejudice in societies such as South Africa and the American South could not be explained by such factors. This, together with other evidence that will be discussed later in this chapter, suggested that social factors in general, and normative conformity specifically, could be responsible for the heightened prejudice in these societies. As Pettigrew wrote in 1961, "conformity to the stern racial norms of southern culture is unusually crucial in the South's heightened hostility to the Negro" (p. 109). This conclusion was widely accepted and helped shift the interest of social psychologists away from psychological explanations of prejudice to social and normative factors. For example, as Turner and Giles (1981) note:

Following the Sherifs, Pettigrew . . . and general social psychological studies of reference groups and social conformity, it seems to have become accepted that prejudice is to be understood as a social or cultural norm, and that, furthermore, where this is not the case, it is unlikely to be of social significance. Thus the problem with personality theories is that they are only likely to be predictive in settings where social factors tend to minimize prejudice. (p. 12)

This normative conformity perspective of prejudice may therefore be summarized as follows: When highly prejudiced beliefs are widespread in a social group or society, they can be viewed as being socially normative; to the extent that this is so, the prejudiced attitudes held by individuals will be determined by normative conformity pressures rather than by psychological factors. Three sets of evidence have been cited to support this perspective:

- First, evidence has been cited to indicate that in highly prejudiced societies the trait of conformity becomes an important predictor of prejudice (Nieuwoudt and Nel, 1975; Orpen, 1971c, 1975; Pettigrew, 1958, 1959).
- Second, it has been argued that in highly prejudiced groups differential exposure to normative pressure should be an important determinant of prejudice. Thus, evidence has been reported indicating that social variables which index the individual's membership in, integration into, and location within social groups seem to predict prejudice more powerfully when the group or society is more normatively prejudiced (Orpen, 1975; Pettigrew, 1958, 1959).
- Third, evidence has been reported showing that psychological factors such as authoritarianism may be less strongly related to prejudice in societies that are normatively prejudiced (Bagley et al., 1979; Orpen, 1971b, 1971c).

Each of these sets of evidence will be discussed in the next three sections. It will be shown that, despite its widespread acceptance, this evidence is actually quite inconclusive and that, as a result, the normative conformity thesis in general, and the interactive hypothesis in particular, have not yet been adequately tested. Finally, more recent evidence, including a direct and systematic test among white South Africans, will be described. This evidence seems to refute the idea that prejudiced attitudes in very highly prejudiced societies are primarily determined by normative conformity pressures and are little influenced by psychological factors such as authoritarianism.

## Conformity and Prejudice

The more prejudice is normative in a particular setting, the more important the trait of conformity is expected to be as a determinant of prejudice (Kinloch, 1974; Nieuwoudt and Nel, 1975; Orpen, 1971c, 1975; Pettigrew, 1958, 1959). For example, Pettigrew (1958), in discussing racism in South Africa and the American South, hypothesized that "susceptibility to conform may be an unusually important psychological component of prejudice in regions where the cultural norms positively sanction intolerance" (p. 40).

A number of attempts have been made to test this proposition. Orpen (1971b, 1971c, 1975) set out to do so by showing that persons who conform more to typical South African norms and values in general would also be more racially prejudiced. He therefore constructed a "South Africanism scale" consisting of statements that raters felt expressed traditional South African values. Highly significant positive correlations were found between this scale and measures of antiblack prejudice in samples of predominantly English-speaking white South African university ($r = .50$ and $r = .53$) and high school students ($r = .43$). Orpen therefore concluded that racial prejudice in these subjects was largely a matter of conforming to a social norm. While this reasoning seems plausible, alternative interpretations are equally feasible. For example, the "South Africanism" scale might largely measure social conservatism. In that case, the correlation between the two scales could be due to the well-established tendency for more conservative persons to be more prejudiced and not necessarily indicate the effects of conformity. A better approach would be to directly assess the relationship between conformity proneness and racial prejudice.

Several studies have employed this approach using a scale devised by Pettigrew (1958, 1960) to measure social conformity. The scale consists of sixteen statements in Likert format expressing the desirability and importance of conforming socially (e.g., "It's better to go along with the crowd than to be a martyr" and "Adherence to convention produces the best kind of citizen"). Pettigrew (1958) originally used this scale with a sample of white South African students (predominantly English-speaking) and found that it correlated strongly with antiblack prejudice (the correlation coefficients were .42 and .46 for Afrikaans and English students, respectively). Four studies using student samples have subsequently replicated this finding (Heaven et al., 1986; Kinloch, 1974; Nieuwoudt & Nel, 1975; Orpen, 1971c).

Although these findings have been accepted rather uncritically as demonstrating that conformity is an important determinant of prejudice in South Africa (cf. Ashmore & DelBoca, 1976; Banton, 1967; Lever, 1978; Turner & Giles, 1981; van den Berghe, 1967), a serious objection exists. Because only one measure of social conformity—that is, Pettigrew's scale—has been used, the conclusion is crucially dependent on the degree to which this scale is a valid measure of behavioral conformity. This seems particularly important because the items of this scale tend to be attitudinal in nature. They reflect individuals' beliefs about and attitudes toward conventional and conforming behavior rather than the degree to which the individuals report actually behaving in this way. Consequently, because it has been shown that attitudes and behavior are not always closely related (Wicker, 1969), the scale could simply be assessing an aspect of social conservatism rather than tendencies to actually behave in a conforming manner.

A survey of the literature revealed that, to date, no evidence has been reported to support the validity of Pettigrew's scale as a measure of behavioral conformity. The only study that could be located did not report supportive findings. Furnham (1974), using samples of black and white South African students, found little association between this scale and conformity in the Asch experimental situation, where subjects conform to or dissent from obviously erroneous perceptual judgments made by the groups to which they are allocated.

To sum up, there does not appear to be any evidence that Pettigrew's scale actually measures behavioral conformity. It might simply reflect conservative social beliefs, which could account for its correlation with prejudice. Because of this, the conclusion that conformity is an important determinant of prejudice in settings such as South Africa, which rests largely on the use of this scale, must be very seriously questioned. Whether conformity actually is an important determinant of prejudice in South Africa would seem to require the use of behaviorally valid measures of conformity. Ideally, such measures could then be related to prejudice under systematically varying conditions of normative pressure.

## Normative Exposure and Prejudice

In social settings where prejudice has become normative, the degree to which individuals are exposed to normative pressures should influence their adoption of these prejudiced norms (Kinloch, 1974; Orpen, 1971c, 1975; Pettigrew, 1958, 1959, 1960). Thus, sociocultural variables that index the degree to which individuals are exposed to the norms of their group should predict prejudice in such settings. Conversely, such variables should be weaker predictors in settings where norms of prejudice are absent or relatively weak. Summing up this argument by comparing the highly prejudiced American South with the less prejudiced North, Pettigrew (1959) proposed that "the anti-Negro complex of the South is more related to socio-cultural and social adjustment factors and less related to externalizing personality factors than in the North" (p. 28). Orpen (1975), on the same basis, argued that "we might thus expect there to be a strong relationship between socio-economic characteristics and prejudice in South Africa and a far weaker relationship between these two variables in the United States (except, possibly, in the South, where racial attitudes have been more clearly articulated)" (p. 103).

In his original research testing this hypothesis, Pettigrew (1958, 1959,

1960) used a number of sociocultural variables that he felt would index differential exposure to normative pressures in the American South and South Africa. His most definitive test of this hypothesis was a comparison of the degree to which six of these variables predicted prejudice in samples drawn from the South and North of the United States. These variables were sex, social mobility, church attendance, political party identification, education, and military service. He reasoned that women, as "carriers of the culture," should experience stronger pressures to conform to social norms than men would. Similarly, upwardly (as opposed to downwardly) mobile persons, high (as opposed to low) church attenders, and persons identifying with conventional political parties (as opposed to independents) should reflect the "mores" of their culture more strongly. On the other hand, military service veterans and the highly educated would be "potential deviants from southern culture simply because their special experience and study have brought them into contact with other ways of life" (Pettigrew, 1958, p. 39).

Pettigrew's findings confirmed his hypotheses. The six sociocultural variables predicted prejudice as expected in the South, with those who were more exposed to Southern norms being more prejudiced. On the other hand, this was not the case in the North where these variables were either not related to prejudice or were related in quite a different fashion (e.g., whereas church attenders and the upwardly mobile were more prejudiced in the South, nonattenders and the downwardly mobile were more prejudiced in the North). Pettigrew (1958) therefore concluded that "southerners who by their roles in the social structure can be anticipated to be conforming to the dictates of the culture, prove to be more prejudiced against Negroes" and "conformity to northern norms—unlike conformity to southern or South African norms—is not associated with hostility for the black man" (p. 38).

These findings, and this conclusion, seem clear-cut. A crucial question, however, is to what extent they have been replicated by subsequent research. Unfortunately, this is not an easy question to answer. An adequate replication should, like Pettigrew's study, compare the importance of sociocultural "normatively relevant" variables in groups that differ markedly in the degree to which they are normatively prejudiced, but which are reasonably equivalent in other respects. Only a few studies have come close to meeting these criteria, and these have rarely used more than a few of the sociocultural normative exposure variables suggested by him. Moreover, the findings have more often than not failed to replicate Pettigrew's findings (e.g., Kinloch's 1974 comparison of Hawaiian and white South African college students). The best study would appear to be that by Middleton (1976), who used national survey data from the United States to compare the degree to which most of the variables originally used by Pettigrew predicted prejudice in the South and North. Unlike Pettigrew, Middleton found that these variables all related to prejudice in essentially the same way in these two regions.

There is a possible objection to Middleton's failure to replicate Pettigrew's findings, however. Middleton's data were collected at least a decade after Pettigrew's. During this time, self-reported antiblack prejudice in the South seems to have begun to decline significantly and to erode the difference between North and South (Condran, 1979; Schuman et al., 1985). The kind of racial attitudes perceived to be normative may have changed even more rapidly among southerners and begun to converge with those held by northerners. These historical shifts might account for Middleton's failure to replicate Pettigrew's findings, and, indeed, might have begun to make overall comparisons between the American South and North inappropriate for testing hypotheses of this kind.

In conclusion, therefore, Pettigrew's original findings strongly supported his hypothesis that sociocultural variables reflecting group norms would be stronger predictors of prejudice in groups that were normatively prejudiced than in those that were not. However, these findings have not been replicated. Few studies have used the kind of comparative research design necessary for an adequate replication, and these have generally not supported Pettigrew's original findings. It is just possible, however, that change in prejudiced attitudes in the American South, and more importantly, in the kinds of attitudes that were viewed as normative, may have been responsible for the failure of the most important of these studies—that by Middleton (1976)—to replicate Pettigrew's findings.

### Authoritarianism and Normative Prejudice

The idea that psychological determinants of prejudice should be less important in highly prejudiced settings where prejudice has become normative has been frequently articulated (Bagley et al., 1979; Colman & Lambley, 1970; Kinloch, 1974; Lever, 1978; Orpen, 1971a, 1975; Pettigrew, 1960; Prothro, 1952; Turner & Giles, 1981; van den Berghe, 1967; Yinger, 1983). Pettigrew (1958, 1959, 1960) was the first to systematically investigate this hypothesis, both in South Africa and by comparing South and North in the United States. His point of departure in the latter context was that "the anti-Negro complex of the South is more related to socio-cultural and social adjustment factors *and less related to externalizing personality factors than in the North*" (1959, p. 28; italics added). His findings, however, did not support the second half of this proposition. The correlation between authoritarianism and prejudice was not significantly greater in the North than in the South. Pettigrew thus concluded that "externalization factors as indexed by F scores are of equal importance in the anti-Negro attitudes of the northern and southern respondents" (1959, p. 35) and attributed the difference in prejudice between the two regions to "socio-cultural and social adjustment factors" (p. 35). This conclusion was buttressed by Pettigrew's (1958, 1960) South African research. The correlations between the F scale and antiblack prejudice in that study were .56 and .46 for English and Afrikaans speakers, respectively. This seemed to indicate that authoritarianism was a powerful predictor of prejudice in South Africa, generating correlations not very much lower than those reported in the United States.

Later, however, Colman and Lambley (1970) challenged this conclusion and pointed out that Pettigrew's findings had been obtained using items taken straight from Adorno et al.'s (1950) original F scale. Because all items were unidirectionally worded, with agreement indicating authoritarianism, scores on the F scale could be spuriously influenced by acquiescent responding. This, they argued, could be an especially serious problem in a society in which prejudice was socially normative and therefore powerfully influenced by conformity: "The point is that in a highly prejudiced society it is something very much like 'acquiescence' which may account for the prejudiced attitudes of many of its (nonauthoritarian) members" (p. 162). This means that correlations between unidirectionally worded F scales and prejudice could be spuriously inflated to a much greater extent in highly prejudiced societies than in societies lower in prejudice. In order to correct for this, Colman and Lambley administered a balanced F scale and measures of racial prejudice to a sample of white, primarily English-speaking, university students. They obtained correlations with two measures of prejudice that were "strikingly lower than those recorded elsewhere" (the correlations were .23 and .33, with only the latter statistically significant) and concluded that in South Africa only a "minimal amount of the variance in race attitudes can be accounted for in terms of authoritarianism" (p. 163).

This argument was later taken up by others, of whom Orpen (1975) and several colleagues were most prominent. They were responsible for a series of studies investigating the correlation of various measures of racial prejudice with balanced or forced-choice F scales that controlled for acquiescence. Most of these studies used English-speaking students as subjects, though samples of high school students and even apprentices were also employed. These studies and all others that have used balanced F scales in South Africa are summarized in Table 9.1. Orpen's conclusion from his studies was that, with acquiescence controlled, the F scale seemed only very weakly predictive of prejudice in South Africa. This, he argued, clearly supported the proposition that "prejudice is not closely related to personality in settings where 'prejudice' is an approved norm" (1971b, p. 78).

**Table 9.1**
**Correlations Between Racial Prejudice and Balanced F-scales in South Africa**

| Study | Sample | Measure of prejudice | Correlation |
|---|---|---|---|
| Colman & Lambley, 1970 | 60 English students | Anti-African scale 1 | .23* |
| | | Anti-African scale 2 | .33 |
| | | Social distance | .27 |
| Heaven, 1983 | 106 residents of Bloemfontein | Antiblack | .39 |
| Heaven, & Rajab, 1980 | 91 residents of Bloemfontein | Antiblack | .18ᵃ |
| Lambley, 1973 | 190 English students | Ethnocentrism scale | .38 |
| | | Social distance | .41 |
| Lambley & Gilbert, 1970 | 106 English students | Anti-African | .32 & .43 |
| | | Social distance | .41 & .47 |
| Orpen, 1971a | 88 English students | Anti-African | .20 |
| | | Social distance | .19 |
| Orpen, 1973a | 90 English students | Social distance | .29 |
| Orpen, 1973b | 81 Rhodesian students | Anti-African, | .22 |
| | | 4 social | .19, .26 |
| | | distance scales | .11, .24 |
| Orpen & Tsapogas, 1972 | 131 English scholars | Anti-African 1 | .15* |
| | | Anti-African 2 | .11* |
| | | Social distance | .05* |
| Orpen & van der Schyff, 1972 | 58 apprentices | Anti-African | .33 |
| | 98 students | Anti-African | .20* |
| Ray, 1980 | 100 residents of Johannesburg | Antiblack | .59 |
| | Mean for 25 reported correlations | | .28 |

*Source*: "Prejudice and Racism." J. Duckitt, in *Social Psychology in South Africa* (p. 183), by
D. Foster & J. Louw-Potgieter (Eds.), 1991, Isando, South Africa: Lexicon. Copyright © 1991 by Lexicon. Reprinted by permission.

*Indicates nonsignificant correlations.

Subsequent studies using balanced F scales (Table 9.1) obtained findings similar to those of Orpen and his colleagues. Only one of these studies reported a reasonably substantial correlation with prejudice (i.e., Ray, 1980b), and the average correlation over all those reported is only .28. Correlations with conceptually related measures such as dogmatism and worldmindedness have produced similarly weak correlations (Orpen, 1971b; Orpen & Rookledge, 1972). Even unidirectionally worded F scales, for which correlations could have been inflated by acquiescence, have sometimes also shown weak and even negligible correlations with prejudice in South Africa (e.g., Heaven, 1979; Kinloch, 1977; Lever, 1978).

These findings have helped bring wide acceptance to the conclusion that authoritarianism has little relevance for prejudice in highly prejudiced settings (cf. Bagley et al., 1979; Lever, 1978; Turner & Giles, 1981; van den Berghe, 1967; Yinger, 1983). For example, Lever (1978), in reviewing South African studies of this kind, concluded that these low correlations "make it necessary to question the effect of personality variables on ethnic attitudes. There are several indicators to suggest that in the South African context . . . group norms and conformity to these norms are far more important for an understanding of ethnic attitudes than are deep-seated personality needs" (p. 127).

However, there are a number of reasons why this conclusion should not be accepted uncritically. One is that the samples used (cf. Table 9.1) have often been small and not very representative of the white South African community. In fact, most have consisted of English-speaking university students, who usually tend to be comparatively low in prejudice by South African standards (Mynhardt, 1980). Another and much more important consideration is that none of these studies reported comparative data. Consequently, while the correlations reported in Table 9.1 do seem low, it is by no means certain that they are lower than what would have been obtained elsewhere for similar samples using the same measures. For one thing, few studies outside South Africa have used balanced F scales. Another problem is that balanced F scales often have very low intercorrelations between their positive and negative items and very poor reliabilities. Low reliabilities could result in weak correlations with other variables. It is difficult to evaluate the seriousness of this problem because most of the studies listed in Table 9.1 did not report internal consistency reliability coefficients. Orpen (1970b), in his doctoral dissertation, however, noted a mean interitem correlation of only .05 for his balanced F scale. This would give low reliabilities, which could have contributed to the relatively weak correlation of such balanced F scales with prejudice.

Overall, therefore, these findings do not permit definitive conclusions about the relationship between authoritarianism and prejudice in social settings characterized by high rather than low levels of prejudice. This would require comparative studies using the same measures (naturally of adequate reliability and validity) in reasonably equivalent samples that differ substantially in normative levels of prejudice. A few studies have reported comparative data for South and North in the United States (Middleton, 1976) and for English and Afrikaans speakers in South Africa (Lever, 1978; Mynhardt, 1980; Nieuwoudt & Nel, 1975). The groups compared, however, have not been appropriately equivalent (cf. Duckitt, 1990b, pp. 227–230). In addition, like Pettigrew's original study (1959), all used unidirectionally worded F scales. These F scales, as Colman and Lambley (1970) showed, could have produced correlations distorted by acquiescence, particularly in the higher prejudice groups.

Summing up, therefore, the idea that psychological factors might be less important determinants of prejudice in settings where prejudice is normative seems plausible and has been widely accepted. Most of the evidence cited for this proposition consists of research done in South Africa, a setting where racial prejudice appears to be socially normative. Thus, studies using balanced F scales have often found that the relationship between authoritarianism and prejudice seems to be unusually weak in South Africa. However, these findings are clearly not definitive. The major problem has been the absence of adequate comparative data. New South African findings providing such data are described in the following section.

## NEW SOUTH AFRICAN FINDINGS

A comparative study of the role of social conformity and psychological determinants of prejudice should ideally contrast relatively similar groups that vary quite markedly in their general levels of prejudice. Pettigrew's (1959) original research, for example, compared samples from the North and South of the United States. A comparison of English- and Afrikaans-speaking white South Africans would be equally feasible. These groups are equivalent in many ways. Despite speaking different languages, they share a common Western European cultural heritage and, as whites in South Africa, they experience similar social, economic, and political conditions. Despite these important similarities, empirical studies have repeatedly shown English speakers to be substantially lower in racial prejudice (Hampel & Krupp, 1977; Kinloch, 1985; Mynhardt, 1980; Nieuwoudt & Nel, 1975; Pettigrew, 1958; Ray, 1980b).

In fact, while Afrikaans speakers have been found to be particularly high in racial prejudice in relation to other societies (Kinloch, 1985; Mynhardt, 1980), this has often not been true for English speakers. For example, Ray (1980b) obtained a mean prejudice score for a sample of white English-speaking residents of Johannesburg that was very similar to that for white Australians. Hampel and Krupp (1977), using large and representative national samples, found that English-speaking South Africans had racial attitudes closer to those of white British than to Afrikaans-speaking South Africans. Finally, Mynhardt (1980) used Adorno et al.'s (1950) original ethnocentrism scale to compare students from two universities, one English and the other Afrikaans, located in Johannesburg only a few kilometers apart. His comparison of the mean scores of these two groups with Adorno's original groups showed that:

Compared with this original research, the Afrikaans group can be described as particularly prejudiced (m = 4.84 per item)....Only one of the 26 original groups of Adorno et al. manifested more negative attitudes than these Afrikaans students. Contrary to this the mean score (3.05 per item) for the English speaking group is comparatively low....Only two of the original 26 groups investigated by Adorno et al. obtained lower mean scores than the present group of English speaking students. (pp. 14–15)

The very low levels of racial prejudice of the English-speaking students in this study undoubtedly reflected the spread of anti-Apartheid sentiment and activism among students at the larger urban English universities at the time. Consequently, it was probably not very representative of the general English-speaking community. Nevertheless, the finding does help illustrate the generally substantial difference in level of racial prejudice in South African research comparing these two groups.

There is, however, an important problem with simply comparing the correlations of authoritarianism and conformity with prejudice in two such large sociocultural groups, as previous studies such as Pettigrew's (1959) have done. Despite quite substantial overall differences, such groups could also be quite heterogeneous in prejudice. Thus, even in a highly prejudiced group such as Afrikaners, considerable subgroup differences in prejudice could exist between, for example, rural and urban persons and persons of high and low education and occupational status. Such differences have been effectively demonstrated in a study by Maykovich (1975), who used a large and nationally representative American sample. He employed a statistical technique termed the Automatic Interaction Detector (Sonquist, 1970) to partition this sample into subgroups defined by sociodemographic factors that were most homogeneous in terms of their racial attitudes. His findings revealed that the highly prejudiced regional subculture of the South naturally partitioned into a number of sociodemographically distinct subgroupings that were much more internally homogeneous in prejudice and which often differed quite substantially from each other in general levels of prejudice.

This means that, in order to adequately test propositions about the relationships of conformity and authoritarianism with prejudice in groups that differ in normative pressures toward prejudice, such subgroupings should be identified. This has not been done in previous research. For example, Pettigrew (1959) and Middleton (1976) simply correlated authoritarianism and prejudice in samples drawn from the American South and North even though both groups would have been quite heterogeneous in prejudice. Younger, highly educated, urban southerners could, for example, have been less prejudiced than older, blue-collar, more rural northerners (cf. Maykovich, 1975). Ideally such subgroupings should be identified, and the correlations of authoritarianism with prejudice should be examined for each subgrouping.

A recent study of racial prejudice in South Africa used this approach (Duckitt, 1988) with a nationally representative sample of white South Africans ($N = 792$). The subgroups that emerged are shown in Figure 9.1 in the dendrogram produced by an XAID (Extended Automatic Interaction Detector) analysis. XAID is an improved version of Sonquist's original AID technique (see Hawkins & Kass, 1982). In its essentials, it involves a step-wise application of a one-way analysis of variance model. At each step the analysis selects the most effective classification by one of a number of sociodemographic predictors to partition the sample into subgroups that are the most homogeneous in racial attitude. Each subgroup is split, in turn, until no further splits are statistically significant.

The most important predictor to emerge from the analysis was language group, which accounted for a fairly substantial 15.6 percent of the variation in prejudice, and on which basis the sample was partitioned into three subgroups. Of these, English speakers were the least and Afrikaans speakers were the most prejudiced, while bilingual persons and speakers of other languages formed an intermediate group. In both the English and the bilingual/other group the best predictor of prejudice was education. Persons with three or more years of education after high school were significantly less prejudiced than were persons with less education in both these groups. In contrast, the best predictor in the Afrikaans group was urbanicity, with persons living in metropolitan areas (given as cities in Figure 9.1) or large towns being less prejudiced than those living in small towns. Finally, among highly educated English speakers, those living in metropolitan areas were less prejudiced than were those living outside the major metropolitan centers.

The XAID analysis, therefore, generated seven sociodemographically distinct groups with maximal homogeneity in prejudice within groups, which varied considerably in mean levels of prejudice across groups. These were not intended to be "real" social groups. For the purpose of the analyses with authoritarianism and conformity proneness, it was merely necessary that their internal homogeneity in terms of antiblack

**Figure 9.1**

**XAID Dendogram for Antiblack Prejudice from Social Variables**

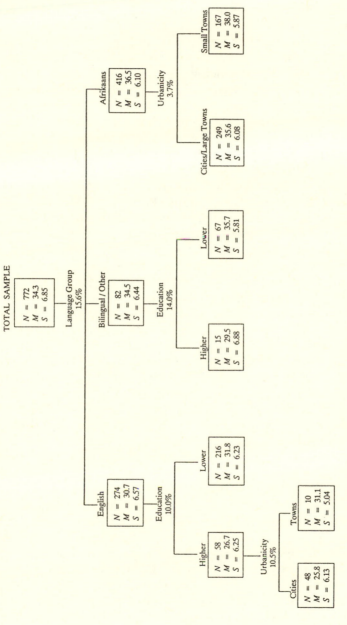

*Source:* "Normative Conformity and Racial Prejudice in South Africa." J. Duckitt, 1988, *Genetic, Social, and General Psychology Monographs, 114,* p. 426. Copyright © by the Helen Dwight Reid Educational Foundation. Reprinted by permission.

*Note:* $N$ = number of subjects; $M$ = mean antiblack prejudice; $S$ = standard deviation.

prejudice be maximized and that there be systematic and substantial variation across groups. If prejudice in South Africa is primarily determined by normative pressures, these "empirical" groups should differ correspondingly in the levels of normative pressure to prejudice characteristic of each.

It is interesting that the groups that emerged from this analysis do resemble important white South African sociopolitical groupings. Thus, of the seven final groups generated by the XAID analysis and shown in Figure 9.1, the English speakers of higher education who reside in metropolitan areas tend to be prototypical supporters of the liberal Democratic Party. The other two English groups, obtaining very similar prejudice means, suggest the somewhat more conservative English speakers who had originally been the backbone of the old United Party opposition. Finally, the larger of the two Afrikaans-speaking groups, those living in metropolitan centers and large towns, tend to constitute the support base of the ruling National Party, while those living in small towns fit the more rural-based right-wing Afrikaner opposition, the Conservative Party. It is evident that these empirically generated groups do seem to have some degree of real world validity. This probably reflects the overwhelming significance that racial attitudes and racial policy have had as the fundamental issues organizing white South African politics (cf. Hanf, Weiland, & Vierdag, 1981, pp. 82–126).

If prejudice in more highly prejudiced social groups is primarily determined by normative conformity pressures, then conformity should be more important and authoritarianism less important as correlates of racial attitude in increasingly prejudiced social groups. The findings from this study, which are shown in Table 9.2, did not support this proposition at all. A measure of social conformity—the Marlowe-Crowne (M-C) approval motivation scale, which has been shown to index behavioral tendencies to conform to social pressure (Marlowe & Crowne, 1961; Strickland, 1970; Strickland & Crowne, 1962)—showed no noteworthy relationship with racial prejudice either in the overall sample, for English and Afrikaans speakers separately, or in any of the seven subgroups derived from the XAID analysis. On the other hand, authoritarianism, measured by Ray's (1979b) balanced F scale, was a generally important predictor of prejudice. The correlation between racism and authoritarianism for the overall sample was .50, and authoritarianism correlated positively with prejudice at a high level of statistical significance in all the subgroups. There was only one subgroup—XAID group 3—in which this correlation, though statistically significant, was rather low in absolute terms (.23). However, this was one of the lower prejudice groups, and there were several extraneous factors operating to depress this correlation: First, the variance in authoritarianism scores was very restricted for this group; second, the reliability of the authoritarianism scale in this

Table 9.2
**Correlations of a Balanced F (BF) Scale and Approval Motivation (M-C) with Racial Prejudice in Different Social Groupings**

| Social group | BF scale | M-C scale | N |
|---|---|---|---|
| XAID 1: English, higher education, metropolitan | .49** | .09 | 46 |
| XAID 2: English, higher education, large and small towns | .63* | -.07 | 10 |
| XAID 3: English, lower education | .23** | .14* | 214 |
| XAID 4: Bilingual/other, higher education | .67** | .04 | 15 |
| XAID 5: Bilingual/other, lower education | .42** | .24 | 68 |
| XAID 6: Afrikaans, metropolitan and large towns | .42** | .01 | 248 |
| XAID 7: Afrikaans, small towns | .38** | .11 | 166 |
| English speakers overall | .36** | .12 | 263 |
| Afrikaans speakers overall | .43** | .03 | 411 |

*Significant at the 5% level.

**Significant at the 1% level.

group was very low. Overall, it is clear from the correlations shown in Table 9.2 that there was no tendency whatsoever either for authoritarianism to become a less important predictor of prejudice or for approval motivation to become a more important predictor in increasingly more prejudiced subgroups.

Frustration and psychological adjustment (see Chapter 8) have also shown relationships with prejudice, but in neither case have significant overall associations emerged for racial prejudice among white South Africans. If this were because the normative character of racial prejudice in South Africa suppresses correlations with psychological predictors of prejudice, then a tendency for such correlations to become stronger could be expected in the less prejudiced XAID groups. This was examined for a number of indices of psychological adjustment (anxiety, depression, cognitive disturbance, and irritability) and frustration (anger, relative deprivation, economic strain, work strain, parenting stress, and marital strain). In all cases, the correlations with racial prejudice were nonsignificant, with no tendency at all for these correlations to become stronger in less prejudiced groups (see Duckitt, 1988).

The data from this study also afforded an opportunity to test Pettigrew's (1959) contention that social variables indexing the degree to which individuals are exposed to normative conformity pressures should be more predictive of prejudiced attitudes in highly prejudiced as opposed to less prejudiced social groups. It was noted earlier that Pettigrew's original finding to this effect from a comparison of samples in the American South and North had not yet been satisfactorily replicated. Seven social variables that seemed to indicate "normative exposure" were compared as predictors of racial prejudice in the overall English- and Afrikaans-speaking groups. These were sex, church attendance, education, the two socioeconomic status indicators of income and occupational status, urbanicity, and marital status.

The first three had been used by Pettigrew in his original analysis. As we noted previously, he had reasoned that women as "carriers of the culture" typically experience stronger pressures to conform to social norms than men experience (cf. also Ehrlich, 1973). Similarly, high (as opposed to low) church attenders should reflect the mores of their culture more strongly, whereas the more highly educated would be potential deviants from traditional social norms because of their special experience and study. Following this general line of reasoning, persons of higher socioeconomic status (i.e., higher income and occupational status) and persons living in large metropolitan areas should, because of their cosmopolitanism and exposure to social and cultural diversity, also deviate more easily from traditional norms (cf. Orpen, 1975; Pettigrew, 1959). Finally, divorced and separated persons, because of their relative social marginality in a rather conservative culture, might also tend to experience weaker conformity pressures than married or widowed persons.

A comparison of the degree to which these social variables predicted prejudice among English and Afrikaans speakers did not confirm Pettigrew's argument, however (cf. Duckitt, 1988, p. 423, Table 1). There was no tendency for these variables to be more strongly associated with racist attitudes in the more highly prejudiced Afrikaans group. Sex, church attendance, and marital status did not show statistically significant associations with prejudice in either group, nor did income once education was statistically controlled. Urbanicity and occupation were associated with prejudice (with urban persons and persons of higher occupational status being less prejudiced) at about the same level in both groups. And, finally, a finding that was directly opposite to what Pettigrew had hypothesized was that education was a reasonably strong predictor of prejudice in the English group ($r = .34$, statistically significant at below the 1 percent level) but not in the Afrikaans group ($r = .10$, which was statistically nonsignificant).

Although totally at variance with Pettigrew's reasoning, this effect for education has been evident in earlier studies as well. For instance, two previous studies using large community samples both found that education had a significantly stronger effect on racial prejudice among English than among Afrikaans speakers (Hampel & Krupp, 1977; Lever, 1980). Overall, these findings raise two issues that require explanation. First, why should education be more strongly related to prejudice in the less prejudiced English group? Second, how can the effects of these social variables—that is, education, occupation, and urbanicity—be explained in general?

The general state of research on the relationship between sociodemographic variables, such as those considered here, and prejudice was reviewed in some detail in Chapter 8 where two alternative explanations for their effects were noted. One was the idea being discussed in this chapter, proposed by Pettigrew (1959) and others, that these variables are related to prejudice because they reflect the degree to which individuals are exposed to social pressures to conform to norms of prejudice. This hypothesis therefore expects these variables to be more strongly related to prejudice the more normatively prejudiced the social context is, which is clearly not supported by current findings. The other explanation was that these variables index cognitive sophistication (Christie, 1954; Glock et al., 1975; Kelman & Barclay, 1963; Selznick & Steinberg, 1969). As such, they should indicate a generalized predisposition to tolerance or intolerance, deriving from the range, variety, and breadth of individuals' environmental and social experience, as well as their cognitive capacity. This hypothesis therefore expects these variables to show basically similar correlations with prejudice across different sociocultural groups and contexts. Thus, the effects of occupation and urbanicity on prejudice obtained in this study can be plausibly accounted for in terms of cognitive sophistication.

Cognitive sophistication may also explain why education was less strongly related to prejudice for Afrikaans than for English speakers. Important differences in education in English- and Afrikaans-language educational institutions in South Africa do exist (Hofmeyer, 1982). Afrikaans institutions have generally implemented the authoritarian approach to education of "Christian National Education" very strictly, with a powerful emphasis on teaching and reinforcing traditional Afrikaner values and group identification. Education has tended to be less authoritarian in English public schools generally, and it is openly liberal in character in the English universities and private schools. It seems feasible, therefore, that the more authoritarian education of young Afrikaners could have inhibited the broadening and liberalizing of social perspectives that are regarded as a crucial component of cognitive sophistication (cf. Kelman & Barclay, 1963; Selznick & Steinberg, 1969). This, then, would account for the generally weaker effect of education on prejudice among Afrikaners.

Summing up, therefore, it appears that the social variables of urbanicity, education, and occupation may influence prejudice through effecting cognitive sophistication and not by indexing exposure to social pressures to conform to norms of prejudice. Their effect on prejudice was quite similar for English and Afrikaans speakers, except for education, in which case the authoritarian character of education among Afrikaans speakers may have been responsible for its weaker effect on prejudice in that group.

While Ray's balanced F scale had been an improvement on the measures of authoritarianism previously used in South Africa, its reliability in the study just described was, in fact, barely adequate (1972). The alpha coefficient was only .63. This raises the possibility that a better and more reliable measure of authoritarianism might produce even stronger correlations with prejudice than were obtained with this measure. The success of Altemeyer's (1981, 1988a) RWA scale as a new measure of authoritarianism in North American research was noted in the previous chapter. Two subsequent South African studies have used the RWA scale, and both have confirmed the finding that authoritarianism is indeed an important determinant of racial prejudice in South Africa (Duckitt, 1990b).

The first of these two studies, which used a sample of 217 students at the University of Natal, also examined the reliability and validity of the RWA scale with highly satisfactory results. For example, the RWA scale was found to be factorially unidimensional and highly reliable (the alpha coefficient was .93). It also correlated strongly and highly significantly with validity criteria of authoritarianism, such as opposing censorship ($r = -.53$), being opposed to detention without trial ($r = -.56$), supporting the right to peaceful protest ($r = -.64$), self-ratings of liberal-conservative ($r = .64$), acceptance of parents' religious views ($r = .46$), and political party preference ($eta = .63$). The correlations between the RWA scale and a number of indices of prejudice and discrimination from this and a second study (using a sample of 303 students at the University of the Witwatersrand) are shown in Table 9.3. They confirm the conclusion that authoritarianism is a powerful determinant of prejudice in South Africa.

In fact, the better and more reliable the measure, the stronger the

Table 9.3
Correlations of the RWA Scale[a] with Measures of Prejudice and Discriminatory
Behavior in Two South African Samples

| Study 1: $N$ = 217 students | | Study 2: $N$ = 303 students | |
|---|---|---|---|
| Measures | r | Measures | r |
| Subtle racism scale | .69 | Subtle racism scale | .63 |
| Antiblack attitudes | .53 | Modified social distance | .65 |
| Social distance to blacks | .56 | Interracial behavior | .36 |
| Modified social distance | .63 | | |

Source: "Prejudice and Racism." J. Duckitt, in Social Psychology in South Africa (p. 188), by
    D. Foster & J. Louw-Potgieter (Eds.), 1991, Isando, South Africa: Lexicon. Copy-
    right © 1991 by Lexicon. Reprinted by permission.

Note. All correlations were significant at beyond the 1% level.

[a]A fourteen item version of the RWA scale was used in Study 2.

correlation seems to be. Thus, Orpen's balanced F scale, which was
highly unreliable, produced weak correlations with racism in South Africa; Ray's balanced F scale, which was somewhat better but still not
adequately reliable, produced stronger correlations; and the RWA scale,
which was found to be highly reliable and valid in South African samples, produced very strong correlations.

Two other subsequent studies, using quite different methodologies,
confirmed the finding that conformity does not appear to be an important
determinant of racial attitudes in South Africa. In fact, these studies
extended this finding as they examined conformity not at the secondary
but at the primary group level. The study described earlier had shown
that racial attitudes do not appear to be determined by normative social
pressure from large-scale sociocultural groups. However, other findings
show that the norms of large secondary social groups are weaker influences than are the norms of primary groups and significant others such
as family and friends (Hare, 1976). Thus, conformity effects might not
be apparent at the secondary group level, but they might well emerge
at the primary group level. In fact, a number of previous studies, mainly
in the United States, had found that measures of perceived social pressure from significant others such as friends and family did correlate
significantly with prejudiced attitudes (e.g., Ewens & Ehrlich, 1972; Fendrich, 1967; Hamblin, 1962; Silverman & Cochrane, 1972). These findings
have often been interpreted as indicating that social pressures cause

prejudiced attitudes. However, alternative interpretations are as feasible. For example, in the case of family, the correlation could simply reflect the learning of prejudiced attitudes from parents and other family members during childhood. In the case of friends, this correlation could reflect the well-established tendency to prefer and select as friends those with similar attitudes.

In the first study, this simple bivariate research design was expanded into an interactional design by incorporating three different measures of conformity proneness (Duckitt, 1990b): the Marlowe-Crowne approval motivation scale discussed earlier, the autonomy scale from Jackson's (1967) Personality Research Form, and Lorr's (1982) conformity scale. The latter two measures had both been well validated by being shown to correlate substantially with self and peer ratings of actual conforming behavior. If the association between perceived social pressures from family and friends and racial attitudes was due to conformity, then this association should be stronger for more than for less conforming persons.

The results from a sample of 303 South African students did not support this. The association between perceived pressure and racial prejudice was not affected by how conforming subjects were. Thus, there was no tendency at all for the correlation between perceived social pressure from significant others to be stronger for highly conforming as opposed to nonconforming subjects for any of the three measures of conformity. This meant that this association could not be accounted for in terms of a conformity mechanism and that it probably reflected the operation of processes such as early learning and homophilic selection. Several other analyses from this study also confirmed the conclusion that conformity to group norms at the primary group level did not appear to be a significant factor in determining students' racial attitudes. Thus, none of the three measures of conformity showed noteworthy correlations with racial prejudice. Nor did the three conformity measures show much association with the degree to which students deviated from the normative levels of prejudice of their class. The strongest of both these sets of correlations was only .19, which indicated very little association between conformity and racial prejudice. Overall, therefore, conformity to primary group norms and social pressure from family and friends appeared to have little impact on the racial attitudes of South African university students.

The second study investigated change in the racial attitudes of British immigrants to South Africa (Tyson & Duckitt, 1990), with assessments immediately prior to their immigrating and again three and twelve months after they settled in South Africa. A marked and highly significant increase in racial prejudice was apparent at the three-month follow up and was maintained at the twelve-month reassessment, as shown in

Figure 9.2. However, this attitude change did not appear to be caused by conformity to social pressure. Racial attitudes at both three and twelve months after migration were not significantly related to the new attitudinal norms subjects experienced. Nor was there any tendency for more conforming persons to show greater change in attitude after migration.

Taken singly, none of these studies was necessarily definitive. The study of British immigrants, for example, used a rather small sample. Data were available for only seventeen subjects for the full one-year follow up and for twenty-four subjects at the three-month postmigration follow up. Nevertheless, the findings are extremely consistent over all these studies. Authoritarianism is strongly related to prejudice in South Africa. This holds even in extremely prejudiced subgroupings such as the nonurban Afrikaners shown in Figure 9.1. Moreover, the better the measure of authoritarianism, the stronger the relationship. On the other hand, conformity is not related to racial prejudice among white South Africans. This finding was confirmed using several well-validated measures of social conformity and was replicated across different research designs.

One question posed by these conclusions is how to account for the earlier findings. Why did earlier studies in South Africa find little association between authoritarianism and racism but strong associations between conformity and racism? This question has important methodological implications that are all too often disregarded. Basically, the validity of the findings from social research using questionnaires or scales to measure constructs such as prejudice, authoritarianism, and conformity is always critically dependent on the validity of the measures used. Very little reliance can be placed on findings from studies that use unreliable, psychometrically unsound, or otherwise invalid measures. Unfortunately, a good deal of social research has involved the use of unsound or unvalidated measures. A classic example has been the original F scale developed by Adorno et al. (1950). In this instance, the accumulation of an immense amount of virtually useless research over a number of decades has been devastatingly documented by Altemeyer (1981).

While the more recent South African research discussed in this section emphasized the use of adequately reliable and valid measures, this was not so in the case of the earlier South African research. For example, much early South African research used the original F scale which, because of its openness to acquiescence, produced findings of very dubious value. Orpen (1970b) and others at least attempted to address one of the original F scale's problems by producing a balanced F scale. However, as we have noted, the interitem correlations for this scale were so low that it could hardly be expected to correlate substantially with any

**Figure 9.2**
**Racial Attitudes of Immigrants to South Africa**

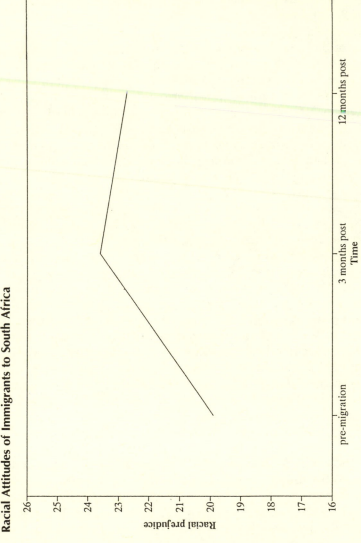

*Source:* "Prejudice and Racism." J. Duckitt, in *Social Psychology in South Africa* (p. 130), by D. Foster & J. Louw-Potgieter (Eds.), 1991, Isando, South Africa: Lexicon. Copyright © 1991 by Lexicon. Reprinted by permission.

other variable. It is remarkable that none of the many published studies using this scale reported alpha coefficients or mentioned the possibility that poor reliabilities could have influenced the weak or nonsignificant correlations that they obtained between authoritarianism and prejudice. Another example of a seriously problematic measure in South African research on prejudice is the use of Pettigrew's conformity scale (e.g., Heaven et al., 1986; Kinloch, 1974; Nieuwoudt & Nel, 1975; Orpen, 1971c; Pettigrew, 1958, 1960). The absence of any published research indicating the validity of this scale as a measure of conformity, as well as the likelihood that it simply measures social conservatism, was noted earlier in this chapter.

## THEORETICAL IMPLICATIONS

The new findings discussed in the preceding section have some important implications for explaining prejudiced attitudes in South Africa and for our understanding of prejudice in general. Three issues seem particularly significant and will be discussed in some detail.

- First, these findings indicate that normative conformity pressures may be much less important in determining prejudiced attitudes in highly prejudiced societies than has generally been assumed. This suggests that a fundamental reappraisal of the normative conformity perspective on prejudice is necessary.

- Second, because it has been shown that the high levels of racial prejudice in societies such as white South Africa cannot be due to psychological factors (Duckitt, 1988; Kinloch, 1974; Middleton, 1976; Pettigrew, 1958, 1960), social factors other than normative conformity pressure must be operative. This implies that social scientists need to redirect their attention to those other social factors that could be responsible for the elevated levels of racial prejudice in societies such as South Africa.

- Third, and perhaps most importantly, these findings help clarify the nature of the interrelationship between social and psychological factors in determining prejudice.

### Reappraising the Normative Conformity Perspective

It is apparent that these new South African findings contradict most of Pettigrew's (1958, 1959, 1960) classic findings that normative conformity pressures are important determinants of prejudiced attitudes in highly prejudiced societies. This normative conformity approach has been a well-established and widely accepted social psychological perspective on prejudice (e.g., Ashmore & DelBoca, 1976; Harding et al., 1969; Orpen, 1975; Pettigrew, 1958, 1959, 1960; Segall et al., 1990; Turner & Giles, 1981). There are several logical and substantive reasons why the role of normative pressure and conformity in determining prejudice may have been overestimated, however.

One consideration is that normative pressures may be easily evaded in natural social contexts. Attitudes are relatively low in social visibility and therefore not as readily subject to surveillance and regulation as behavior. As the research on what has been termed "modern racism" in the United States demonstrates, it is not difficult for racist sentiments to be cloaked in egalitarian-sounding beliefs and widely accepted traditional values (McConahay & Hough, 1976). Presumably, this is also possible in the opposite direction: Essentially unprejudiced individuals may superficially espouse some of the beliefs characteristic of a prejudiced social milieu without sharing the underlying prejudiced affect. In addition, individuals in modern industrial societies usually have a great deal of scope for selecting situations, information, and reference others that will support or at least not challenge internalized attitudes (Byrne, 1971). This may help explain a well-established, though rather puzzling, finding: Persons who espouse racist sentiments that are, in reality, quite deviant in their social settings or societies, nevertheless often perceive a great deal of social support, if not majority support, for these views (O'Gorman, 1975; O'Gorman & Garry, 1976; Silverman & Cochrane, 1972).

A second consideration is that the conformity paradigm tends to presuppose a rather simplistic and unidirectional relationship between group and individual. Thus, it implies that norms are arbitrary external impositions upon individuals who are passively and mechanistically molded by group pressures. It is doubtful whether this is ever true outside certain experimental laboratory situations or very exceptional and unusual social circumstances. In natural social groups and settings, norms emerge and crystallize out of group members' beliefs about their shared goals and interests (Hare, 1976, pp. 19–20). This means that behavior or beliefs that accord with group norms typically would not involve conformity as a psychological process, at least for the majority of group members most of the time. More recent research on minority influence has also shown that majorities do not necessarily overwhelm minority viewpoints, even in small group situations, and that compliance with social pressure is not a particularly effective route for beliefs to become accepted and internalized (Hoffman, 1977; Maass & Clark, 1984). As a result, it has been cogently argued that the traditional conformity paradigm substantially overevaluated the group's impact on individuals and seriously neglected the impact of individuals on the group (Moreland & Levine, 1982).

A number of empirical findings that have emerged during the past few decades are not really consistent with the idea that normative conformity is an important cause of prejudiced attitudes. For instance, it

has been shown that racial attitudes do not tend to be relatively superficial feelings that alter reasonably readily in response to situational
pressures. This is illustrated by research on the concept of modern or
symbolic racism, which suggests that, despite substantial change in
American norms, the underlying affective basis of racial prejudice has
been remarkably resistant to change. Racial prejudice has simply come
to be expressed through somewhat different beliefs (Crosby et al., 1980;
McConahay & Hough, 1976; Sears & Kinder, 1985). This literature has
therefore argued that the basic prejudiced affect must have been established through early learning and childhood socialization (e.g., Mc-
Conahay & Hough, 1976).

Another set of findings, indicate that once racial attitudes have been
internalized, they do not appear to change very readily. These findings
concern the manner in which historical change in prejudice has actually
taken place. It has been shown, for instance, that most of the decline
in racial prejudice and anti-Semitism in North America and Western
Europe has come about through successive age cohorts tending to be
less prejudiced (Firebaugh & Davis, 1988; Martire & Clark, 1982; Wuthnow, 1982). Once again, this suggests that these attitudes are acquired
through social learning in childhood and that, once internalized, these
attitudes tend to be rather resistant to change.

Overall, therefore, there are a number of empirical and substantive
reasons why conformity to normative pressure need not be an important
general factor in determining prejudiced attitudes. However, this does
not mean that conformity may never be important. It is possible that
certain circumstances, or combinations of circumstances, may well exist
under which conformity pressures could influence prejudice. This is
suggested by experimental studies that demonstrate quite dramatic instances of conforming behavior under specific laboratory conditions
(e.g., Asch, 1952; Milgram, 1974). Bagley and Verma (1979) have also
found some effects of conformity to classroom norms on the racial attitudes of British high school students. Instead of viewing conformity
to normative pressure as a general determinant of individual prejudice
levels, it might be more appropriately seen as a highly specific factor
that operates only under certain sets of circumstances.

Some pertinent points were made by Singer (1981) in the context of
a more general critique of the utility of explanation in terms of conformity
to reference group norms. She suggested that, in this kind of situation,
such concepts stand for "a combination of other characteristics—visibility, salience, reward, to name only a few. Use of the term 'reference
group' serves to obscure rather than illuminate these characteristics; it
begs the question of why conformity occurs" (p. 91). Consequently, it
"gives the illusion of explanation while simply pushing the crucial explanatory task one step further back" (p. 72). Therefore, an important

task for theory and research would seem to be that of elucidating the particular conditions under which conformity to normative pressures might actually become a factor in racial prejudice.

### Alternative Social Influences

If conformity pressures are not important general determinants of prejudice even in very highly prejudiced settings, then an obvious question arises: How do individuals come to hold attitudes that are widely shared in their social groups? More specifically, how can we account for the intensely prejudiced attitudes shared by most members of highly prejudiced social groups, such as white South Africans? Pettigrew's studies (1958, 1959, 1960) had long ago demonstrated that this is not explicable in terms of psychological factors such as authoritarianism. Although authoritarianism was somewhat higher among white South Africans, this difference did not account for the very high levels of racial prejudice observed in these subjects. The study discussed in the previous section also found that, although Afrikaners were markedly more authoritarian than English speakers, controlling for this accounted for only a small part of the difference in racist attitudes between them (Duckitt, 1988). It seems clear that social influences must be responsible for the elevated levels of prejudice in the members of highly prejudiced groups such as these. Because conformity pressures do not appear to be a significant factor in this respect, other social influences and processes must be operative.

Several alternative social processes could provide explanations as plausible as conformity of how individuals may acquire prejudiced attitudes that are widely shared in their social groups. These processes were discussed in detail in Chapter 7. Very briefly, shared attitudes toward an outgroup (a) can result from the perception that ingroup members have common interests in relation to an outgroup; (b) may have been acquired through social learning, particularly during childhood socialization; or (c) could have arisen from shared experiences with and perceptions of outgroup members when groups are differentiated on socially valued dimensions. Thus, racial prejudice in South Africa could be seen as serving the interests of a dominant white group by rationalizing and justifying its domination and privileges. Typically, such attitudes would originally be acquired through social learning during childhood socialization. Later they would be reinforced by their utility in justifying an advantageous situation. In addition, whites' perception of the "social reality" that most blacks occupy inferior social roles, statuses, and circumstances would tend to result in blacks being attributed traits consistent with and responsible for these roles and circumstances (e.g., victim-blaming attributions).

It is not just South African research that has neglected such social factors; in general, very little adequate research has examined their role in determining prejudiced attitudes. For example, although a good deal of research has looked at the developmental aspects of prejudice in childhood (reviewed in Chapter 7), hardly any research has considered how important childhood socialization might actually be in determining prejudice in adulthood. The dominance of the normative conformity perspective has clearly been a factor in this neglect and has been particularly salient in the case of South African research. Because of the assumption that white racial attitudes are largely a product of conformity to social norms, this research has expended a great deal of energy on the futile enterprise of trying to demonstrate that psychological factors have little significance for racial attitudes among white South Africans (e.g., Colman & Lambley, 1970; Edwards, 1985; Heaven, 1980, 1981, 1983a; Louw-Potgieter, 1988; Orpen, 1971a, 1973a, 1973b, 1975; Ray & Heaven, 1984). An important priority, therefore, would appear to be a fundamental redirection of attention and research toward investigating the kind of alternative social processes noted here.

## Social and Psychological Interaction

The idea that social and psychological factors interact in the determination of prejudice has been the basis of an important criticism of psychological, or personality-based, theories of prejudice. Turner and Giles (1981), for example, point out that "the problem with personality theories is that they are only likely to be predictive of prejudice in settings where social factors tend to minimize prejudice" (p. 12). These would be circumstances in which prejudice would usually not be of much social significance. Consequently, they assert that "the consensus in social psychology seems to be not to doubt personality determinants of prejudice but to question their importance" (p. 12).

The new findings discussed in this chapter do not support this assertion. Instead, they suggest that authoritarianism remains an important factor in prejudice in highly prejudiced settings. Moreover, there is no tendency for its importance to be reduced in progressively more prejudiced groups or settings. This has a crucial implication for the understanding of prejudice: It suggests that social and psychological theories of prejudice are not competing explanations, but are complementary. Both seem to be important, and the role or importance of each does not appear to be affected by the operation of the other. Precisely how they may complement each other will be discussed in the remainder of this chapter.

The broad theoretical framework proposed in Chapter 4 to integrate and organize the variety of theories that have tried to explain prejudice suggested that four basic processes are involved in the causation of prejudice and are necessary for its explanation. To recapitulate: First, certain universal psychological processes build in an inherently human potentiality for prejudice. Second, social and intergroup dynamics delineate the conditions of intergroup contact and interaction that elaborate this potentiality into socially shared patterns of prejudice in these groups. Third, mechanisms of transmission indicate how these intergroup dynamics and shared patterns of prejudice are socially transmitted to individual members of these groups. Fourth and finally, individual-difference dimensions determine individual susceptibility to prejudice and so operate to modulate the impact of these social-influence mechanisms on these individuals.

These four processes are seen as complementary, with each delineating a qualitatively different but equally essential aspect of the causation of prejudice. Two of these processes, the social transmission of prejudice and individual-difference dimensions governing susceptibility, are necessary to account for the formation of prejudice in individuals. They therefore correspond broadly with the distinction between social and psychological determinants of prejudice made in the psychological literature.

The proposal that individual-difference or psychological factors operate to modulate the impact of social influences toward prejudice on the individual was discussed in Chapter 8. It was noted in the introduction to that chapter that prejudice tends to be a generalized attitude, and as Prothro's (1952) findings indicated, this generality has to be interpreted in a relative rather than in an absolute sense. Thus, although more prejudiced individuals do not necessarily dislike all outgroups, they do tend to be generally less favorable to outgroups relative to the prevailing feeling to that outgroup characteristic of their social milieu. An important implication of this was pointed out earlier in this book: that is, the generality of prejudice can not be seen as resulting from an inner need for hostility to outgroups, but, rather, it reflects a generalized susceptibility or receptiveness to the prejudiced ideas present in the social environment. Individual differences in prejudice can therefore be viewed in terms of differential susceptibility, with this susceptibility modulating the degree to which social influences to prejudice against a particular group actually affect a particular individual's attitude toward that group.

From this it is clear how both social-influence factors and individual-difference susceptibility factors can be complementary and equally relevant for the determination of prejudice in individuals. Social-influence factors will tend to be a generalized characteristic of a social setting and will therefore determine the general level of individual prejudice within that setting—that is, whether persons in that environment tend to be generally high or low in prejudice. Susceptibility factors could also account for some of this effect by being generally elevated in a particular social setting, but this would not usually be of major significance. The primary role of susceptibility factors would tend to be in the area of within-group individual differences.

Because susceptibility factors, such as authoritarianism, modulate the impact of social influence on individuals, they will account for much of the variation between individuals in prejudice in a social setting. Susceptibility factors would not determine all the individual-difference variation as some of this could also be due to variability in the exposure of individuals to social-influence factors. However, the degree of variability in exposure to these social influences would not necessarily vary in different social settings. There is no reason why the amount of variability in the impact of social influences favoring high prejudice on individuals should be any different from the amount of variability in the impact of social influences favoring low prejudice. This means that susceptibility factors would account for much of the individual differences in prejudice in any social setting, and the degree to which they did so would usually not vary across settings, irrespective of whether social influences in these settings favored high prejudice or low prejudice. In its essence, this question of the interrelationship between social influence and individual susceptibility can be seen as directly analogous to the person-versus-situation issue—a debate that has been broadly resolved with the conclusion that both person and situation factors are necessary and complementary factors for the explanation of behavior (Kendrick & Fundar, 1988).

In a social setting such as South Africa, for example, social-influence factors would result in a mean level of racial prejudice much higher than in a setting such as Britain. Thus, the social learning of prejudice during childhood will be more intensive in South Africa. There will be a greater perception of threat to white interests from black equality in South Africa, and the interracial differences and inequities in social roles, status, and circumstances, which stimulate perceptual and attributional processes conducive to prejudice and stereotyping, will also be greater. Consequently, white South Africans will be generally higher in racial prejudice than will white British (Hampel & Krupp, 1977). However, individual-difference dimensions, such as authoritarianism, that determine individuals' generalized susceptibility to adopt prejudiced attitudes should be of similar importance in explaining the variation of individuals around the mean level of prejudice in each setting. The only proviso here, as Thomas (1974) noted, would be that the overall variation in prejudice in any setting should not be markedly reduced compared to the other. In such a case, the amount of variation accounted for by individual-difference variables would naturally be correspondingly lower.

This does not mean that any specific individual-difference variable must necessarily always be invariant in its relation to prejudice in different settings. It is possible, for example, that, because authoritarianism seems to involve a hypersensitivity to threat in individuals (cf. Altemeyer, 1988; and the discussion in Chapter 8), authoritarianism might be more strongly related to prejudice in a society in which intergroup relations involve the perception of threat and conflict. Thus, the correlations between Altemeyer's RWA scale and racial prejudice for white South African students discussed in this chapter seem stronger than those obtained by Altemeyer (1981, 1988a) with student samples in Canada. If comparative research does show this to be the case, it would not, however, mean that individual-difference or "psychological" variables were any less important in Canada. It could simply mean that one particular individual-difference factor accounted for less of the variance in prejudice there. As a result, one or more other individual-difference variables would probably account for a correspondingly greater proportion of the variation in prejudice.

The most fundamental conclusion, therefore, would seem to be that the issue of the relative importance of social and psychological factors in the determination of prejudice has largely been a pseudo-problem. Basically, social-influence factors and individual-susceptibility factors have different and complementary roles in determining prejudice in individuals. In practice, the former will tend to determine the general or mean level of prejudice in any particular social setting, whereas the latter will account for much of the variation around this mean. Consequently, any attempt to provide an adequate explanation for the prejudiced attitudes held by individuals in any particular social setting would necessarily have to encompass both sets of factors.

# 10

# The Future of Prejudice

There has been a significant upsurge of interest in prejudice and related phenomena among psychologists during the past decade and a half. In fact, the number of books appearing on the subject seems to be increasing at an almost exponential rate (e.g., Aboud, 1988; Bar-Tal et al., 1989; Dovidio & Gaertner, 1986; Fisher, 1990; Hewstone & Brown, 1986a; Hogg & Abrams, 1988; Katz & Taylor, 1988; Stroebe, Kruglanski, Bar-Tal, & Hewstone, 1988; van Oudenhoven & Willemsen, 1989a). Most of these books and most of the published research reflect the influence of the currently dominant cognitively based approach. In this volume, I have argued that this approach, like previously dominant paradigms, is only a partial approach. It illuminates only one aspect of the causation of prejudice and obscures others. Like its predecessors, it attempts to answer one particular question about the nature and causation of prejudice, which circumstances have helped make particularly salient for social scientists during this historical period.

The historical analysis in Chapter 4 suggested that the shifts in social scientists' understanding of prejudice have involved four fundamentally different but equally valid questions about the causation of prejudice. It was argued that these four questions seem to correspond to four basic and qualitatively different causal processes in the determination of prejudice. First, certain universal psychological processes build in an inherently human potentiality for prejudice. Second, social and intergroup dynamics of contact and interaction between groups elaborate this potentiality into socially consensual patterns of prejudice in these groups. Third, mechanisms of social influence are responsible for the transmission of these intergroup dynamics and shared patterns of prejudice to individual members of these groups in the form of prejudiced attitudes. Fourth, certain individual-difference dimensions determine individual susceptibility to prejudice and so operate to modulate the impact of these social transmission mechanisms on individual attitudes. It was argued that this perspective provides a rudimentary integrative framework involving four complementary processes, which gives a reasonably complete overall explanation of prejudice as both a group and an individual phenomenon. Thus, all existing theories, approaches, and empirical findings concerning the explanation of prejudice can be seen as pertaining to at least one of these four complementary causal mechanisms and can, therefore, be logically and coherently subsumed within this framework. The theories and findings relating to each of these four causal processes were reviewed in Chapters 5 to 8.

This review indicates considerable advances in our knowledge since Allport's comprehensive overview in 1954. In broad outline, we seem to have a fairly good general idea of what universal cognitive and motivational processes underlie the human propensity for prejudice, the kind of macrosocial and intergroup dynamics that elaborate these potentialities into socially shared patterns of prejudice in groups and societies, the social influence factors that condition prejudiced attitudes in the individual members of these groups and societies, and the kind of individual-difference dimensions that make individuals more or less susceptible to these social influences. On the other hand, it is equally clear that a great deal remains to be done. There are very few, if any, areas in which clear-cut and unequivocal conclusions can be drawn. We currently have a canvas on which the broad brush strokes can be seen but the details are not yet clear.

In spite of the seriously incomplete state of our knowledge, some important practical issues must be confronted. Prejudiced and hostile intergroup attitudes have become increasingly dysfunctional for human social existence. It is possible that in earlier times prejudice may well have been functional for human survival in an evolutionary sense. In an era when human groups often competed intensely for resources essential for survival, prejudice may have had some adaptive function. Dislike, mistrust, and suspicion of outgroups may have helped cement loyalty to the ingroup and facilitated a readiness to defend and, if necessary, die in the interests of the group. The development of modern and technologically advanced mass societies that possess enormously destructive weaponry has changed the situation dramatically, however. From a possible evolutionary advantage, prejudiced intergroup attitudes—with their potential for periodic eruption in overt intergroup conflict—have now become an extremely serious threat to the continued survival of human society and civilization.

## REDUCING PREJUDICE: A MULTILEVEL APPROACH

Can the social scientific knowledge that has been amassed about prejudice help alleviate this threat? It is unlikely that the universal psychological processes that have been shown to underlie a fundamentally human propensity for prejudice can be changed. However, the degree to which they come to be expressed in prejudice can be. This would require action at three different levels, corresponding to the three causal processes described in Chapters 6, 7, and 8. Thus, change would be required—first, at the level of social structure and intergroup relations; second, in the social influences to which individuals are exposed; and third, in individual susceptibility. Since the causal processes that establish and maintain prejudice are operative at all three levels, changing well-established prejudiced attitudes ideally requires a multilevel approach. This is probably the single most important implication of the multilevel causal framework used for the explanation of prejudice in this volume. Isolated, single interventions, such as those often favored by psychologists in attempts to change the attitudes of individuals, are unlikely to be effective in the long run if they leave the social milieu and influences impacting on these individuals unchanged. In fact, unless such interventions have some effect on the basic susceptibility of the individual to prejudice, they may not even generalize beyond the attitude to the group that has been specifically targeted for improvement.

Another implication is that the higher the level of the intervention, the greater will be its potential impact. Changes at the macrolevel in social structure or nature of the intergroup relations will generally have far more fundamental and extensive impacts than will interventions that target individuals, no matter how many are actually involved in the latter case. Unfortunately, such changes are often very difficult and may seem far beyond the ability and competence of social psychologists. However, this is not always so. Social scientists played a significant role in the judicial decisions leading to the desegregation of American schools (Cook, 1979). Social scientists have also begun to play a role in designing constitutions and political systems to reduce or channel interethnic conflicts (Horowitz, 1985). In fact, the potential contribution that social scientists can make in the reduction or control of prejudice at all levels is beginning to seem considerable. Surprisingly little systematic attention has been given to this in the scientific literature, which, thus far, has placed its primary emphasis on trying to understand prejudice rather than on changing it. Nevertheless, a great deal of relevant knowledge has gradually been accumulated to assist in reducing prejudice at each of the causal levels that have been identified here.

It has already been noted that, because of their universal and inherently human nature, it is unlikely that the cognitive and motivational fundamentals underlying the propensity for prejudice can be modified. However, an understanding of how basic processes operate, such as cognitive categorization and the ingroup-favoring tendencies that it elicits, is still important for the design of effective interventions to reduce prejudice. The more interventions are designed to be compatible with rather than contrary to these processes, the more effective they will ultimately be. Thus, to be effective, interventions must generally not make ingroup-outgroup distinctions more salient or more generalized over social situations. They must not make outgroups seem more homogeneous or more dissimilar to the ingroup, lower or illegitimately higher on socially valued dimensions regarded as indicative of worth, and frustrating, competitive, or threatening to the ingroup.

This can be illustrated by a number of well-meaning interventions or activities which, it is popularly believed, should reduce prejudice and further harmonious intergroup relations, but which, in practice, tend to have the opposite effect. These include international student exchange programs (Stroebe, Lenkert, & Jonas, 1988), competitive sporting tournaments or matches between groups (Sherif & Sherif, 1953), international tourism (Ben-Arie & Amir, 1988), international aid or welfare (Staub, 1989), and simply bringing members of hostile groups or groups of different status into contact with each other (Allport, 1954; Sherif & Sherif, 1953). In each of these cases, ingroup-outgroup distinctions are in some way or another made more salient, generalized, or threatening, with the result that intergroup attitudes become less rather than more favorable. In contrast, interventions that successfully improve intergroup attitudes should generally make ingroup-outgroup distinctions less salient and less generalized. Outgroups should be made to seem more differentiated and less homogeneous, less threatening, less dissimilar, cooperating to achieve mutual goals rather than competing, rewarding rather than frustrating to the ingroup, not lower in status and worth to the ingroup, and, if higher in status, legitimately so.

A number of interventions have been used or proposed that seem able to reduce prejudice successfully under appropriate circumstances. These interventions have typically involved action at one of the three levels identified—that is, social structure and intergroup relations, social influence, and individual attitude and susceptibility. The kind of interventions at each of these levels will be briefly discussed in the next three sections.

## SOCIAL STRUCTURE AND INTERGROUP RELATIONS

In the case of interventions at the level of social structure and intergroup relations, the most crucial factor in any society with a history or background of prejudice and discrimination against a minority group almost certainly involves the complete removal of all legal and institutional supports for discrimination or any overt expressions of prejudice. Typically, this requires the dismantling of formal segregation and resolute steps to combat both formal and informal barriers to minority advancement. Although desegregating previously segregated groups will not in itself reduce prejudice or improve minority conditions, it is generally important in creating the kind of conditions under which improvements can occur. As the experience in the United States indicates, desegregation needs to be accompanied by a number of other measures. These include clear and vigorously enforced antidiscriminatory laws, which not only markedly raise the costs of discriminatory behavior but also establish unequivocal social and institutional supports for new norms of tolerance and nondiscrimination. This should usually also involve concerted affirmative action programs to break entrenched cycles of exclusion and to redress the often severe social and economic inequities that result from histories of injustice and discrimination. Reducing or eliminating such inequities has a number of important effects, such as helping to make group boundaries less salient and lessening negative stereotyping and victim-blaming tendencies.

Fundamental to this scenario are the issues of political power and political will. Even in democracies, political majority groups may have little motivation to try and reduce prejudice and discrimination against minorities, particularly when this risks a governing party losing political support from majority voters. Sometimes broader international considerations and pressures may make the maintenance of a discriminatory system too costly for a majority group. It seems highly likely that global geopolitical considerations may have helped influence desegregation in the United States. International pressure on white South Africa, though of quite a different kind, has certainly been a very potent factor in motivating whites to move away from Apartheid. Another and potentially more important factor consists of the political organization and pressure for change that has been exerted by minorities themselves. A considerable sociological literature is available, detailing the kind of social circumstances and strategies that are likely to result in failure or success for minority movements seeking to legitimize their demands for equality and justice (Altemeyer, 1988a; Simpson & Yinger, 1985). As it happens, there are some very interesting parallels with the social psychological research on how minorities can influence majorities in experimental laboratory research on small groups (Moscovici, 1976). Even though circumstances vary enormously, it is often important for minority groups, who are also numerical minorities in democratic societies, to gain allies within the majority group. Sometimes this may be possible by appealing to important majority group values, such as equity and democracy, or by embedding minority demands within broader campaigns against social injustice in general (cf. Deutsch, 1971).

Political factors are often crucial for either exacerbating or mitigating intergroup animosities. Once salient ethnic or cultural divisions assume political significance and become infused with threat, conflict, and competition for power, intergroup attitudes and relations usually deteriorate markedly. Such situations, however, can be avoided or defused by designing constitutional and political systems to channel political processes and tensions away from dangerous ethnic cleavages. Horowitz (1985) illustrated this very effectively with reference to a number of severely divided societies. An excellent example is provided by the two federal Nigerian constitutions separated by thirteen years of military rule. In the first federal constitution (1960–1966), state boundaries largely followed important lines of ethnic cleavage, setting off a struggle for power at the center, which seriously exacerbated ethnic hostilities and culminated in a disastrous civil war. The second constitution (1979–1983), which was devised in consultation with constitutional experts, markedly mitigated interethnic conflict largely by restructuring the federal states to channel political tensions along much less dangerous subethnic cleavages.

Thus, societies can be structured to facilitate either intergroup tolerance or prejudice. In general, a tolerant society will be structured so that ethnic, cultural, religious, occupational, socioeconomic, and other group distinctions are not convergent but cut across each other so that different identities are salient at different times and in different situations. All such groups should on at least some occasions share some important superordinate identity. Groups should generally be of similar status, wealth, or power, and, if differences exist, they should be viewed as legitimate and not due to some or other inequity, shared disadvantage, or lack of worth. Discriminatory barriers or actions should be absent and, if necessary, legally and normatively proscribed. The political system should encourage parties to gain broad-based support over as wide a spectrum of groups as possible to compete successfully in the political arena, and it should penalize parties that are pursuing narrowly sectional and divisive constituencies.

## SOCIAL-INFLUENCE PROCESSES

The influence of social structure on the intergroup attitudes held by individuals is transmitted in a variety of ways. These were discussed in some detail in Chapter 7. Typically, these social influences will tend to mediate social structure fairly directly. However, they need not always simply reflect structure. Their own characteristics may independently influence attitudes, perhaps to some extent weakening the negative impact of even an "apartheid" social structure, or partly countering the positive impact of a society structured for tolerance. At this level, three kinds of intervention to improve intergroup attitudes seem particularly feasible. These involve the mass media, the educational system, and the way in which interpersonal contact between individuals from different groups is organized in important settings such as work organizations.

In modern industrial societies the media have come to play an increasingly important role in conditioning the image that individuals have of their societies. The manner in which the media present and portray social and intergroup "realities" can markedly influence the perceived salience of (a) intergroup distinctions, roles, and inequities; (b) negative stereotyping; (c) the social acceptability of prejudice; and (d) norms that govern intergroup behavior. A good deal has been done to identify the negative and biased portrayals of minorities that have undoubtedly contributed to and reinforced prejudice against them (e.g., Milner, 1983) and to eliminate or at least reduce this kind of media presentation, particularly in the case of racism in the United States (cf. Greenberg & Mazingo, 1976). Relatively little has yet been done, however, to establish clear and systematic guidelines of how minorities should be portrayed to actively promote tolerance and positive attitudes toward them. In this respect, Stephan (1987) suggested that more positive attitudes would probably be facilitated to the extent that minority members were presented frequently, positively, and in individuating ways. The effect of media portrayals are not always as obvious as this. Thus, Levin and Levin (1982) noted some evidence that antiprejudice campaigns or media programs in which the persecution and victimization of minorities are emphasized may reinforce rather than reduce prejudice against them. They suggested that programs which show the costs of prejudice and discrimination for the majority group may be much more effective in improving intergroup attitudes.

A great deal of emphasis is usually placed on the role of education and educational systems in reducing prejudice. The formal educational system is not only a major agent of socialization but also one of the most important sites for direct interpersonal contact between individuals from different groups. Education itself has been shown to reduce prejudice, but, as Chapter 7 indicated, this does not apply to all education. Authoritarian approaches to education—such as Christian National Education in South Africa and the approach that Inbar, Resh, and Adler (1984) termed conservative achievement-orientated education in the Israeli context—do not seem to reduce prejudice, whereas more liberal or progressive approaches to education do.

The composition of curricula and the content of what is taught have also received increasing attention. Staub (1989), for example, emphasized the importance of teaching about prejudice and intergroup hostility and how to combat them. Glock et al. (1975) suggested that education can counter stereotyping and prejudice by emphasizing how intergroup differences can be due to social and historical circumstances to reduce the tendency to attribute such differences to the nature of the groups concerned. More comprehensive approaches have stressed that an unambiguously multicultural approach to education should be designed into all aspects of the school—its administrative policy, teaching, liaison with parents, staff development, language and religious policy, and so forth (e.g., Leicester, 1989). This should include programs such as antiracism awareness with the objective of directly changing student and teacher attitudes.

The way in which intergroup contact is structured in classroom and learning situations also has important influences on intergroup attitudes. The traditional approach of whole class instruction, in which students work on their own and compete for grades, tends not to improve intergroup attitudes in desegregated classrooms, particularly when majority and minority children differ in social status and achievement level (e.g., Sharan & Rich, 1984). In this situation prejudice will even be exacerbated if academic tracking is introduced. On the other hand, research on cooperative education has shown that, when learning and teaching situations are structured so that children cooperate with each other in mixed-ethnic groups, there are marked gains not only in minority performance but also in intergroup acceptance. A number of cooperative learning strategies have been developed, and these positive outcomes have been consistently and powerfully demonstrated (Johnson & Johnson, 1989; Sharan, 1990). In general, therefore, the kind of educational system that would reduce prejudice and promote tolerance should emphasize a broadly liberal-progressive approach to education, would clearly commit itself to multicultural policies and curricula, and would use cooperative teaching and learning techniques with multiethnic groups.

Next to the educational setting, the context of work is the area in which personal contact between members of different groups is most likely and common. Work organizations can structure or influence this contact to facilitate positive intergroup attitudes in a number of ways. In South African work organizations, for example, interracial animosities or issues can be responsible for costly strikes and the interracial climate can markedly influence the effectiveness of organizations. This situation typically requires a clear and totally unambiguous commitment from the organization to equal opportunity—incorporating measures that actively demonstrate the unacceptability of racism or discrimination in any guise, the complete desegregation of all facilities and activities, and training programs to change prejudiced attitudes directly. This should be accompanied by affirmative action to promote blacks to management and supervisory levels to blur the management-labor racial boundary, by an emphasis on superordinate goals through building greater organizational commitment, by eliminating situations of interracial competition, and by restructuring work activities to maximize cooperative activity in mixed-race groupings.

A currently problematic area in South Africa is the relationship between white supervisor and black worker. The changing political situation has increased the tensions associated with this relationship markedly. Typically, a good deal of ambiguity exists about the specific role, status, and authority of supervisors. This ambiguity tends to be useful for organizations as rigid definitions may impair flexibility and reduce efficiency (as in "working to rule"). However, when intergroup tensions exist between supervisors and workers, such areas of ambiguity can become extremely hazardous. In essence, this ambiguity results in no clear differentiation between the legitimate aspects of supervisory authority and those aspects that are expressions of racist supremacy and therefore illegitimate. Supervisors, on their part, may find it difficult to appropriately differentiate between workers' assertion of the right to be treated with basic respect and direct challenges to their legitimate status and authority. In such circumstances, it becomes crucial that the roles, functions, and legitimate authority of supervisors be very much more clearly defined by the organization than is customary and that the basic rights of workers be clarified and unambiguously supported.

The contemporary situation that confronts black persons in countries such as the United States, where formal discriminatory barriers and overt prejudice have largely been eliminated in work organizations, tends to be somewhat different. A major problem here, noted by Pettigrew and Martin (1989), is that blacks are confronted by subtle stereotyping and covert prejudice that is often seriously exacerbated by being viewed as tokens and occupying solo statuses (a single black person in a group of whites). Their remedies include sanctions by organizational authorities, training programs to reduce prejudice, structuring interethnic work activities in a more cooperative manner, and establishing systems to reward supervisors for the progress of their black subordinates or trainees. In addition, they suggest that the disadvantages of solo status should be avoided wherever possible by clustering blacks to comprise about 20 percent of work groups and by obtaining higher black numbers in the organization by funding special training and educational programs.

## INDIVIDUAL ATTITUDES AND SUSCEPTIBILITY

Interventions aiming at changing individuals are broadly of two kinds: They may attempt to change, first, individual's generalized susceptibility to prejudice and, second, specific intergroup attitudes. Changing individuals' generalized susceptibility to prejudice usually involves trying to change well-established and often deeply ingrained traits, values, or characteristics. This approach may engender considerable resistance, and, with good reason, it is not viewed as easily done. The most common approach to changing susceptibility to prejudice uses psychotherapeutically based techniques. Bagley et al. (1979), for example, described group counseling sessions in multiracial British schools that reduced racial prejudice by increasing the self-esteem of the students who participated. Altemeyer (1988a) also described a number of nontherapeutic techniques that he found to be effective in reducing authoritarianism in college students.

The alternative approach of trying to change specific intergroup attitudes has an important limitation. Changing the attitude to one particular outgroup in a positive direction does not necessarily mean that other intergroup attitudes will also become more positive. However, changing an attitude is usually much easier than changing more enduring traits or characteristics. As a result, this approach tends to be much more commonly employed. A variety of change programs have been used. Some can be classified as broadly cognitive, focusing on information, knowledge, awareness, and understanding. Others seem to rely more on affective changes toward outgroup members, precipitated by experiences shared with them in mixed workshop settings.

Cognitively orientated programs can be overtly didactic, consisting of lectures, films, discussions, and extracurricular readings. The emphasis may often be on the minority or outgroup's history and achievements, though knowledge and skills pertinent to intergroup problems and relations can also be included. Effects have usually been found to be positive, particularly for more extensive programs, programs that emphasize intergroup similarities rather than differences, and programs that require active participation (Fisher, 1990; Stephan & Stephan, 1984). Racism awareness training (Katz, 1978) has a somewhat different emphasis. Here the focus is on making participants aware of the forms and manifestations of racism in society, particularly in its more covert and subtle expressions. Typically, this should not only change racial attitudes but engender a readiness in the individual to actively combat racism in his or her environment (Leicester, 1989). Finally, a somewhat different approach is employed in intercultural training. In this case, the emphasis is usually on cultural differences, with the objective of developing an empathic understanding of the outgroup's subjective culture. Techniques such as the cultural assimilator, for example, teach subjects to perceive and interpret incidents conducive to intercultural misunderstanding and stereotyping from the outgroups' points of view and have been shown to have positive effects on intergroup attitudes (van den Heuvel & Meertens, 1989).

A number of workshop approaches that bring together members of different groups have also been used. Human relations or sensitivity training brings members of different ethnic or cultural groups together in small interaction groups (e.g., Doob & Foltz, 1973). Generally these groups diagnose and discuss typical intergroup problems and issues in intensive, quasi-therapeutic encounters. The focus tends to be on using personal reactions and group dynamics to enhance awareness and self-insight to change attitudes. Problem-solving or conflict-resolution workshops have a somewhat different focus. Participants are drawn from two "opposing" groups with the specific objective of developing solutions for the dysfunctional intergroup relationship. This usually involves steps such as defining and reviewing the problem, debating alternatives, evaluating solutions, and developing action plans (e.g., Blake & Mouton, 1984). A number of exercises may be included in the workshop, such as the two sides exchanging and discussing the image each has of itself and the other. These processes and the interaction between the two groups are intended to break down old negative attitudes and replace them with more positive ones (Fisher, 1990).

In practice, intervention programs and workshops aimed at changing prejudiced attitudes often employ an eclectic mix of methods and exercises. Such programs have been used in organizational, military (e.g., Landis, Hope, & Day, 1984), and educational settings (e.g., Ijaz, 1982). Empirical evaluations have generally confirmed their effectiveness (cf. Fisher, 1990; Stephan & Stephan, 1984). However, it is not clear how enduring these changes are, particularly if they are not accompanied by change in social structures and the social influences that impact on the individuals who have experienced the interventions. In addition, the changed attitudes are also necessarily limited to those individuals who have participated in the programs, although attempts to broaden this have been made by involving community leaders or other "influentials" (e.g., Doob & Foltz, 1973). It seems likely that the greatest potential impact for such programs will come if they can be systematically and comprehensively integrated into school education.

## DEVELOPING INTERVENTION POLICIES

The previous three sections very cursorily surveyed a variety of measures that could be used to reduce prejudice. Two further issues are also relevant here: one concerns the integration of specific measures over different levels into broad and coherent policies; the other concerns the issue of when and where particular measures or policies would be most appropriate and effective. In the first case, a very broad and fundamental distinction can be made between the two general approaches or policies of assimilation and multiculturalism. These two approaches can be seen as the opposite poles of a dimension that reflects the degree to which multiethnic societies are prepared to tolerate and accept important subgroup distinctions and identities. The policy of assimilation has the objective of blurring and ultimately merging these identities completely into a single broader superordinate identity—a melting pot ideology. The multicultural approach, on the other hand, views cultural diversity as both inevitable and valuable in its own right, and it has the objective of accepting, recognizing, and maintaining subgroup identities.

To the extent that a policy of assimilation progressively blurred and weakened interethnic differences, interactions between persons from these different groups would become individualized and would ultimately remove any basis for interethnic prejudice. In interracial terms this should eventually create a truly colorblind society. Brewer and Miller (1984) argued, on the basis of social categorization theory, that this approach of reducing category-based interaction between individuals from different groups and personalizing these interactions should be the most effective way of reducing intergroup prejudice. Recent experimental research has supported this by showing that intergroup bias and discrimination is effectively reduced to the extent that different group identities become submerged in a new superordinate identity (Gaertner, Mann, Dovidio, Murrell, & Pomare, 1990; Gaertner et al., 1989).

The assimilationist approach, however, is open to certain criticisms. For example, it has been shown that in majority-minority situations an assimilationist and supposedly colorblind approach can be very disadvantageous to minorities because it might conceal a good deal of covert prejudice and discrimination against them and reinforce an intolerant attitude toward cultural differences (Saharso, 1989; Schofield, 1986). Hewstone and Brown (1986b) also noted that the goal of a homogenized society without significant intergroup differences may be very difficult, if not impossible, as these group identities and a sense of positive distinctiveness from other groups will often be highly valued. They argue that this need not necessarily lead to prejudice. Intergroup contact in such situations could instead involve what they term mutual intergroup differentiation. Thus, each group would see itself as superior to the other on those values and dimensions important to it and concede inferiority on values and dimensions important to the outgroup. However, this may be a somewhat idealized situation. It has been pointed out, for example, that whenever groups differ in status or power, as is very often the case, there is a very strong tendency for the characteristics of the higher status group to become normatively desirable and those of the lower status group to be devalued (Mummendey & Simon, 1989). In such situations mutual intergroup differentiation may simply not be possible in a way that does not adversely affect the self-respect of lower status outgroups and minorities.

Although assimilation was traditionally regarded as the preferred strategy for multiethnic societies, the multicultural alternative seems to be increasingly favored today (e.g., Berry, 1984; van Oudenhoven & Willemsen, 1989b). However, these two approaches may not be as incompatible as they appear. First, it has been pointed out that a strong superordinate identity and strong subgroup identities are not inconsistent with each other. In fact, it is not at all uncommon for a superordinate *cultura franca*—that is, a common body of culture that is not specifically tied to any one particular cultural group—to emerge quite naturally in culturally diverse communities or societies (van Oudenhoven & Willemsen, 1989b, p. 248). Second, most interventions to reduce prejudice are reasonably compatible with both approaches. Third, a balanced approach that both accepts and tolerates diversity, yet at the same time seeks to make group distinctions less salient and generalized, particularly when these distinctions are associated with prejudiced attitudes and potential conflict, is by no means unfeasible. Indeed, this may well be the most appropriate policy in most situations.

The latter point suggests that the multicultural versus assimilationist debate might be best viewed as not involving a choice of one or the other policy but, rather, as striking the balance between the two that is most appropriate for particular circumstances. Thus, in stable societies with a strong and well-established superordinate identity, the emphasis may be better placed on the need to tolerate and accept diversity. On the other hand, in newly emergent societies that are riven by strong ethnic or tribal divisions with a high potential for divisive conflict, the emphasis may be more appropriately placed on measures to defuse and weaken these distinctions and to build a strong superordinate identity.

This raises the second issue, noted at the beginning of this section, of selecting those measures and policies that would be most appropriate in particular situations. In general, the nature of the intergroup situation will dictate what objectives for improving intergroup attitudes and relations are feasible and what measures and policies should be most effective. Thus, a careful analysis of the historical intergroup situation and the nature of the present intergroup relations should precede attempts to set goals and develop policies. Although some attention has been given to this issue in the literature (e.g., Amir & Ben-Arie, 1989; Simpson & Yinger, 1985), there has been little work thus far on developing systematic and comprehensive guidelines on the situational and intergroup dimensions that determine the suitability of different intervention strategies. Amir and Ben-Arie (1989), however, recently made some interesting suggestions. Noting three intergroup situations in Israel—between Western Jews and Middle Eastern Jews, between Arabs and Jews, and between religious and secular Jews—they argued that the different intergroup relationship in each case means that different objectives and policies will be appropriate for each.

When groups question each other's legitimacy and do not seem to agree on the principle of coexistence, as Amir and Ben-Arie (1989) suggested is the case for religious and secular Jews, the focus of change has to be at the macrosocial level. Often such situations, such as the one in

Northern Ireland between Catholics and Protestants and the conflict in Nigeria following the first federal Republic, seem to require political conflict resolution and the design of constitutional and political systems that will defuse the intergroup conflict before other measures become possible. The second intergroup situation is one in which groups broadly agree on coexistence but do not desire close contact or integrated facilities. Amir and Ben-Arie suggested that this characterized the Arab-Jewish relationship, though the past few years of intifada suggest that this may have been an overly optimistic assessment. Nevertheless, at this somewhat more advanced stage of intergroup relations, they suggest an informational approach may be most appropriate. This would involve using the mass media and educational systems to improve intercultural awareness and understanding and to break down negative stereotypes and attitudes. Finally, the most advanced intergroup situation discussed is that between Western and Middle Eastern Jews, where the groups not only agree on the principle of coexistence but also have common objectives and support closer contact. In this case, it is argued, policies such as comprehensive desegregation and facilitating equal status and positive intergroup contact should prove particularly effective.

## A WORLD WITHOUT PREJUDICE?

Finally, given the state of our knowledge, the question may be posed whether a world in which prejudice has been eliminated is at all possible. On the one hand, there are some positive factors. Contrary to the currently fashionable conclusion that stereotyping and even prejudice may be inevitable and universal outcomes of basic and unchangeable human cognitive processes, I have argued here that it is only the potential for prejudice that is inherently human, and this potential is realized only under particular social circumstances. No matter how depressingly common these circumstances may be today, it does create the possibility of structuring societies and circumstances in order to make tolerance rather than prejudice the norm.

Pettigrew (1986) pointed out that situations of reasonable intergroup harmony are not necessarily uncommon. Willemsen and van Oudenhoven (1989) also noted that "relations between majority and minority groups are not necessarily problematic. In Switzerland, for instance, relations between the German-speaking majority and the French, Italian, and Retroroman minorities are rather harmonious" (p. 11). It is, of course, unlikely that petty prejudices and some negative stereotyping can be totally eliminated in even relatively ideal social circumstances. As long as intergroup differentiations exist, some form of prejudice and stereotyping, even if mild, will probably be present.

Nevertheless, it is not difficult to find examples of social settings in which interethnic prejudice is not a significant social issue or problem. Moreover, the kind of measures briefly reviewed in this chapter, which tend to reduce prejudice and intergroup hostilities, are not incompatible with democracy and social justice. In fact, most of these measures would help create fairer, more just, and more equitable societies. To the extent that we can create such societies, it is likely that we will be realizing the very conditions in which different groups and peoples can coexist in relative harmony.

# Bibliography

Abelson, R. P., Kinder, D. R., Peters, M. D., & Fiske, S. T. (1982). Affective and semantic components in political person perception. *Journal of Personality and Social Psychology, 42*, 619–630.

Aboud, F. E. (1988). *Children and prejudice*. Oxford: Blackwell.

Aboud, F. E., & Skerry, S. A. (1984). The development of ethnic attitudes: A critical review. *Journal of Cross-Cultural Psychology, 15*, 3–34.

Abrams, D., & Hogg, M. A. (1988). Comments on the motivational status of self-esteem in social identity and intergroup discrimination. *European Journal of Social Psychology, 18*, 317–334.

Ackerman, N., & Jahoda, M. (1950). *Anti-Semitism and emotional disorders: A psycho-analytic interpretation*. New York: Harper.

Adams, F., & Osgood, C. (1973). A cross-cultural study of the affective meanings of color. *Journal of Cross-Cultural Psychology, 4*, 135–156.

Adorno, T., Frenkel-Brunswick, E., Levinson, D., & Sanford, R. (1950). *The authoritarian personality*. New York: Harper.

Ajzen, I., & Fishbein, M. (1977). Attitude-behavior relations: A theoretical analysis and a review of empirical research. *Psychological Bulletin, 84*, 888–918.

Ajzen, I., & Fishbein, M. (1980). *Understanding attitudes and predicting social behavior*. Englewood Cliffs, New Jersey: Prentice-Hall.

Allen, R. O., & Spilka, B. (1967). Committed and consensual religion: A specification of religion-prejudice relationships. *Journal for the Scientific Study of Religion, 6*, 191–206.

Allen, V., & Wilder, D. (1975). Categorization, belief similarity, and intergroup discrimination. *Journal of Personality and Social Psychology, 32*, 971–977.

Allport, G. W. (1954). *The nature of prejudice*. Reading, Massachusetts: Addison-Wesley.

Allport, G. W. (1966). Religious context of prejudice. *Journal for the Scientific Study of Religion, 5*, 447–457.

Allport, G. W., & Kramer, B. M. (1946). Some roots of prejudice. *Journal of Psychology, 22*, 9–39.

Allport, G. W., & Ross, J. M. (1967). Personal religious orientation and prejudice. *Journal of Personality and Social Psychology, 5,* 432–443.

Altemeyer, B. (1981). *Right-wing authoritarianism.* Winnipeg: University of Manitoba Press.

Altemeyer, B. (1988a). *Enemies of freedom: Understanding right-wing authoritarianism.* San Francisco: Jossey-Bass.

Altemeyer, B. (1988b, March/April). Marching in step: A psychological explanation of state terror. *The Sciences,* pp. 30–38.

Amir, Y. (1976). The role of intergroup contact in change in prejudice and ethnic relations. In P. A. Katz (Ed.), *Towards the elimination of racism* (pp. 245–308). New York: Pergamon.

Amir, Y., & Ben-Arie, R. (1989). Enhancing intergroup relations in Israel: A differential approach. In D. Bar-Tal, C. F. Graumann, A. W. Kruglanski, & W. Stroebe (Eds.), *Stereotyping and prejudice: Changing conceptions* (pp. 243–257). Berlin: Springer.

Apostle, R., Glock, C., Piazza, T., & Suelze, M. (1983). *The anatomy of racial attitudes.* Berkeley: University of California Press.

Appelgryn, A.E.M., & Nieuwoudt, J. M. (1988). Relative deprivation and the ethnic attitudes of blacks and Afrikaans speaking whites in South Africa. *Journal of Social Psychology, 128,* 311–324.

Applezweig, D. G. (1954). Some determinants of behavioral rigidity. *Journal of Abnormal and Social Psychology, 49,* 224–228.

Argyle, M., & Beit-Hallahmi, B. (1975). *The social psychology of religion.* London: Routledge & Kegan Paul.

Asch, S. E. (1952). *Social psychology.* New York: Prentice-Hall.

Ashmore, R. (1970). The problem of intergroup prejudice. In B. E. Collins (Ed.), *Social Psychology* (pp. 245–296). Reading, Massachusetts: Addison-Wesley.

Ashmore, R., & DelBoca, F. (1976). Psychological approaches to understanding intergroup conflict. In P. Katz (Ed.), *Towards the elimination of racism* (pp. 73–123). New York: Pergamon.

Ashmore, R., & DelBoca, F. (1981). Conceptual approaches to stereotypes and stereotyping. In D. Hamilton (Ed.), *Cognitive processes in stereotyping and intergroup behavior* (pp. 1–36). Hillsdale, New Jersey: Erlbaum.

Aumack, L. (1955). The effects of imprisonment on authoritarian attitudes. *American Psychologist, 10,* 342.

Babad, E. Y., Birnbaum, M., & Benne, K. D. (1983). *The social self: Group influences on personal identity.* Beverly Hills: Sage.

Bagley, C., & Verma, G. (1979). *Racial prejudice, the individual and society.* Westmead, England: Saxon House.

Bagley, C., Verma, G., Mallick, K., & Young, L. (1979). *Personality, self-esteem and prejudice.* Westmead, England: Saxon House.

Banton, M. (1967). *Race relations.* London: Tavistock.

Bar-Tal, D., Graumann, C. F., Kruglanski, A. W., & Stroebe, W. (Eds.). (1989). *Stereotyping and prejudice: Changing conceptions.* Berlin: Springer.

Bass, B. M. (1955). Authoritarianism or acquiescence? *Journal of Abnormal and Social Psychology, 51,* 616–623.

Bass, B. M. (1956). Development and evaluation of a scale for measuring social acquiescence. *Journal of Abnormal and Social Psychology, 53,* 296–299.

Batson, C. D., Flink, C. H., Schoenrade, P. A., Fultz, J., & Pych, V. (1986). Religious orientation and overt versus covert racial prejudice. *Journal of Personality and Social Psychology, 50,* 175–181.

Batson, C. D., Naifeh, S. J., & Pate, S. (1978). Social desirability, religious orientation, and racial prejudice. *Journal for the Scientific Study of Religion, 17,* 31–41.

Beloff, H., & Coupar, S. (1969). Some transactional perceptions of African faces. *British Journal of Social and Clinical Psychology, 7,* 169–175.

Bem, D. (1970). *Beliefs, attitudes and human affairs.* Belmont, California: Brooks/Cole.

Bem, D. (1972). Self-perception theory. In L. Berkowitz (Ed.), *Advances in experimental social psychology, Vol. 6* (pp. 1–62). New York: Academic.

Ben-Arie, R., & Amir, Y. (1988). Intergroup contact, cultural information and change in ethnic attitudes. In W. Stroebe, A. Kruglanski, D. Bar-Tal, & M. Hewstone (Eds.), *The social psychology of intergroup conflict* (pp. 151–166). Berlin: Springer.

Bentler, P. M., & Speckart, G. (1981). Attitudes "cause" behavior: A structural equation analysis. *Journal of Personality and Social Psychology, 40,* 226–238.

Berg, K. (1966). Ethnic attitudes and agreement with a Negro person. *Journal of Personality and Social Psychology, 4,* 215–220.

Berkowitz, L. (1959). Anti-Semitism and the displacement of aggression. *Journal of Abnormal and Social Psychology, 59,* 182–187.

Berkowitz, L. (1962). *Aggression: A social psychological analysis.* New York: McGraw-Hill.

Berkowitz, L., & Green, J. A. (1962). The stimulus qualities of the scapegoat. *Journal of Abnormal and Social Psychology, 64,* 293–301.

Berry, J. W. (1984). Cultural relations in plural societies: Alternatives to segregation and their sociopsychological implications. In N. Miller & M. Brewer (Eds.), *Groups in contact: The psychology of desegregation* (pp. 11–27). San Diego: Academic.

Best, D., Naylor, C., & Williams, J. (1975). Extension of color bias research to young French and Italian children. *Journal of Cross-Cultural Psychology, 6,* 390–405.

Beswick, D. G., & Hills, M. D. (1972). A survey of ethnocentrism in Australia. *Australian Journal of Psychology, 24,* 153–163.

Bettelheim, B., & Janowitz, M. (1964). *Social change and prejudice.* London: Collier-MacMillan.

Bielby, W. T. (1987). Modern prejudice and institutional barriers to equal employment opportunity for minorities. *Journal of Social Issues, 43,* 79–84.

Bierly, M. M. (1985). Prejudice toward contemporary outgroups as a generalized attitude. *Journal of Applied Social Psychology, 15,* 189–199.

Billig, M. (1976). *Social psychology and intergroup relations.* London: Academic.

Billig, M. (1978). *Fascists: A social psychological view of the National Front.* London: Academic.

Bird, C., Monachesi, E. D., & Burdick, H. (1952). Infiltration and the attitudes of white and Negro parents and children. *Journal of Abnormal and Social Psychology, 47,* 688–699.

Blackwell, J. (1982). Persistence and change in intergroup relations: The crisis upon us. *Social Problems, 29,* 325–346.

Blake, R. R., & Mouton, J. S. (1979). Intergroup problem solving in organizations: From theory to practice. In W. G. Austin and S. Worchel (Eds.), *The social psychology of intergroup relations* (pp. 19–32). Monterey, California: Brooks/Cole.

Blake, R. R., & Mouton, J. S. (1984). *Solving costly organizational conflicts.* San Francisco: Jossey-Bass.

Blalock, H. (1967). *Towards a theory of minority-group relations.* New York: Wiley.

Blauner, R. (1972). *Racial oppression in America.* New York: Harper & Row.

Block, J. (1955). Personality characteristics associated with fathers' attitudes towards child-rearing. *Child Development, 26,* 41–48.

Block, J., & Block, J. (1951). An investigation of the relationship between intolerance of ambiguity and ethnocentrism. *Journal of Personality, 19,* 303–311.

Bobo, L. (1983). Whites' opposition to busing: Symbolic racism or realistic group conflict? *Journal of Personality and Social Psychology, 45,* 1196–1210.

Bobo, L. (1988). Attitudes toward the black political movement: Trends, meaning, and effects on racial policy preferences. *Social Psychology Quarterly, 51,* 287–302.

Bogardus, E. (1925). Measuring social distance. *Journal of Applied Sociology, 9,* 299–308.

Bogardus, E. (1928). *Immigration and race attitudes.* Boston: Heath.

Bonacich, E. (1972). A theory of ethnic antagonism: The split labor market. *American Sociological Review, 37,* 447–559.

Boswell, D., & Williams, J. (1975). Correlates of race and color bias among preschool children. *Psychological Reports, 36,* 147–154.

Bourhis, R., & Hill, P. (1982). Intergroup perceptions in British higher education: A field study. In H. Tajfel (Ed.), *Social identity and intergroup relations.* Cambridge: Cambridge University Press.

Bowser, B. P. (1985). Race relations in the 1980s: The case of the United States. *Journal of Black Studies, 15,* 307–324.

Boyanowsky, E., & Allen, V. (1973). Ingroup norms and self-identity as determinants of discriminatory behavior. *Journal of Personality and Social Psychology, 25,* 408–418.

Branch, C. W., & Newcombe, N. (1986). Racial attitude development among young black children as a function of parental attitudes: A longitudinal and cross-sectional study. *Child Development, 57,* 712–721.

Branthwaite, A., Doyle, S., & Lightbown, N. (1979). The balance between fairness and discrimination. *European Journal of Social Psychology, 9,* 149–163.

Bray, D. W. (1950). The prediction of behavior from two attitude scales. *Journal of Abnormal and Social Psychology, 45,* 64–84.

Brewer, M. B. (1968). Determinants of social distance among East African tribal groups. *Journal of Personality and Social Psychology, 10,* 279–289.

Brewer, M. B. (1979). In-group bias in the minimal intergroup situation: A cognitive-motivational analysis. *Psychological Bulletin, 86,* 307–324.

Brewer, M. B. (1981). Ethnocentrism and its role in interpersonal trust. In M. B. Brewer & B. Collins (Eds.), *Scientific inquiry in the social sciences* (pp. 345–360). San Francisco: Jossey-Bass.

Brewer, M. B., & Campbell, D. T. (1976). *Ethnocentrism and intergroup attitudes: East African evidence.* New York: Sage.

Brewer, M. B., Campbell, D. T., & LeVine, R. (1971). Cross-cultural test of the relationship between affect and evaluation. *Proceedings of the 79th Annual Convention of the American Psychological Association, 6,* 213–214.

Brewer, M. B., & Kramer, R. (1985). The psychology of intergroup attitudes and behavior. *Annual Review of Psychology, 36,* 219–243.

Brewer, M. B., & Miller, N. (1984). Beyond the contact hypothesis: Theoretical perspectives on desegregation. In N. Miller & M. B. Brewer (Eds.), *Groups in contact: The psychology of desegregation* (pp. 281–302). San Diego: Academic.

Brewer, M. B., & Silver, M. (1978). Ingroup bias as a function of task characteristics. *European Journal of Social Psychology, 8,* 393–400.

Brewster-Smith, M. (1965). An analysis of two measures of authoritarianism in Peace Corps teachers. *Journal of Personality, 33,* 513–535.

Brigham, J. C. (1971a). Ethnic stereotypes. *Psychological Bulletin, 76,* 15–38.

Brigham, J. C. (1971b). Racial stereotypes, attitudes, and evaluations of and behavioral intentions toward Negroes and whites. *Sociometry, 34,* 360–380.

Brigham, J. C. (1972). Racial stereotypes: Measurement variables and the stereotype-attitude relationship. *Journal of Applied Psychology, 2,* 63–76.

Brigham, J. C., Woodmansee J., & Cook, S. (1976). Dimensions of verbal racial attitudes: Interracial marriage and approaches to racial equality. *Journal of Social Issues, 32,* 9–21.

Brown, C. E. (1981). Shared space invasion and race. *Personality and Social Psychology Bulletin, 7,* 103–108.

Brown, R. (1965). *Social psychology.* New York: Free Press.

Brown, R. J. (1978). Divided we fall: An analysis of relations between sections of a factory workforce. In H. Tajfel (Ed.), *Differentiation between social groups: Studies in the social psychology of intergroup relations* (pp. 395–430). London: Academic.

Brown, R. J. (1984a). The effects of intergroup similarity and cooperative vs. competitive orientation on intergroup discrimination. *British Journal of Social Psychology, 23,* 21–33.

Brown, R. J. (1984b). The role of similarity in intergroup relations. In H. Tajfel (Ed.), *The social dimension, Vol. 2* (pp. 603–623). Cambridge, England: Cambridge University Press.

Brown, R. J., & Abrams, D. (1986). The effects of intergroup similarity and goal interdependence on intergroup attitudes and task performance. *Journal of Experimental Social Psychology, 22,* 78–92.

Brown, R. J., Condor, S., Matthews, A., Wade, G., & Williams, J. (1986). Explaining intergroup differentiation in an industrial organization. *Journal of Occupational Psychology, 59,* 273–286.

Brown, R. J., & Turner, J. C. (1979). The criss-cross categorization effect in intergroup discrimination. *British Journal of Social and Clinical Psychology, 18,* 371–383.

Brown, R. J., & Turner, J.C. (1981). Interpersonal and intergroup behaviour. In

J. Turner & H. Giles (Eds.), *Intergroup behaviour* (pp. 33–65). Oxford: Blackwell.

Brown, R. J., & Williams, J. A. (1984). Intergroup identification: The same thing to all people? *Human Relations, 37*, 547–564.

Brown, R. W. (1953). A determinant of the relationship between rigidity and authoritarianism. *Journal of Abnormal and Social Psychology, 48*, 469–476.

Bush, D. F., Gallagher, B. J., & Weiner, W. (1982). Patterns of authoritarianism between generations. *Journal of Social Psychology, 116*, 91–97.

Buss, A. H. (1961). *The psychology of aggression*. New York: Wiley.

Byrne, D. (1965). Parental antecedents of authoritarianism. *Journal of Personality and Social Psychology, 1*, 369–373.

Byrne, D. (1966). *An introduction to personality*. Englewood Cliffs, New Jersey: Prentice-Hall.

Byrne, D. (1971). *The attraction paradigm*. New York: Academic.

Byrne, D., & Bounds, C. (1964). The reversal of F scale items. *Psychological Reports, 14*, 216.

Byrne, D., & Wong, T. J. (1962). Racial prejudice, interpersonal attraction, and assumed dissimilarity of attitudes. *Journal of Abnormal and Social Psychology, 65*, 246–253.

Camilleri, S. F. (1959). A factor analysis of the F scale. *Social Forces, 37*, 316–323.

Campbell, A. (1971). *White attitudes toward black people*. Ann Arbor: University of Michigan Institute for Social Research.

Campbell, A., Converse, W., Miller, W., & Stokes, D. (1960). *The American voter*. New York: Wiley.

Campbell, A. A. (1947). Factors associated with attitudes toward Jews. In T. M. Newcomb & E. L. Hartley (Eds.), *Readings in social psychology*, New York: Holt, Rinehart & Winston.

Campbell, D. T., & McCandless, B. R. (1951). Ethnocentrism, xenophobia, and personality. *Human Relations, 4*, 186–192.

Carlson, J. M., & Iovini, J. (1985). The transmission of racial attitudes from fathers to sons: A study of blacks and whites. *Adolescence, 20*, 233–237.

Carmichael, S., & Hamilton, C. (1967). *Black power*. New York: Random House.

Cattell, R. B., Eber, H. W., & Tatsuoka, M. M. (1970). *Handbook for the sixteen personality factor questionnaire (16PF)*. Champaign, Illinois: Institute for Personality and Ability Testing.

Cheek, J. M. (1982). Aggregation, moderator variables, and the validity of personality tests: A peer rating study. *Journal of Personality and Social Psychology, 43*, 1254–1269.

Chesler, M., & Schmuck, R. (1964). Student reactions to the Cuban crisis and public dissent. *Public Opinion Quarterly, 28*, 467–482.

Chesler, M. A. (1976). Contemporary sociological theories of racism. In P. Katz (Ed.), *Towards the elimination of racism* (pp. 21–71). New York: Pergamon.

Cheson, B. D., Stricker, G., & Fry, C. L. (1970). The repression-sensitization scale and measures of prejudice. *Journal of Social Psychology, 80*, 197–200.

Christie, R. (1954). Authoritarianism reexamined. In R. Christie & M. Jahoda (Eds.), *Studies in the scope and method of "the authoritarian personality"* (pp. 123–196). Glencoe, Illinois: Free Press.

Christie, R., & Garcia, J. (1951). Subcultural variation of the authoritarian personality. *Journal of Abnormal and Social Psychology, 46,* 457–469.

Christie, R., Havel, J., & Seidenberg, B. (1958). Is the F scale irreversible? *Journal of Abnormal and Social Psychology, 56,* 143–159.

Clark, K. B., & Clark, M. P. (1947). Racial identification and preference in Negro children. In T. M. Newcomb & E. L. Hartley (Eds.), *Readings in social psychology* (pp. 169–178). New York: Holt.

Cohen, J. M. (1977). Sources of peer group homogeneity. *Sociology of Education, 50,* 227–241.

Colman, A., & Lambley, P. (1970). Authoritarianism and race attitudes in South Africa. *Journal of Social Psychology, 82,* 161–164.

Commins, B., & Lockwood, J. (1979). The effects of status differences, favoured treatment and equity on intergroup comparisons. *European Journal of Social Psychology, 9,* 281–289.

Comrey, A. L., & Newmeyer, J. A. (1965). Measurement of radicalism-conservatism. *Journal of Social Psychology, 67,* 357–369.

Condor, S., & Brown, R. (1988). Psychological processes in intergroup conflict. In W. Stroebe, A. Kruglanski, D. Bar-Tal, & M. Hewstone (Eds.), *The social psychology of intergroup conflict* (pp. 3–26). Berlin: Springer.

Condran, J. G. (1979). Changes in white attitudes toward blacks: 1963–1979. *Public Opinion Quarterly, 43,* 463–476.

Converse, P. E. (1964). The nature of belief systems in mass publics. In D. E. Apter (Ed.), *Ideology and discontent* (pp. 206–261). Glencoe, Illinois: Free Press.

Cook, S. W. (1972). Motives in a conceptual analysis of attitude-related behavior. In J. Brigham & T. Weissbach (Eds.), *Racial attitudes in America: Analyses and findings of social psychology.* New York: Harper & Row.

Cook, S. W. (1978). Interpersonal and attitudinal outcomes in cooperating interracial groups. *Journal of Research in Developmental Education, 12,* 97–113.

Cook, S. W. (1979). Social science and school desegregation: Did we mislead the court? *Personality and Social Psychology Bulletin, 5,* 420–437.

Cooper, J., & Fazio, R. (1979). The formation and persistence of attitudes that support intergroup conflict. In W. Austin & S. Worchel (Eds.), *The social psychology of intergroup relations* (pp. 149–159). Monterey, California: Brooks/Cole.

Cooper, J., & McGaugh, J. (1963). *Integrative principles of social psychology.* Cambridge, Massachusetts: Schenkman.

Coser, L. A. (1956). *The functions of social conflict.* London: Routledge & Kegan Paul.

Couch, A., & Keniston, K. (1960). Yeasayers and naysayers: Agreeing response set as a personality variable. *Journal of Abnormal and Social Psychology, 60,* 151–171.

Cowen, E., Landes, J., & Schaet, D. (1959). The effects of mild frustration on the expression of prejudiced attitudes. *Journal of Abnormal and Social Psychology, 58,* 33–38.

Cox, O. (1948). *Caste, class and race: A study in social dynamics.* New York: Doubleday.

Crabbe, B. D. (1974). Are authoritarians sick? In J. J. Ray (Ed.), *Conservatism as heresy*. Sydney: A.N.Z. Book Co.

Crocker, J., & Luhtanen, R. (1990). Collective self-esteem and ingroup bias. *Journal of Personality and Social Psychology, 58*, 60–67.

Crocker, J., & Schwartz, I. (1985). Prejudice and ingroup favoritism in a minimal intergroup situation: Effects of self-esteem. *Personality and Social Psychology Bulletin, 11*, 379–386.

Crocker, J., Thompson, L. L., McGraw, K. M., & Ingerman, C. (1987). Downward comparison, prejudice, and evaluations of others: Effects of self-esteem and threat. *Journal of Personality and Social Psychology, 52*, 907–916.

Crosby, F., Bromley, S., & Saxe, L. (1980). Recent unobtrusive studies of black and white discrimination and prejudice: A literature review. *Psychological Bulletin, 87*, 546–563.

Darley, J. M., & Darley, S. A. (1976). Conformity and deviation. In J. W. Thibault, J. T. Spence, R. C. Carson et al. (Eds.), *Contemporary topics in social psychology*. Morristown, New Jersey: General Learning Press.

Davey, A. (1983). *Learning to be prejudiced: Growing up in multi-ethnic Britain*. London: Edward Arnold.

DeFleur, M., & Westie, F. (1958). Verbal attitudes and overt acts: An experiment on the salience of attitudes. *American Sociological Review, 23*, 667–673.

DeFriese, G., & Ford, W. S. (1969). Verbal attitudes, overt acts, and the influence of social constraint in interracial behavior. *Social Problems, 16*, 493–504.

de Kiewiet, C. .W. (1957). *A history of South Africa: Social and economic*. London: Oxford University Press.

Deschamps, J-C., & Doise, W. (1978). Crossed category memberships in intergroup relations. In H. Tajfel (Ed.), *Differentiation in social groups: Studies in the social psychology of intergroup relations* (pp. 141–158). London: Academic.

Deutsch, M. (1971). Strategies for powerless groups. In G. T. Marx (Ed.), *Racial conflict* (pp. 223–228). Boston: Little, Brown.

Deutsch, M., & Gerard, H. B. (1955). A study of normative and informational social influence upon individual judgment. *Journal of Abnormal and Social Psychology, 51*, 629–636.

Deutscher, I. (1973). *What we say? What we do?* Glenview, Illinois: Scott, Foresman.

Dickens, L., & Hobart, C. (1959). Parental dominance and offspring ethnocentrism. *Journal of Social Psychology, 49*, 297–303.

Diehl, M. (1988). Social identity and minimal groups: The effects of interpersonal and intergroup attitudinal similarity on intergroup discrimination. *British Journal of Social Psychology, 27*, 289–300.

Dion, K. L. (1979). Intergroup conflict and intragroup cohesiveness. In W. G. Austin & S. Worchel (Eds.), *The social psychology of intergroup relations* (pp. 211–224). Monterey, California: Brooks/Cole.

Doise, W., & Sinclair, A. (1973). The categorization process in intergroup relations. *European Journal of Social Psychology, 3*, 145–157.

Dollard, J., Doob, L., Miller, N. E., Mowrer, O., & Sears, R. (1939). *Frustration and aggression*. New Haven: Yale University Press.

Donahue, M. J. (1985). Intrinsic and extrinsic religiousness: Review and meta-analysis. *Journal of Personality and Social Psychology, 48,* 400–419.

Donnerstein, E., Donnerstein, M., Simon, S., & Ditrichs, R. (1972). Variables in interracial aggression: Anonymity, expected retaliation and a riot. *Journal of Personality and Social Psychology, 22,* 236–245.

Doob, L. W. (1964). *Patriotism and nationalism: Their psychological foundations.* New Haven: Yale University Press.

Doob, L. W., & Foltz, W. J. (1973). The Belfast Workshop: An application of group techniques to a destructive conflict. *Journal of Conflict Resolution, 17,* 489–512.

Dovidio, J. F., & Gaertner, S. L. (Eds). (1986). *Prejudice, discrimination, and racism.* Orlando, Florida: Academic.

Duckitt, J. (1982). Directiveness and authoritarianism: Some research findings and a critical reappraisal. *South African Journal of Psychology, 13,* 10–12.

Duckitt, J. (1983a). Culture, class, personality and authoritarianism among white South Africans. *Journal of Social Psychology, 121,* 191–199.

Duckitt, J. (1983b). Authoritarianism and adjustment in an authoritarian culture. *Journal of Social Psychology, 121,* 211–212.

Duckitt, J. (1984). Reply to Ray's directiveness and authoritarianism: A rejoinder to Duckitt. *South African Journal of Psychology, 14,* 65–66.

Duckitt, J. (1985a). Prejudice and neurotic symptomatology among white South Africans. *Journal of Psychology, 119,* 15–20.

Duckitt, J. (1985b). Social class and F scale authoritarianism: A reconsideration. *The High School Journal, 68,* 279–286.

Duckitt, J. (1988). Normative conformity and racial prejudice in South Africa. *Genetic, Social, and General Psychology Monographs, 114,* 413–437.

Duckitt, J. (1989). Authoritarianism and group identification: A new view of an old construct. *Political Psychology, 10,* 63–84.

Duckitt, J. (1990a). Response to Ray. *Political Psychology, 11,* 633–635.

Duckitt, J. (1990b). *A social psychological investigation of racial prejudice in South Africa.* Unpublished doctoral dissertation, University of the Witwatersrand, Johannesburg, South Africa.

Duckitt, J. (1991). Prejudice and racism. In D. Foster & J. Louw-Potgieter (Eds.), *Social psychology in South Africa* (pp. 171–203). Isando, South Africa: Lexicon.

du Preez, J. M. (1983). *Africana Afrikaner: Master symbols in South African school textbooks.* Alberton, South Africa: Librarius.

du Preez, P. D. (1977). Explanations of racial antagonism. *Social Dynamics, 3,* 17–25.

Eagly, A. H., & Steffin, V. J. (1984). Gender stereotypes stem from the distribution of women and men into social roles. *Journal of Personality and Social Psychology, 46,* 735–754.

Edwards, D. (1985). Authoritarianism in South Africa: A conceptual challenge to social science. *The High School Journal, 68,* 261–268.

Edwards, O. L. (1972). Intergenerational variation in racial attitudes. *Sociology and Social Research, 57(1),* 22–31.

Ehrlich, H. J. (1973). *The social psychology of prejudice.* New York: Wiley.

Ellemers, N., van Knippenberg, A., de Vries, N., & Wilkie, H. (1988). Social identification and permeability of group boundaries. *European Journal of Social Psychology, 18,* 479–513.

Ellemers, N., van Knippenberg, A., & Wilkie, H. (1990). The influence of the permeability of group boundaries and stability of group status on strategies of individual mobility and social change. *British Journal of Social Psychology, 29,* 233–246.

Elliot, G., & Tyson, G. (1983). The effects of modifying color-meaning concepts on the racial attitudes of black and white South African preschool children. *Journal of Social Psychology, 121,* 181–190.

Epstein R., & Komorita, S. S. (1965). Parental discipline, stimulus characteristics of outgroups, and social distance in children. *Journal of Personality and Social Psychology, 2,* 416–420.

Epstein, R., & Komorita, S. S. (1966). Prejudice among Negro children as related to parental ethnocentrism and punitiveness. *Journal of Personality and Social Psychology, 4,* 643–647.

Epstein, S. (1983). Aggregation and beyond: Some basic issues in the prediction of behavior. *Journal of Personality, 51,* 360–392.

Ewens, W. L., & Ehrlich, H. J. (1972). Reference-other support and ethnic attitudes as predictors of intergroup behavior. *The Sociological Quarterly, 13,* 348–360.

Eysenck, H. J. (1954). *The psychology of politics.* London: Routledge & Kegan Paul.

Fairchild, H., & Gurin, P. (1978). Traditions in the social psychological analysis of race relations. *American Behavioral Scientist, 21,* 757–778.

Farris, C. D. (1960). Selected attitudes on foreign affairs as correlates of authoritarianism and anomie. *Journal of Politics, 22,* 50–67.

Feagin, J. R. (1964). Prejudice and religious types: A focused study of southern fundamentalists. *Journal for the Scientific Study of Religion, 4,* 3–13.

Feagin, J. R. (1970). Home defense and the police: Black and white perspectives. *American Behavioral Scientist, 13,* 717–726.

Feagin, J. R., & Eckberg, D. R. (1980). Discrimination: Motivation, action, effects, and context. *Annual Review of Sociology, 6,* 1–20.

Feldman, R. S., & Donohoe, L. F. (1978). Nonverbal communication of affect in interracial dyads. *Journal of Educational Psychology, 70,* 979–987.

Fendrich, J. M. (1967). Perceived reference group support: Racial attitudes and overt behavior. *American Sociological Review, 32,* 960–969.

Fensterwald, B. (1958). The anatomy of American isolationism and expansionism, II. *Journal of Conflict Resolution, 2,* 280–309.

Feshbach, S., & Singer, R. (1957). The effects of personal and shared threats on social prejudice. *Journal of Abnormal and Social Psychology, 54,* 411–416.

Festinger, L. (1957). *A theory of cognitive dissonance.* Stanford, California: Stanford University Press.

Finchilescu, G. (1986). Effect of incompatibility between internal and external group membership criteria on intergroup behaviour. *European Journal of Social Psychology, 16,* 83–87.

Finchilescu, G. (1988). Interracial contact in South Africa within the nursing context. *Journal of Applied Psychology, 18,* 1207–1221.

Fink, H. C. (1971). Fictitious groups and the generality of prejudice: An artifact of scales without neutral categories. *Psychological Reports, 29,* 359–365.

Firebaugh, G., & Davis, K. E. (1988). Trends in anti-black prejudice, 1972–1984: region and cohort effects. *American Journal of Sociology, 94,* 251–272.

Fishbein, M., & Ajzen, I. (1975). *Belief, attitude, intention and behavior: An introduction to theory and research.* Reading, Massachusetts: Addison-Wesley.

Fisher, R. J. (1990). *The social psychology of intergroup and international conflict resolution.* Berlin: Springer.

Foley, L. A. (1976). Personality and situational influences on changes in prejudice: A replication of Cook's railroad game in a prison setting. *Journal of Personality and Social Psychology, 34,* 846–856.

Forbes, H. D. (1985). *Nationalism, ethnocentrism, and personality,* Chicago: University of Chicago Press.

Foster, D. (1986). The development of racial orientation in children: A review of South African research. In S. Burman & P. Reynolds (Eds.), *Growing up in a divided society: The contexts of childhood in South Africa.* Johannesburg: Ravan Press.

Foster, D. (1991). Social influence I: Ideology. In D. Foster & J. Louw-Potgieter (Eds.), *Social Psychology in South Africa* (pp. 345–394). Johannesburg: Lexicon.

Foster, D., & Finchilescu, G. (1986). Contact in a non-contact society: The case of South Africa. In M. Hewstone & R. Brown (Eds.), *Contact and conflict in intergroup encounters* (pp. 119–136). Oxford: Blackwell.

Foster-Carter, O. (1984). Racial bias in children's literature: A review of the research on Africa. *Sage Race Relations Abstracts, 9(4),* 1–11.

Fredricks, A. J., & Dossett, D. L. (1983). Attitude-behavior relations: A comparison of the Fishbein-Ajzen and the Bentler-Speckart models. *Journal of Personality and Social Psychology, 45,* 501–512.

Frenkel-Brunswick, E. (1949). Intolerance of ambiguity as an emotional and perceptual variable. *Journal of Personality, 18,* 108–143.

Frenkel-Brunswick, E., & Havel, J. (1953). Prejudice in the interviews of children: Attitudes toward minority groups. *Journal of Genetic Psychology, 82,* 91–136.

Freud, A. (1946). *The ego and the mechanisms of defense.* London: Hogarth.

Frey, D., & Gaertner, S. (1986). Helping and the avoidance of inappropriate interracial behavior: A strategy that perpetuates a nonprejudiced self-image. *Journal of Personality and Social Psychology, 50,* 1083–1090.

Friedman, M., Webster, H., & Sanford, N. (1956). A study of authoritarianism and psychopathology. *Journal of Psychology, 41,* 315–322.

Fromm, E. (1941). *Escape from freedom.* New York: Rinehart.

Furnham, A. (1974). *The conforming behaviour of black and white South Africans.* Unpublished master's thesis, University of Natal, Pietermaritzburg, South Africa.

Furnham, A. (1985). Just world beliefs in an unjust society: A cross cultural comparison. *European Journal of Social Psychology, 15,* 363–366.

Gaertner, S. L. (1973). Helping behavior and racial discrimination among liberals and conservatives. *Journal of Personality and Social Psychology, 25,* 335–341.

Gaertner, S. L., Mann, J., Dovidio, J. F., Murrell, A., & Pomare, M. (1990). How does cooperation reduce intergroup bias? *Journal of Personality and Social Psychology, 59,* 692–704.

Gaertner, S. L., Mann, J., Murrell, A., & Dovidio, J. F. (1989). Reducing inter-group bias: The benefits of recategorization. *Journal of Personality and Social Psychology, 57*, 239–249.

Gage, N. L., Leavitt, G. S., & Stone, G. G. (1957). The psychological meaning of acquiescence set for authoritarianism. *Journal of Abnormal and Social Psychology, 55*, 98–103.

Gaier, E. L., & Bass, B. L. (1959). Regional differences in interrelations among authoritarianism, acquiescence, and ethnocentrism. *Journal of Social Psychology, 49*, 47–51.

Gardiner, G. (1972). Complexity training and prejudice reduction. *Journal of Applied Social Psychology, 2*, 326–342.

Gardner, R. C. (1973). Ethnic stereotypes: The traditional approach, a new look. *Canadian Psychologist, 14*, 133–148.

Genthner, R., & Taylor, S. (1973). Physical aggression as a function of racial prejudice and the race of the target. *Journal of Personality and Social Psychology, 27*, 207–210.

Gergen, K. J., & Gergen, M. M. (1981). *Social psychology*. New York: Harcourt Brace Jovanovich.

Glock, C., Wuthnow, R., Piliavin, J., & Spencer, M. (1975). *Adolescent prejudice*. New York: Harper & Row.

Goertzel, T. D. (1987). Authoritarianism of personality and political attitudes. *Journal of Social Psychology, 127*, 7–18.

Goldstein, M., & Davis, E. E. (1972). Race and belief: A further analysis of the social determinants of behavioral intentions. *Journal of Personality and Social Psychology, 22*, 346–355.

Goodman, M. E. (1952). *Race awareness in young children*. Reading, Massachusetts: Addison-Wesley.

Gordon, A. I. (1943). Frustration and aggression among Jewish university students. *Jewish Sociological Studies, 5*, 27–42.

Gorsuch, R. L., & Aleshire, D. (1974). Christian faith and ethnic prejudice: A review and interpretation of research. *Journal for the Scientific Study of Religion, 13*, 281–307.

Gorsuch, R. L., & Ortberg, J. (1983). Moral obligation and attitudes: Their relation to behavioral intentions. *Journal of Personality and Social Psychology, 44*, 1025–1028.

Gough, H. G. (1957). *California Psychological Inventory Manual*. Palo Alto, California: Consulting Psychologists Press.

Gough, H. G., Harris, D. B., Martin, W. E., & Edwards, M. (1950). Children's ethnic attitudes: I. Relationship to certain personality factors. *Child Development, 21*, 89–91.

Gray, D. B., & Revelle, W. (1972). A cluster analytic critique of the Multifactor Racial Attitude Inventory. *Psychological Record, 22*, 103–112.

Green, J. A. (1972). Attitudinal and situational determinants of intended behavior toward blacks. *Journal of Personality and Social Psychology, 22*, 13–17.

Greenberg, B. S., & Mazingo, S. L. (1976). Racial issues in mass media institutions. In P. A. Katz (Ed.), *Towards the elimination of racism* (pp. 309–340). New York: Pergamon.

Greenberg, J., & Rosenfield, J. (1979). Whites' ethnocentrism and their attributions for the behavior of blacks: A motivational bias. *Journal of Personality, 47*, 644–657.

Greenwald, A. (1968). On defining attitude and attitude theory. In A. Greenwald, T. Brock, & T. Ostrom (Eds.), *Psychological foundations of attitudes.* (pp. 361–388). New York: Academic.

Guilford, J. P. (1931). Racial preferences of a thousand American university students. *Journal of Social Psychology, 2*, 199–208.

Guimond, S., Begin, G., & Palmer, D. (1989). Education and causal attributions: The development of "person-blame" and "system-blame" ideology. *Social Psychology Quarterly, 52*, 126–140.

Guimond, S., Dube-Simard, L. (1983). Relative deprivation theory and the Quebec nationalist movement: The cognition-emotion distinction and the personal-group deprivation issue. *Journal of Personality and Social Psychology, 44*, 526–535.

Gurr, T. R. (1970). *Why men rebel.* Princeton: Princeton University Press.

Guttman, L. L. (1944). A basis for scaling qualitative data. *American Sociological Review, 9*, 139–150.

Haller, J. (1971). *Outcasts from evolution: Scientific attitudes of racial inferiority: 1859–1900.* Urbana: University of Illinois Press.

Hamblin, R. L. (1962, Fall). The dynamics of racial discrimination. *Social Problems, 7*, 102–121.

Hamilton, D. (Ed.) (1981a). *Cognitive processes in stereotyping and intergroup behavior.* Hillsdale, New Jersey: Erlbaum.

Hamilton, D. (1981b). Illusory correlation as a basis for stereotyping. In D. Hamilton (Ed.), *Cognitive processes in stereotyping and intergroup behavior* (pp. 117–144). Hillsdale, New Jersey: Erlbaum.

Hamilton, D. (1981c). Stereotyping and intergroup behavior: Some thoughts on the cognitive approach. In D. Hamilton (Ed.), *Cognitive processes in stereotyping and intergroup behavior* (pp. 333–353). Hillsdale, New Jersey: Erlbaum.

Hamilton, D. L., & Sherman, S. J. (1989). Illusory correlations: Implications for stereotype theory and research. In D. Bar-Tal, C. F. Graumann, A. W. Kruglanski, & W. Stroebe (Eds.), *Stereotyping and prejudice: Changing conceptions* (pp. 59–82). Berlin: Springer.

Hamilton, D. L., & Trolier, T. K. (1986). Stereotypes and stereotyping: An overview of the cognitive approach. In J. F. Dovidio & S. L. Gaertner (Eds.), *Prejudice, discrimination, and racism* (pp. 127–164). Orlando, Florida: Academic.

Hamilton, R. (1972). *Class and politics in the United States.* New York: Wiley.

Hampel, R., & Krupp, B. (1977). The cultural and political framework of prejudice in South Africa and Great Britain. *Journal of Social Psychology, 103*, 193–202.

Haney, C., & Zimbardo, P. G. (1976). Social roles and role playing: Observations from the Stanford prison study. In E. P. Hollander & R. C. Hunt (Eds.), *Current perspectives in social psychology* (pp. 266–274). New York: Oxford University Press.

Hanf, T., Weiland, H., & Vierdag, G. (1981). *South Africa: The prospects of peaceful change*. London: Rex Collings.

Hanson, D. J. (1983). Authoritarianism and dogmatism: Political orientations. In V. K. Kool & J. J. Ray (Eds.), *Authoritarianism across cultures* (pp. 122–141). Bombay: Himalaya Publishing House.

Harding, J., Proshansky, H., Kutner, B., & Chein, I. (1969). Prejudice and ethnic relations. In G. Lindzey & E. Aronson (Eds.), *The handbook of social psychology, Vol. 5* (pp. 1–76). Reading, Massachusetts: Addison-Wesley.

Hare, A. P. (1976). *Handbook of small group research*. New York: Free Press.

Harris, D. B., Gough H. G., & Martin, W. E. (1950). Children's ethnic attitudes: II. Relationship to parental belief concerning child training. *Child Development, 21*, 169–181.

Hart, I. (1957). Maternal child-rearing practices and authoritarian ideology. *Journal of Abnormal and Social Psychology, 55*, 232–237.

Hartley, E. L. (1946). *Problems in prejudice*. New York: King's Crown Press.

Hassan, M. K. (1975). Religious prejudice among college students: A sociopsychological investigation. *Journal of Social and Economic Studies, 3*, 101–107.

Hassan, M. K. (1976). Self-image, social prejudice and child-rearing practices. *Asian Journal of Psychology and Education, 1*, 30–37.

Hassan, M. K. (1978). A study of ethnocentrism, prejudice and related personality factors in Hindu and Muslim college students. *Psychologia, 21*, 150–154.

Hawkins, D., & Kass, G. (1982). Automatic interaction detection. In D. Hawkins (Ed.), *Topics in applied multivariate analysis* (pp. 267–299). Cambridge: Cambridge University Press.

Heaven, P.C.L. (1979). *A cross-cultural study of conservatism in South Africa and its relation to ethnic attitudes*. Unpublished doctoral dissertation, University of South Africa, Pretoria, South Africa.

Heaven, P.C.L. (1980). Authoritarianism, prejudice, and alienation among Afrikaners. *Journal of Social Psychology, 110*, 39–42.

Heaven, P.C.L. (1981). Correlates of authoritarian personality. *South African Journal of Psychology, 11*, 85–86.

Heaven, P.C.L. (1983a). Individual vs intergroup explanations of prejudice among Afrikaners. *Journal of Social Psychology, 121*, 201–210.

Heaven, P.C.L. (1983b). Self-esteem and associated variables among white South Africans. *Journal of Social Psychology, 119*, 283–284.

Heaven, P.C.L., Conners, J., & Trevethan, R. (1987). Authoritarianism and the EPQ. *Personality and Individual Differences, 8*, 677–680.

Heaven, P.C.L., & Rajab, D. (1980). Authoritarianism and patriotism: A study among Afrikaners and Indians in South Africa. In P.C.L. Heaven (Ed.), *Authoritarianism: South African Studies* (pp. 9–15). Bloemfontein, South Africa: P. J. de Villiers Publishers.

Heaven, P.C.L., Stones, C., & Bester, C. (1986). Attitudes to a South African liberation movement. *Journal of Conflict Resolution, 30*, 487–496.

Hewstone, M. (1988). Attributional bases of intergroup conflict. In W. Stroebe, A. Kruglanski, D. Bar-Tal, & M. Hewstone (Eds.), *The social psychology of intergroup conflict* (pp. 47–72). Berlin: Springer.

Hewstone, M., & Brown, R. (Eds.) (1986a). *Contact and conflict in intergroup encounters*. Oxford: Blackwell.

Hewstone, M., & Brown, R. (1986b). Contact is not enough: An intergroup perspective on the "Contact Hypothesis." In M. Hewstone & R. Brown (Eds.), *Contact and conflict in intergroup encounters* (pp. 1–44). Oxford: Blackwell.

Hewstone, M., & Ward, C. (1985). Ethnocentrism and causal attribution in Southeast Asia. *Journal of Personality and Social Psychology, 48,* 614–623.

Hills, M. (1976, July). A measure of attitudes toward cultural pluralism in New Zealand. Paper presented at the Annual Conference of the International Association of Cross-Cultural Psychology, Tilburg, The Netherlands.

Hinkle, S., & Schopler, J. (1979). Ethnocentrism in the evaluation of group products. In W. G. Austin & S. Worchel (Eds.), *The social psychology of intergroup relations* (pp. 160–173). Monterey, California: Brooks/Cole.

Hinkle, S., Taylor, L. A., & Fox-Cardamone, D. L. (1989). Intragroup identification and intergroup differentiation: A multicomponent approach. *British Journal of Social Psychology, 28,* 305–317.

Hodge, R. W., & Treiman, D. J. (1966). Occupational mobility and attitudes toward Negroes. *American Sociological Review, 31,* 93–102.

Hoffman, M. L. (1977). Moral internalization: Current theory and research. In L. Berkowitz (Ed.), *Advances in experimental social psychology, Vol. 10* (pp. 86–135). New York: Academic.

Hofmeyer, J. M. (1982). *An examination of the influence of Christian National Education on the principles underlying white and black education in South Africa 1948–1982.* Unpublished master's thesis, University of the Witwatersrand, Johannesburg, South Africa.

Hogg, M. A., & Abrams, D. (1988). *Social identifications*. London: Routledge.

Hoogvelt, A.M.M. (1969). Ethnocentrism, authoritarianism, and Powellism. *Race, 11,* 1–12.

Horowitz, D. (1985). *Ethnic groups in conflict*. Berkeley: University of California Press.

Horowitz, E. L., & Horowitz, R. E. (1938). Development of social attitudes in children. *Sociometry, 1,* 307–338.

Hovland, C., & Sears, R. (1940). Minor studies of aggression V1. Correlation of lynchings with economic indices. *Journal of Psychology, 9,* 301–310.

Hughes, A. (1975). *Psychology and the political experience*. London: Cambridge University Press.

Hyman, H. H., & Sheatsley, P. B. (1954). The authoritarian personality—A methodological critique. In R. Christie & M. Jahoda (Eds.), *Studies in the scope and method of "the authoritarian personality"* (pp. 50–122). Glencoe, Illinois: Free Press.

Hyman, H. H., & Sheatsley, P. B. (1964). Attitudes toward desegregation. *Scientific American, 211 (July),* 16–23.

Hyman, H. H., & Wright, C. R. (1979). *Education's lasting influence on values*. Chicago: University of Chicago Press.

Ijaz, M. A. (1982). "We can change our childrens' racial attitudes." *Multiculturalism, 5,* 11–17.

Inbar, D., Resh, N., & Adler, C. (1984). Integration and school variables. In Y.

Amir, S. Sharan, & R. Ben-Arie (Eds.), *School desegregation: Cross-cultural perspectives* (pp. 119–132). Hillsdale, New Jersey: Erlbaum.

Insko, C. A., Nacoste, R. W., & Moe, J. L. (1983). Belief congruence and racial discrimination: Review of the evidence and critical evaluation. *European Journal of Social Psychology, 13*, 153–174.

Isaacs, H. R. (1975). *Idols of the tribe: Group identity and political change.* New York: Harper & Row.

Iverson, M., & Schwab, H. (1967). Ethnocentric dogmatism and binocular fusion of racially discrepant stimuli. *Journal of Personality and Social Psychology, 7*, 73–81.

Iwawaki, S., Sonoo, K., Williams, J., & Best, D. (1978). Color bias among young Japanese children. *Journal of Cross-Cultural Psychology, 9*, 61–73.

Jackman, M. R. (1977). Prejudice, tolerance, and attitudes towards ethnic groups. *Social Science Research, 6*, 145–169.

Jackman, M. R. (1978). General and applied tolerance: Does education increase commitment to racial integration? *American Journal of Political Science, 22*, 302–324.

Jackman, M. R., & Muha, M. J. (1984). Education and intergroup attitudes: Moral enlightenment, superficial democratic commitment, or ideological refinement? *American Sociological Review, 49*, 751–769.

Jackson, D. N. (1967). *Personality research form manual.* Goshen, New York: Research Psychologists Press.

Jackson, D. N., & Messick, S. J. (1957). A note on ethnocentrism and acquiescent response sets. *Journal of Abnormal and Social Psychology, 54*, 132–134.

Jacobson, C. (1985). Resistance to affirmative action: Self-interest or racism? *Journal of Conflict Resolution, 29*, 306–329.

Jahoda, M. (1960). *Race relations and mental health.* Paris: UNESCO.

Jaspers, I. (1978). The nature and measurement of attitudes. In H. Tajfel & C. Fraser (Eds.), *Introducing social psychology* (pp. 256–276). Middlesex, England: Penguin.

Johnson, D. W., & Johnson, R. T. (1989). *Cooperation and competition: Theory and research.* Edina, Minnesota: Interaction Book Company.

Jones, J. M. (1972). *Prejudice and racism.* Reading, Massachusetts: Addison-Wesley.

Jones, R. A. (1982). Perceiving other people: Stereotyping as a process of social cognition. In A. G. Miller (Ed.), *In the eye of the beholder: Contemporary issues in stereotyping* (pp. 41–91). New York: Praeger.

Judd, C. M., & Park, B. (1988). Out-group homogeneity: Judgments of variability at the individual and group levels. *Journal of Personality and Social Psychology, 54*, 778–788.

Kalin, R., & Berry, J. W. (1980). Geographic mobility and ethnic tolerance. *Journal of Social Psychology, 112*, 129–134.

Kates, S., & Diab, N. (1955). Authoritarian ideology and attitudes on parent-child relationships. *Journal of Abnormal and Social Psychology, 51*, 13–16.

Katz, D., & Braly, K. (1933). Racial stereotypes in one hundred college students. *Journal of Abnormal and Social Psychology, 28*, 280–290.

Katz, D., & Stotland, E. (1959). A preliminary statement of a theory of attitude structure and change. In S. Koch (Ed.), *Psychology: A study of a science*, *Vol. 3* (pp. 423–475). New York: McGraw-Hill.

Katz, I. (1978). *White awareness: A handbook for anti-racism training*. Norman, Oklahoma: University of Oklahoma Press.

Katz, P. A. (1976). The acquisition of racial attitudes in children. In P. A. Katz (Ed.), *Towards the elimination of racism* (pp. 125–154). New York: Pergamon.

Katz, P. A., & Taylor, D. A. (1988). *Eliminating racism: Profiles in controversy*. New York: Plenum.

Kaufman, W. C. (1957). Status, authoritarianism, and anti-Semitism. *American Journal of Sociology, 62*, 379–382.

Kelley, J., Ferson, J., & Holtzman, W. (1958). The measurement of attitudes towards the Negro in the South. *Journal of Social Psychology, 48*, 305–317.

Kelly, C. (1988). Intergroup differentiation in a political context. *British Journal of Social Psychology, 27*, 319–332.

Kelman, H. (1961). Processes of opinion change. *Public Opinion Quarterly, 25*, 57–78.

Kelman, H., & Barclay, J. (1963). The F scale as a measure of breadth of perspective. *Journal of Abnormal and Social Psychology, 67*, 608–615.

Kelman, H., & Pettigrew, T. (1959). How to understand prejudice. *Commentary, 28*, 436–441.

Kendrick, D. T., & Fundar, D. C. (1988). Profiting from controversy: Lessons from the person-situation debate. *American Psychologist, 43*, 23–34.

Kerlinger, F. (1984). *Liberalism and conservatism: The nature and structure of social attitudes*. Hillsdale, New Jersey: Erlbaum.

Kerlinger, F., & Rokeach, M. (1966). The factorial nature of the F and D scales. *Journal of Personality and Social Psychology, 4*, 391–399.

Kidder, L., & Stewart, V. (1975). *The psychology of intergroup relations: Conflict and consciousness*. New York: McGraw-Hill.

Kiesler, C. A. (1969). Group pressure and conformity. In J. Mills (Ed.), *Experimental social psychology* (pp. 235–278). London: Macmillan.

Kinder, D. R. (1986). The continuing American dilemma: White resistance to racial change 40 years after Myrdal. *Journal of Social Issues, 42*, 151–171.

Kinder, D. R., & Rhodebeck, L. A. (1982). Continuities in support for racial equality. *Public Opinion Quarterly, 46*, 195–215.

Kinder, D. R., & Sears, D. O. (1981). Prejudice and politics: Symbolic racism versus racial threats to the good life. *Journal of Personality and Social Psychology, 40*, 414–431.

Kinloch, G. (1974). Racial prejudice in highly and less racist societies: Social distance preferences among white college students in South Africa and Hawaii. *Sociology and Social Research, 59*, 1–13.

Kinloch, G. (1977). Intergroup stereotypes and social distance among white college students in Durban, South Africa. *Journal of Psychology, 95*, 17–23.

Kinloch, G. (1985). Racial attitudes in South Africa: A review. *Genetic, Social and General Psychology Monographs, 111*, 261–281.

Kirscht, J. P., & Dillehay, R. C. (1967). *Dimensions of authoritarianism*. Lexington: University of Kentucky Press.

Kleugel, J., & Smith, E. (1983). Affirmative action attitudes: Effects of self-interest, racial affect, and stratification beliefs on whites' views. *Social Forces 61*, 797–824.

Klineberg, O. (1968). Prejudice: The concept. In D. Sills (Ed.), *Encyclopedia of the social sciences, Vol. 12* (pp. 439–448). New York: Macmillan.

Knapp, R. J. (1976). Authoritarianism, alienation, and related variables: A correlational and factor-analytic study. *Psychological Bulletin, 83*, 194–212.

Kohn, P. M. (1974). The authoritarianism-rebellion scale: A balanced F scale with left wing reversals. *Sociometry, 35*, 176–189.

Konecni, V. J. (1979). The role of aversive events in the development of intergroup conflict. In W. Austin & S. Worchel (Eds.), *The social psychology of intergroup relations* (pp. 85–102). Monterey, California: Brooks/Cole.

Kovel, J. (1970). *White racism: A psychological history*. New York: Pantheon.

Krech, D., & Crutchfield, R. (1948). *Theory and problems of social psychology*. New York: McGraw-Hill.

Krech, D., Crutchfield, R., & Ballachey, E. (1962). *Individual in society*. New York: McGraw-Hill.

Kuhn, T. S. (1962). *The structure of scientific revolutions*. Chicago: University of Chicago Press.

Kutner, B., Wilkins, C., & Yarrow, P. (1952). Verbal attitudes and overt behavior involving racial prejudice. *Journal of Abnormal and Social Psychology, 47*, 649–652.

Lalonde, R. N., Moghaddam, F. M., & Taylor, D. M. (1987). The process of group differentiation in a dynamic intergroup setting. *Journal of Social Psychology, 127*, 273–287.

Lambert, W. W., & Lambert, W. E. (1964). *Social psychology*. Englewood Cliffs, New Jersey: Prentice-Hall.

Lambley, P. (1973). Authoritarianism and prejudice in South African student samples. *Journal of Social Psychology, 91*, 341–342.

Lambley, P. (1980). *The psychology of apartheid*. London: Secker & Warburg.

Lambley, P., & Gilbert, L. (1970). Forced choice and counterbalanced versions of the F scale. *Psychological Reports, 27*, 547–550.

Landis, D., Hope, R. O., & Day, H. R. (1984). Training for desegregation in the military. In N. Miller & M. Brewer (Eds.), *Groups in contact: The psychology of desegregation* (pp. 256–278). San Diego: Academic.

Landsberger, H., & Saavedra, A. (1967). Response set in developing countries. *Public Opinion Quarterly, 31*, 214–229.

Lanternari, V. (1980). Ethnocentrism and ideology. *Ethnic and Racial Studies, 3*, 52–67.

LaPiere, R. T. (1934). Attitudes vs actions. *Social Forces, 13*, 230–237.

Larsen, K., Colen, L., von Flue, D., & Zimmerman, P. (1974). Situational pressure, attitudes toward blacks, and laboratory aggression. *Social Behavior and Personality, 2*, 219–221.

Larson, K., & Schwendiman, G. (1969). Authoritarianism, self-esteem, and insecurity. *Psychological Reports, 25*, 229–230.

Lauderdale, P., Smith-Cunnien, P., Parker J., and Inverarity J. (1984). External threat and the definition of deviance. *Journal of Personality and Social Psychology, 46*, 1058–1068.

Lee, R. E., & Warr, P. B. (1969). The development and standardization of a balanced F-scale. *Journal of General Psychology, 81*, 109–129.

Leicester, M. (1989). *Multicultural education: From theory to practice.* Windsor, England: NFER-Nelson.

Lemyre, L., & Smith, P. M. (1985). Intergroup discrimination and self-esteem in the minimal group paradigm. *Journal of Personality and Social Psychology, 49*, 660–670.

Lenski, C., & Leggett, J. (1960). Caste, class, and deference in the research interview. *American Journal of Sociology, 65*, 463–467.

Leonard, K. E., & Taylor, S. P. (1981). Effects of racial prejudice and race of target on aggression. *Aggressive Behavior, 7*, 205–214.

Lerner, M. J. (1980). *The belief in a just world: A fundamental delusion.* New York: Plenum.

Lerner, M. J., & Miller, D. T. (1978). Just world research and the attribution process. *Psychological Bulletin, 85*, 1030–1051.

Le Roux, P. (1986). Growing up an Afrikaner. In S. Burman & P. Reynolds (Eds.), *Growing up in a divided society* (pp. 184–207). Johannesburg: Ravan Press.

Lever, H. (1976). Frustration and prejudice in South Africa. *Journal of Social Psychology, 100*, 21–33.

Lever, H. (1978). *South African society.* Johannesburg: Jonathan Ball Publishers.

Lever, H. (1980). Education and ethnic attitudes in South Africa. *Sociology and Social Research, 64*, 53–69.

Lever, H., Schlemmer, L., & Wagner, O. (1967). A factor analysis of authoritarianism. *Journal of Social Research, 16*, 41–48.

Levin, J., & Levin, W. C. (1982). *The functions of prejudice and discrimination.* New York: Harper & Row.

LeVine, R. A., & Campbell, D. T. (1972). *Ethnocentrism: Theories of conflict, ethnic attitudes and group behavior.* New York: Wiley.

Levinson, D. J. (1957). Authoritarian personality and foreign policy. *Journal of Conflict Resolution, 1*, 37–47.

Levinson, D. J., & Huffman, P. E. (1955). Traditional family ideology and its relation to personality. *Journal of Personality, 23*, 251–273.

Lewin, K. (1948). *Resolving social conflicts.* New York: Harper.

Likert, R. (1931). *A technique for the measurement of attitudes.* New York: Columbia University Press.

Lilli, W., & Rehm, J. (1988). Judgmental processes as bases of intergroup conflict. In W. Stroebe, A. W. Kruglanski, D. Bar-Tal, & M. Hewstone (Eds.), *The social psychology of intergroup conflict* (pp. 29–46). Berlin: Springer.

Lindzey, G. (1950). An experimental examination of the scapegoat theory of prejudice. *Journal of Abnormal and Social Psychology, 45*, 297–309.

Linn, L. (1965). Verbal attitudes and overt behavior: A study of racial discrimination. *Social Forces, 43*, 353–364.

Lippman, W. (1922). *Public opinion.* New York: Harcourt Brace Jovanovich.

Lipset, S. M. (1963). *Political man.* New York: Doubleday.

Locksley, A., Ortiz, V., & Hepburn, C. (1980). Social categorization and discriminatory behavior: Extinguishing the minimal intergroup discriminatory effect. *Journal of Personality and Social Psychology, 39*, 773–783.

Longshore, D., & Prager, J. (1985). The impact of school desegregation: A situational analysis. *Annual Review of Sociology, 11,* 75–91.

Lord, C., Lepper, M., & Mackie, D. (1984). Attitude prototypes as determinants of attitude-behavior consistency. *Journal of Personality and Social Psychology, 46,* 1254–1266.

Lorr, M. (1982). *Interpersonal style inventory manual.* Unpublished test manual, Catholic University of America, Washington, D.C.

Louw-Potgieter, J. (1988). The authoritarian personality: An inadequate explanation for intergroup conflict in South Africa. *Journal of Social Psychology, 128,* 75–87.

Lutterman, K. G., & Middleton, R. (1970). Authoritarianism, anomia and prejudice. *Social Forces, 48,* 485–492.

Lyle, W, H., & Levitt, E. E. (1955). Punitiveness, authoritarianism, and parental discipline of grade school children. *Journal of Abnormal and Social Psychology, 51,* 42–46.

Maass, A., & Clark, R. D. (1984). Hidden impact of minorities: Fifteen years of minority influence research. *Psychological Bulletin, 95,* 428–450.

Mabe, P., & Williams, J. (1975). Relation of racial attitudes to sociometric choices among second grade children. *Psychological Reports, 37,* 547–554.

MacCrone, I. D. (1937). *Race attitudes in South Africa: Historical, experimental and psychological studies.* London: Oxford University Press.

MacKinnon, W. J., & Centers, R. (1957). Authoritarianism and internationalism. *Public Opinion Quarterly, 20,* 621–630.

MacNeil, L. W. (1974). Cognitive complexity: A brief synthesis of theoretical approaches and a concept attainment task analogue to cognitive structure. *Psychological Reports, 34,* 3–11.

Malof, M., & Lott, A. J. (1962). Ethnocentrism and the acceptance of Negro support in a group pressure situation. *Journal of Abnormal and Social Psychology, 65,* 254–258.

Mann, J. (1959). The relationship between cognitive, affective, and behavioral aspects of racial prejudice. *Journal of Social Psychology, 49,* 223–228.

Mann, M. (1970). The social cohesion of liberal democracy. *American Sociological Review, 35,* 423–439.

Manstead, A.S.R., Proffit, C., & Smart, J. L. (1983). Predicting and understanding mothers' infant-feeding intentions and behavior: Testing the theory of reasoned action. *Journal of Personality and Social Psychology, 44,* 657–671.

Marden, C., & Meyer, G. (1962). *Minorities in American society.* New York: American Book Company.

Marlowe, D., & Crowne, D. (1961). Social desirability and response to perceived situational demands. *Journal of Consulting Psychology, 25,* 109–115.

Martin, J. G. (1964). *The tolerant personality.* Detroit: Wayne State University Press.

Martin, J. G., & Westie, F. R. (1959). The tolerant personality. *American Sociological Review, 24,* 521–528.

Martire, G., & Clark, R. (1982). *Anti-Semitism in the United States: A study of prejudice in the 1980s.* New York: Praeger.

Marx, G. T. (1967). *Protest and prejudice.* New York: Harper & Row.

Masling, M. (1954). How neurotic is the authoritarian? *Journal of Abnormal and Social Psychology, 49*, 316–318.

Maslow, A. H. (1943). The authoritarian character structure. *Journal of Social Psychology, 18*, 401–411.

May, J., & May, G. (1979). Color preference for black and white by infants and young children. *Perceptual and Motor Skills, 49*, 143–148.

May, J., & May G. (1981). Effects of age on color preference for black and white by infants and young children. *Perceptual and Motor Skills, 52*, 255–261.

Maykovich, M. (1975). Correlates of racial prejudice. *Journal of Personality and Social Psychology, 32*, 1014–1020.

McCauley, C., Stitt, C. L., & Segal, M. (1980). Stereotyping: From prejudice to prediction. *Psychological Bulletin, 87*, 195–208.

McClean, H. V. (1946). Psychodynamic factors in racial relations. *Annals of the American Academy of Political and Social Science, 244*, 159–166.

McClendon, M. J. (1985). Racism, rational choice, and white opposition to racial change: A case study of busing. *Public Opinion Quarterly, 49*, 214–233.

McClosky, H. (1958). Conservatism and personality. *American Political Science Review, 52*, 27–45.

McClosky, H. (1967). Personality and attitude correlates of foreign policy orientations. In J. N. Rosenau (Ed.), *Domestic sources of foreign policy*. New York: Free Press.

McConahay, J. (1982). Self-interest versus racial attitudes as correlates of anti-busing attitudes in Louisville: Is it the buses or the blacks? *Journal of Politics, 44*, 692–720.

McConahay, J. (1983). Modern racism and modern discrimination: The effects of race, racial attitudes, and context on simulated hiring decisions. *Personality and Social Psychology Bulletin, 9*, 551–558.

McConahay, J. (1986). Modern racism, ambivalence, and the modern racism scale. In J. Dovidio & S. L. Gaertner (Eds.), *Prejudice, discrimination, and racism: Theory and research*. New York: Academic.

McConahay, J., Hardee, B. B., & Batts, V. (1981). Has racism declined in America? *Journal of Conflict Resolution, 25*, 563–579.

McConahay, J., & Hough, J. C. (1976). Symbolic racism. *Journal of Social Issues, 32*, 23–45.

McCord, W, McCord, J., & Howard, A. (1960). Early familial experiences and bigotry. *American Sociological Review, 25*, 717–722.

McDill, E. L. (1961). Anomie, authoritarianism, prejudice, and socio-economic status: An attempt at clarification. *Social Forces, 39*, 239–245.

McGuire, W. J. (1966). Attitudes and opinions. *Annual Review of Psychology, 17*, 475–514.

Mehryar, A. (1970). Authoritarianism, rigidity, and Eysenck's E and N dimensions in an authoritarian culture. *Psychological Reports, 27*, 326.

Meindl, J. R., & Lerner, M. J. (1984). Exacerbation of extreme responses to an out-group. *Journal of Personality and Social Psychology, 47*, 71–84.

Melamed, L. (1970). The relationship between actions and attitudes in a South African setting. *South African Journal of Psychology, 1*, 19–23.

Meloen, J. D. (1983). *De autoritaire reaktie in tijden van welvaart en krisis* [The authoritarian response in times of prosperity and crisis]. Unpublished doctoral dissertation, University of Amsterdam, Holland.

Meloen, J. D., Hagendoorn, L., Raaijmakers, Q., & Visser, L. (1988). Authoritarianism and the revival of political racism: Reassessments in the Netherlands of the reliability and validity of the concept of authoritarianism by Adorno et al. *Political Psychology, 9*, 413–429.

Merton, R. K. (1970). Discrimination and the American creed. In P. I. Rose (Ed.), *The study of society* (pp. 449–457). New York: Random House.

Messick, D. M., & Mackie, D. M. (1989). Intergroup relations. *Annual Review of Psychology, 40*, 45–81.

Mezei, L. (1971). Perceived social pressure as an explanation of shifts in the relative influence of race and belief on prejudice across social situations. *Journal of Personality and Social Psychology, 19*, 69–81.

Michael, S. (1967). Authoritarianism, anomie and the disordered mind. *Acta Psychiatrica Scandinavica, 43*, 286–299.

Middleton, R. (1976). Regional differences in prejudice. *American Sociological Review, 41*, 94–117.

Milgram, S. (1963). Behavioral study of obedience. *Journal of Personality and Social Psychology, 63*, 371–378.

Milgram, S. (1974). *Obedience to authority: An experimental view*. New York: Harper & Row.

Miller, A. G. (1982). Stereotyping: Further perspectives and conclusions. In A. G. Miller (Ed.), *In the eye of the beholder: Contemporary issues in stereotyping* (pp. 466–505). New York: Praeger.

Miller, N. E., & Bugelski, R. (1948). Minor studies of aggression: II. The influence of frustration imposed by the in-group on attitudes expressed toward outgroups. *Journal of Psychology, 25*, 437–442.

Milner, D. (1975). *Children and race*. Harmondsworth, England: Penguin.

Milner, D. (1981). Racial prejudice. In J. Turner & H. Giles (Eds.), *Intergroup behaviour* (pp. 102–143). Oxford: Blackwell.

Milner, D. (1983). *Children and race: Ten years on*. London: Ward Lock Educational.

Minard, R. (1952). Race relationships in the Pocahontas coal field. *Journal of Social Issues, 8*, 29–44.

Mischel, W. (1977). On the future of personality measurement. *American Psychologist, 32*, 246–254.

Mischel, W., & Schopler, J. (1959). Authoritarianism and reactions to "Sputniks." *Journal of Abnormal and Social Psychology, 59*, 142–145.

Moe, J. L., Nacoste, R. W., & Insko, C. A. (1981). Belief versus race as determinants of discrimination: A study of Southern adolescents in 1966 and 1979. *Journal of Personality and Social Psychology, 41*, 1031–1050.

Moghaddam, F. M., & Stringer, P. (1986). Trivial and important criteria for social categorization in the minimal group paradigm. *Journal of Social Psychology, 126*, 345–354.

Moghaddam, F. M., & Stringer, P. (1988). Outgroup similarity and intergroup bias. *Journal of Social Psychology, 128*, 105–115.

Montgomery, R. L., & Enzie, F. E. (1973). Predicting behavior in a social influence-situation from attitude-scale measures of prejudice. *Psychological Reports, 32*, 235–240.

Moore, J. W., Hauk, W. E., & Denne, T. C. (1984). Racial prejudice, interracial contact, and personality variables. *Journal of Experimental Education, 52,* 168–173.

Moreland, R. L., & Levine, J. M. (1982). Socialization in small groups: Temporal changes in individual-group relations. In L. Berkowitz (Ed.), *Advances in experimental social psychology, Vol. 2* (pp. 137–192). New York: Academic.

Morse, C., & Allport, F. (1952). The causation of anti-Semitism: An investigation of seven hypotheses. *Journal of Psychology, 34,* 197–233.

Moscovici, S. (1976). *Social influence and social change.* London: Academic.

Moscovici, S., & Paicheler, G. (1978). Social comparison and social recognition: Two complementary processes of identification. In H. Tajfel (Ed.), *Differentiation in social groups: Studies in the social psychology of intergroup relations* (pp. 251–266). London: Academic.

Mosher, D. L., & Scodel, A. (1960). A study of the relationship between ethnocentrism in children and the ethnocentrism and authoritarian rearing practices of their mothers. *Child Development, 31,* 369–376.

Mowrer, O. H. (1960). *Learning theory and behavior.* New York: Wiley.

Mulford, C. L. (1968). Ethnocentrism and attitudes toward the mentally ill. *Sociological Quarterly, 9,* 107–111.

Mullen, B. (1983). Operationalizing the effect of the group on the individual: A self-attention perspective. *Journal of Experimental Social Psychology, 19,* 295–322.

Mummendey, A., & Simon, B. (1989). Better or different? III: The impact of importance of comparison dimension and relative in-group size upon intergroup discrimination. *British Journal of Social Psychology, 28,* 1–16.

Murphey, G., & Likert, R. (1938). *Public opinion and the individual.* New York: Harper.

Mynhardt, J. (1980). Prejudice among Afrikaans- and English-speaking South African students. *Journal of Social Psychology, 110,* 9–17.

Newcomb, T. (1943). *Personality and social change: Attitude formation in a student community.* New York: Holt, Rinehart & Winston.

Newcomb, T. (1961). *The acquaintance process.* New York: Holt, Rinehart & Winston.

Newcomb, T., Turner, R., & Converse, E. (1965). *Social Psychology.* New York: Holt, Rinehart & Winston.

Nieuwoudt, J. M., & Nel, E. (1975). The relationship between ethnic prejudice, authoritarianism and conformity among South African students. In S. Morse & C. Orpen (Eds.), *Contemporary South Africa: Social psychological perspectives* (pp. 99–102). Johannesburg: Juta and Co.

Nieuwoudt, J. M., & Plug, C. (1983). South African ethnic attitudes: 1973–1978. *Journal of Social Psychology, 121,* 163–171.

Nieuwoudt, J. M., Plug, C., & Mynhardt, J. (1977). White ethnic attitudes after Soweto: A field experiment. *South African Journal of Sociology, 16,* 1–12.

Ng, S. H. (1982). Power and intergroup discrimination. In H. Tajfel (Ed.), *Social identity and intergroup relations* (pp. 179–206). Cambridge: Cambridge University Press.

Ng, S. H. (1985). Biases in reward allocation resulting from personal status, group status, and allocation procedure. *Australian Journal of Psychology*, *37*, 297–307.

Oaker, G., & Brown, R. J. (1986). Intergroup relations in a hospital setting: A further test of social identity theory. *Human Relations*, *39*, 767–778.

Oakes, P., & Turner, J. (1980). Social categorization and intergroup behaviour: Does minimal intergroup discrimination make social identity more positive? *European Journal of Social Psychology*, *10*, 295–301.

O'Gorman, H. J. (1975). Pluralistic ignorance and white estimates of support for racial segregation. *Public Opinion Quarterly*, *39*, 313–330.

O'Gorman, H. J., & Garry, S. L. (1976). Pluralistic ignorance—a replication and extension. *Public Opinion Quarterly*, *40*, 449–458.

Olson, J. M., & Zanna, M. P. (1983). Attitudes and beliefs. In D. Perlman & P. C. Cozby (Eds.), *Social Psychology* (pp. 75–96). New York: Holt, Rinehart & Winston.

Orpen, C. (1970a). Authoritarianism in an "authoritarian" culture: The case of Afrikaans-speaking South Africa. *Journal of Social Psychology*, *81*, 119–120.

Orpen, C. (1970b). *Authoritarianism within an "authoritarian" culture: A critical reexamination of the "theory" of the authoritarian personality.* Unpublished doctoral dissertation, University of Cape Town, Cape Town, South Africa.

Orpen, C. (1971a). Authoritarianism and racial attitudes among English-speaking South Africans. *Journal of Social Psychology*, *84*, 301–302.

Orpen, C. (1971b). The effect of cultural factors on the relationship between prejudice and personality. *Journal of Psychology*, *78*, 73–79.

Orpen, C. (1971c). Prejudice and adjustment to cultural norms among English-speaking South Africans. *Journal of Psychology*, *77*, 217–218.

Orpen, C. (1972a). A cross-cultural investigation of the relationship between conservatism and personality. *Journal of Psychology*, *81*, 297–300.

Orpen, C. (1972b). The cross-cultural validity of the Eysenck Personality Inventory: A test in Afrikaans-speaking South Africa. *British Journal of Social and Clinical Psychology*, *11*, 244–247.

Orpen, C. (1973a). Sociocultural and personality factors in prejudice: The case of white South Africa. *South African Journal of Psychology*, *3*, 91–96.

Orpen, C. (1973b). The reference group basis of racial attitudes: An empirical study with white and black Rhodesians. *South African Journal of Sociology*, *6*, 67–73.

Orpen, C. (1975). Authoritarianism revisited: A critical examination of "expressive" theories of prejudice. In S. Morse & C. Orpen (Eds.), *Contemporary South Africa: Social psychological perspectives* (pp. 103–111). Johannesburg: Juta and Co.

Orpen, C., & Rookledge, Q. (1972). Dogmatism and prejudice in white South Africa. *Journal of Social Psychology*, *86*, 151–153.

Orpen, C., & Tsapogas, G. (1972). Racial prejudice and authoritarianism: A test in white South Africa. *Psychological Reports*, *30*, 441–442.

Orpen, C., & van der Schyff, L. (1972). Prejudice and personality in white South Africa: A "differential learning" alternative to the authoritarian personality. *Journal of Social Psychology*, *87*, 313–314.

Owen, C. A., Eisner, H. C., & McFaul, T. R. (1981). A half-century of social distance research: National replication of the Bogardus studies. *Sociology and Social Research, 66,* 80–98.

Pagel, M. D., & Davidson, A. R. (1984). A comparison of three social-psychological models of attitude and behavioral plan: Prediction of contraceptive behavior. *Journal of Personality and Social Psychology, 47,* 517–533.

Park, R. E. (1924). The concept of social distance. *Journal of Applied Sociology, 8,* 339–344.

Patchen, M. (1982). *Black-white contact in schools: Its social and academic effects.* West Lafayette, Indiana: Purdue University Press.

Patchen, M. (1983). Students' own racial attitudes and those of peers of both races, as related to interracial behaviors. *Sociology and Social Research, 68,* 59–77.

Patchen, M., Davidson, J., Hoffman, G., & Brown, W. (1977). Determinants of students' interracial behavior and opinion change. *Sociology of Education, 50,* 55–75.

Peabody, D. (1961). Attitude content and agreement set in scales of authoritarianism, dogmatism, antisemitism and economic conservatism. *Journal of Abnormal and Social Psychology, 63,* 1–11.

Pearlin, L. (1954). Shifting group attachments and attitudes towards Negroes. *Social Forces, 33,* 47–50.

Peterson, W. (1958). Prejudice in American society: A critique of some recent formulations. *Commentary, 26,* 342–348.

Pettigrew, T. F. (1958). Personality and socio-cultural factors in intergroup attitudes: A cross-national comparison. *Journal of Conflict Resolution, 2,* 29–42.

Pettigrew, T. F. (1959). Regional differences in anti-Negro prejudice. *Journal of Abnormal and Social Psychology, 59,* 28–36.

Pettigrew, T. F. (1960). Social distance attitudes of South African students. *Social Forces, 38,* 246–253.

Pettigrew, T. F. (1961). Social psychology and desegregation research. *American Psychologist, 16,* 105–112.

Pettigrew, T. F. (1971). *Racially separate or together?* New York: McGraw-Hill.

Pettigrew, T. F. (1975). *Racial discrimination in the U.S.* New York: Harper & Row.

Pettigrew, T. F. (1979). The ultimate attribution error: Extending Allport's cognitive analysis of prejudice. *Personality and Social Psychology Bulletin, 5,* 461–476.

Pettigrew, T. F. (1981). Extending the stereotype concept. In D. Hamilton (Ed.), *Cognitive processes in stereotyping and intergroup relations* (pp. 303–331). Hillsdale, New Jersey: Erlbaum.

Pettigrew, T. F. (1986). The intergroup contact hypothesis reconsidered. In M. Hewstone & R. Brown (Eds.), *Contact and conflict in intergroup encounters* (pp. 169–195). Oxford: Blackwell.

Pettigrew, T. F., & Martin, J. (1987). Shaping the organizational context for black American inclusion. *Journal of Social Issues, 43,* 41–78.

Pettigrew, T. F., & Martin, J. (1989). Organizational inclusion of minority groups: A social psychological analysis. In J. P. van Oudenhoven & T. M. Willemsen (Eds.), *Ethnic minorities: Social psychological perspectives* (pp. 169–200). Amsterdam: Swets & Zeitlinger.

Porter, D. T. (1974). An experimental investigation of the effects of racial prejudice and racial perception upon communication effectiveness. *Speech Monographs, 41,* 179–184.

Prentice, N. M. (1961). Ethnic attitudes, neuroticism, and culture. *Journal of Social Psychology, 54,* 75–82.

Press, L., Burt, I., & Barling, J. (1979). Racial preferences among South African white and black preschool children. *Journal of Social Psychology, 107,* 125–126.

Preston-Whyte, E. (1976). Race attitudes and behaviour: The case of domestic employment in white South African homes. *African Studies, 35,* 75–89.

Proshansky, H. M. (1966). The development of intergroup attitudes. In L. W. Hoffman & M. L. Hoffman (Eds.), *Review of child development research* (pp. 311–371). New York: Russell Sage.

Prothro, E. T. (1952). Ethnocentrism and anti-Negro attitudes in the deep South *Journal of Abnormal and Social Psychology, 47,* 105–108.

Prothro, E. T., & Jensen, J. A. (1950). Interrelations of religious and ethnic attitudes in selected southern populations. *Journal of Social Psychology, 34,* 252–258.

Prothro, E.T., & Miles, O.K. (1952). A comparison of ethnic attitudes of college students and middle class adults from the same state. *Journal of Social Psychology, 36,* 53–58.

Purdue, C. W., Dovidio, J. F., Gurtman, M. B., & Taylor, R. B. (1990). Us and them: Social categorization and the process of intergroup bias. *Journal of Personality and Social Psychology, 59,* 475–486.

Quinley, H. E., & Glock, C. Y. (1979). *Anti-Semitism in America.* New York: Free Press.

Rabbie, J. M., & Horwitz, M. (1969). Arousal of ingroup-outgroup bias by a chance win or loss. *Journal of Personality and Social Psychology, 13,* 269–277.

Rabbie, J. M., & Wilkens, C. (1971). Intergroup competition and its effect on intra- and intergroup relations. *European Journal of Social Psychology, 1,* 215–234.

Rajecki, D. (1982). *Attitudes: Themes and advances.* Sunderland, Massachusetts: Sinauer Associates.

Rand, T. M., & Wexley, K. M. (1975). Demonstration of the effect "similar to me" in simulated employment interviews. *Psychological Reports, 36,* 535–544.

Raper, A. (1933). *The tragedy of lynching.* Chapel Hill: University of North Carolina Press.

Ray, J. J. (1972). A new balanced F scale—and its relation to social class. *Australian Psychologist, 7,* 155–166.

Ray, J. J. (1974). Introduction. In J. J. Ray (Ed.), *Conservatism as heresy.* Sydney: A.N.Z. Book Co.

Ray, J. J. (1976). Do authoritarians hold authoritarian attitudes? *Human Relations, 29,* 307–325.

Ray, J. J. (1979a). Is the dogmatism scale irreversible? *South African Journal of Psychology, 9,* 104–107.

Ray, J. J. (1979b). A short balanced F scale. *Journal of Social Psychology, 109,* 309–310.

Ray, J. J. (1980a). Authoritarianism in California thirty years later—with some cross-cultural comparisons. *Journal of Social Psychology, 111,* 9–17.

Ray, J. J. (1980b). Racism and authoritarianism among white South Africans. *Journal of Social Psychology, 110,* 29–37.

Ray, J. J. (1981a). Do authoritarian attitudes or authoritarian personalities reflect mental illness? *South African Journal of Psychology, 11,* 153–157.

Ray, J. J. (1981b). The new Australian nationalism. *Quadrant, 25,* 1–2.

Ray, J. J. (1983). Reviving the problem of acquiescent response set. *Journal of Social Psychology, 121,* 81–96.

Ray, J. J. (1984). Authoritarianism and achievement motivation in contemporary West Germany. *Journal of Social Psychology, 122,* 3–19.

Ray, J. J. (1988a). Cognitive style as a predictor of authoritarianism, conservatism, and racism: A fantasy in many movements. *Political Psychology, 9,* 303–308.

Ray, J. J. (1988b). Racism and personal adjustment: Testing the Bagley hypothesis in Germany and South Africa. *Personality and Individual Differences, 9,* 685–686.

Ray, J. J., & Furnham, A. (1984). Authoritarianism, conservatism, and racism. *Ethnic and Racial Studies, 7,* 406–412.

Ray, J. J., & Heaven, P.C.L. (1984). Conservatism and authoritarianism among urban Afrikaners. *Journal of Social Psychology, 122,* 163–170.

Ray, J. J., & Lovejoy, F. H. (1986). The generality of racial prejudice. *Journal of Social Psychology, 126,* 563–564.

Rehm, J., Lilli, W., & Eimeren, B. (1988). Reduced intergroup differentiation as a result of self-categorization in overlapping categories. A quasi-experiment. *European Journal of Social Psychology, 18,* 375–379.

Reich, M. (1972). The economics of racism. In R. C. Edwards, M. Reich, & T. E. Weisskopf (Eds.), *The capitalist system* (pp. 313–321). Englewood Cliffs, New Jersey: Prentice-Hall.

Reich, W. (1975). *The mass psychology of fascism.* Harmondsworth, England: Penguin.

Rex, J. (1970). *Race relations in sociological theory.* New York: Schocken.

Rhyne, E. H. (1962). Racial prejudice and personality scales: An alternative approach. *Social Forces, 41,* 44–53.

Richards, S. A., & Jaffee, C. L. (1972). Blacks supervising whites: A study of interracial difficulties in working together in a simulated organization. *Journal of Applied Psychology, 56,* 234–240.

Richert, K. C. (1963). Explorations into the specific behavioral determinants of authoritarians. *Psychological Reports, 13,* 950.

Roberts, A. H., & Rokeach, M. (1956). Anomie, authoritarianism, and prejudice: A replication. *American Journal of Sociology, 61,* 355–358.

Rogers, R. W. (1983). Race variables in aggression. In R. G. Geen & E. I. Donnerstein (Eds.), *Aggression: Theoretical and empirical reviews, Vol. 2* (pp. 27–50). New York: Academic.

Rogers, R. W., & Prentice-Dunn, S. (1981). Deindividuation and anger-mediated interracial aggression: Unmasking regressive racism. *Journal of Personality and Social Psychology, 41,* 63–73.

Rokeach, M. (1948). Generalized mental rigidity as a factor in ethnocentrism. *Journal of Abnormal and Social Psychology, 43,* 259–278.

Rokeach, M. (1954). The nature and meaning of dogmatism. *Psychological Review, 61,* 194–204.

Rokeach, M., & Fruchter, B. (1956). A factorial study of dogmatism and related concepts. *Journal of Abnormal and Social Psychology, 53,* 356–360.

Rokeach, M., & Mezei, L. (1966). Race and shared belief as factors in social choice. *Science, 151,* 167–172.

Rokeach, M., Smith, P., & Evans, R. (1960). Two kinds of prejudice or one? In M. Rokeach, *The open and the closed mind* (pp. 132–168). New York: Basic Books.

Roof, W. C. (1978). *Community and commitment: Religious plausibility in a liberal Protestant church.* New York: Elsevier.

Rorer, L. G. (1965). The great response style myth. *Psychological Bulletin, 63,* 129–156.

Rorer, L. G., & Widger, T. A. (1983). Personality structure and assessment. *Annual Review of Psychology, 34,* 431–463.

Rose, A. (1956). Intergroup relations vs prejudice. *Social Problems, 4,* 173–176.

Rose, A. (1964). Race and minority group relations. In J. Gould & W. L. Kolb (Eds.), *A dictionary of the social sciences* (pp. 570–571). New York: Free Press.

Rose, S. (1951). *The roots of prejudice.* Paris: UNESCO.

Rosenblith, J. F. (1949). A replication of "some roots of prejudice." *Journal of Abnormal and Social Psychology, 44,* 470–489.

Rosenfield, D., & Stephan, W. (1981). Intergroup relations among children. In S. Brehm, S. Kassim, & F. Gibbons (Eds.), *Developmental social psychology* (pp. 271–297). New York: Oxford University Press.

Ross, L. (1977). The intuitive psychologist and his shortcomings: Distortions in the attribution process. In L. Berkowitz (Ed.), *Advances in experimental social psychology, Vol. 10* (pp. 174–220). New York: Academic.

Rothbart, M. (1976). Achieving racial equality: An analysis of resistance to social reform. In P. Katz (Ed.), *Towards the elimination of racism* (pp. 341–376). New York: Pergamon.

Rothbart, M., & John, O. P. (1985). Social categorization and behavioral episodes: A cognitive analysis of effects of intergroup contact. *Journal of Social Issues, 41,* 81–84.

Rubin, I. M. (1967). Increased self-acceptance: A means of reducing prejudice. *Journal of Personality and Social Psychology, 5,* 233–238.

Ryan, W. (1971). *Blaming the victim.* New York: Random House.

Sachdev, I., & Bourhis, R. Y. (1984). Minimal majorities and minorities. *European Journal of Social Psychology, 14,* 35–52.

Sachdev, I., & Bourhis, R. Y. (1987). Status differentials and intergroup behaviour. *British Journal of Social Psychology, 17,* 277–293.

Saenger, G. H., & Gilbert, E. (1950). Customer reactions to the integration of Negro personnel. *International Journal of Opinion and Attitude Research, 4,* 57–76.

Saharso, S. (1989). Ethnic identity and the paradox of equality. In J. P. van

Oudenhoven, & T. M. Willemsen (Eds.), *Ethnic minorities: Social psychological perspectives* (pp. 97–114). Amsterdam: Swets & Zeitlinger.

Samelson, F. (1978). From "race psychology" to "studies in prejudice": Some observations on the thematic reversal in social psychology. *Journal of the History of the Behavioral Sciences, 14,* 265–278.

Samelson, F., & Yates, J. (1967). Acquiescence and the F scale: Old assumptions and new data. *Psychological Bulletin, 68,* 91–103.

Sappington, A. (1974). Behavior of biased and non-biased whites towards blacks in a simulated interaction. *Psychological Reports, 35,* 487–493.

Schermerhorn, R. (1970). *Comparative ethnic relations: A framework for theory and research.* New York: Random House.

Schofield, J. W. (1986). Causes and consequences of the colorblind perspective. In J. F. Dovidio & S. L. Gaertner (Eds.), *Prejudice, discrimination, and racism* (pp. 231–254). Orlando, Florida: Academic.

Schönbach, P., Gollwitzer, P. M. Stiepel, G., & Wagner, U. (1981). *Education and intergroup attitudes.* London: Academic.

Schuman, H., & Bobo, L. (1988). Survey-based experiments on white racial attitudes toward residential integration. *American Journal of Sociology, 94,* 273–299.

Schuman, H., & Harding, J. (1964). Prejudice and the norm of rationality. *Sociometry, 27,* 353–371.

Schuman, H., Steeh, C., & Bobo, L. (1985). *Racial attitudes in America.* Cambridge, Massachusetts: Harvard University Press.

Schwartz, S. H., & Tessler, R. C. (1972). A test of a model for reducing measured attitude-behavior discrepancies. *Journal of Personality and Social Psychology, 24,* 225–236.

Schwarzwald, J. (1984). Integration as a situational contingent: Secular versus religious public education. In Y. Amir & S. Sharon (Eds.), *School desegregation: Cross-cultural perspectives* (pp. 99–117). Hillsdale, New Jersey: Erlbaum.

Schwarzwald, J., & Yinon, Y. (1978). Physical aggression: Effects of ethnicity of target and directionality of aggression. *European Journal of Social Psychology, 8,* 367–376.

Schwendiman, G., Larson, K. S., & Cope, S. C. (1970). Authoritarian traits as predictors of preference in 1968 United States presidential elections. *Psychological Reports, 27,* 629–630.

Sears, D. O., & Allen, H. M. (1984). The trajectory of local desegregation controversies and whites' opposition to busing. In N. Miller & M. B.. Brewer (Eds.), *Groups in contact: The psychology of desegregation* (pp. 123–151). New York: Academic.

Sears, D. O., Hensler, C., & Speer, L. (1979). Whites' opposition to busing: Self-interest or symbolic politics? *American Political Science Review, 73,* 369–384.

Sears, D. O., & Kinder, D. R. (1971). Racial tensions and voting in Los Angeles. In W. Z. Hirsch (Ed.), *Los Angeles: Viability and prospects for metropolitan leadership.* Cambridge, Massachusetts: Harvard University Press.

Sears, D. O., & Kinder, D. R. (1985). Whites' opposition to busing: On conceptualizing and operationalizing "group conflict." *Journal of Personality and Social Psychology, 48,* 1141–1147.

Secord, P. E., & Backman, C. W. (1964). *Social psychology*. New York: McGraw-Hill.

Seeman, M. (1975). Alienation studies. *Annual Review of Sociology, 1*, 91–123.

Seeman, M. (1977). Some real and imaginary consequences of social mobility: A French-American comparison. *American Journal of Sociology, 82*, 757–782.

Seeman, M. (1981). Intergroup relations. In M. Rosenberg & R. H. Turner (Eds.), *Social psychology: Sociological perspectives* (pp. 378–410). New York: Basic Books.

Seeman, M., Rohan, D., & Argeriou, M. (1966). Social mobility and prejudice: A Swedish replication. *Social Problems, 14*, 187–197.

Segall, M. H., Dasen, P. R., Berry, J. W., & Poortinga, Y. (1990). *Human behavior in global perspective*. New York: Pergamon.

Selznick, G., & Steinberg, S. (1969). *The tenacity of prejudice: Anti-Semitism in contemporary America* New York: Harper.

Serum, C. S., & Myers, D. G. (1970). Note on prejudice and personality. *Psychological Reports, 26*, 65–66.

Sharan, M. B., & Karan, L. W. (1974). Relationship between prejudice and adjustment. *Psychologia, 17*, 99–102.

Sharan, S. (Ed.) (1990). *Cooperative learning: Theory and research*. New York: Praeger.

Sharan, S., & Rich, Y. (1984). Field experiments on ethnic integration in Israeli schools. In Y. Amir, S. Sharan, & R. Ben-Arie (Eds.), *School desegregation: Cross-cultural perspectives* (pp. 189–218). Hillsdale, New Jersey: Erlbaum.

Sherif, M. (1967). *Group conflict and cooperation*. London: Routledge & Kegan Paul.

Sherif, M., & Sherif, C. W. (1953). *Groups in harmony and tension*. New York: Harper.

Sherif, M., & Sherif, C. W. (1964). *Reference groups: Exploration into conformity and deviation of adolescents*. New York: Harper.

Sherif, M., & Sherif, C. W. (1979). Reseach on intergroup relations. In W. G. Austin & S. Worchel (Eds.), *The social psychology of intergroup relations* (pp. 7–18). Monterey, California: Brooks/Cole.

Shills, E. A. (1954). Authoritarianism: Right and left. In R. Christie & M. Jahoda (Eds.), *Studies in the scope and method of "the authoritarian personality"* (pp. 24–49). Glencoe, Illinois: Free Press.

Sidanius, J. (1985). Cognitive functioning and sociopolitical ideology revisited. *Political Psychology, 6*, 637–662.

Sidanius, J. (1988). Intolerance of ambiguity, conservatism, and racism—Whose fantasy, whose reality?: A reply to Ray. *Political Psychology, 9*, 309–316.

Silverman, B. I. (1974). Consequences, racial discrimination, and the principle of belief congruence. *Journal of Personality and Social Psychology, 29*, 497–508.

Silverman, B. I., & Cochrane, R. (1972). Effect of the social context on the principle of belief congruence. *Journal of Personality and Social Psychology, 22*, 259–269.

Silverman, I., & Kleinman, D. (1967). A response deviance interpretation of the effects of experimentally induced frustration on prejudice. *Journal of Experimental Research in Personality, 2*, 150–153.

Simpson, G. E., & Yinger, J. M. (1972). *Racial and cultural minorities: An analysis of prejudice and discrimination* (4th ed.). New York: Harper & Row.

Simpson, G. E., & Yinger, J. M. (1985). *Racial and cultural minorities: An analysis of prejudice and discrimination* (5th ed.). New York: Plenum.

Singer, E. (1981). Reference groups and social evaluations. In M. Rosenberg & R. H. Turner (Eds.), *Social psychology: Sociological perspectives* (pp. 66–93). New York: Basic Books.

Sinha, A. K., and Upadhyaya, O. P. (1960). Change and persistence in the stereotypes of university students toward different ethnic groups during the Sino-Indian border dispute. *Journal of Social Psychology, 52,* 31–39.

Sinha, R. P., & Hassan, M. K. (1975). Some personality correlates of social prejudice. *Journal of Social and Economic Studies, 3,* 225–231.

Skevington, S. (1981). Intergroup relations and nursing. *European Journal of Social Psychology, 11,* 43–59.

Smith, C. R., Williams, L., & Willis, R. (1967). Race, sex, and belief as determinants of friendship acceptance. *Journal of Personality and Social Psychology, 5,* 127–137.

Smith, E.W.L., & Dixon, T. R. (1968). Verbal conditioning as a function of race of the experimenter and prejudice of the subject. *Journal of Experimental Social Psychology, 4,* 285–301.

Smith, H. P., & Rosen, E. W. (1958). Some psychological correlates of world-mindedness and authoritarianism. *Journal of Personality, 26,* 170–183.

Sniderman, P. M., & Tetlock, P. E. (1986a). Symbolic racism: Problems of motive attribution in political analysis. *Journal of Social Issues, 42,* 129–150.

Sniderman, P. M., & Tetlock, P. E. (1986b). Reflections on American racism. *Journal of Social Issues, 42,* 173–187.

Snyder, M. (1981). On the self-perpetuating nature of social stereotypes. In D Hamilton (Ed.), *Cognitive processes in stereotyping and intergroup behavior* (pp. 183–212). Hillsdale, New Jersey: Erlbaum.

Sonquist, J. (1970). *Multivariate model building: The validation of a search strategy.* Ann Arbor, Michigan: Braun & Brumfield.

Spangenberg, J., & Nel, E. M. (1983). The effect of equal-status contact on ethnic attitudes. *Journal of Social Psychology, 121,* 173–180.

Spencer, M. (1983). Children's cultural values and parental child rearing strategies. *Developmental Review 3,* 351–370.

Spencer, M., & Horowitz, F. (1973). Effects of systematic social and token reinforcement on the modification of racial and color concept attitudes in black and white preschool children. *Developmental Psychology, 9,* 246–254.

Srole, L. (1956). Social integration and certain corollaries: An exploratory study. *American Sociological Review, 21,* 709–716.

Stagner, R., & Congdon, C. (1955). Another failure to demonstrate displacement of aggression. *Journal of Abnormal and Social Psychology, 51,* 695–696.

Staub, E. (1989). *The roots of evil: The origins of genocide and other group violence.* Cambridge: Cambridge University Press.

Stein, D. D. (1966). The influence of belief systems on interpersonal preference: A validation study of Rokeach's theory of prejudice. *Psychological Monographs: General and Applied, No. 616.*

Stein, D. D., Hardyck, J. A., & Smith, M. B. (1965). Race and belief: An open and shut case. *Journal of Personality and Social Psychology, 1*, 281–289.

Steiner, I. D. (1974). Whatever happened to the group in social psychology? *Journal of Experimental Social Psychology, 10*, 94–108.

Stember, C. H. (1961). *Education and attitude change.* New York: Institute of Human Relations Press.

Stephan, W. G. (1983). Intergroup relations. In D. Perlman & P. Cozby (Eds.), *Social psychology* (pp. 414–441). New York: Holt, Rinehart & Winston.

Stephan, W. G. (1985). Intergroup relations. In G. Lindzey & E. Aronson (Eds.), *The handbook of social psychology* (pp. 599–638). New York: Random House.

Stephan, W. G. (1987). The contact hypothesis in intergroup relations. In C. Hendrick (Ed.), *Group processes and intergroup relations: Review of personality and social psychology, Vol. 9* (pp. 13–40). Newbury Park, California: Sage.

Stephan, W. G. (1989). A cognitive approach to stereotyping. In D. Bar-Tal, C. F. Graumann, A. W. Kruglanski, & W. Stroebe (Eds.), *Stereotyping and prejudice: Changing conceptions* (pp. 37–58). Berlin: Springer.

Stephan, W. G., & Rosenfield, D. (1978). Effects of desegregation on racial attitudes. *Journal of Personality and Social Psychology, 36*, 795–804.

Stephan, W. G., & Rosenfield, D. (1982). Racial and ethnic stereotypes. In A. G. Miller (Ed.), *In the eye of the beholder* (pp. 93–135). New York: Praeger.

Stephan, W. G., & Stephan, C. W. (1984). The role of ignorance in intergroup relations. In N. Miller & M. Brewer (Eds.), *Groups in contact: The psychology of desegregation* (pp. 229–255). New York: Academic.

Stone, W. F. (1980). The myth of left-wing authoritarianism. *Political Psychology, 2*, 3–19.

Stricker, G. (1963). Scapegoating: An experimental investigation. *Journal of Abnormal and Social Psychology, 67*, 125–131.

Strickland, B. (1970). Individual differences in verbal conditioning, extinction and awareness. *Journal of Personality, 38*, 364–378.

Strickland, B., & Crowne, D. P. (1962). Conformity under conditions of simulated group pressure as a function of the need for social approval. *Journal of Social Psychology, 58*, 171–181.

Stroebe, W., & Insko, C. A. (1989). Stereotype, prejudice, and discrimination: Changing conceptions in theory and research. In D. Bar-Tal, C. F. Graumann, A. W. Kruglanski, & W. Stroebe (Eds.), *Stereotyping and prejudice: Changing conceptions* (pp. 3–34). Berlin: Springer.

Stroebe, W., Kruglanski, A. W., Bar-Tal, D., & Hewstone, M. (Eds.). (1988). *The social psychology of intergroup conflict.* Berlin: Springer.

Stroebe, W., Lenkert, A., & Jonas, K. (1988). Familiarity may breed contempt: The impact of student exchange on national stereotypes and attitudes. In W. Stroebe, A. W. Kruglanski, D. Bar-Tal, & M. Hewstone (Eds.), *The social psychology of intergroup conflict* (pp. 167–187). Berlin: Springer.

Sumner, W. G. (1906). *Folkways.* New York: Ginn.

Surgeon, G., Mayo, J., & Bogue, D. (1976). *Race relations in Chicago. Second survey: 1975.* Chicago: University of Chicago.

Tabachnick, B. R. (1962). Some correlates of prejudice towards Negroes in elementary age children. *Journal of Genetic Psychology, 100*, 193–203.

Tajfel, H. (1969). Cognitive aspects of prejudice. *Journal of Social Issues, 25*, 79–97.

Tajfel, H. (1970). Experiments in intergroup discrimination. *Scientific American, 223(2)*, 96–102.

Tajfel, H. (1981). *Human groups and social categories.* Cambridge: Cambridge University Press.

Tajfel, H. (1982a). Instrumentality, identity and social comparisons. In H. Tajfel (Ed.), *Social identity and intergroup relations* (pp. 483–507). Cambridge: Cambridge University Press.

Tajfel, H. (1982b). Social psychology of intergroup attitudes. *Annual Review of Psychology, 33*, 1–39.

Tajfel, H. (1984). Intergroup relations, social myths and social justice in social psychology. In H. Tajfel (Ed.), *The social dimension, Vol. 2* (pp. 695–715). Cambridge: Cambridge University Press.

Tajfel, H., Flament, C., Billig, M., & Bundy, R. (1971). Social categorization and intergroup behaviour. *European Journal of Social Psychology, 1*, 149–177.

Tajfel, H., & Turner, J. (1979). An integrative theory of intergroup conflict. In W. Austin & S. Worchel (Eds.), *The social psychology of intergroup relations* (pp. 33–47). Monterey, California: Brooks/Cole.

Tajfel, H., & Wilkes, A. (1963). Classification and quantitative judgment. *British Journal of Psychology, 54*, 101–114.

Taylor, D. M., & Moghaddam, F. M. (1987). *Theories of intergroup relations: International social psychological perspectives.* New York: Praeger.

Taylor, M. L. (1980). Fraternal deprivation and competitive racism: A second look. *Sociology and Social Research, 65*, 37–55.

Terhune, K. W. (1984). Nationalism among foreign and American students: An exploratory study. *Journal of Conflict Resolution, 8*, 256–270.

Tetlock, P. E. (1983). Cognitive style and political ideology. *Journal of Personality and Social Psychology, 45*, 118–126.

Thomas, D. R. (1974). The relationship between ethnocentrism and conservatism in an "authoritarian" culture. *Journal of Psychology, 94*, 179–186.

Thomas, D. R. (1987). Authoritarianism and child-rearing practices. *Australian Psychologist, 22*, 197–201.

Thompson, L. L., & Crocker, J. (1990). Downward social comparison in the minimal intergroup situation: A test of a self-enhancement interpretation. *Journal of Applied Social Psychology, 20*, 1166–1184.

Thurow, L. (1969). *Poverty and discrimination.* Washington, D.C.: Brookings Institute.

Thurstone, L., & Chave, E. (1929). *The measurement of attitudes.* Chicago: University of Chicago Press.

Tomkins, S. S. (1963). Left and right: A basic dimension of ideology and personality. In R. W. White (Ed.), *The study of lives* (pp. 388–411). Chicago: Atherton.

Traynham, R., & Witte, K. (1976). The effects of modifying color-meaning concept attitudes in five and eight year old children. *Journal of Experimental Child Psychology, 21*, 165–174.

Trent, R. D. (1957). The relation between expressed self-acceptance and expressed attitudes towards Negroes and whites among Negro children. *Journal of Genetic Psychology, 91,* 25–31.

Triandis, H. C. (1961). A note on Rokeach's theory of prejudice. *Journal of Abnormal and Social Psychology, 62,* 184–186.

Triandis, H.C. (1967). Towards an analysis of the components of interpersonal attitudes. In W.C. Sherif & M. Sherif (Eds.), *Attitude, ego involvement and change.* New York: Wiley.

Triandis, H. C., & Davis, E. E. (1965). Race and belief as determinants of behavioral intention. *Journal of Personality and Social Psychology, 2,* 715–726.

Triandis, H. C., Davis, E. E., & Takezawa, S. (1965). Some determinants of social distance among American, German, and Japanese students. *Journal of Personality and Social Psychology, 2,* 540–551.

Triandis, H. C., & Triandis, L. M. (1960). Race, social class, religion, and nationality as determinants of social distance. *Journal of Abnormal and Social Psychology, 61,* 110–118.

Tripathi, R. C., & Srivastava, R. (1981). Relative deprivation and intergroup attitudes. *European Journal of Social Psychology, 11,* 313–318.

Turner, J. C. (1975). Social comparison and social identity: Some prospects for intergroup behaviour. *European Journal of Social Psychology, 5,* 5–34.

Turner, J. C. (1981). The experimental social psychology of intergroup behaviour. In J. Turner & H. Giles (Eds.), *Intergroup behaviour* (pp. 66–101). Oxford: Blackwell.

Turner, J. C. (1985). Social categorization and the self concept: A social cognitive theory of group behavior. In E. J. Lawler (Ed.), *Advances in group process: Theory and research, Vol. 2* (pp. 77–121). Greenwich, Connecticut: JAI Press.

Turner, J. C., & Brown, R. J. (1978). Social status, cognitive alternatives and intergroup relations. In H. Tajfel (Ed.), *Differentiation between social groups* (pp. 201–234). London: Academic.

Turner, J. C., & Giles, H. (1981). Introduction. In J. C. Turner & H. Giles (Eds.), *Intergroup behaviour* (pp. 1–32). Oxford: Blackwell.

Tygart, C. E. (1984). Political liberalism-conservatism among clergy: The question of dimensionality. *Human Relations, 37,* 853–861.

Tyson, G. A. (1985). *Children's racial attitudes: A review.* Unpublished report submitted to the H.S.R.C. Investigation into Intergroup Relations. Pretoria, South Africa: Human Sciences Research Council.

Tyson, G. A., & Duckitt, J. (1990). Racial attitudes of British immigrants to South Africa: A longitudinal study. In D. M. Keats, D. Munro, & L. Mann (Eds.), *Heterogeneity in cross-cultural psychology.* Amsterdam: Swets & Zeitlinger.

Tyson, G. A., Schlachter, A., & Cooper, S. (1988). Game playing strategy as an indicator of racial prejudice among South African students. *Journal of Social Psychology, 128,* 473–486.

Vanbeselaere, N. (1987). The effects of dichotomous and crossed social categorizations upon intergroup discrimination. *European Journal of Social Psychology, 17,* 143–156.

van den Berghe, P. L. (1962). Race attitudes in Durban, South Africa. *Journal of Social Psychology, 57,* 55–72.

van den Berghe, P. L. (1967). *Race and racism.* New York: Wiley.

van den Heuvel, H., & Meertens, R. W. (1989). The culture assimilator: Is it possible to improve interethnic relations by emphasizing ethnic differences? In J. P. van Oudenhoven & T. M. Willemsen (Eds.), *Ethnic minorities: Social psychological perspectives* (pp. 221–236). Amsterdam: Swets & Zeitlinger.

van der Spuy, H.I.J., & Shamley, D.A.F. (Eds.). (1978). *The psychology of apartheid: A psycho-social perspective on South Africa.* Washington, D.C.: University Press of America.

van Knippenberg, A. (1978). Status differences, comparative relevance and intergroup differentiation. In H. Tajfel (Ed.), *Differentiation between social groups* (pp. 171–200). London: Academic.

van Knippenberg, A. (1989). Strategies of identity management. In J. P. van Oudenhoven & T. M. Willemsen (Eds.), *Ethnic minorities: Social psychological perspectives* (pp. 59–76). Amsterdam: Swets & Zeitlinger.

van Knippenberg, A., & van Oers, H. (1984). Social identity and equity concerns in intergroup perception. *British Journal of Social Psychology, 23,* 351–362.

van Oudenhoven, J. P., & Willemsen, T. M. (Eds.). (1989a). *Ethnic minorities: Social psychological perspectives.* Amsterdam: Swets & Zeitlinger.

van Oudenhoven, J. P., & Willemsen, T. M. (1989b). Towards a useful social psychology for ethnic minorities. In J. P. van Oudenhoven & T. M. Willemsen, (Eds.), *Ethnic minorities: Social psychological perspectives* (pp. 237–251). Amsterdam: Swets & Zeitlinger.

Vanneman, R., & Pettigrew, T. (1972). Race and relative deprivation in the urban United States. *Race, 13,* 461–486.

Vaughan, G. M. (1988). The psychology of intergroup discrimination. *New Zealand Journal of Psychology, 17,* 1–14.

Wagner, U., Lampen, L., Syllwasschy, J. (1986). In-group inferiority, social identity and out-group devaluation in a modified minimal group study. *British Journal of Social Psychology, 25,* 15–23.

Wagner, U., & Schönbach, P. (1984). Links between educational status and prejudice: Ethnic attitudes in West Germany. In N. Miller & M. B. Brewer (Eds.), *Groups in contact: The psychology of desegregation* (pp. 29–52). San Diego: Academic.

Ward, D. (1985). Generations and the expression of symbolic racism. *Political Psychology, 6,* 1–18.

Ward, D. (1988). A critic's defense of the criticized. *Political Psychology, 9,* 317–320.

Warner, L., & DeFleur, M. L. (1969). Attitude as an interactional concept: Social constraint and social distance as intervening variables between attitudes and action. *American Sociological Review, 34,* 153–169.

Warner, L., & Dennis, R. (1970). Prejudice versus discrimination: An empirical example and theoretical extension. *Social Forces, 38,* 473–478.

Watson, J. (1950). Some social and psychological situations related to change in attitude. *Human Relations, 3,* 15–56.

Weatherley, D. (1961). Anti-Semitism and the expression of fantasy aggression. *Journal of Abnormal and Social Psychology, 62,* 454–457.

Webster, A. C., & Stewart, R.A.C. (1973). Theological conservatism. In G. D. Wilson (Ed.), *The psychology of conservatism* (pp. 129–147). London: Academic.

Weigel, R. H., & Howes, P. W. (1985). Conceptions of racial prejudice: Symbolic racism reconsidered. *Journal of Social Issues, 41,* 117–138.

Weigel, R. H., & Newman, L. S. (1976). Increasing attitude-behavior correspondence by broadening the scope of the behavioral measure. *Journal of Personality and Social Psychology, 33,* 793–802.

Weitz, S. (1972). Attitude, voice and behavior: A repressed affect model of interracial interaction. *Journal of Personality and Social Psychology, 24,* 14–21.

Westie, F. R. (1964). Race and ethnic relations. In R.E.L. Faris (Ed.), *Handbook of modern sociology* (pp. 576–618). Chicago: Rand McNally.

Wexley, K. N., & Nemeroff, W. F. (1974). The effects of racial prejudice, race of applicant and biographical similarity on interviewer evaluations of job applicants. *Journal of Social and Behavioral Sciences, 20,* 66–78.

Whitehead, G. I., Smith, S. H., & Eichhorn, J. A, (1982). The effect of subject's race and other's race on judgments of causality for success and failure. *Journal of Personality, 50,* 194–202.

Wicker, A. (1969). Attitudes vs actions: The relationship of verbal and overt behavioral responses to attitude objects. *Journal of Social Issues, 25,* 41–78.

Wilder, D. A. (1986). Social categorization: Implications for creation and reduction of intergroup bias. In L. Berkowitz (Ed.), *Advances in experimental social psychology, Vol. 19* (pp. 291–355). New York: Academic.

Willemsen, T. M., & van Oudenhoven, J. P. (1989). Social psychological perspectives on ethnic minorities: An introduction. In J. P. van Oudenhoven & T. M. Willemsen (Eds.), *Ethnic minorities: Social psychological perspectives* (pp. 11–21). Amsterdam: Swets & Zeitlinger.

Williams E. I., & Williams, C. D. (1963). Relationships between authoritarian attitudes of college students, estimation of parents' attitudes, and actual parental attitudes. *Journal of Social Psychology, 61,* 43–48.

Williams, J. (1964). Connotations of color names among Negroes and Caucasians. *Perceptual and Motor Skills, 18,* 721–731.

Williams, J. (1969). Individual differences in color-name connotations as related to measures of racial attitude. *Perceptual and Motor Skills, 29,* 383–386.

Williams, J., Boswell, D., & Best, D. (1975). Evaluative responses of preschool children to the colors white and black. *Child Development, 46,* 501–508.

Williams, J., & Morland, J. (1976). *Race, color and the young child.* Chapel Hill: University of North Carolina Press.

Wills, T. A. (1981). Downward comparison principles in social psychology. *Psychological Bulletin, 90,* 245–271.

Wilson, G. D. (Ed.). (1973). *The psychology of conservatism.* New York: Academic.

Wilson, G. D., & Shutte, P. (1973). The structure of social attitudes in South Africa. *Journal of Social Psychology, 90,* 323–324.

Wilson, T. C. (1986). The asymmetry of racial distance between white and black. *Sociology and Social Research, 70,* 161–163.

Wilson, W. (1973). *Power, racism, and privilege: Race relations in theoretical and sociohistorical perspective.* New York: Macmillan.

Woodmansee, J., & Cook, S. (1967). Dimensions of verbal racial attitudes: Their identification and measurement. *Journal of Personality and Social Psychology, 7,* 240–250.

Worchel, S., & Cooper, J. (1976). *Understanding social psychology*. Homewood, Illinois: Dorsey Press.

Wrightsman, L. S., Radloff, R. W., Horton, D. L., & Mecherikoff, M. (1961). Authoritarian attitudes and presidential voting preferences. *Psychological Reports, 8*, 43–46.

Wuthnow, R. (1982). Anti-Semitism and stereotyping. In A. Miller (Ed.), *In the eye of the beholder* (pp. 137–187). New York: Praeger.

Wylie, R. C. (1979). *The self-concept: Vol. 2. Theory and research on selected topics* (2nd ed.). Lincoln: University of Nebraska Press.

Yinger, J. M. (1983). Ethnicity and social change: The interaction of structural, cultural, and personality factors. *Ethnic and Racial Studies, 6*, 395–409.

Zawadzki, B. (1948). Limitations of the scapegoat theory of prejudice. *Journal of Abnormal and Social Psychology, 43*, 127–141.

Zippel, B., & Norman, R. (1966). Party switching, authoritarianism, and dogmatism in the 1974 elections. *Psychological Reports, 19*, 667–670.

Zuckerman, D. M., Singer, D. G., & Singer, J. L. (1980). Children's television viewing, racial and sex-role attitudes. *Journal of Applied Social Psychology, 10, 281–294*.

Zuckerman, M., Barrett-Ribback, B., Monashkin, I., & Norton, J. (1958). Normative data and factor analysis on the Parental Attitude Research Instrument. *Journal of Consulting Psychology, 22*, 165–171.

Zuckerman, M., & Reis, H. T. (1978). Comparison of three models for predicting altruistic behavior. *Journal of Personality and Social Psychology, 36*, 498–510.

# Index

## ABOUT THE AUTHOR

JOHN DUCKITT, a South African, studied at the University of Cape Town, Natal, and then Witwatersrand, where he focused on social psychology. He has been involved in a series of research studies on racial attitudes and authoritarianism among white South Africans, and has published a number of articles on these and other topics in both international and South African journals.